AF529066

Financial Inclusion and Inclusive Growth

Scope and Dimension

Financial Inclusion and Inclusive Growth

Scope and Dimension

Edited by
K. GANGADHARAN

New Delhi-110 002

Financial Inclusion and Inclusive Growth
Scope and Dimension

ISBN: 978-81-077-6

Rs.1950/-

First Published 2012

Published by:
Reference Press
4831/24, Ansari Road,
Darya Ganj,
New Delhi-110 002.
INDIA
Phones: 23260807, 41563444
Fax: 41563334
E-mail: info@essessreference.com
www.essessreference.com

Cover Design by *Patch Creative Unit*

Printed and bound in India at Salasar Imaging Systems.

Contents

SECTION IV : BANKS FRAUD AND INSTABILITY

SECTION V : BANKING INNOVATION AND FINANCIAL INCLUSION

SECTION VI : FINANCIAL INCLUSION AND PRIORITY SECTOR

Preface

Conventional concept of banking has been changed with the advancement of technologies and now banks are so close to us that we can avail banking services from anywhere at any time. But this is only the glittering part of the scene. On the other side there is a vast majority of public who is unaware of these innovations. There is a vast section that has no knowledge, no access and no availability of the so called hi - tech services. There is still another group who has the knowledge and access but still not using these innovative banking services due to one reason or other. Here comes the question: Can we claim the pride of technological advancement / innovations in banking when majority of the Indian people are not using these services. At this juncture the present attempt of studying about innovation and inclusion is of high relevance in the era of propagating inclusive growth.

Despite making significant improvements in all the areas relating to financial viability, profitability and competitiveness, there are concerns that banks have not been able to include vast segment of the population, especially the underprivileged sections of the society, into the fold of basic banking services. Internationally efforts are being made to study the causes of financial exclusion and designing strategies to ensure financial inclusion of the poor and disadvantaged. The reasons may vary from country to country and hence the strategy could also vary but all out efforts are being made as financial inclusion can truly lift the financial condition and standards of life of the poor and the disadvantaged.

Financial inclusion is the delivery of banking services at an affordable cost to the vast sections of disadvantaged and low income groups. Unrestrained access to public goods and services is the *sine qua non* of an open and efficient society. As banking services are in the nature of public good, it is essential that availability of banking and payment services to the entire population without discrimination is the prime objective of the public policy. Consequences of financial exclusion will vary depending on the nature and extent of services denied. It may lead to increased travel requirements, higher incidence of crime, general decline in investment, difficulties in gaining access to credit or getting credit from informal sources at exorbitant rates, and increased unemployment, etc. The small business may suffer due to the loss of access to middle class and higher-income consumers, higher cash handling costs and delays in remittances of money. According to certain researches, financial exclusion can lead to social exclusion.

It is becoming increasingly apparent that addressing financial exclusion will require a holistic approach on the part of the banks in creating awareness about financial products, education, and advice on money management, debt counselling, savings and affordable credit. Banks need to redesign their business strategies to incorporate specific plans to promote financial inclusion of low income group treating it both a business opportunity as well as a corporate social responsibility. They have to make use of all available resources including technology and expertise available with them as well as the MFIs and NGOs. It may appear in the first instance that taking banking to the sections constituting "the bottom of the pyramid", may not be profitable but it should always be remembered that even the relatively low margins on high volumes can be a very profitable proposition. Financial inclusion can emerge as commercial profitable business. Only the banks should be prepared to think outside the box!

The present volume is an outcome of the two days international conference on Innovation and Inclusion in Banking : Issues Strategies and Options organized by the Department of Applied Economics of Kannur University during February 3rd and 4th 2011. The conferences succeeded in bringing together scholars, teachers, financial economist, banking persons, social scientists, NGOS, to discuss inclusion - innovation strategies on the part of banks, share experiences and deliberate on strategies to build capacity to identify and improve the financial e empowerment of people in the rock bottom level. It also suggests measures to help the planners and policy makers and administrators to attend service for more financial accessibility to the people at the lower strata of the society. The NABARD, RBI, ICSSR and UGC sponsored the conference. We finally considered 40 papers with proper revision after the conference. I hope that this volume will prove to be an enriching authentic work for the students of financial economics and financial inclusion and will be a useful reading text for the research scholars, teachers, financial and banking experts, administrators, bankers, policy makers and planners involved with rural development and financial empowerment.

First of all, I would like to express my thanks to all the contributors of the papers and delegates of the conference for their valuable contributions. All my colleagues in the department extended their help, co-operation and support in the completion of the exercise. I would like to particularly convey my thanks to Vineesh Kumar K.V , the project fellow attached to my major research project who worked very hard during the course of the conference and also took in charge of all typing and record keeping assistance both during the course of the conference and at the preparation of the manuscript. My thanks are all also due to Reference Press, New Delhi for efficiently bearing the responsibility for the publication of the book.

K. Gangadharan

Contributors

Alimullah Miyan
Vice-Chancellor & Founder
International University of Business Agriculture and Technology, Dhaka, Bangladesh

Annamalai. S
Professor and Head
Department of Bank Management
Alagappa University, Karaikudi

Anupam Mitra
Assistant Professor
Department of Commerce
RPM College, University of Calcutta, India

Arabi. U
Associate Professor
Department of Studies and Research in Economics
Mangalore University

Asokan .T
Professor & Head
Department of Management Studies
Kannur University

Balamurugan. S
M.Phil Scholar
Department of Economics
Bharathiar University, Coimbatore

Baligatti Y.G.
Associate Professor
K.R.C.E.S's Degree College, Bailhongal

Basin Hans. V
Associate Professor and Head
Department of Economics
St. Aloysius Evening College
Mangalore, Changanacherry

Clifford G Machougu
Lecturer, Faculty of Business Administration
St Augustine University of Tanzania

Dhanya K.A
Lecturer in Commerce
Amal College of Advanced Studies, Nilambur

Dileep A. S
Assistant Professor, Department of Commerce
N.S.S College, Pandalam

Feroze P. S
Assistant Professor , Dept. of Commerce
Sree Narayana College, Nattika

Gangadharan.K
Head, School of Development Studies
Kannur University, Kerala

George K.M
Former United Nations Advisor

Govindarajalu.K
Professor, Department of Economics
Bharathiar University, Coimbatore

Harsha Aturupane
Lead Education Specialist
Human Development Unit
South Asia Region, World Bank, Colombo.

Hemalatha A .V
Associate Professor in Commerce
PRNSS College Mattanur, Kannur

Isabella George
CEO, AGES

Jairus B Amayi
Lecturer, Faculty of Business Administration
St Augustine University of Tanzania

Janardhanan V.K
Professor & Head
Department of Commerce & Management Studies
University of Calicut, Kerala.

Jiya Shahani
Research Scholar
Centre for studies in Economics and Planning
Central University of Gujarat

Joseph M.A
Associate Professor
Department of Commerce and Management Studies
University of Calicut, Kerala

Joseph Sebastian Thekkedam
Associate Professor, St. Berchmans' College,
Chanyanacherry

Joshy Andrews
Assistant Professor
Nehru School of Management, Pampadi

Madhava Menon N
Associate Professor in Economics
N S S College, Cherthala

Manohar V Serraro
Research Scholar, Manipal University

Michael Raj M
Associate Professor, Department of Economics
St. Stephen's College, Pathanapuram

Mohammed Razik Parakandi
Assistant Professor
Department of Management Studies
Kannur University

Nicas Nibengo
Assistant Lecturer
Faculty of Business Administration
St Augustine University of Tanzania

Philip P. J
Former Principal, Kozancheri College

Pradeep Kumar.B
Assistant Professor
P.G. Department of Economics
P.M.Govt.College, Chalakudy

Rajesh. T
Assistant Professor
Department of Commerce, Mannaniya college

Rajesh. K
Assistant Professor
Dept. of Economics, St.Aloysius College, Thrissur.

Ramanjaneyulu M
Professor of Economics
Bangalore University, Bangalore

Sabu Thomas
Assistant Professor in Politics
SGTDS, MG University, Kottayam, Kerala

Sajan. K
Ph D Scholar, Dravidian University
Kuppam, Andhra Pradesh

Salini. K
Faculty, IIPS, Kanattukara, Thrissur

Sandhya. P
Research Scholar in Economics
Kannur University

Sequeira A. H
Professor, Department of Humanities
Social Sciences and Management
National Institute of Technology
Karnataka, Surathkal

Shankaran Nambiar
Senior Research Fellow & Head
Policy Studies Division
Malaysian Institute of Economic Research
Kuala Lumpur

Shivakumar. D
Selection Grade Lecturer, ICICI Manipal Academy

Shridevi V Patted
Assistant Professor, Govt. First Grade College
Tyamagondlu

Sulaiman. E
Reader, School of Management and Business Studies
Mahatma Gandhi University

Ushakumari L
Associate Professor
Department of Commerce, S D College, Alappuzha

Venugopalan K. V
Associate Professor
P.G. Department of Commerce, Govt. College Madappally

Vinesh Kumar K.V
Research Scholar, Department of Applied
Economics, Kannur University

Vipin Chnadran K. P
Assistant Professor
P.G. Department of Economics
Zamorin's Guruvayurappan College, Calicut

Visalakshi C. A
Assistant Professor
Dept. of Commerce, Govt. College, Chittur

Introduction

K. Gangadharan

One of the prime objectives of for the creation of an inclusive and efficient economy is access and availability of banking and payment services to the entire population. It is also essential for the Indian growth story to become sustainable. Since inclusive economic growth is crucial for achieving sustainable economic development, financial inclusion and extension of financial services to every citizen of the country is an important goal for the government.

The Banking industry has sown tremendous growth in volume and complexity during the last few decades. Significant improvements are made in all the areas relating to financial viability profitability and competitiveness. That is commendable since banking industry is framed on a commercial platform. As a commercial organization the Banks are always concerned with viability and performing assets as part of maximizing profit. But unlike other commercial institutions, Banks have responsibility to the weaker sections of society. Mere profit making should not be the only motto. A more proactive role by the banks is needed specially to include a vast segment of the underprivileged section of the society in to the fold of basic banking services. Financial inclusion is therefore the delivery of banking and other financial services at affordable costs to the vast sections of disadvantaged and low income groups.

The statistics on banking operations in India in terms of its reaching out to the poor in India are not encouraging. Approximately only 40% of the country's population has bank accounts and only about 38% of the branches of the scheduled commercial banks are in rural areas. Over half of the 90 million farmer households in the country today still do not have access to credit either from institutional or non-institutional sources. In urban India, 9400 people are covered by one branch. But in semi urban and rural India one branch covers 13,900 people.

INTERNATIONAL EXPERIENCE IN PROMOTING FINANCIAL INCLUSION

An interesting feature which emerges from the international practice is that the more developed the society is, the greater the thrust on empowerment of the common person and low income groups. It may be worthwhile to have a look at the international experience in tackling the problem of financial exclusion, so that we can learn from the international experience.

The Financial Inclusion Task Force in UK has identified three priority areas for the purpose of financial inclusion, viz., access to banking, access to affordable credit and access to free face-to-face money advice. UK has established a Financial Inclusion Fund to promote financial inclusion and assigned responsibility to banks and credit unions in removing financial exclusion. No frills accounts were also introduced once permitted in banks for augmenting financial accessibility and affordability for opening bank accounts. An enhanced legislative environment for credit unions has been established, accompanied by tighter regulations to ensure greater protection for investors. A Post Office Card Account (POCA) has been created for those who are unable or unwilling to access a basic bank account. The concept of a

Savings Gateway has been piloted. This offers those on low-income employments £1 from the state for every £1 they invest, up to a maximum of £25 per month. In addition, the Community Finance Learning Initiatives (CFLIs) were also introduced with a view to promoting basic financial literacy among housing association tenants.

FINANCIAL INCLUSION THROUGH BANKING

A strategic approach is therefore needed to cover the vast rural habitation through banking facilities. To bring this financially excluded population within the fold of the formal banking system, the Government and Reserve Bank of India have taken several steps to ease the entry of the rural population and the urban slum population into the banking system. Based on the recommendations of the C.Rangarajan Committee Report on Financial Sector Reform, the Government created the financial inclusion fund for meeting the cost of developmental and promotional interventions for ensuring financial inclusion and "The Financial Inclusion Technology Fund " to meet the cost of technology adoption with an overall corpus of Rs.500crore each. To address the problem of high transaction costs, Banks were advised to migrate all their branches to computer based core banking solutions that allows for real time transactions, increasing use of IT based solutions such as smart cards, mobile phones and hand held devises to extend their reach.

Measures were also taken to simplify account opening. These included the no frills account which is a financial inclusion scheme that has reached out to and benefited even the tribals. Direct effort by the Government towards financial inclusion include Self Help Group-Bank Linkage Programme, Kissan Credit Card Scheme, Rashtriya Swasthya Bima Yojana and financing of RRBS, Co-operatives and public sector Banks that lend to the rural clients. Technology can be a very effective tool in providing access to Banking products in remote areas. ATMS, cash dispensing machines can be modified to make them more user friendly for the people who are illiterate or semi illiterate. The recent simplification of know your customer norms are another milestone in ensuring financial inclusion. Self Help Groups are playing a predominant role in the process of financial inclusion Through SHGs nearly 40 million households are linking with Banks

RBI has liberalized its branch authorization policy for the rural areas as well as the policy for location of ATMs. The most recent change in the Bank-Branch policy of RBI allows scheduled Commercial Banks other than Regional Rural Banks to open branches in towns and villages with population below 50,000 without seeking permission from RBI. To expand the branch network in the North East, the RBI is working with State Governments and the Banks on a viability gap funding model by providing the capital and the running cost of branches for the first five years to the states which provide premises and security.

From savings accounts and recurring or Fixed deposits the banking services needs to develope credit cards, insurance, shares, mutual funds etc. ATMs, smart cards, internet banking have also become common services. Whatever be the development in Information Technology, this reflects in banking service also. Cheques are replaced by RTGS (Real Time Gross Settlement) and NEFT (National Electronic Funds Transfer) and other electronic forms of money transfer – so that customers receive credit real time online.

The nationalization of commercial banks in India under the dynamic leadership of Prime Minister Mrs. Indira Gandhi in 1969 and 1980 was a bold step taken towards financial inclusion. Ever since Indira Gandhi nationalized 14 commercial banks, India has tried to extend more credit to the poor through priority sector lending schemes of RBI in which all public sector banks are required to set aside 40% of net bank credit as loan for weaker sections and agricultural sector, 18% of the net credit should go to agriculture lending as more than 80% of the population depend directly or indirectly on agriculture. RBI also stipulated that bank open at least 25% of total number of branches in rural and semi urban areas. But this target has not been fulfilled. The nationalization of commercial Banks marked a paradigm shift in the focus of banking from 'Class Banking" to Mass Banking. Again the establishment of Regional Rural Banks in 1975, during Indira Gandhi' Prime Minister ship, also took banking service to the people in the remote villages of India. The branches of commercial banks and RRBs have increased from 8321 in the year 1969 to 78,882 branches at the end of March 2010. It is interesting to note that as part of financial inclusion strategy, around 40% of all branches of commercial banks are established in rural areas of the country. However, there are some under banked states such as Bihar, Orissa, Rajasthan, Uttarpradsh, Chattisgarh, Jharkhand, West Bengal and large number of North Eastern States, where the average population per branch office continues to be a quite high compared to national average. Now the Reserve Bank of India has decided to encourage opening of more branches in these under banked areas as part of its policy for banking inclusion. Government also seeks to ensure that all governmental subsidies and allied financial support is routed about through designated accounts About 4.41 crore poor households in 626 districts who benefit every year from MGNREGS receive their payments in their bank accounts.

We need to examine why the entire population of our country could not be brought into the gamut of banking services. Although there are many reasons for this the main reason is that banking is seen primarily as a commercial venture. In the remote areas of the country where income levels are so low, where do the banks get deposits and to whom will they lend to earn profit? This focusing on profitability has been the main reason for not reaching banking services to the rural areas

Banks need to redesign their business strategies to incorporate specific plans to promote financial inclusion of low income groups treating it both a business opportunity as well as a corporate social responsibility.

It was against this backdrop to study the spatial, social and economic aspects of financial inclusion and inclusive growth through innovative banking services, the Department of Applied Economics, Kannur University organized an international conference on Innovation and Inclusion in Banking: Issues, Strategies and Options on 3rd and 4th February 2011. It was sponsored and funded by NABARD, ICSSR, New Delhi and University Grants Commission. The conference was devoted to acquire a broad understanding of the linkage of financial inclusion and economic development through inclusive growth. The conference succeeded in eliciting the basic issues and constraints connected with financial inclusion and inclusive growth and suggested various policy measures for attaining financial inclusion and inclusive growth so as to attain the Millennium Development goal of removal of abject poverty. Experts from multiple disciplines participated in the conference and presented their papers with subsequent in-depth discussions on each aspect of the subject. In all, thirty five papers finally revised after the conference has been received from the experts belonging to multi-disciplinary boundaries for publication. These papers are accordingly categorized into six sections and presented subsequently in the book. The major sub-themes are micro finance and financial inclusion, banks frauds and instability, financial inclusion and human resource development, banking innovation and financial inclusion and financial inclusion and priority sector.

SECTION I : FINANCIAL INCLUSION, HUMAN DEVELOPMENT AND INCLUSIVE GROWTH

Alimullah Miyan in his paper challenges of financing higher education from inclusion perspectives focus on the need for promoting higher education through bank finance as part of the financial inclusion strategy. As part of the financial inclusion strategy to promote higher education, he advocates the world Knowledge Based Area Development Scheme (K B A D). Students can avail loans refundable after gainful employment. K B A D can be made sustainable through initial funding by the state donor agencies, community and civil society. In this paper he provides the IUBAT model of KBAD providing repayable loans to students enabling them to break out poverty trap which if extended in wider scale in any society could lead to community self-reliance through ensuring growth with equity.

Harsha Aturupane in his paper 'human development foundations of innovations in banking' argues for undertaking high-tech innovations in higher education especially at the university level to promote research and expand opportunities for innovation and knowledge generation which ultimately benefit the expansion and diversification of business and commerce in the country, betterment of living condition of people and development of nation.

S Annamalai in his paper 'furthering financial inclusion through financial literacy and credit counselling' advocates the need for formal literacy as a precondition for widening the financial inclusion strategy. The paper typically advocates the need for evaluating the people in rural and urban areas with regard to various financial products and services for the formal financial sector.

Shankaran Nambiar in his paper 'micro credit and capability enhancement in institutional perspective' examines few case studies to illustrate how the institutional frame work of microfinance, that has been proposed so far has indeed practical values in capability enhancement.

Financial inclusion and inclusive growth through banking lessons from India by **K. Gangadharan** examines the history of banking, its growth land marks and its business dimension in the past and present. The paper explores the basic innovation carried out in the banking arena and how it percolated as benefit to the vulnerable and deprived communities and ultimately for their economic empowerment. The paper also examines the trends and progress of financial inclusion strategy of Indian banks and the emerging challenges.

Mohammed Razik and T. Asokan in their paper 'Human Capital Preparedness for banking sector productivity, empirical evidence from major public sector and private sector banks in India' provides a way out for enhancing banking productivity by giving human dimension to banking business.

K Govindarajalu and S Balamurugan in their paper 'role of banks in financing higher education aspirants' provides the vital role of banks in extending financial support to the higher education sector in India as a strategy of financial inclusion. In the paper an attempt has been made to elicit the problem faced by aspirants of higher education in getting educational loans, problems of the bankers in extending loans and provides a strategy to overcome the issues.

SECTION II : MICRO FINANCE AND FINANCIAL INCLUSION

New dimension of microfinance under NGO's to ensure sustainable development through corporate social responsibilities under millennium development goals of the UN by **K M George** is a paper focusing on the CSR of NGOs with micro finance approach. The basic theme of the paper is to ascertain whether CSR of business adequately empower NGO's with micro finance. The general perception of CSR is to plough back part of the profits of companies and business for sustainable development oriented activities. This paper is a cross checking models in this regard to ascertain whether CSR of business adaptability empower NGOs with micro finance.

Y.G. Baligatti and Shridevi V Patted in their paper aims at a comparative evaluation of financial inclusion as promoted by PSBs, RRBs, Foreign and Private sector banks from 2005-2009.Further, the study offers suggestions for promoting financial inclusion.

Sabu Thomas in his paper 'Discredited credit-examining the politics of financial exclusion in India' describes the pitfall in the policies pursued for providing financial access to vulnerable sections. The question he focuses is about the political morality of growth rates in the same bed with never ending farmer suicides. He advocates the new technology to play of vital role in providing accessibility of credit in rural segments of the country.

Promotion strategies for banking services, a study by **Joseph Sebastian Thekedam** provides a better picture about the promotion strategies adopted as part of marketing strategies by new generation banks in India. The paper reveals that even new generation banks have used all promotion tools in the promotion mix for the promotion of banking services. According to him the personal selling is the most important tool used for promoting banking services. The study reveals that external factors like cultural aspects, technology intensity of the industry, the competitive environment of the market and economic factors etc also influence greatly on the choice of promotion strategy. The study concludes with basic remarks that new generation banks keep its identity by helping a contingency approach of the promotion strategy for providing banking services instead of pure adaptation or a pure standardization strategy.

Manohar V Serrao, A H Sequeira and Basil Hans in their paper 'designing a methodology to investigate accessibility and impact of financial inclusion' attempts to devise a research methodology to measure the impact of access to financial services by the poor and marginalized sections of the society. The team of authors also examined the multi dimensional concept of financial inclusion giving an account of the social initiatives of financial inclusion in India, the experience gained and challenges ahead. They suggest an amalgamation of technological approach and human approach for strengthening, enabling and evaluating mechanisms of financial inclusion.

U Arabi's paper 'Regional Rural Banks Potential role in in financial inclusion in India: The challenges ahead' are the outcome of a study based on secondary data on Regional Rural Banks. The study focuses on the potential role of Grameen Banks in financial inclusion and the basic challenges that face in achieving the goals of financial inclusion in the rural financial system in India.

A V Hemalatha in her paper 'Micro finance for women A study of Self Help Groups in Kerala' argues the need for a supplementary credit delivery system which could provide required credit on cordial terms to women to make them economically empower and self dependent. The SHG- Bank linkage programme of NABARD is a novel project in this direction and the SHG work as an organization at the grass root level based on the principle of self help and mutual help. This paper shed light on the working of SHG and the role played by SHGS in empowering poor women at the rock bottom level.

Sajan K and Joseph M A in their joint paper 'Credit Requirements and Credit Sources of low income groups- Need for New Credit facility Models and Products' is an attempt to study the genuine credit requirement of low income groups. The low income groups consist of small fixed shop traders, hawkers, peddlers and regular but small income earning persons who use informal credit source for their credit requirements. The study proved that the credentials suggested by financial institutions for getting credit and financial products do not go well with the qualifications of these small income groups. The study spotted out the need of having new models of credit facility and financial products for vulnerable sectors.

K.V.Vinesh Kumar in his paper 'micro credit and self-help groups in India: An Evaluation' discusses the innovative and forward-looking policies based on the ground realities of micro finance institutions in India. This paper provides a commercial approach to micro finance institutions in making micro finance financially sustainable and providing financial services to the poor. The paper focuses on the growth and performance of self-help group and micro credit in India and its challenges.

Jairus Amayi and Clifford Machogu in their paper 'financial capital paradigm and income poverty reduction in Tanzania: perceptions of customers of financial institution and Markets in Mwanaza city in Tanzania,' an attempt has been made to analyze public perception on the contribution of financial capital and income poverty reduction. The paper determined the level of public awareness on financial capital services, the driving forces and constraints for public demand and supply of financial capital and the level of magnitude of financial capital contribution on income poverty reduction.

Rajesh and Salini K in their paper 'micro financing in India, diverging from objectives' provides an indepth analysis of the sustainability of microfinance among financial institution in the Indian context. The basic premise of this paper is to empirically analyze the operational framework of this institution and provides a critical assessment of the major issues of micro finance in India.

Ushakumari in her paper "Financial Inclusion Without Financial Literacy does more harm than good" aims to seek answer to two important questions. 1. Whether the loaners of banks depend on informal sources for meeting any of their financial requirements.2. If there is any dependency with the dire need that push them to the hands of the money lenders? The paper indirectly focuses on the relevance and need of financial literacy to check the intensity of financial exclusion.

B Pradeep Kumar and P.J Philip, in their paper "Financial Exclusion A Theoretical Approach" discuss various theories of financial exclusion viz the share holder wealth maximization theory and the theory of asymmetric information. While the former has assured more relevance in recent times and the latter has been the centre of discussion on financial inclusion for many decades. The paper present important theoretical strategies to address the problem of financial exclusion, viz the supply leading financial development, demand following financial development and compares the efficiency of both in tackling the problem of financial exclusion. The paper sheds light on active and passive exclusion and also on the extent of banking exclusion in India particularly in the case of marginalized and weaker sections.

SECTION III : FINANCIAL INCLUSION AND CO OPERATIVES

Anupam Mithra in his paper "an Overview of Credit Risk and NPA of Urban Cooperative banks in India," an attempt has been made to manage the credit risk to minimize NPA of the Urban CO-Operative Banks in India.

X-efficiency in district co-operative banks in Kerala by **Feroze P S** is an attempt to measure the level of technical efficiency, pure technical efficiency and scale efficiency with data on development analysis. It also examines the sources of inefficiency in District Co- Operative Banks. The paper suggests potential improvement in the efficiency of inefficient district cooperative banks in terms of potential reduction in inputs and potential addition in outputs.

SECTION IV : BANKS FRAUDS AND INSTABILITY

In the paper "Frauds and Security Threats Associated With the Use of ATM-A case study" by **A S Dileep and K.Rajesh** presents a few findings of an empirical research on the fraudulent practices in connection with ATM in some major banks in Thiruvanathapuram, the capital city of Kerala. It throws light on the modes operandi of ATM fraud and puts forward a few security suggestions that should be adhered to both by banks and ATM users in order to eliminate or reduce the threat to the barest minimum.

"Global Financial Crisis and Indian Banks" by **K Venugopalan** examines the origin and causes of financial crisis, its effect on world economy and the impact of crisis in Indian Banks. The paper also sheds light on the need for and expansion of more and more public sector banks to achieve the target of financial inclusion.

SECTION V : BANKING INNOVATION AND FINANCIAL INCLUSION

Joshy Andrews's paper "Investment in gold exchange traded funds: A safe and Novel approach to investment in gold" is an indepth analysis of gold exchange traded funds available in India.The paper provides a comparison of performance of various gold exchange traded funds available in India. The paper also focuses on the superiority of Gold exchange traded funds over investment in physical form of gold and also covers the dynamics of gold exchange traded fund market in India.

E Sulaiman in his paper "An Islamic Microfinance model -The missing dimension attempts to discuss the concept and approaches of Islamic microfinance and practices adopted by the Islamic micro finance institution. The practices discussed in this paper are valuable in drawing the attention of the Islamic Banking practices to the fact that microfinance without undermining the institutional viability, competitiveness and sustainability,

In the paper Technology Innovations in Banking: "Do They Reach Out the Common man" by **Dhanya K A and V. K. Janardhanan** an attempt is made to identify the extent of usage of new technologies in banking by common people and also detect the reason for non usage. The study also focuses on the role played by banks in promoting the technology usage.

Jiya K Shahani in her paper "Banking and Corporate Social Responsibility" identifies the needs for development of an adequate banking and credit structure in the rural areas to increase the flow of credit to agriculture and allied activities, use of information and communication technology and intermediaries that can increase the outreach, scale and depth of banking service at affordable cost to unbanked segments. She lays stress for changing the trade linked functions of commercial banks to the frontier areas of social commitment to lift up those at the bottom of social pyramid and makes those left behind by inflation and consumerism to be able to join the economic bandwagon.

D Shivakumar in his paper "Developments in Payment and Settlement Systems: A study of RTGS" provides a vivid picture of the working advantage of Real Time Gross Settlement as a latest electronic payment system. This paper tries to evaluate the improvements in payment systems brought out in recent past, its impact and examine specifically the RTGS as a convenient, fast and efficient mode of payment.

C. A. Visalakshi in her paper "Innovations in Modern Banking a tool for Inclusive Growth" provides the real issues of limiting banking technology to the urban community and denying the accessibility to majority of the rural segments of the country. She is optimistic that the use of smart card technology, mobile ATMS, Coverage of post offices under electronic payments network in remote areas could play a significant role in providing financial services in un-banked and under banked people. The paper gives a message that technology based banking activities will be a milestone in the way of achieving inclusive growth in India.

Raman Janeyalu in his paper "Electronic Banking in India: Issues and Challenges" examines the pivotal role played by banking technology in extending banking services to more and more customers and also the expansion of volume of business technology, plastic money, barcode, hologram, magnetic strip, capital memory card, ATM, NEFT, RTGS, Mobile banking , core banking solutions etc. The paper also provides the advantages of the banking technology and the scope for further expansion in the immediate future.

SECTION VI : FINANCIAL INCLUSION AND PRIORITY SECTOR

K. P. Vipin Chnadran and P. Sandhya in their paper "Financial Inclusion in India: Emerging Trends and Challenges of Banking Services" provides description of the history of financial inclusion in India. The paper suggests that the banks need to redesign their business strategies to incorporate specific plans to promote financial inclusion of low income group, treating it both a business opportunity as well as a corporate social responsibility.

Michael Raj in his paper "An Analysis of agriculture credit and capital formation in Indian agriculture: A pre reform and post reform comparison" checks the growth and trend of institutional credit in India. It also examines the growth of short term and long term credit in Indian agriculture and it also provides a comparative analysis of long term credit and capital formation in Indian Agriculture in pre reform and post reform period.

The paper "Financial de-regulation and financial exclusion with special reference to Priority Lending" by **Madhava Menon** examines financial exclusion in the era of liberalization in India. The first section deals with the meaning, process, causes and consequences of financial exclusion. The second section deals with the extent of financial exclusion in the priority sector especially small and medium scale industries and farm sectors.

CONCLUSION

The banking development of the world has witnessed an unprecedented growth in volume and complexity mainly over the past five decades and both developed and developing countries have enjoyed the benefits of banking and financial innovations. One of the prime objectives of the inclusive and efficient economy is access and availability of banking and payment services to the entire population. Since inclusive economic growth is crucial for achieving sustainable economic development, financial inclusion and extension of financial services to every citizen of the country is an important goal for the Government.

Innovative products combined with superior service are vital for the survival of banks today. Retail banking is assuming greater importance. The customer now has a wide selection of banks and products to choose from. 54% of Indians are under 25 years of age. They are a good target market for investment and innovative products. Adopting new state of the art technology and continuously accelerating business process are essential to cater to the increasing demands and expectations of the customers. Continuous innovation on the product offered by banks is paramount to ensure that the products stand out above that of their competitors and is the preferred choice of the customer The needs of the customer today is far different from what it was say 10 years ago. Quickness and diversity in services is expected and should be ensured

In India, we have certain worrying features in our system. Even after 6 decades of planned development and banking development, still a major chunk of Indian population still depends on money lenders and non-institutional sources for credit and financial requirements and the rare availability of public sector banks are the only hope for majority of them. While competition generally brings in more options and services at lower costs to the consumers, this has unfortunately not happened in the banking sector while the private sector and new generation banks levy a plethora of miscellaneous hidden charges on the services provided. But now even this scenario has undergone a change. As part of reforms measures and banking sector reform policies it is unfortunate that public sector banks are now competeting with private banks in charging the customers on miscellaneous services. In this juncture any financial and innovative banking system should see to it that the financial protection and financial inclusion is extend against any economic and social catastrophe and the poor people who are really worst affected with high cost of banking and financial services are not constrained to seek financial care. So banking and financial inclusion agenda must be planned in such a way that the fruits of banking development must be able to percolate to the downtrodden, marginalized and vulnerable sections of the society in a better, accessible and affordable manner so as to ensure social justice to the vast sections from the octopus hold of money lenders and non-institutional agencies.

Section I : Financial inclusion, Human Development and Inclusive Growth

1
Challenges of Financing Higher Education from Inclusion Perspectives

M. Alimullah Miyan

INTRODUCTION

Knowledge is the engine of growth for any nation. Advanced level of instrumental knowledge and skills enable people to contribute towards national development. All over the world, economies are changing as more and more, knowledge supplants physical capital as the source of present and future growth. As knowledge becomes more important, so does higher education. The quality of knowledge generated within higher education institutions, and its availability to the wider economy, is becoming increasingly critical to national competitiveness. According to UNESCO, higher education is a long term social investment in productivity, social cohesion and cultural development. Basic and applied research within higher education in collaboration with international universities and national business and industry fosters innovation and economy in resource utilization with properly addressing environmental concerns. Higher education enhances knowledge generation and cultural development including institutional autonomy, intellectual freedom and a culture of peace based on democracy, tolerance and mutual respect. A well-functioning higher education sector can lead to enhanced quality in basic education too.

Funding is central to the success of higher education system in terms of both intuition building and facilitation of access. The traditional public funding is falling far short in meeting quantitative expansion and qualitative parameters. Hence, alternative funding modalities are gaining ground. Non-government universities are emerging as a substantial supplement and more importantly, as a model for market-driven, dynamic and quality higher education.

In developing societies, despite notable expansion in both government and non-government universities, the question of accessibility and equity remains as a burning policy issue. Wider social mobility through increased accessibility by marginal communities to higher education is an emerging strategy adopted by many developing societies. This Knowledge Based Area Development (KBAD) approach envisages equitable and balanced proliferation of higher educational benefits to underdeveloped regions and marginalized communities embracing them into the mainstream development process for attaining community self reliance through inclusion.

CRITICAL ROLE OF HIGHER EDUCATION IN A DEVELOPING COUNTRY

The quality of human resource of a nation is easily judged by the educational attainment of its people. For the development of any field or area such as business, science, economics, religion education is deemed necessary. It is said that education is a must if a nation aspires to achieve growth and development and more importantly sustain it. This may well explain the fact that rich and developed nations of the world have very high literacy and productive human resource.

As per the Worlds Education Indicators (WEI) program report published by the UNESCO Institute for Statistics which analyzes the progress made by 19 middle income and developing countries, member states of the Organization for Economic Cooperation and Development (OECD) and additional twelve countries on educational performance as of 2005, China has the most tertiary graduates in the world. As of 2005, more students entered and graduated in the 19 WEI countries than all the OECD countries combined. In terms of numbers about 5.7 millions WEI attained tertiary degree compared to 5.2 millions from OECD countries. This figure would increase substantially if data from India would be added. From the WEIs data it is observed that China had most tertiary graduates in the world of 2.4 millions which is more than the top three OECD countries combined: USA (1.4 millions), Japan (0.6 millions) and France (0.3 millions). This largely accounts for rapid growth of Chinese economy. Although WEI countries achieved substantial growth in education in general and more particularly in tertiary education, graduation ratios remain lower in WEI countries than those of the OECD and there is also wide scale problem of discrimination in term of access to tertiary education.

Higher education is more critical to the developing countries as it needs to cater to increasing numbers of students, specially from disadvantaged backgrounds, promote general education in edition to technical skills to ensure flexibility, innovation and continual renewal of socio-economic structures in a fast-changing world, adopt dynamic curricula and emphasize on research to select, absorb, and create new knowledge more efficiently and rapidly. Higher education in developing societies can ensure optimum utilization of limited resources and effectively make up for scarcity of material resources through developing human resources as an alternative to achieve socio-economic development. Developing societies are endowed with people, but has very limited natural resources and financial capital. By developing the people into human capital, they can overcome some of the limitations of financial capital and at the same time lay the basis of generating capital resources. Education and skill development may be chosen as the route for creating human capital.

Higher education also acts as a means of attaining enhanced social mobility. A vast number of people in the developing countries are captive in a vicious poverty trap. Spread of higher education among underdeveloped segments of the population can empower them to move up to a higher level of enlightenment and prosperity. Individual achievement benefits the wider community and acts as propellant for inducing others to pursue higher education. In terms of intellectual capacity building from individual, family, community level up to the national administration and policy making, higher education plays the most vital role. A quality higher education can result in more pro-poor and pro-development policy framework and increased income generation from home and abroad by skilled human resources. Effective higher education plays central role in developing productivity, innovation, entrepreneurship, gender mainstreaming and overall socio-cultural advancement in a developing society. A new vision of higher education in developing societies should combine the demands for universality of higher learning with the imperative for greater relevance to the society. This vision stresses on the principles of academic freedom and institutional autonomy simultaneously emphasizing on social accountability.

DIMENSIONALITY OF HIGHER EDUCATION

To achieve its anticipated goals, higher education must be relevant, internationalized, effective, dynamic and accessible by all. Relevance dictates being responsive to market and society in terms of learning contents. Relevance is not confined to gainful employment alone. It also covers capacity building in policy issues and induction to ethical standards, democracy, peace and equity. Internationalization and cross-border cooperation can enhance relevance and marketability of higher education through exchange of experience and expertise between universities in the developed and developing countries and also through continuously adapting to the ever-changing skill requirements in a global perspective. Simultaneously, to be effective, the quality of education must also be of the highest standard encompassing the existing body of knowledge along with dynamic exploration to emerging frontiers. Besides, to ensure propagation of learning and diffusion of resultant benefits to all segments of the society, higher education must also be accessible specifically by women and low income groups.

Quality of higher education hinges on adequacy of infra-structure, curriculum, faculty, management and governance. Infrastructure in terms of premises, lab, library and modern teaching aids (internet, multimedia) constitute the basic prerequisite of quality in higher education. The curriculum must cover all the basic skills and knowledge required in the present and future context of market and society home and abroad. Research should focus on creating newer knowledge on the local and international context. Competent faculty is a function of education, training, experience and research for continued advancement. Management signifies efficient administration of the higher education institutes in operational terms while governance relates to institutional autonomy and academic freedom in terms of meeting the quality parameters.

In developing societies, conventional approaches to meet the different dimensions of higher education are having a limited success. Increased public funding and emergence of new public and non-government universities only partially met the quantitative and qualitative challenges. More remains to be done in terms of devising a comprehensive solution to the issues of relevance, internationalization, effectiveness, dynamism and accessibility. Policy makers and stakeholders in developing societies are searching for viable and sustainable alternatives.

PRESENT SCENARIO IN HIGHER EDUCATION

Pressure on higher education is on the rise due to boosting demand worldwide. Today, higher education worldwide confronts the new realities including expansion, differentiation and knowledge revolution. The challenge gets more pronounced in developing countries, forcing policymakers to think creatively. Previously, higher education in developing countries was characterized by small number of students. Today, a dramatic shift from 'Class to Mass' has occurred and half of the world's higher education students live in developing countries. As children complete primary and secondary education, demand for higher education keeps rising. Developing countries have also seen rising real income bringing higher education within reach.

Expansion has produced a variety of consequences. Existing institutions have grown in size and traditional institutions have been replicated by public or private means. A more creative response has been differentiation leading to new types of institutions and providers. Non-government institutions have joined public ones, while a range of vocational and professional schools now complement the traditional universities.

The public universities, despite substantial expansion, can not cope with the rising demand. Emergence of non-government universities has proven instrumental in making higher education responsive to changing demand while complying with quality parameters. The proportion of students in private institutions is on the increase, reaching over 50 per cent of total enrolments in some countries, mostly developing ones.

According to Nuffic Conference 'A Changing Landscape', The Hague, 23-25 May 2005, the major challenges facing governments and higher education institutes in the developing societies are related to Access, Massification, Privatization, Commoditization, Quality Assurance and Maintenance, Relevance, Digital Divide, International Mobility of Staff and Trends in Donor Policies.

Access relates to improved chances for women and students from poor families or regions. Massification relates to coping with the enormous growth in number of students. Privatization signifies growing need of private funds and means to attract private investment without compromising the accessibility and quality.

Commoditization implies maneuvers by the developed countries to create a free global market for higher education as a commodity. The challenge for developing countries is to resist flooding by second-rate, standard courses that do not match their cultural setting or socio-economic needs. Regarding Quality Assurance and Maintenance in a backdrop of proliferation by national, private and cross-border institutes, the challenge is to ensure minimum quality and pursue continuous improvement.

Relevance signifies connection to the world of work where curricula are geared to the local circumstances, developed in conjunction with employers avoiding blind replication of irrelevant foreign values and ideas. Digital Divide relates to new ICT opportunities implicating huge investments. The challenge is to attract donor support and private funds to facilitate ICT access and simultaneously matching online theoretical teaching with guidance and practical assignments. International Mobility of Staff while offering great opportunities for the individuals can easily lead to a brain-drain for the developing societies. Challenge is to resist the brain-drain and create better perspectives for well educated staff within the country. Finally, Trends in Donor Policies related to minimizing the cost of donor support and maximizing the benefits.

PREMISE FOR KNOWLEDGE BASED AREA DEVELOPMENT (KBAD)

The pressure of quantitative expansion, though uneven across countries and region, is more pronounced in case of the developing countries. Apart from population growth, facilitation in primary and secondary education under "Education For All" (EFA) has created rising demand for higher education in developing societies. Moreover, higher education is considered instrumental in developing societies for ushering social, cultural and political changes to counteract the legacies of colonialism and more recent undemocratic systems. Besides, the ongoing process of globalization has accentuated the efficacy of investment in higher education.

In many developing countries, the local higher education institutions and specially the ones in the public sector is failing dismally in being responsive to changes or even to be operational in their traditional and stagnant way of delivering obsolete body of knowledge. As a result, a vast number of students from these countries are migrating to developed countries for higher education. Few return to the country of origin, leading to a gaping brain-drain, that further stagnates the development prospect of the developing societies. Absence of competent faculty and policy-makers also acts adversely on the overall quality of higher education creating a vicious circle.

Although, higher education is hugely subsidized even in developed economies, the growth of non-government universities is on the rise in the developing world to meet quantitative as well as qualitative demands. The latter is more critical as it helps to fight back rampant brain-drain and creates dynamic internationalization within local non-government institutions. The issue of relevance is also ensured by default as the very existence of such institutions hinges on delivering marketable knowledge and skills. Thus, despite being expensive, enrollment in non-government universities is rising persistently.

The public universities are to some extent accessible by the low income segments as it is hugely subsidized. Yet, owing to the socio-economic reality, the prerequisite higher secondary education available to poor students are not at par with that available to the well off segments of the society. As a result the poor can have access to the public universities more as an exception than as rule. Moreover, due to lack of responsibility and ownership in the funding process, education in public universities are taken by the students less as a long term investment and more as a windfall advantage. Consequently, the pressure for being market driven is also much less in case of public universities. In many developing countries, the public universities are beset with myriads of problems. Both students and teachers indulge in partisan politics, the administration is also stagnant and the curriculum is obsolete. Disruptions in academic schedule result in very long tenure of study that ultimately proves to be devastating for the students, the society and the nation. On the other hand, the non-government universities are dictated by the market forces making it more responsive to the changing demand by default. But, access to these universities are expensive and hence out of reach of the vast majority of population in developing societies.

Governments in the developing world are making continuous efforts to expand the educational base at all levels despite serious resource constraints. The targeted education of women with stipend and tuition waiver up to Higher Secondary (12th Grade) level is an example of this effort in the context of Bangladesh. Although there is uneven spread of education in the developing societies, most urban/rural communities have many young men and women with higher secondary level education, if not higher. However, most of these people are educated in non-marketable skills or cannot pursue higher education due to opportunity/resource constraints and hence remain unemployed. A way out should be found to transform their previous investment in education into productive outcome through further investment in marketable knowledge and skills. This is the basic premise of Knowledge Based Area Development concept.

In many developing societies, area based development approach (rural and urban) is going on under the umbrella of micro-credit by the government and non-government organizations (NGOs) targeted to ultra-poor and certain special segments of population. This micro-credit has obviously contributed to alleviation of poverty to some extent but has not created prosperity for the recipients for many reasons. Thus the people continue to remain in the cycle of poverty and do not get an opportunity to break out of the poverty trap.

FUNDING HIGHER EDUCATION

Traditional public funding is shrinking and more alternative funding approaches are being tried involving all stakeholders to ensure social accountability and ownership. No country nowadays is able to support a comprehensive system of higher education from public funding alone.

Alternative funding is gaining ground in the 'policy landscape' in higher education. The consequence demands a modified distribution of cost-sharing responsibilities, increasing or introducing tuition fees and other charges and through various income-generating activities such as contract research, a broad range of academic and cultural services and short-term courses.

The search for alternative funding has proved much more difficult for the developing countries. In most instances, growth in enrolment has not been matched by allocation of resources leading institutions to cutback budgets, study programs, modernization of infrastructure, library holdings, international co-operation and even academic staff. Shortage of funds combined with growing public debate on the issue of allocation brought about a reduction of state funding for higher education, in both developed and developing countries.

Rising social expectations from higher education under diminishing resources presents a major dilemma for the developing countries. According to UNESCO's statistics, developing countries spend a much higher proportion of their GNP on the public higher education sector. Yet, these countries are far from able to allocate the level of support they need or that given in developed societies. On average expenditure per student in absolute terms is ten times lower in the developing countries than in the industrialized world. Such problems reveal a policy dilemma with regard to public spending on higher education: the poorer the region, the higher the relative cost per student, estimated in terms of the percentage of GNP allocated to higher education.

Funding is central in both capacity building and facilitation of access to higher education. It dictates extent of achievement in terms of both quality and quantity. The conventional mode of public funding suffers from some inherent limitations in quality and quantity. More and more, governments, specifically in developing world, are finding it difficult to expand and improve delivery of higher education, chiefly due to dearth of fund. Private funding in the form of non-government universities has been able to address some of the inherent deficiencies in public universities. Yet, the extent of coverage is limited for obvious reasons and the education tends to be expensive and hence inaccessible to the low income groups. The middle ground is a quasi-public funding with participation of the stakeholders. In the short run, it can prove more effective in facilitating accessibility while the issue of funding for institution-building may also be addressed in the long run through participatory funding modalities.

KNOWLEDGE BASED AREA DEVELOPMENT (KBAD)

Under KBAD, young men/women from each urban/ rural locality would be given opportunity to go for higher education and acquire a degree/diploma/post higher secondary certificate in marketable (within and outside the country) knowledge and skills. Such educated/trained person would be expected to make efforts to pull up his/her family, neighbors and the village/urban/community through access to knowledge for economic and social development. The achievement of the individual will also have a demonstration effect in the village/locality and act as an eye opener to other young people in the area. This can also bring hopes and dreams to the impoverished village community. The young men or women should reach the minimum qualification (Higher Secondary, i.e. 12 years of formal education) or equivalent to gain entry to university level institutions.

Financing of education and skill development would be a barrier to realization of Knowledge Based Area Development concept. It is expected that the family of the individual would bear the cost of such education/training.

However, economic situation in developing societies may not permit most families to bear the cost of such education. The introduction of an Educational Loan Scheme can partially alleviate this problem. The government and/or NGOs should consider developing and operating such an Educational Loan Scheme. Eventually an Educational Bank may be established to facilitate access of the middle class and poor to market oriented higher education for social mobility and as a step towards realizing the vision of Knowledge Based Area Development approach. In this process, it may be possible to break away from the poverty cycle. The Education Bank could be the conduit to finance such persons on easy terms but on a repayable basis. This would be a radical approach to break the poverty cycle but this might also work as a catalyst as well as a role model.

The Education Bank can also finance educational institutions on easy terms for institution building but on repayable basis and also provide loans to teachers for higher education and training. The capital for Education Bank can be mobilized through aids and loans from development organizations and share subscription from individuals with expectation of reasonable return on capital and philanthropic orientation. Development of human capital of the society would be the intrinsic return to donors, while financial return at a reasonable rate (?) would be the additional return to subscribers to the capital. The Education Bank is to be operated on business principles but targeted to investment in education, skill development and institution building activities relating to the same. The Education Bank can take the form of an educational cooperative.

BANGLADESH SCENARIO

Historically, higher education in Bangladesh was organized in the public sector only. That is, all universities were funded by the government through its budgeting process and there was hardly any involvement of the community in running and managing of these institutions of learning.

The university teaching systems had been mostly back dated or antiquated with two year/three year basis examination system leaving little opportunity for frequent or continuous evaluation of students, feedback to the students in terms of their performance, as well as providing a climate of interactive learning process.

The universities in the country had been passing through a chaotic situation and there was hardly any professionalism available in managing the educational programs prevailing in the universities. The faculty members were not attentive to their duties; in most cases, classes were not held on many occasions due to political unrest, intra-fighting of the faculty members, students and administration that created a condition where the universities could hardly function as academic entities. Most university academic sessions were behind schedule by three to four years with the outdated curricula irrelevant to the needs of the society leading to widespread unemployment in the country.

On the other hand, government was not in a position to create job facilities for the people. This resulted in a large group of educated, unemployed young people in the society who felt very frustrated but were not in the position to translate their knowledge and skill into any meaningful productivity. The public universities had all the elements of a good university in terms of structures and system but, unfortunately, there was hardly any professionalism in terms of academic decisions related to student admission, teaching, training, research, faculty promotion, motivation and evaluation that resulted in campus irregularities that again caused qualified faculty to move out of the country.

This again led brighter students to leave the country if financially solvent. Parents felt that it may be cheaper in the long run to send their children abroad for education because of the more than double the time period required for educational degree attainment in Bangladesh as well as the poor quality from which they are protected if their children go out and get their education.

Phenomenal quantitative expansion in higher education chiefly during the last decades was an outcome of widespread advancement of free primary and secondary education through state financing and donor funding. More and more, the public universities found themselves incapable of handling the quantitative expansion, despite the fact that good numbers of new public universities have been established to meet the growing demand. Thus, the government induced by the leading academicians and policymakers, decided to introduce private initiative in the field of higher education. Ultimately, the Non-Government University Act 1992 was enacted facilitating establishment of non-government universities. Today, there are 54 non-government universities delivering modern, market driven education through international cooperation, competent faculty and modern teaching methods. They account for 53% of student enrollment in higher education as opposed to 47% in government universities excluding enrolments in colleges and Open University. As per Annual Report of 2009 of the University Grants Commission (UGC) of Bangladesh enrollment in private universities grew rapidly from 8,718 in 2001 to more than 200,000 by the end of 2009. As of 2010 the estimated number of students in non-government universities is around 225,000. The enactment of 1992 in Bangladesh is a pioneering one among the SAARC countries which provided the framework for establishment of different universities without resorting to separate enactment for each university. The legislation survived changes in government and went through minor amendment in 1998, and substantive change in 2010. Thus, the non-government university concept has been accepted across the political divide and has become a social reality in Bangladesh.

Although, non-government universities have succeeded in supplementing the capacity of the public sector, their contribution is more commendable in terms of modernization of content and delivery. By definitions, non-government universities are tuned to the demand of the market at home and abroad, facilitating propagation of critical expertise and resisting the abysmal brain-drain that is considered devastating to the nation.

It is important to note that access to higher education in Bangladesh is not only limited - 7% of cohorts aged 17-23, as compared to 12% in India, 30% in Malaysia and 48% in Thailand - but also highly inequitable. In Bangladesh, the children of professionals, businessmen, civil servants and teachers are almost exclusively represented in higher education institutions. A World Bank review of 1990 found that "the financing arrangements in the education system and the structure of enrollments result in highly inequitable distribution of public spending on education, with the 10 percent best educated people in a generation receiving as much as 76 percent of the cumulative public spending appropriate to the entire generation through publicly financed education". Although around 10 percent of the budget for higher education is allocated to students in the form of stipends and subventions, these do not benefit the poorest because they are awarded on the basis of merit, not on economic need. Thus, the marginal impact of public spending on the disadvantaged section is quite clear. A large segment continues to be excluded from the opportunity of social mobility by having access to higher education: be it public or private. Inclusion for social equity remains to be a big challenge.

In terms of funding, non-government universities are run on self-reliant funding on full-cost-recovery approach.

Thus a big chunk of the cost is passed on to the students in the form of full fees. Yet, many of the non-government universities suffer from dearth of capital that limits their capacity to deliver in compliance with quantity and quality. As far as students are concerned, education in non-government universities is expensive by definition, barring the low income groups from availing the more modern education available within the country. The emergence of non-government universities was a condition of necessity but far from being sufficient to address the challenges facing the higher education sector in Bangladesh. Any alternative funding modality both for institution-building and for financing accessibility can play a vital role in enhancing the contribution of non-government universities to the higher education scenario. KBAD can provide such a strategic alternative.

IUBAT AND KBAD

IUBAT has set out the long term vision of producing one technical graduate from each village/ward under the KBAD concept as a step towards community self reliance. To materialize this vision and to translate the concept into reality, IUBAT has special provision for supplementing the family resources of a student through scholarship, grant, fee waiver, deferred payment, campus job, student loan and the like. It is IUBAT policy to cater to needs of all qualified students who aspire for higher professional education regardless of the income level of his/her family through appropriate educational financing arrangements.

To institutionalize the educational financing IUBAT has established an educational cooperative in the form of IUBAT Multipurpose Cooperative Society Ltd. (IMCSL), with a share capital of 50 million taka divided in 500 thousand shares of Tk 100 each. One of the prime objectives of IMCSL is to mobilize funds for providing educational loan and scholarship to the members and their dependents to help them pursue higher education and professional training. IMCSL is looked upon as a prelude to establishment of an Educational Bank (Shikkha Bank) with a wider mandate. Anyone can contribute to the share capital by becoming a member and pave the way for educational financing.

IUBAT has also introduced Career Development Loan scheme for students out of the IMCSL as well as Financial Assistance Fund (FAF) established at IUBAT. Besides facilities of deferred fees payment have been introduced at IUBAT. Loan under FAF is free of any service charge, while the loan from IMCSL or deferred payment from the university carry service charge. Students after graduation and employment are required to repay the loan on easy monthly installments, consistent with the earning potential of the degree/diploma/certificate.

Through this process, IUBAT is already practicing the concept of Knowledge Based Area Development to a limited extent. To materialize the concept on a wider scale, it is proposed to pick up one young man or woman from each village/ward and give him/her degree/diploma/certificate in marketable skills on the basis of self financing or in combination with deferred tuition payment facilities to be extended by IUBAT or Career Development Loan to be availed from IMCSL or from the FAF of IUBAT.

EXTENDING KBAD

To make the KBAD concept operational, each educated member in the developing society who made productive use of education, could be urged to motivate one 12th grade or equivalent passed young man or woman belonging to his/ her place of to enroll in any of the degree/diploma / certificate programs in a quality non-government university. Professional educational programs available at such universities (for example in IUBAT) include subjects like business administration, computer science, engineering, agriculture, economics, hospitality and tourism and nursing.

Besides motivation to enroll, the referee should make an assessment of the individual's/ family's ability to pay the relevant university fees during the study period and recommend to the university authority for granting of loan under the deferred payment facility or other alternatives for those who do not have the ability to pay the full fees during the study period.

Furthermore, the concerned member of the society should assist in development of the referred student through encouragement and psychological support during his/her difficult educational transition period. The university would send a copy of the result of the student every semester, until graduation, to the referee for information and continued motivational support. This will enable the individual to observe the outcome of his/her referral effort for development of an individual.

Through such enrollment motivation, facilitation, and encouragement through the study period each educated person will have an opportunity to repay his/her debt to the place of birth by facilitating knowledge/skill acquisition for area development and lay the seeds for community self reliance.

CONCLUDING REMARKS

Under KBAD concept, an approach is sought to make a bold attempt to prepare a section of the population to break out of poverty and enter into an era of prosperity. If replicated in a sustainable manner, the approach can go a long way in achieving socio-economic advancement in developing societies through facilitating wide scale accessibility.

This knowledge based development will require considerable capital resource as well as institutional infra-structure which can be addressed through establishment of

Educational Bank(s) in communities.

Active participation of every educated individual of a country in building a prosperous society based on knowledge will give rise to a drive towards nation building. This will be worth emulating paving the way for development of the country as a self-reliant, prosperous and self-respecting nation through meeting the challenge of financing higher education for inclusive growth at community, state and national levels.

REFERENCES

1. Annual Report 2009, University Grants Commission of Bangladesh.
2. Bangladesh Higher Education, Richard Johanson, Bangladesh Education Sector Review, Part Two, The World Bank, 2000
3. Expert Group Report 2005, University Grants Commission of Bangladesh
4. Higher Education in Developing Countries: Peril and Promise, The World Bank Task Force, 2000
5. Highlights from the UIS report: Education Counts, Benchmarking progress in 19 WEI Countries, UNESCO Institute for Statistics, www.uis.unesco.org/wei2007
6. Knowledge Based Area Development - A Step Towards Community Self-Reliance, Prof Dr M Alimullah Miyan, IUBAT, ISBN Number 984-70060-0003-7
7. Non-Government University (Amendment) Law of Bangladesh 1998
8. Non-Government University Law of Bangladesh 1992
9. Non-Government University Law of Bangladesh 2010
10. Non-Government University Movement In Bangladesh: April, 1989 Prof Dr M Alimullah Miyan
11. Nuffic Conference 'A Changing Landscape', The Hague, 23-25 May 2005

12. Nurturing Non-Government (Private) Universities of Bangladesh, Prof M Alimullah Miyan, PhD, Roundtable on Non-Government Initiatives in University Education of Bangladesh, Association of Private Universities of Bangladesh (APUB), March 15, 2010

13. Policy Paper for Change and Development in Higher Education, UNESCO 1995

14. Role of Non-Government Universities in Higher Education, Prof Dr M Alimullah Miyan, Journal of Bangladesh Studies, Volume 8 No. 1, 2006, ISSN 1529-0905

15. Strategic Plan for Higher Education in Bangladesh: 2005-2025, University Grants Commission of Bangladesh, January, 2006.

2
Human Development Foundations of Innovations in Banking

Harsha Aturupane

INTRODUCTION

Banking and finance have seen many innovations in recent years. Several of these innovations have been driven by developments in technology and communications. The internet and mobile phones have transformed and revolutionized banking. Internet banking and mobile banking are becoming increasingly common in both developed and developing countries. There are even bankers who argue that the future of banking will be in mobile banking. The mobile phone, according to them, will also become the purses and wallets of people. The mobile phone will allow contactless payments, enable deposits and transfers among deposits, and also act as a credit card. And this is just one example of the many innovations in banking.

Innovations, in all sectors including banking, arise from a variety of sources. The most frequent and sustained sources of innovation, however, are teams of highly qualified researchers, and groups of well-educated and creative professionals. Universities contain some of the best educated, most intelligent professionals and individuals in society. Hence, universities should be among the leading sources of innovations, including in banking and finance. And some universities are, indeed, sources of important innovations. But these universities tend to be a small cluster of academic institutions, mostly located in rich countries. It is important that some universities in the developing countries, too, become sources of innovation.

UNIVERSITIES AND RESEARCH AND INNOVATION

The reputation of a university is established, almost entirely, by the quality and impact of the research conducted by its academic staff. The best-known and highest-ranked universities in the world are the institutions that make the most significant contributions to the advancement of knowledge through their research. Other factors, such as the availability of innovative curricula and the quality of teaching, are far less important for the international reputation of a university. The main reason for this is that important research outcomes are known widely, and extend the reputation of a university far beyond the campus of that institution itself. In contrast, the quality of teaching and curricula are normally known only within that institution. For instance, the famous universities of the world, such as Cambridge, Harvard, Oxford and Stanford, are primarily well-known due to their research, innovation and knowledge generation, and to the quality of their teaching only secondarily.

A further reason why research is the central correlate of the reputation of a university is that the factors which help to create high class research universities also help to improve the quality of curricula and teaching. Academics who are up-to-date with the literature and thinking of their subjects and disciplines are potentially better teachers than academics who are outdated and obsolete.

CONDITIONS FOR HIGH QUALITY RESEARCH AND INNOVATION CAPACITY IN UNIVERSITIES

The development of good research universities requires an abundance of resources. Research in most fields is expensive. And universities around the world are willing to pay high salaries to attract well-known researchers as staff. Research-intensive universities are also complex organizations to develop, operate and expand. All these require very generous resources. All the famous research universities are well-endowed financially. And wealthy universities have resources not only to promote research, but to introduce innovations in curricula and to attract good teachers.

A second factor needed to develop good research universities is a concentration of talent. The top research universities have both outstanding academics and outstanding students. The latter often proceed to become the well-known academics of the next generation. The best known universities in the world draw their talent pool of academic staff and students not from within their national boundaries but from across the entire globe. The top universities in the US and UK have about 20-25 percent of their students and around 30-35 percent of their staff from overseas. And clearly a concentration of talent not only helps promote research but also enables a university to pitch courses and teach to a higher level of academic content and rigor.

A third factor required to produce good research universities is a high degree of autonomy. This is clearly seen in the experience of North American universities as against many university systems in continental Europe. The majority of the leading research universities in the world are in the

U.S.A., and the American higher education sector is characterized by a high degree of autonomy and flexibility. American universities are able to set fees and influence their revenues; establish institutional arrangements through which academics can generate resources for and from research, and devote substantial time to engage in research activities; award benefit packages and incentives to attract high quality researchers, including paying differential salaries to academics; and create admissions criteria and processes to lure highly talented students. Many university systems in continental Europe have found difficulty competing with the American universities due to their highly centralized governance structures. This includes common salary scales and benefits for academics in all universities; incentive systems that do not necessarily promote research; centralized admissions that sometimes seek to distribute talented students "equitably" among all universities; and relatively inflexible distributions of workloads that may not allow academics to specialize in research according to their comparative advantages. The national context, too, requires a high degree of autonomy. Good quality research needs freedom for academics to engage in and disseminate research findings with minimal control from the state or other social institutions.

Given this context, universities in developing countries face considerable challenges to the promotion of research. First, resources are scarce. As a result, various types of research that require expensive equipment and material are not feasible. Second, mainly and as a consequence of the scarcity of resources, universities do not have an adequate concentration of talent, whether of staff or students. Most university departments have a few good researchers, at best. And the brain drain weakens the talent pool. Third, the governance structure of many university systems does not facilitate research. For instance, most universities lack a mechanism to attract and utilize resources for research efficiently and speedily. Also, the incentive system does not necessarily promote research, especially at the level of institutions such as departments and faculties. Academics who engage in research usually have to swim against the tide.

However, there are also opportunities. First, the current generations of university academics contain several individuals who consider research and the production of knowledge as a vitally important component of their work programs. There are probably more research papers published by the present generations of academics than all the academics of past generations, when lecturers perceived themselves mainly as teachers, combined. Second, modern communications technology has reduced the information and technology gap between the developed countries and the developing countries. There is a vast and rapidly growing body of knowledge and information available electronically, now, which can be accessed from anywhere in the world. Consider, for instance, the availability of e-journals and e-libraries. This means that knowledge can and does travel faster across the world, and academics in developing counties can tap into this body of knowledge relatively easily. Third, research is increasingly being done by cross-institutional and trans-institutional teams collaborating across national and even continental boundaries. This provides opportunities for academics in developing country universities to collaborate with academics in developed countries on research projects, and to tap into the resources of wealthier and better funded universities.

POLICY MEASURES TO PROMOTE RESEARCH AND INNOVATION IN UNIVERSITIES

There are a number of steps that the university system in South Asia can take to minimize the constraints to the promotion of research and to expand opportunities for innovation and knowledge-generation.

First, universities need to establish formal institutions to facilitate and promote research, such as technology brokering centers and business offices. This would benefit universities by increasing the revenues they can generate by offering intellectual services to the world of industry and commerce. It would also benefit the national economy, as firms and companies can tap into the considerable intellectual resources available in universities for their research and development, and monitoring and evaluation, activities.

Second, universities need to set up institution-wide incentive systems to promote research. For instance, if an academic can attract resources for research, there can be a system by which she/her can " buy " time off from her/his teaching and administration, with a payment from the research grant. This payment can be used to recruit the additional teaching and administrative help needed to substitute for that academics' teaching and administration time. And a part of the grant can be made available to the university, faculty and department of the academic, to upgrade facilities and improve equipment.

Third, the distinction between "research" and "consulting" work is increasingly blurred, and should be discarded completely. If an academic can attract research resources from which the individual is paid for her/his skills and time, that is a positive outcome of the demand for that academics knowledge and capabilities. It should be encouraged in terms of the incentives and rewards it offers for university academics to engage in research. And it will benefit the national university system, as the increase in earnings that academics receive will decrease, at the margin, the propensity of researchers to emigrate out of the country.

Fourth, the funding of education and higher education seriously needs to be re-visited. For instance, India invests relatively little on education, approximately 3.7 percent of GDP. This is well below the average for developing countries and middle-income countries. Lower middle income countries invest around 4.3 percent of GDP on education, and upper-middle income countries invest about 4.6 percent of GDP on education. Yet, the scope for increasing public investment in education is restricted over the medium-term. Hence, alternative strategies to increase education financing, including expanding the scope for the higher education sector to draw resources from the private sector, needs to be developed and facilitated.

SUGGESTIONS FOR RESEARCH IN THE CONTEXT OF INNOVATIONS IN BANKING AND INCLUSION

The technology driven innovations in banking, including internet banking and mobile banking, are accessible to the rich and affluent. However, in developing countries there are large numbers and proportions of people who are not able to afford the computers and technology devices to benefit from these opportunities. In a country such as India, hundreds of millions of people are excluded from these benefits. The marginalized, illiterate and other vulnerable populations are likely to take generations before they can access these technological benefits.

It would be very useful if economists and social scientists could explore the equity implications of this dimension of innovations in banking. At the same time, engineers and scientists need to undertake research into areas that will enable technology based banking to be more accessible for the poor and vulnerable.

3

Furthering Financial Inclusion through Financial Literacy and Credit Counselling

S. Annamalai

It has been universally accepted that Financial Inclusion can act as an effective tool to accelerate the economic growth and alleviate poverty in the world. Various countries including United Kingdom, United States, Canada, France, Brazil and Australia are taking efforts to bring the underprivileged segment of the society into banking fold thus improving their financials and living standards.

Financial Inclusion in the Indian Context has been defined as the provision of affordable financial services, viz., access to payments and remittance facilities, savings, loans and insurance services by the formal financial system to those who tend to be excluded. Financial Inclusion is important for the poor as it provides them opportunities to build savings, avail credit, make investments and equips them to meet emergencies.

FINANCIAL EXCLUSION SCENARIO IN INDIA

- India is second largest populated country in the world and 72.17% population is living in villages.
- Out of 6.0 lakh habitations in the Country, only about 30,000 have a commercial Bank branch
- Just about 40% of the population across the country has bank accounts and only 26.2% of the rural population is covered through bank accounts.
- Out of 89.3 million farmer households, about 45.9 million (51.4%) do not have access to credit either from credit institutions or from non-institutional sources
- Proportion of people with life insurance cover is as low as 10% and non life insurance cover is at abysmal 0.6%
- Only 2% of population has access to credit card.
- Only 13% of population has ATM/ Debit card.
- Exclusion is as high as over 75% in North Eastern States and ranging between 25-50% in other States.
- Financial Exclusion is noticeable predominantly in large sections of rural areas and slums in Urban areas.

INITIATIVES FOR FINANCIAL INCLUSION IN INDIA

Phase I

- Starting in the late 60's through the 80's, the focus was on channeling of credit to the neglected sector of the society with special emphasis on weaker section.
- Nationalization of major commercial Banks- 14 Banks in 1969 & 6 Banks in 1980.
- Strengthening of Co-operative sector in rural areas.
- Introduction of Lead Bank Scheme in 1969, to expand outreach to rural & semi urban areas
- Creation of Regional Rural Banks, in 1975.

- Targets for Priority sector, Agriculture, Small Scale Industries, DRI, etc
- Service Area Approach introduction in 1989.
- 20 point economic programme & Integrated Rural Development Programme (IRDP) in rural & Semi urban areas

Phase II

- Early 90's to March 2005, the focus was on strengthening the financial institutions as a part of financial sector reforms. Financial inclusion in this phase was encouraged mainly by the introduction of Self Help Group (SHG) - Bank linkage in early 90's and Kisan Credit Card (KCC) to farmers.

Phase III

- In April 2005, Financial Inclusion was explicitly made as a major policy objective and thrust was on providing safe facility of saving deposits through no frill accounts.
- General Credit Card (GCC) and Overdraft (OD) were introduced in 2006.
- RBI permitted banks to utilize the services of NGOs, SHGs, MFIs as Business Facilitators (BFs) and Business Correspondents (BCs).
- Establishment of Rural Self Employment Training Institutes (RSETI) and Financial Literacy and Credit Counseling (FLCC) Centres.
- Proposed to extend insurance and other services also to the targeted beneficiaries.
- Encouraging Business Correspondent and other banking services delivery models with appropriate technology back up.
- Setting up of Unique Identification Authority of India (UIDAI) for providing UID number to all citizens

which will help in solving KYC issues and enable interoperability which will facilitate customer of one bank to transact with business correspondent of another banking using smart card through Point of Sale (POS) Machine (Micro ATMs).

ROLE OF FLCC

- To educate the people in rural and urban areas with regard to various financial products and services available from the formal financial sector.
- To make the people aware of the advantages of being connected with the formal financial sector.
- To provide face-to-face financial counseling services, including education on responsible borrowing and offering debt counseling to individuals who are indebted to formal and/or informal financial sectors.
- To formulate debt restructuring plans for borrowers in distress and recommend the same to formal financial institutions, including cooperatives, for consideration.
- To take up any such activity that promotes financial literacy, awareness of the banking products, financial planning and amelioration of debt-related distress of an individual.
- To create awareness among the public about various financial management.

4
Microcredit and Capability Enhancement: An Institutional Perspective

Shankaran Nambiar

INTRODUCTION

Organisations that extend microcredit have been accepted as having a useful role to play in improving the well-being of the disadvantaged sections of many economies. In this context, the Grameen Bank experience comes to mind. Indeed, the question of how credit can be extended to the least advantaged, especially when they do not have the resources to apply for loans with conventional banks, is a vexing issue for policy makers. But more than merely relaxing the credit constraint for the disadvantaged, many of the attempts at providing microcredit go beyond supplying loans. Some of the organisations try to encourage entrepreneurial skills and income-generating strategies, while others attempt to change the attitudes of the target audience.

Sen's capability approach is a useful tool to analyse the design and operation of microcredit organisations. This is because organisations that offer credit seek to improve the capabilities of the disadvantaged in a broader sense than merely offering loans so that the individuals concerned can buy capital, resources, or whatever else it might be that they require. Sen does not specify a list of capabilities, but by capabilities he means anything that can improve the way an individual lives and does what he values. This list could include obvious elements such as enjoying good nutrition, health, adequate access to nutrition; but it could also include enjoying healthy relationships, and the freedom to participate socially. Aside from extending loans, microcredit agencies certainly wish to improve the well-being of individuals, an issue that is central to Sen's capability approach.

This paper seeks to explore the relevance of Sen's capability approach to microcredit. The paper is organised as follows. The first section provides an overview of Sen's capability approach. The second section illustrates how Sen's framework can be applied to a case study of a microcredit initiative in Malaysia. This is followed by a discussion of how microcredit initiatives can be employed to improve capabilities. Finally, some concluding remarks are made.

THE CAPABILITY APPROACH

Sen's capability approach is based on the notion that people seek commodities because they possess certain characteristics[1]. For instance, we are interested in a plate of rice for the nutrients and calorific value that it possesses. The characteristics approach leads to functionings because a good's characteristics make possible a functioning. People derive the functioning of energy from rice and the functioning of mobility from the car. Goods, because of the characteristics that they possess, make possible functionings. To pursue our example, a person values a plate of rice for its nutritional and calorific value rather than for the whiteness of rice. A commodity would be chosen because it contains a sub-set of characteristics that are valuable for the functionings that they make possible and which are valued[2].

The concepts of functionings and capabilities figure prominently in Sen's capability approach. Functionings are referred to as the "beings and doings" of a person[3]. Functionings are the more foundational term in that they refer to all that a person is and does. But they do not fully encapsulate a person's abilities since they do not include the choice that a person would exert in determining what exactly a person would be or do. The element of choice, and hence, of freedom to exercise choice is more properly present in the notion of capabilities. Capability is a broader concept since it is a set of vectors of functionings. It is because it is a set of functionings that specific configurations of functionings can be selected from it. This act of choosing specific combinations endows a person with the "freedom to lead one type of life or another" (Sen, 1992:40).

Sen establishes a link between commodities and freedom through his capability approach. A chain of instruments is necessary to facilitate the movement from commodities to freedom. The first link in this chain is provided by a number of 'conversion factors'[4]. These factors make it possible for commodities to be converted into functionings since the mere availability of commodities does not automatically guarantee functionings. The acknowledgement of conversion factors is important for two reasons. Sen recognises that the possession of commodities does not by itself ensure that people are able to extract the benefits of these commodities to improve their well-being.

Also, there are obstacles to the achievement of capabilities that hinder the achievement of capabilities

There are three conversion factors that inhibit or encourage the transformation of characteristics into functionings[5]. These factors are: a) personal characteristics, b) social characteristics, and c) environmental characteristics. By personal characteristics are meant those characteristics that a person is endowed with and which affect his bodily operation as well as his psychological make-up and operation. Examples of such characteristics include a person's intelligence, psycho-motor skills, metabolism, physical or mental handicaps, and height. Thus a person who receives ample supplies of food may not be able to convert them into the functioning of nutrition if he suffers from a persistent medical condition that affects his absorptive capacity. Similarly, a person who is given a car cannot convert it into the functioning of mobility if he cannot coordinate the movement of his feet with his hands, as when he has to simultaneously use the steering wheel and engage the gear.

Social characteristics include gender practices in a society, social norms, social hierarchies, and government policies[6]. Many striking examples can be given to illustrate the efficacy of social characteristics in inhibiting the conversion of commodities into functionings[7]. In a society where women are not allowed to walk along streets, an otherwise good transportation system cannot be converted into the functioning of travel. Similarly, if there are religious constraints to women assuming positions of authority in society, then education and individual talent will obstruct women from gaining the functioning of power. An example can be given from caste-ridden societies, where members of lower castes may be prevented from using specified public tanks or wells, although they may have pots. This makes water as a commodity more difficult to obtain, it also makes the functionings of cleanliness and health more problematic for those households that belong to the lower castes in such societies.

The third conversion factor is made up of environmental characteristics such as the provision of public goods (such as parks, street lighting, water supply), climate, and infrastructural facilities. It will be useful to give some examples to illustrate how these conversion factors can act as a constraint to the acquisition of functionings. The absence of street lighting, for instance, can restrict the ability of people to gain the functioning of mobility at night even if they have cars. If governments do not provide parks, people who have the time for leisure may not be able to enjoy the functioning of leisure that is specifically associated with walking through a park, or having a picnic in a park. When the infrastructure in a country is inadequate it hinders trading, commerce, and the distribution of goods. This will discourage businessmen and could suppress the flourishing of the functioning of entrepreneurship, although businessmen may not have problems in obtaining the necessary inputs and credit.

The notion of conversion factors and the associated examples show the relationship between commodities and functionings. Commodities, by themselves, are not an assurance of happiness or well-being, as we have seen. In fact, personal handicaps of one form or another, social restrictions and constraints, as well as environmental factors can act to restrict functionings. But if the conversion factors are of such manner as to enable the person to make full use of the commodities at his disposal, then the set of functionings that a person will possess will be at the its maximum, or close to any such notional level. When the set of functionings is at its maximum, then the person has the fullest level of freedom that can be obtained with the given set of commodities. Alternatively, a person can have the same bundle of commodities as was the case previously, but if the conversion factors are a heavily restricting, then the set of functionings that a person can derive from the commodities will be much smaller. Commodities cannot, therefore, be taken by themselves to denote the functionings that a person has access to. A set of commodities cannot be an indicator of the freedom that a person has at his hands without considering the quality of the conversion factors. The same set of commodities in combination with favourable conversion factors can give a high degree of freedom, but with unfavourable conversion factors the resulting functionings, and the consequent freedom, will be more modest.

The capability approach derives its name from the capabilities that a person possesses. Capability is used in this approach in a very special sense. Here capability refers to a person's ability to function, or to choose from a set of functionings. Functionings are distinct from capabilities. Functionings indicate what a person is and does. On the other hand, a person's capability is determined by the combination of functionings that a person can choose from a given vector of functionings. A person's capability is thus tied to freedom in so far as he can exert his choice over a vector of functionings to select the precise combination that he has reason to value. A person with a wider range of functionings at his disposal, quite naturally, has more opportunities to exploit. To the extent that he has a wider array of functionings at his disposal, to that extent does a person have more opportunities available to him. It is in this sense that a person can exercise his capability and by so doing enjoy the freedom that he obtains.

Microcredit is geared towards ensuring that the poor and disadvantaged have a wider range of opportunities. The purpose of extending microcredit is to permit the disadvantaged to enjoy more functionings. However, the fundamental challenge that is confronted by the disadvantaged is the restrictions they face in terms of the capabilities that they have access to. The constraints to capabilities can be physical, but there is almost always an institutional component that has to be overcome in seeking to enhance capabilities. [8] The institutions that enable economic transactions can also restrict them; and it is these institutions that must be overcome if individuals are enjoy a wider space of capabilities.

Organisations that seek to provide microcredit have to engage themselves with relaxing the institutional constraints that restrict the fulfilment of capabilities. Many of these institutions have the characteristics of path dependence in that they tend to be self-enforcing and are resistant to change. The restrictions that are imposed by caste are one example of a path dependent capability-constraining institution. Similarly, gender restrictions that prevent a female child from attending school are another constraint that can be a path dependent institution. The flowering of capabilities can be achieved only if path dependent institutional constraints are overcome. [9] The provision of microcredit has to grapple with the wider issues posed by institutional constraints rather than limiting itself simply to extending credit. In the discussion that follows, the case of a Malaysian microcredit organisation is examined so as to highlight how the institutional constraints to capability improvement can be removed.

CREDIT UNION MOVEMENT: A MALAYSIAN CASE

The operation of a microfinance institution in Malaysia offers an interesting instance of how our analytical framework can be used to examine the achievement of capabilities. In other words, the capabilities approach, once it incorporates an institutional approach, becomes a suitable tool for the analysis of development programmes.

The organisation, *Koperasi Kredit Rakyat* (KKR) (or, the People's Credit Cooperative Society), that is the subject of our case analysis, initially functioned as a youth social club in the early 70s. As a social club its goal was to improve the socio-economic status of estate workers, which it endeavoured to do by conducting tailoring classes and offering tuition and pre-school instruction to the children of plantation workers. In 1975, the club became a member of the Credit Union Promotion Club (CUPC) and was registered as a credit cooperative. The CUPC, which was registered a year earlier under the Society Act of Malaysia, was together with the National Federation of Credit Unions in Malaysia (NAFCUM), a pioneers in introducing credit unions throughout the country. NAFCUM was established in 1970, but has remained an informal organisation. Following the success of KKR, credit unions were established for workers (*Koperasi Kredit Pekerja* or the Workers's Credit Cooperative) and tribals (the Indigenous Peoples' Credit Union). These cooperatives may be collectively referred to as the Credit Union Movement (CUM), a title by which the founders refer to these organisations.

Initial encouragement for the establishment of credit unions came from the Church, with the general sense of agreement that this was the right approach to adopt in Malaysia. Early support in the form of inspiration came from the Catholic Welfare Services of Malaysia and the Asian Confederation of Credit Unions. The local church and Misereor were the first organisations to provide funding. Founding members of the project were sent to Searsolin in the Philippines and the Indian Social Institute, India for the necessary training. Participation in the Cendhrra Network provided exposure and capacity building in the founding of the credit movement in Malaysia.

The CUM was committed to three objectives: a) to eradicate poverty, b) to eradicate ignorance, and c) to identify and nurture grassroots leaders. One must note that these objectives were formed against the backdrop of the changing economic scenario in Malaysia. Primary among the influences that affected the country at that time was the shift to export-oriented growth, spurred by the influx of multinational companies, and along with it the winding-down of the agriculture sector. These factors led to rural-urban migration and a general neglect of the rural sector. By the late 70s rubber plantations ceased to be as important as they used to be and the problems of estate workers - the locus of CUM's attention - were exacerbated.

It, thus, stands to reason why CUM, in the early years of its founding, was concerned with the rural poor. One of CUM's principle goals has been to "consolidate and strengthen the existing human and financial resources among the poor" (Sinnappan, undated). This statement is a clear indication that the agents of this organisation are willing to accept the pre-existing resources of the communities that they work with as a starting point and something that can be built upon. Consonant with this goal is that of preparing "ordinary men and women to participate in national economic programmes through small grassroots economic initiatives" (Sinnappan, undated). Although it is doubtful whether or not the communities that CUM have worked with are able to participate in national economic programmes, there is no doubt that it has been true to its goal in working with small communities for their uplift. Other goals that CUM has sought to achieve include helping members' children attain higher levels of academic and technical education and networking with 'progressive' NGOs. CUM has also been keen on achieving social justice and gender-based egalitarianism.

CUM has laid much emphasis on volunteerism in executing its activities. There are five areas where CUM has been very active (Kuala Lumpur, Batang Berjuntai, Seremban, Bagan Serai and Sungai Petani) and each of these areas has a team of volunteers who promote the organisation's agenda. Most of the leaders of the organisation hold jobs of their own and pursue CUM's activities on their own time and initiative. It is not surprising, therefore, that there are only 30 full-time staff and about 2,000 community-based volunteer leaders for an organisation that has some 40,000 members. This feature of the NGO, besides reinforcing the philosophy of volunteerism, keeps the cost of staff maintenance low, and, by extension, keeps the costs of loans low.

Central to the CUM programme is the generation of savings from its members. Before we come to the issue of savings we would do well to indicate the criteria of membership that CUM draws. CUM permits only the poor to join its groups. It classifies the poor, for membership purposes, as being hard-core, below the poverty line or upward mobility poor. The hard core poor are defined as those households earning less than RM350 per month. The poor beneath the poverty line includes all households earning less than RM500 per month but more than RM350 per month, whereas those categorised as upward mobility poor are those earning less than RM1,000 per month but more than RM500 per month. The following categories of people are encouraged to become members: tribals, single mothers, widows, the physically challenged and youths who have no gainful employment. CUM envisions poverty as the common bond among its members, and uses its categories of poverty as a stringent measure for excluding certain groups from membership. Thus, politicians, landlords, plantation managers and supervisors and money-lenders are not granted membership into any of its groups.

The cornerstone of CUM is based on the generation of savings from among its members. Savings are mobilised by encouraging members to save. This is done on an entirely voluntary basis. Since CUM's members are poor, the biggest obstacle faced by facilitators is in pointing out that it is, indeed, possible for them to save. This is done by analysing the family and personal budgets of members followed by an examination of expenditure patterns, before showing how savings can be made. The requisite support for savings is garnered by developing the necessary administration of the community's savings. This takes the form of adequate management and book-keeping systems that are transparent to the members of the community and by establishing norms of accountability. Reports of accounts are discussed at the community level in annual meetings.

The success of the CUM is apparent from its membership of 40,367 persons in 2003[11]. This population is drawn from a total of 462 credit unions, 50 per cent of which are based in rural areas. About RM35 million was generated, by the end of 2003, in the form of savings, and loans amounting to RM106 million were extended by CUM from its inception to the year 2003. The total capital that CUM had mobilised by the same year was (approximately) an astounding RM58 million. With this huge source of funds it is easy to see how CUM can offer services ranging from loans to assistance in small business development, agricultural business development, housing for the rural poor and assistance for single mothers and widows.

Network formation is the primary tool that is used to organise people into becoming members of the group as well as pursuing the goals of the various groups that are members of CUM. As mentioned by Sinappan (personal communication), this involves forging connections among members in a number of ways. The usual methodology that is followed includes a five-step process that is organised along the following lines:

1. encouraging the community to undertake a socio-economic survey of itself
2. introductory meeting to discuss findings of above-mentioned survey and present initial concepts

regarding the notion of a credit union

3. conducting a pre-membership course
4. engaging in a decision-making process as to whether it would serve the community to form a credit union
5. election of leaders from within the community to manage a credit union

As is apparent, the methodology revolves around the participation of the community, and, in particular, it encourages the formation of networks among members of the community. The first step is primarily one that prods the community into organising themselves into organising a survey so that the intuition of the community is verified through the socio-economic survey that they undertake. This step is useful in understanding the final outcome of the community, but it does not re-present to the community the processes that constrain the community. In that sense, the first step is a partial learning process because a more complete process would incorporate an understanding of the path dependent nature of various elements that individuals in the community are subject to. The second step is a natural sequel to the first: it is a self-reflexive exercise that objectively mirrors to the members of the community the status of their socio-economic condition[12]. This step offers a juncture for presenting the concept of a credit union. This is followed by a pre-membership course. This course introduces the potential members into an understanding of what the formation of a credit union would entail in terms of obligations and commitment that would be expected of the members. The fourth step, again, requires network formation. Notwithstanding the fact that individuals in the community are already engaged in links, the meetings that are organised by the CUM facilitators presses individuals into forming networks with a different view, that is, with a view to overcoming elements of path dependence within the community. The decision-making process elicits network formation since individuals, in the course of discussing issues relating to the problem at hand, come to know each other better and so pave the way for the final step, which is the election of leaders. Encouraging the formation of networks under the ambit of CUM is very much the focus of the programme. This is, in part, done through courses of different strands (e.g. lessons on leadership, membership empowerment and refresher courses). Meetings are held for a variety of reasons, including planning, implementing and evaluating programmes.

Perhaps, the function of providing credit remains the central, palpable function that CUM offers. Because of its visible and immediate nature the exercise of lifting the constraint on access to credit attracts and sustains membership. In the rural communities, the individuals borrowed money from the credit unions, for the repayment of debts, to meet marriage and funeral expenses and to cover the costs of celebrating festivals. More recently, the shift in borrowing patterns is for purposes such as increasing agricultural production, starting businesses, covering the cost of education and for the purchase or renovation of houses. One, thus, sees a change in the pattern for which individuals borrow. There is a shift from borrowing for social purposes to borrowing for more economic or business-oriented purposes. At any rate these reasons work to improve the capabilities of individuals in the community, and they permit the groups to address wider issues of interest to the community.

Aside from providing credit CUM takes an active position on gender issues. It has instituted gender programmes which seek to help women struggle against the stronghold of patriarchy[13]. At a more concrete and micro-level, there are programmes to help its female members acquire managerial skills as well as to conduct micro-enterprises. Women are also provided with leadership training to improve their self-esteem and confidence. Programmes are also conducted to conscientise men, so that they become more responsible husbands and fathers and equal partners in the house. The aim of this move is to reduce domestic violence and to get men to share household chores with their wives, besides inducing men to spend more judiciously.

Aside from gender issues, CUM attempts to address a wide range of issues as would befit an organisation that seeks to achieve social mobilisation. In choosing the variety of issues that it selects, CUM takes into account the socio-economic context and spatial location of the target groups. Broadly, CUM distinguishes between groups based in plantations, urban squatter communities, and indigenous villages and land settlement schemes[14]. In the case of its activities in the plantation sector, CUM addresses issues such as monthly wages, rights to basic amenities, sale of estates for development purposes, health security and issues relating to migrant workers. CUM in its work with urban squatters provides support in issues relating to the eviction of squatters, the sale of squatter land and the provision of basic amenities (for example, water, drainage and play centres) in squatter areas. Finally, the set of issues that are addressed in regard to indigenous people is quite distinct. One of the prime problems that indigenous people face is with regard to their customary rights of land, which is often not respected by land developers. Similarly, the threat of deforestation poses difficulties for their livelihoods and presents challenges when it comes to relocation.

In keeping with its objectives of striving for social justice and helping the disadvantaged participate in the broader national economic activities, CUM provides training and education in many areas. These areas include youth, gender and children development programmes. Education is also provided in consumer and environmental issues.

CUM has also attempted to organise farmers and agricultural workers to fight for their rights. Indeed, it has also run programmes to provide para-legal training. A brief listing of these areas as well as recognition of the fact that it works towards "gender egalitarianism" suggests that CUM takes its role of social mobilisation very seriously. Although CUM works with target groups that have varying levels of education, this has not discouraged it from conducting workshops on issues as diverse and topical as globalisation and the World Trade Organisation. It has also sought to increase the awareness of individuals in its communities on specific issues such as the impact of the Agreement on Agriculture and the Trade Related Intellectual Property Rights on consumers.

An example such as CUM illustrates how a group of people can offer the necessary agency in order to help disadvantaged individuals achieve the capabilities that will improve their livelihoods. Looked at differently, a capability approach that is devoid of institutions fails to capture the mechanics through which the enhancement of capabilities can be achieved. In the case of CUM, we find that this organisation provides the agency through which disadvantaged individuals form connections. These individuals, be they the poor or women, are able to form connections with other disadvantaged individuals and by doing so are able to achieve certain capabilities that they value. Thus, these individuals are able to enjoy capabilities such as education, nutritious food, housing, and a life free from violence, to mention some examples. As we have seen, higher incomes are not the only thing that CUM assists individuals in achieving. Self-esteem and self-confidence are equally important in their scheme of objectives.

One cannot lose sight of the fact that much of the work that is done by CUM is of an institutional nature. The institutional aspect of being in a disadvantaged situation refers to the cognitive systems that the disadvantaged take upon themselves as part of a lived process. Clearly, the disadvantaged, be they the poor, women or the unemployed, adopt certain cognitive systems and with these systems are associated specific rules and mental models. Part of the work that CUM does is to help change aspects of the mental models and cognitive systems, if not the model in its totality. As we have seen, this is done in many ways, one of which is to mirror these debilitating rules to the disadvantaged so that they can develop routines that help them overcome their disadvantage. Of course, it is not only new routines that are transferred. As part of the system of providing credit, incomes are expanded, and this is something that Sen distinguishes from capabilities. While CUM attempts to improve incomes, it pays no less attention to the improvement of capabilities; and it does this by teaching the members of the community appropriate ways of developing suitable routines.

There are several levels at which institutions are touched upon in an effort such as CUM's. The first relates to developing new routines, since the disadvantaged have to learn routines that are in consonance with their attempts to move away from their initial positions of disadvantage. For women who have no familiarity with doing business or being employed, it is necessary to develop appropriate routines. As a consequence of participating in the leadership and planning programmes that are offered by CUM these women gain the confidence to create suitable routines to handle the tasks that they now have to undertake. Similarly, by equipping the poor to acquire the necessary skills to set up their own micro-enterprises the poor are being encouraged to develop the necessary routines, be it to apply for licences or in matters relating to farming.

Learning, which is central to any theory of institutions, plays an important role in the activities of the CUM. One may add, without running the risk of stating the obvious, that disadvantage individuals know their condition. However, an explicit awareness of this condition is brought out through meetings, and, particularly, through the socio-economic survey that is carried out at the start of CUM's programmes with any community. The regular meetings fulfil two functions: a) they aid in making explicit and sharing in the public domain what the disadvantage realise, anyway, and, b) they help forge connections among fellow disadvantaged individuals, which is necessary for the execution of the programmes. Meetings as well as the training programmes are used in two ways: 1) to learn about the pre-existing capability situation, and 2) to learn routines that would help overcome the norms and conventions that support the path dependent nature of capability-restricting institutions.

The third manner in which institutions are drawn upon in our framework is through the formation of networks. These connections which go to constitute networks lay the basis for a fresh set of institutions (rules and routines) that are able to overcome path dependent institutions. Meetings of all manner help to create these networks. As mentioned previously, the disadvantaged individuals in a community would have their own ties prior to the agency of an NGO such as CUM. Nevertheless, with the arrival of CUM (and through its activities) a set of networks would be formed that help to execute the NGO's objectives. Thus, as we have observed in our record of CUM's case, networks are formed that assist in improving capabilities.

MICROCREDIT INITIATIVES FOR CAPABILITY IMPROVEMENT

Microcredit initiatives such as CUM should be viewed as undertaking a broad range of efforts that go towards providing credit. In that sense there are two issues that are at stake in analysing the functioning of micro credit organisations. First, it should be recognised that micro credit organisations seek to improve capabilities, rather than restricting themselves to increasing the incomes of the disadvantaged. This is an important distinction that arises from Sen's exposition of capabilities. There is frequent stress on income in the literature on microcredit rather than on the other factors that contribute to well-being, not the least of which is freedom. Second, as the CUM case illustrates, microcredit organisations should (and often do) assist in altering the institutions that surround the disadvantaged individuals who participate in these schemes. By this is meant that the norms, rules and mental models that affect the behaviour of recipients of credit should be changed by micro credit institutions, as CUM illustrates.

CUM targets tribals, single mothers, widows and the physically challenged. As with other microcredit institutions the disadvantaged are the centre of focus. CUM does not restrict itself with the provision of credit, but it casts its net wider and attempts to address the problems that these disadvantaged groups confront. Correspondingly, the activities that are undertaken include those faced by urban squatters, activities relating to land rights for indigenous people, and the issue of monthly wages for plantation workers.

Rather than confining itself to relaxing the credit constraints that these groups have, CUM makes an effort to expand the space of freedom that the disadvantaged groups can enjoy. Sen's notion of capabilities goes beyond the narrow scope of income, and the case of CUM shows how microcredit institutions can effectively engage in achieving a broader set of capabilities. Sen does not propose a list of capabilities, but the efforts of CUM suggest that against the overarching objective of maximising the freedom that the disadvantaged can obtain, there are other more specific capabilities that need to be sought.

Consequently, it is not surprising that the services that are offered include arranging loans both for personal and professional purposes as well as assistance with business development. The latter service is important and signifies an interest in creating and promoting the entrepreneurial spirit among the disadvantaged. It is possible for the disadvantaged to move out of their circle of dependence to the extent that they are better entrepreneurs and can thereby exercise greater freedom in taking advantage of opportunities. This exemplifies that the capability to exercise entrepreneurial skills is an important one that institutions should seek to develop.

From the foregoing discussion it is clear that possessing entrepreneurial skills is a capability that is worthy of pursuit. This capability is all the more important given the limited financial and physical resources at the disposal of the disadvantaged. In the face of these, and other social constraints, microcredit is a necessary instrument for the facilitation of entrepreneurship. As Sen argues, the achievement of capabilities is necessary to be able to live a life that one values; there is no doubt that entrepreneurship permits this. However, microcredit is necessary for the disadvantaged to live the sort of lives that they value; and this is where institutions such as CUM have a role to play.

The applicability of the capability approach in analysing institutions that provide microcredit seems to be a direct application of the capability approach. However, there is a less direct aspect to Sen's capability approach that has to be developed in explaining how microcredit institutions can improve the capabilities of the disadvantaged. CUM, quite clearly, is interested in raising the self-esteem and dignity of its target group. This is a broader objective than that of raising the incomes of the disadvantaged. This requires a change in the cognitive structure of individuals involved. Similarly, to gain and exercise entrepreneurial skills demands a reorientation of the individuals' manner of thinking, and exercising their mental models. In other words, this involves a change in the institutions that govern the way they interact so as to seize the opportunities that come their way. Sen does not have much to say on this. However, this is a crucial way in which microcredit institutions can contribute to the capabilities of the disadvantaged.

CONCLUSION

The capability approach shifts attention away from the traditional focus on income to a set of capabilities that allows individuals to enjoy the life that they value. Institutions that seek to provide microcredit have within their capacity the possibility of providing a wider range of capabilities to the disadvantaged. To think of improving the lives of individuals by increasing their incomes would be to take a rather narrow view of well-being since it omits important considerations such as freedom and access to being and enjoying a life that one thinks worthwhile.

The case study of a microcredit provider in Malaysia that has been narrated and analysed shows how organisations can extend themselves in a manner that assists them in achieving an improved set of capabilities. Indeed, dignity and self-esteem are important aspects of an individual's life and deserve attention, aspects that CUM, for instance, attempts to address. There are useful lessons that emerge from our discussion of CUM. Perhaps the most important lesson that emerges is that it is necessary to change the institutions that help foster individual agency so as to improve capabilities.

ENDNOTES

1 Sen (1985:9-10) acknowledges the contribution of Lancaster

(1966), but adds that in addition to commodities and characteristics we "have to consider the 'functionings' of persons", that is how commodities and characteristics are used to deliver well-being.

2 Robeyns (2000:12) correctly stresses that commodities are valuable within the capability approach not merely because they are exchangeable for income or money, but because of the characteristics that enable a functioning. She gives the example of a bike which is valued not only because it is object made of certain materials, with certain features, but because it enables the functioning of mobility.

3 Sen (2000:75) states that the "concept of "functionings," which has distinctly Aristotelian roots, reflects the various things a person may value doing or being." He, further, clarifies that to get a fuller picture of the well-being of a person "we clearly have to move on to 'functionings', to wit, what the person succeeds in *doing* with the commodities and characteristics at his or her command" (Sen, 1985a:10). Nussbaum, similarly, relates human functioning to what humans actually do and are (Nussbaum,1999:34)

4 Robeyns (2000, 2001) discusses the use of conversion factors in the capability approach.

5 The notion of conversion factors (Robeyns, 2005:99) can be based on Sen's typology of "instrumental freedoms". In Sen (2000) he mentions the following instrumental freedoms: 1) political freedoms, 2) economic facilities, 3) social opportunities, 4) transparency guarantees and 5) protective security. It can be argued that one can derive a set of conversion factors that encourage (or limit) the flowering of instrumental freedoms from the list of instrumental freedoms that Sen offers.

6 "Social characteristics" is a rather sweeping term that spans a broad range of issues that would more properly be sub-divided into social, political and institutional practices. However, in keeping with Robeyns' (2001) use of the term, I retain its usage. I recognise that Robeyns uses "social characteristics" to encapsulate "variations in social climate" and "differences in relational perspectives", no less wide

categories that Sen ((1999:70-71) himself uses to classify the sources of variation between incomes and advantage

7 On gender in relation to the capabilities approach see Sen (1992, Chapter 8; 2000, Chapter 8), Robeyns (2001, 2003) and Nussbaum (2003).

8 See Nambiar (forthcoming) for a full account of the role of institutions in constraining the achievement of capabilities.

9 Nambiar (2010) discusses the path dependent nature of institutions and how networks can be used to overcome these constraints.

10 Most of this section was based on data collected from and discussions with Paul Sinappan, a founder member of Credit Union Malaysia.

11 See Siwar, C. and B. Quinones (2000) for an economic evaluation of CUM.

12 In our terms, this would be equivalent to facilitating an understanding of the capability situation among the capability disadvantaged.

13 In other words, CUM works towards addressing the gender-biased institutional constraints that limit the capabilities of women.

14 Clearly, there is a need to separately address the different mental models, rules and routines as they apply in different sectors of society.

REFERENCES

1. Lancaster, K.J. (1966), "A New Approach to Consumer Theory," *Journal of Political Economy*, Vol. 74.
2. Nambiar, S. (2010), *Sen's Capability Approach and Institutions*, New York: Nova Science Publishers.
3. Nambiar, S. (forthcoming), "Capabilities and Constraints," *Forum for Social Economics.*
4. Nussbaum, M.C. (2003), "Capabilities as Fundamental Entitlements: Sen and Social Justice," *Feminist Economics*, Vol.9, No.2-3

5. Robeyns, I. (2000), "An Unworkable Idea or a Promising Alternative? Sen's Capability Approach Re-examined," Discussion Paper 00.30, Center for Economic Studies, Katholieke Universiteit Leuven.

6. Robeyns, I. (2001), "Understanding Sen's Capability Approach," Mimeo, Wolfson College, University of Cambridge

7. Robeyns, I. (2001), "Sen's Capability Approach and Feminist Concerns," Paper prepared for the Conference on Sen's Capability Approach, St. Edmunds College, June 5-7.

8. Robeyns, I. (2003), "Sen's Capability Approach and Gender Equality: Selecting Relevant Capabilities", *Feminist Economics*, Vol.2

9. Sen, A.K. (1985a), *Commodities and Capabilities*, Amsterdam: North-Holland.

10. Sen, A.K. (1992), *Inequality Re-examined*, (Expanded edition with a substantial annexe by James Foster and Amartya Sen), Oxford: Clarendon Press.

11. Sen, A.K. (1999), *Development as Freedom*, Oxford: Oxford University Press

12. Sinnappan, P. (undated), "Women's Empowerment through Micro-Finance and Micro-Enterprises: The Malaysian Experience, Unpublished paper.

13. Siwar, C. and B. Quinones (2000), "Microfinance in Malaysia: Aiming at Success," In J. Remenyi and B. Quinones Jr. (eds.) (2000), *Microfinance and Poverty Alleviation – Case Studies from Asia and the Pacific*, London and New York: Pinter

5

Financial Inclusion and Inclusive Growth through Banking: Lessons from India

K. Gangadharan

INTRODUCTION

The concept inclusion should be seen as a process of including the excluded as agents whose participation is essential in the very design of the development process and not simply as welfare targets of development programmes (Planning Commission, 2007).It is the process of ensuring access to financial services and timely and adequate credit were needed by vulnerable groups such as weaker sections and access groups at an affordable cost (Rangarajan, 2008). The inclusive growth as a strategy of economic development received attention owing to a rising concern that the benefits of economic growth have not been equitably shared. Growth is inclusive when it creates economic opportunities along with ensuring equal access to them. Apart from addressing the issue of inequality, inclusive growth may also make poverty reduction efforts more effectively by explicitly creating productive economic opportunities for the poor and vulnerable sections of the society. The inclusive growth by encompassing the hitherto excluded population can bring in several other benefits as well to the economy.

Some of the glaring facts about financial exclusion are very much clear from the following figures. It is estimated that 45.9 million farmer households out of a total of 89.3 million households do not have access to credit either from the institutional or non institutional sources (NSSO, 2008). One branch is catering to the banking needs of 16,000 (June, 2007), only 13% are availing loans from the banks in the income brackets of less than Rs. 50,000 and 53% are still taking loans from the institutional and non institutional sources only for emergency purposes. The number of branches per lakh population was 6.33 as on 2010 March where as it was 25 to 40 for developed countries .These figures tell us the urgent needs for extending the banking services to every part of the country and to every people of the country for achieving the objective of inclusive growth through financial inclusion. In this context it is very significant to examine the financial inclusion and inclusive growth strategy followed by Indian banks in the past and the strategy and innovative schemes perused in the present and challenges in widening the inclusive base in the future

WHAT IS FINANCIAL INCLUSION?

Financial inclusion represents reliable access to affordable savings, loans, remittances and insurance services. We believe that financial inclusion primarily implies access to a bank account backed by deposit insurance, access to affordable credit and the payments system. It is strongly believed that increasing financial inclusion reduces the economic vulnerability of households, promotes economic growth, alleviate poverty and improves the quality of people's lives. Thus expansion of banking lads to increasing availability of finance to spur economic growth and helps to alleviate poverty (Usha Thorat 2010) There are supply side and demand side factors driving inclusive growth (Chakarabarty 2009). Banks largely are expected to mitigate the supply side processes that prevent poor and disadvantaged social groups from gaining access to the financial system. Apart from the supply side factors demand side factors such as lower income and asset holdings also have a significant bearing on financial inclusion.

WHY FINANCIAL INCLUSION SO SIGNIFICANT?

It is a necessary condition for generating equitable and sustaining inclusive growth. There are only few instances of an economy transiting from an agrarian system to a post industrial modern society without broad based financial inclusion. Economic opportunity is strongly intertwined with financial access. Such access is to empower for the poor as it provides them opportunities to build savings, make investments and avail credit. Access to financial services also helps the poor to insure themselves against income shocks and equip them to meet emergencies such as illness or loss of employment.

SIZE OF FINANCIAL EXCLUSION

Out of the 600000 habitations in the country only about 30,000 or just 5 percent have a commercial branch. Just about 40% of the population across the country has bank accounts and this rate is much lower in the north eastern part of the country. The proportion of people having any kind of life insurance cover is as low as 10 percent and the proportion having a non life insurance cover is an abysmally low 0.6 percent. People having debit card comprise only 13% and those having credit cards are a marginal 2% only.

Even where bank accounts are claimed to have been opened verification has shown that a significant portion of these accounts are dormant. Very few conduct banking transaction and even fewer receive any credit. Millions of people across the country are thereby denied the opportunity to harness their earning capacity and entrepreneurial talent and are condemned to marginalization and poverty. But this aspect has a brighter story and it is similar to that of the business strategy case of a shoe company.

FINANCIAL INCLUSION A VIABLE BUSINESS MODEL.

The success story of Dharavi, a bustling industrial slum in Mumbai reveals how banks can augment the ambit of financial empowerment. Dharavi exports goods worth $500-$650 million every year. Ironically, even though Dharavi is situated right in the heart of Mumbai, the most banked city in the country and adjoins the Bhandra Kurla complex, Mumbai's financial district, it did not have a commercial bank branch for a long period of time not withstanding its celebrated entrepreneurial spirit and export performance. The first commercial bank branch was opened in February 2007 and in Just 3 years the bank registered business in excess of Rs. 44 crores. One more branch opened again and now 9 ATMs in Dharavi all of them being actively used.

FINANCIAL INCLUSION- INITIATIVES AND STRATEGIES FOLLOWED

The RBI asked state governments and banks to identify centers where there is need for setting up branches that are full-fledged, offer forex facilities, handling government business and meet currency needs. RBI will then find the capital and running cost for 5 years and state government should provide the premises and appropriate security arrangements.

Government of India has set up 2 funds

a) Financial inclusion fund for meeting the costs of developmental and promotional intervention towards financial inclusion

b) Financial inclusion technology fund for meeting the cost of technology adoption. Each of these fund has an overall corpus of Rs.500 crores

c) The announcement of finance minister in the last budget speech that every village in the country with over 2000 population must have access to banking services by march 2013

d) Aadhar- The unique Identification Number UID project of Government of India. The main aim of UID is to provide a unique ID number for every one in the country. It will be a powerful instrument for helping the poor to establish their identity to meet the banks Know your Customer norms. This will reduce cash and non cash transaction cost both to banks and potential customers.

e) RBI has very domestic commercial bank, public and private sector to prepare its own financial inclusion plan.

f) The FIPs are meant to b rolled out over the next 3 years and included performance evaluation indicators. The main challenge in this regard is to make the no frills account operational. Because of dire poverty , the account or the branch services are rarely or nominally used This can b gauged through

g) Scalable Technology solution on the part of banks

h) RBI should put under core banking solution

i) Business correspondent model coupled with biometric technology application

j) Fixing financial inclusion targets for staff members as criteria of performance.

ROLE OF FINANCIAL INCLUSION IN ACHIEVING INCLUSIVE GROWTH

Access to financial products is constrained by several factors which include lack of awareness about the financial products, unaffordable products, high transaction costs and products which are not convenient, inflexible, not customized and of low quality. Financial inclusion promotes thrift and develops culture of savings and also enables efficient payment mechanism, strengthening the resource base of the financial institution which benefits the economy as resource become available for efficient payment mechanism and allocation. The empirical evidence shows that countries with large proportion of population excluded from the formal financial system also show higher poverty ratios at higher inequality (Thorat, 2008).

A quick look at the data on the sources of loans and also percentage of person's annual income less than Rs. 50,000 show that 28.3% had bank accounts and only 13% had availed of bank finance and even in higher income brackets exclusion existed. So the need to financial inclusion has to be strengthened in the years to come. (Table 1)

Table 1. Earner's having a bank account-2007

Annual income (in Rs.)	*Urban*	*Rural*	*Total*
<50,000	43.1	26.8	28.3
50,000-1,00,000	75.5	71.7	73.0
1,00,000-2,00,000	91.8	87.4	89.9
2,00,000-4,00,000	95.5	93.6	94.9
>4,00,000	98.0	96.3	97.6
All	61.7	38.0	44.9

Source: Report on Currency and Finance 2006-08, IIMS-2007.

The process of financial inclusion in India can be broadly classified in to four phases. First phase from the formation of banking establishment in the country up to 1969

(1870-1969).No such financial establishment was carried out in this stage. Second Stage 1969-1990. The focus was on channeling of credit to the neglected sectors of the economy. Special emphasize was laid on weaker sections of the society. The third phase 1990-2005, focused mainly on strengthening the financial institutions as by the introduction of Self Help Groups, Bank Linkage Programme in the early 1990s and Kisan Credit Cards (KCCs) for providing credit to farmers. The fourth stage (2005 onwards) , the financial inclusion was explicitly made as a policy objective and thrust was on providing safe facility of saving deposits through "no frills" accounts (Table 2).

Table 2. Sources of loans (percent of indebtedness)

Annual income (in Rs.)	*Banks*	*Money lenders*	*Other institutional & non institutional sources*	*Total*
<50,000	13	34	52.1	100
50,000-1,00,000	34.5	19.6	45.9	100
1,00,000-2,00,000	49.3	12.0	38.7	100
2,00,000-4,00,000	51.6	11.8	36.6	100
>4,00,000	62.8	5.5	31.7	100

Source : Report on Currency and Finance 2006-07, IIMS Survey-2007.

FINANCIAL INCLUSION IN INDIA- A HISTORICAL SKETCH (1870-1969)

The East India Company in India in the 18th century itself had taken initiative to form banks for the smoothening of their trade and commerce. In 1870 itself the Presidency Bank of Bengal and Bank of Madras were formed and later this bank was called as Imperial Bank in 1935 and finally it nationalized in 1950 and renamed as the Central Bank of the country namely the RBI. Table 3 shows the growth path of banking institution in India from 1870-1934. It can be seen that in 1870 a total of 8 banks were in the country (3 Presidency banks, 3 Exchange banks and 2 Class A banks with capital base of 5 lakhs) and by the end of 1934 this has fetched to 123 banks (Table 3). The deposits mobilized these banks also increased from Rs. 1263 lakhs in 1870 to Rs. 23,428 lakhs by the 1934 (Table 4).

Table 3. Number of Banks 1870-1934

Number of Reporting Commercial Banks					
As on Dec.	*Presidency/ Imperial Bank*	*Class A (Cap 5L+)*	*Exchange bank*	*Class B (Cap 1-5L)*	*Total*
1870	3	2	3	-	8
1880	3	3	4	-	10
1890	3	5	5	-	13
1900	3	9	8	-	20
1910	3	16	11	-	30
1913	3	18	12	23	56
1920	3	25	15	33	76
1930	1	31	18	57	107
1934	1	36	17	69	123

The coverage and distribution of banks in different provinces of India in 1930 reveals that Bengal province accounted with highest number of banks with 933 banks followed by Madras province with 167(Table 5). The picture of financial inclusion and capital base of banks augmented widely by the span of 14 years and the table 6 shows the distribution of commercial banks both scheduled and non scheduled with their total paid up capital. It reveals that the strong capital base of Indian banks exhibiting the capacity for a take off in the arena of financial inclusion. The capital base shows that it had total paid up capital of Rs.454 crores

Table 4. Bank Deposits 1872-1934

Deposits (Lakhs)

As on Dec.	*Presidency/ Imperial Bank*	*Class A*	*Exchange Bank*	*Class B*	*Total*
1870	1,197	14	52	-	1,263
1880	1,140	14	52	-	1,543
1890	1,836	271	754	-	2,861
1900	1,569	808	1,050	-	3,241
1910	3,654	2,566	2,479	-	8,699
1913	4,236	2,259	3,104	151	9,750
1920	8,629	7,115	7,481	23	23,458
1930	8,397	6,326	6,811	439	21,973
1934	8,100	7,677	7,140	511	23,428

operating through 637 banks throughout the country. Even during this period 6 banks were identified as big banks with deposit liability of 100 crores and above. They are Imperial Bank, Central Bank of India Ltd., Punjab National Bank, Bank of India Ltd. and UCO Bank Ltd. The Banking Regulation Act was amended in 1961 for the compulsory amalgamation of a banking company in order to broaden capital base and also to check them from bank failures which occurred in the case of Palai Central Bankin Kerala. The sketch of bank failures in India from 1936 to 1955 reveals that the maximum number of chronological failures was occurred in 1939. It paved as an eye opener for the authorities to amend the Banking Regulation Act in 1961(Table 7).

A picture of financial inclusion and care given to the priority sector of the economy at the time of independence was very weak. Though agriculture contributed 55% of GDP the share of bank credit to agriculture was only 1.9%. Similarly at the time of independence rural population exceed to 80% whereas the share of bank credit to this

Table 5: Province wise Distribution of Banks in India-1930

No	*State*	*No. of Reporting Banks*
1	Madras	167
2	Bombay	30
3	Bengal	919
4	United provinces of Agra and Oudh	33
5	Punjab	29
6	Burma	4
7	Bihar and Orissa	18
8	Central provinces and Berar	3
9	Assam	51
10	N.W.F. province	1
11	Delhi province	3
	Total	1258

segment has been only 7% and farmer borrowed 75 crores, but the share contributed by banks was only 0.9%.and 69.7% was contributed and financed by money lenders. Similarly per branch population was 1, 36,000 and saving rate of people was little below 10%of national income. Thus the picture of financial inclusion has been very bleak in India at the time of independence and banks were small, weak and concentrated in urban centers, owned by business houses and lacked expertise. Rural Co-operatives were weak and ineffective.

The stage of financial inclusion was also not much attractive during the phase of independence to nationalization. Though an array of schemes and agendas like promotion of co-operatives, nationalization of Imperial bank, Refinance support extended by RBI, formulation of ARC, DIC, social control on banks, National Credit Council

Table 6. Distribution of Commercial Banks-Dec. 1947.

State (Rs. In crore)	*Scheduled Banks*		*Non Scheduled Banks*		*Total*	
	No of Banks	*Paid up capital*	*No of Banks*	*Paid up capital*	*No of Banks*	*Paid up capital*
Assam	1	1	14	2	15	3
Bihar	2	6	10	1	12	6
Bombay	13	71	27	7	40	78
Madras	14	24	186	20	200	45
West Bengal	22	146	84	12	106	158
Delhi	5	32	3	1	8	33
East Punjab	7	14	20	5	27	19
Central provinces and Berar	2	4	3	1	5	5
United provinces	5	15	20	2	25	17
Ajmer Mewar	0	0	1	-	1	-
Indian States	11	53	187	38	198	91
Total	82	365	555	89	637	454

Table 7. Number of Banks Failed-1936-1955

Year (Jan-Dec.)	*Number of Banks Failed*	*Year (Jan-Dec.)*	*Number of Banks Failed*
1936	88	1947	38
1937	65	1948	45
1938	73	1949	55
1939	117	1950	45
1940	107	1951	60
1941	94	1952	31
1942	50	1953	31
1943	59	1954	27
1944	29	1955	29
1945	27		

and Multi-agency Approach were implemented. It did not gain momentum for providing banking for masses. The advances given by Scheduled Commercial bank in 1951 and 1967 for various purposes are given as Table 8.

Table 8. Advances of SCBs to various Sectors

Sector	*March 1951*		*March 1967*	
	Amount (crores)	*Share to total advances*	*Amount (crores)*	*Share to total advances*
Industry	199	34.05%	1747	64.3%
Commerce	211	36.0%	527	19.4%
Financial	74	12.7%	97	3.6%
Personal	40	6.8%	115	4.2%
Agriculture	12	2.1%	57	2.2%
Others	49	8.4%	174	6.3%
Total	585	100.0%	2716	100.0%

Source: Evolution of Banking in India, T &P 2007-08

The share of SCB to total bank advances to industry was 34%in 1951 and it increased to 64.3% In 1967 it indicating the extent of financial percolation carried out India towards industrial sector. Similarly the loan given to commerce and agriculture did not widened during this period rather shrinked as the priorities has given the profitary industries owned and operated by proprieties of S.C.Bank.

SECOND PHASE OF FINANCIAL INCLUSION (1969-1990)

The era of nationalization actually witnessed a land mark in the financial inclusion strategy of Indian commercial banks. The policy of rapid branch expansion, Lead Bank scheme, Credit Guarantee Scheme, Directed Lending, Creation of RRBs, NABARD, LABs, and the Service Area Approach and Credit Authorization Scheme etc. were really milestones in the financial inclusion path of banking industry of India. The branch expansion have really witnessed a revolution with enactment of nationalization as rural branches of commercial banks increased from 13.3% in 1952 to 32% in 2008.At the same time urban branches from 47.8% in 1952 to 25% in 2008 (Table 9). Another interesting thing to indicate here is that agriculture and allied sectors begun to attract by banking institutions and the share of advances given to agriculture sector increased from 2.1% in 1951 to 12.4% in 2008.This change in allocation itself is the signal of financial inclusion carried out by the SCBs in India.

Table 9. Number of Offices of Scheduled Commercial Banks in India

March	*Rural*	*Semi Urban*	*Urban*	*Metro*	*Total*	*Population per office in '000*
1969	1443	3337	1911	1496	8187	65
1970	4817	4401	2504	1900	13622	41
1975	6807	5598	3489	2836	18730	32
1980	15105	8122	5178	4014	32419	20
1985	30185	9816	6578	4806	51385	14
1990	34791	11324	8042	5595	59752	14
1995	33004	13341	8868	7154	62367	15
2000	32734	14407	10052	8219	65412	15
2005	32082	15403	11500	9370	68355	16
2008	31076	17675	14391	12908	76000	15

Source: Report on Currency and Finance 2006-08, RBI for 2008 http:#rbi.org.in (accessed on Tue 22 June 2010).

Similarly the personal loan provided by the scheduled commercial banks also increased from 6.8% of the total advances in 1951 to 22.9% of the advances in 2008(Table 10). This also reveals the individual empowerment and initiative taken for the individual credit needs of the people of the country and remarked as another golden feather on the part of financial inclusion strategy of Indian commercial banks.

Table 10. Advances of SCBs to various Sectors

Sector	*March 1951*		*March 1967*		*March 2008*	
	Amount (crores)	*Share to total advances*	*Amount (crores)*	*Share to total advances*	*Amount (crores)*	*Share to total advances*
Industry	199	34.05%	1747	64.3%	871900	39.6%
Commerce	211	36.0%	527	19.4%		
Financial	74	12.7%	97	3.6%		
Personal	40	6.8%	115	4.2%	505390	22.9%
Agriculture	12	2.1%	57	2.2%	273658	12.4%
Others	49	8.4%	174	6.3%		
Total	585	100.0%	2716	100.0%	2247437	100.0%

Source : Evolution of Banking in India, T &P 2007-08

The achievement of Indian commercial banks in the arena of financial inclusion can also be justified with some other basic indicators. They are number of rural bank branches, average population per branch, hike in bank deposit as percentage of GDP, bank credit as percentage of GDP, rural deposit in total deposit and rural credit in total credit. All these indicators show a rapid jerk for the period from 1967 to 1990 though slight change occurred in the approach and perception of financial inclusion in the era of financial reform (Table 11).

THE THIRD PHASE OF FINANCIAL INCLUSION (1990-2005)

The third phase of development of financial inclusion can be seen from the expansion occurred in the SHG, Bank Linkage Programme and Kisan Credit Cards.

Table 11. Other Achievements

	1967	*1990*
Number of bank branches	6985	59752 (58.2% rural and semi-urban)
Average population per branch	65,000	14,000
Bank deposit (as % of GDP)	13%	38%
Bank credit (as % of GDP)	10%	24%
Rural deposit in total deposit	3%	16%
Rural credit in total credit	3.3%	14.2%

Source : Evolution of Banking in India, Report on Currency and Finance, RBI Page 109.

Kisan Credit Cards : KCC is one outstanding example which has considerably reduced transaction costs and has arguably facilitated credit delivery. Kisan Credit Cards Scheme was first introduced in India by Andhra Bank in 1998. The Scheme aims to facilitate access to short term credit to farmers and to simplify the credit mechanism so that farmers can receive credit on time. The different commercial banks, Regional Rural Banks and Co-Operative Banks issue the Kisan Credit Cards (Table 12)

Merits of Kisan Credit Cards

1. The card can be used like an ordinary credit card, thus giving a feeding to the farmers that there is an underlying guarantee of getting loan from the bank as long as the earlier loan is repaid.
2. The facility is given for three to five years instead of one year, thus reducing the procedural delays.
3. There is flexibility in operation of the facility in terms of number of withdrawals and in repayment of loans.
4. A certain new features such as personal insurance for all the card holders ranging from Rs. 25,000 to Rs.

Table 12. Agency wise and Period wise Progress of KCC. (Rs. In crore & No. of cards in lakh)

Year	*Co-operatives*		*RRBs*		*Commercial Banks*		*Over all*	
	No. of cards issued	*Amt. sanc.*	*No. of cards issued*	*Amt. sanc.*	*No. of cards issued*	*Amt. sanc.*	*No. of cards issued*	*Amt. sanc.*
1998-1999	1.55	826	0.06	11	6.22	1473	7.83	2310
1999-2000	35.95	3606	1.73	405	13.66	3537	51.34	7548
2000-2001	56.14	9412	6.48	1400	23.9	5615	86.52	11642
2001-2002	54.36	15952	8.34	2382	30.71	7524	93.41	25858
2005-2006	25.98	20339	12.49	8483	41.65	18779	80.12	47601
2006-2007	22.98	13141	14.06	7373	48.08	26215	85.12	46729
2007-2008	20.91	20492	17.73	9074	46.06	20421	84.70	49987
2008-2009	13.44	13172	14.14	7632	58.34	25865	85.92	46669

Source: NABARD

50,000 against permanent disability or accidental death, an effective measure for risk mitigation were also incorporated in the scheme.

Features of Kisan Credit Cards

1. Revolving cash credit facilities involving any number of withdrawals and repayment within the sanctioned credit limit is available to the card holder.
2. Personal Accident Insurance Scheme providing cover to all KCC holders up to Rs. 50,000 to cover accidental death/ permanent disability under a master policy at a nominal premium of Rs. 15 per annum or Rs. 45 under three years is available to the card holder.
3. RBI has stipulated uniform security and margin for loans for all card holders.
4. Each withdrawal made by the card holder is to be paid within 12 months.
5. Card valued for three years subject to annual renewal.

6. Credit limit can be enhanced depending on performance and needs.
7. All branches engaged in agricultural lending could issue the KCC.

The KCC scheme increased the farmer's access to credit from institutional sources. The objective of the scheme is to provide adequate and timely assistance from the banking system to farmers to enable them to meet all their cultivation needs including purchase of inputs in a flexible and cost effective manner. The scheme is being operated by Co-Operative Banks,

RRBs, Scheduled commercial banks, through out the country. Loans disbursed under KCC are also eligible for personal accident insurance cover and Rs. 50,000 for accident death and Rs. 25,000 for permanent disability. The table 12 provides the success indicators of KCC as a vital tool of financial inclusion.

SHG BANK LINKAGE PROGRAMME

Studies by various agencies have shown that the self help savings and credit groups have the potential to bring together the formal banking structure and the poor for mutual benefit. The benefit to the formal banking credit institutions lies in the externalization of the part of the credit cycle, assessment of credit needs, identification of borrowers, disbursal of loans tailored to borrower needs and requirements, more effective supervision of end use of loans lending to better loan repayment, reduction in the formal paper work involved and a consequent reduction in transaction cost and perhaps most significant improved discoveries. In 1990, the NABARD initiated the project of linkage of 500 SHGs with banks. In 1996, the SHG Linkage Programme linking the non-formal sector represented by the SHGs and the institutional credit delivery system of Commercial Banks, Co-Operatives and the RRBs was operationalised through out the country. In 1996, the RBI included financing of SHGs as a mainstream activity of banks under priority sector lending.

The SHG Bank Linkage model was launched by NABARD in 1992 to facilitate collective decision making and door step banking to the poor. As on 31st March 2009, a total number of 42, 24,338 SHGs having outstanding bank loan of Rs. 22,680 crores. In 2008-09 the number of SHGs financed was 16, 09586 and the amount disbursed was Rs. 12,254 crores. In 2008-09 alone Rs. 15,986 crores had been disbursed which is 5.5% of the ground level credit flow and this has increased from around 1% in 2001-02.

THE FOURTH PHASE OF FINANCIAL INCLUSION (2005 ONWARDS)

Safe facility of saving deposit through "no frills" account (NFA) is the main motto during this phase. A number of schemes of services were introduced for augmenting the operationalisation of NFA.

NEW CHALLENGES FOR BANKS IN FINANCIAL INCLUSION

1. Policy Reforms are necessary to ensure the development, growth and efficient functioning of rural financial markets.
2. Legal and regulatory reforms.
3. Inadequate financial infrastructure is another challenge. It includes legal, information regulatory and supervisory systems for financial institution and markets.
4. Limited retail level institutional capacity. The poor still have inadequate access to credit, saving and insurances commensurate with their need for these services. Poverty, low population density, isolated markets,

highly covariate risk and seasonality often result in high transaction cost, lack of traditional collateral, high income fluctuations and limited opportunities for risk diversification.

5. Inadequate investment in agriculture and rural development. The insufficient investment in physical infrastructure (especially irrigation, roads, and electricity and support services for marketing, business development and extension) continues to increase the risk and cost of financial inclusion and particularly discourage investment in the provision of micro finance services on a significant scale.
6. Inadequate investments in social intermediation. This is particularly true with respect to the poorest women in poor households, poor in resource poor and remote areas and ethnic minorities.
7. Banking services need to increase products and financial services and business plan that encourage talents in rural areas and also design bouquets of products for the poor. They include,
    a. Benefits to the poor like preferential interest rates for the poor and self Help groups in rural areas, extended loan tenures for the investment made by them and also help artisan to market their products to cities and towns
    b. A pure savings products, ideally recurring or variable recurring deposits.
    c. Entrepreneurial credit such as GIC and KCC.
    d. Financial Inclusion plan integrated with bank business plan. Bank must view financial inclusion as a huge business opportunity and perfect their delivery models.
8. Monitoring-Need for a structured approach: A closely monitoring of the progress made by banks as per the

priority of financial inclusion plans is inevitable. A structured approach enable to overcome the defects of institutions occurred earlier and will be an improvement over the previous one.

9. Bank should take initiative to guard against technology barrier between the bank and customer. As we all recognize technology is a great enabler for making banking more efficient and more inclusive. At the same time it is also faceless and the absence of a human touch can be quite intimidating, if not threatening to those just entering the banking network.

CONCLUSION

Financial inclusion and inclusive growth strategy are two closely connected programs. The achievement of the latter depends on the attainment and deepening of the former. In order to augment the ambit of financial inclusion banking services have to spread to all regions and all communities must be brought under its ambit irrespective of caste, colour and creed to enjoy the benefits of banking services. The saving tendency can be augmented only when they learn the lessons of creating a surplus after the day to day subsistence and banks can definitely chalk out credit schemes for such sections for creating a surplus after meeting their subsistence. No doubt, the banking system in the country has grown, but it has enormous possibilities of expansion considering that it is still to reach the unbanked areas, and make banking services available to all individuals. The lessons of banking development and financial services delivered and extended by Banks in India reveals that Banking is the panacea for financial inclusion and inclusive growth.

REFERENCES

1. Chakarabarty (2009), Banking: Key driver for inclusive

growth, Reserve Bank of India Bulletin, September.

2. Thorat U (2008) Inclusive growth, the role of Banks in emerging economies. Lecture delivered at independence commemoration Lecture 2008 at the Central Bank of Sri lanka, Colombo
3. RBI (2008) Report on currency and Finance 2006-2008, RBI, Mumbai
4. RBI (2009) 100 percent financial inclusion -Evaluation by External agencies, Broad findings, RBI, Mumbai
5. Chakrabarty (2010) financial deepening by putting financial inclusion campaiagn into mission mode, RBI Bulletin, Vol.7 July
6. Usha Thorat(2010)Financial regulation and financial inclusion working together or at cross purposes, RBI Bulletin, vol.7, July
7. Planning Commission (2007) Towards Inclusive growth, the gender dimension, The Planning Commission, New Delhi
8. NABARD (2009) Status of Micro finance in India 2008-09, NABARD, Mumbai
9. Report of the Task force on credit related issues of farmers Submitted to Ministry of Agriculture, Government of India
10. Website: http:#rbi.org.in(accessed on Tue 22 June 2010).

6
Human Capital Preparedness for Banking Sector Productivity: Empirical Evidence from Public Sector and Private Sector Banks

Mohammed Razik Parakandi
T. Asokan

INTRODUCTION

Economies tend to follow a developmental progression that takes them from a heavy reliance on primary, toward the development of manufacturing and finally toward a more service based structure. Historically, manufacturing tend to be more open to international trade and competition than service sector. As a result, there has been a tendency for the first economies which industrialized to come under competitive attack from those seeking to industrialize later. The resultant shrinkage of manufacturing activity in the leading developed economies of the world might explain their growing reliance on the service sector. However as of now with the dramatic reduction of cost, attainment of newer levels of speed and improvements in the reliability of transportation of people the service sector is one of the most intensive international competitive spheres. In every economy, service sector is fast emerging as a dominant contributor to GDP and this increases need to focus on improving ways to enhance quality of service organizations as it will dictate the future of such economies. Service sector now accounts for more than half the GDP marks a watershed in the evolution of the Indian economy and takes it closer to the fundamentals of a developed economy. Indian service industry covers a wide gamut of activities among which banking sector plays a leading role.

SIGNIFICANCE OF THE STUDY

The service sector is the most common workplace in India. In service-sector, people use time to deploy knowledge assets, collaboration, and process-engagement to create productivity, effectiveness, performance improvement potential and sustainability. The focus is on people interacting with people and serving the customer rather than transforming physical goods. Comparing to past era, more and more banks recognize the fact that key element of success of any service oriented business is human capital. In today's era of borderless trade and commerce, banks are offering more or less identical products and services and are compelled to ensure that their human recourses are equipped with necessary competency and preparedness to influence their own performance and that of others so as to differentiate one banks' service experience from that of another. This need is driving the market to search for value additions to make banks more productive and humane. Advent of globalization and the resultant competition has brought in a new paradigm of banking service quality creation and delivery. A shift from tangible physical assets to human assets consists of intangible knowledge and skill sets. The traditional styles of leadership becoming less effective, administrators expect their teams to be proactive and better prepared to meet the demands of the customer and the industry. Today, banking administrators directly deal with their diverse employees and clients on a regular basis. Their leadership qualities and generic competencies ultimately determine their style of leadership, performance and growth of their business. More and more banking firms around the world are recognizing the fact that, in order to gain competitive advantage, empowered human capital is critical and thus, empowers to be more productive.

This is the context where a need felt for analyzing the human capital preparedness for banking productivity and finding newer ways of visible value addition to the service quality. Understanding role of individuals and teams within business is the foundation for developing higher-level organizational performance. Therefore, it is imperative that a positive human experience is the ultimate objective of any banking business and it is the factor that determines performance of such organizations. This is the context where an effort is made to examine human capital preparedness for delivering banking service quality. The study was conducted among 360 executives in public sector and private sector banks in India.

HUMAN CAPITAL PROFILE IN BANKING SECTOR

A comparative analysis of human capital profile such as age, gender, educational qualifications, team size and service duration is made here. Each of these components of human capital profile was compared between public sector and private sector banking organizations. Table 3.1 presents observations on the age distribution of executive workforce in public and private sector banking organizations. It is observed from the table that, in public sector banks 38.9% of executive workforce are aged between 35 and 45; followed by 35.6% falling to age category above 45; 22.2% belong to age group 25-35; and only 3.3% are below the age of 25. Where as in private sector banking firms 61.7% of executives are aged between 25 and 35; 25% are less than 25 years old, 12.8% belong to age class 35-45 and only 0.6% is aged above 45. It can be further derived that 86.7 of executives in private sector are aged below 35, which shows a youth dominance among private sector executives. It can be summarized that more than half of the executive workforce in the banking sector are below 35 years old.

Table 3.1. Age Distribution

Sector		*Age Categories*				*Total*
		Below 25	*25-35*	*35-45*	*Above 45*	
Public Sector	Frequency	6	40	70	64	180
	% within Sector	3.3%	22.2%	38.9%	35.6%	100%
Private Sector	Frequency	45	111	23	1	180
	% within Sector	25.0%	61.7%	12.8%	.6%	100%
Total	Frequency	51	151	93	65	360
	Percentage	14.2%	41.9%	25.8%	18.1%	100%

Source: Primary data

Comparative analysis of the age distribution shows evidence of a significant difference in the age distribution of the executive workforce between the public and private sector service organizations. 86.7 of the executives in the private sector are aged below 35, where as this is 25.5% in the public sector, which shows a youth dominance among the executives of the private sector. Typical age group to which most of the private sector executives falls is 25-35 years age group. Table 3.2 reveals gender distribution of executive workforce in public and private sector banks. It is observed from the above table that, among the executives of public sector banks 56.7% are male and 43.3% are females; where as in private sector banking firms 63.9% of executive workforce are male and 36.1% are female.

Table 3.2. Gender Distribution

Sector		*Sex*		*Total*
		Male	*Female*	
Public Sector	Frequency	102	78	180
	% within Sector	56.7%	43.3%	100%
Private Sector	Frequency	115	65	180
	% within Sector	63.9%	36.1%	100%
Total	Frequency	217	143	360
	Percentage	60.3%	39.7%	100%

Source: Primary data

Even though there does not exist a significant variation in sex distribution of public and private banks, it can be observed that public sector employs relatively more number of females.

Table 3.3 reveals some important information on educational qualifications of executives in public and private sector banks. It can be observed that in public sector organizations 32.8% executives are postgraduates; 56.7% are graduates; 1.1% have plus-two qualification; 3.9% have SSLC qualification; 3.3% are diploma holder and 2.2% have other qualifications. Where as in private sector 37.8% of executives are postgraduates; 46.7% are graduates; 1.7% are plus-two holders, 4.4% are diploma holder; 9.4% have other qualifications and nobody falls to the category SSLC qualification.

Table 3.3. Distribution of Educational Qualification

Sector		*Educational qualification*						
		SSLC	*+ 2*	*Diploma*	*Graduation*	*PG*	*Others*	*Total*
Public Sector	Frequency	7	2	6	102	59	4	180
	% within Sector	3.9%	1.1%	3.3%	56.7%	32.8%	2.2%	100%
Private Sector	Frequency	0	3	8	84	68	17	180
	% within Sector	.0%	1.7%	4.4%	46.7%	37.8%	9.4%	100%
Total	Frequency	7	5	14	186	127	21	360
	Percentage	1.9%	1.4%	3.9%	51.7%	35.3%	5.8%	100%

Source: Primary data

It can be concluded from the above statistics that a vast majority of the executives, i.e. 87%, are either graduates or post graduates. A comparative analysis between sectors shows existence of highly significant difference in the educational qualifications of the executives between private and public sector banking organizations. It was observed that private sector had higher number of post graduates, and none of the executives belong to SSLC qualification in the private sector. This doesn't imply that the public sector executives are inferior in terms of their qualification; it is noted that majority of the public sector workforce belong to the graduate category, and a cumulative percentage of graduates and post graduates in the public sector exceeds that of private sector. It is observed from table 6.1.9 that, in public sector banks majority of teams, i.e., 51.7% , have less than 10 members; 26.1% have members above 40 members; 18.3% have members 10 to 20; 2.8% teams have member size class 20-30; 1.1% of the executive team have a member class between 30 and 40. In private sector firms 56.7% of executive teams have members below 10; 31.7% are between 10 and 20; 4.4% have a team size class 20-30; 3.9% are with more than 40 members. 3.3% belong to member size class 30 to 40.

It can be summarized from the above statistics that more than half of the teams have less than 10 members; considering the other statistics, usual team size can be interpreted as 0-20 members. Since span of control often determine the effective management of a team a special attention was given on the comparative analysis of span of control practiced between public and private sector banking firms. The study revealed statistical evidence for a significant difference in the span of control between the sectors. Private sector has 88.4% of their teams with less than 20 members, where as this is 70% in public sector. It is also worth noting that more than one in every four team in the public sector has more than 40 members where as is it less than 4% in the private sector. It is inferred from table 3.5 that in public sector, 26.1% of employees are working for more than 20 years in same company; 24.4% of them have been working with present organization for less than 5 years; 23.3% are working for 15 to 20 years,; 15.6% are between 10 & 15 years; and 10.6% belong to 5-10 years. 0.6% with 15 to 20 years and 1.7% are more than 20 years.

Table 3.4. Distribution of Span of Control

Sector		*No. of Subordinates/ Team Members*					*Total*
		Below 10	*10 - 20*	*20 - 30*	*30 - 40*	*Above 40*	
Public Sector	Frequency	93	33	5	2	47	180
	% within Sector	51.7%	18.3%	2.8%	1.1%	26.1%	100%
Private Sector	Frequency	102	57	8	6	7	180
	% within Sector	56.7%	31.7%	4.4%	3.3%	3.9%	100%
Total	Frequency	195	90	13	8	54	360
	Percentage	54.2%	25.0%	3.6%	2.2%	15.0%	100%

Source: Primary data

The above general statistics show that a total of about 60% of the banking executives have less than 5 years service with the current organization. A comparative analysis between sectors would show a completely different picture, i.e., in the private sector banks about 95% of the executives have less than 5 years association with the current banks where as this is only 25% in the public sector, this is due to either the increased number of young executives or increased trend with the job shifting in the private sector. In addition to this, it is also found from the study that 50% of the executives in public sector banks have more than 15 year of service with the current organization, where as this category is 2% in the private sector.

Table 3.5. Distribution Length of service

Sector		*Years of service in present organization*					
		Below 5	*5 - 10*	*10-15*	*15-20*	*Above 20*	*Total*
Public Sector	Frequency	44	19	28	42	47	180
	% within Sector	24.4%	10.6%	15.6%	23.3%	26.1%	100%
Private Sector	Frequency	170	4	2	1	3	180
	% within Sector	94.4%	2.2%	1.1%	.6%	1.7%	100%
Total	Frequency	214	23	30	43	50	360
	Percent	59.4%	6.4%	8.3%	11.9%	13.9%	100%

Source: Primary data

HUMAN CAPITAL PROFILE IN BANKING SECTOR: SECTOR COMPARISONS

Below chi-square tests examines statistical evidences of any significant difference in the human capital profile between private sector and public sector banking organizations. Chi-square statistics in table 4.1 examine the existence of significant difference in age distribution of executive workforce between public sector and private sector banks. The level of significance is .000, which shows statistical evidence for a highly significant difference between age distribution of executives in public and private sector service banks. This leads to acceptance of the hypothesis H.4.1 that states that there is significant difference in age distribution of executive workforce between the public and private sector service organizations. In table 4.2, the chi-square statistics of significance is 0.161, which is well above the acceptable statistical limit of 0.05. Thus, it can be inferred that the gender distribution of executive workforce between public and private sector banks is not statistically significant. This leads to rejection of the hypothesis H.4.2, which states that there is significant relationship in gender distribution of executive workforce between public and private sector organizations.

Table 4.1. Age Distribution: Sector Comparison – Chi-square Test

Chi-Square Tests	*Value*	*df*	*Asymp. Significance (2-sided)*
Pearson Chi-Square	148.022[a]	3	.000
Likelihood Ratio	173.153	3	.000
Linear-by-Linear Association	139.267	1	.000
Valid Cases	360		

a. 0 cells (.0%) have expected count less than 5. The minimum expected count is 25.50.

Source: Primary data

Table 4.2. Gender distribution: Sector Comparison – Chi-square Test

Chi-Square Tests	*Value*	*df*	*Asymp. Sig. (2-sided)*	*Exact Sig. (2-sided)*	*Exact Sig. (1-sided)*
Pearson Chi-Square	1.961[a]	1	.161		
Continuity Correction[b]	1.671	1	.196		
Likelihood Ratio	1.963	1	.161		
Fisher's Exact Test				.196	.098
Linear-by-Linear Association	1.955	1	.162		
Valid Cases	360				

a. 0 cells (.0%) have expected count less than 5. The minimum expected count is 71.50.

Source: Primary data)

Chi-square statistics in table 4.3 analyze differences in educational qualifications of executives between private and public sector organizations. Since 33.3% of the cells have expected count less than 5, likelihood ratio is taken as a valid tool for analysis. A significance level 0.001 implies a highly significant difference in educational qualifications of executives between public and private sectors. This leads to acceptance of the hypothesis H.4.3, which states that there is significant difference in educational qualifications of executives in private and public sector organizations. It can be seen from table 4.4 that the level of significance is .000, which shows the existence of a highly significant difference in the span of control between the sectors. This leads to acceptance of the hypothesis H.4.4: there is significant difference in size of the executive teams in public and private sector service organizations. It can be seen from table 4.5 that level of significance is .000, which shows existence of a highly significant difference between sectors in the length of service with current employer in public and private organizations. This leads to acceptance of the hypothesis H.4.5: There is significant difference in the length of service of executives in public and private banking organizations.

Table 4.3. Distribution of Educational Qualification: Sector Comparison- Chi square Test

Chi-Square Tests

	Value	*df*	*Asymp. Sig. (2-sided)*
Pearson Chi-Square	17.913[a]	5	.003
Likelihood Ratio	21.237	5	.001
Linear-by-Linear Association	10.164	1	.001
Valid Cases	360		

a. 4 cells (33.3%) have expected count less than 5. The minimum expected count is 2.50.

Source: Primary data

Table 4.4. Classification of Span of Control: Sector Comparison – Chi-square Test

Chi-Square Tests	*Value*	*df*	*Asymp. Sig. (2-sided)*
Pearson Chi-Square	39.137[a]	4	.000
Likelihood Ratio	42.891	4	.000
Linear-by-Linear Association	19.127	1	.000
N of Valid Cases	360		

a. 2 cells (20.0%) have expected count less than 5. The minimum expected count is 4.00.

Source: Primary data

Table 4.5. Distribution of Length of Service: Sector Comparison – Chi-square Test

Chi-Square Tests	*Value*	*df*	*Asymp. Sig. (2-sided)*
Pearson Chi-Square	184.316[a]	4	.000
Likelihood Ratio	213.463	4	.000
Linear-by-Linear Association	155.604	1	.000
Valid Cases	360		

a. 0 cells (.0%) have expected count less than 5. The minimum expected count is 11.50.

Source: Primary data

HUMAN CAPITAL SKILL INVENTORY IN BANKING SECTOR

Executive soft skills inventory between public sector and private sector banking firms are compared in this section. To analyze various components of skills inventory the skills have been classified into Self Management Skills, Interpersonal Skills and Technology Skills. It can be observed from table 5.1 statistics that in public sector banks, 20.6% of executives have very good Self Management skills; 56.1% are good, 16.7% have Average self management skills ratings, 5.6% are poor and 1.1% are very poor in Self management skills. In private sector banks, 15% of executives are very good in self management skills, 48.9% have good self management skill, 26.7% have average self management skills, 6.1% are poor, and 3.3% are very poor in self management skills.

Table 5.1. Self Management Skills Ratings

Sector		*Self Management Skills*					*Total*
		Very Poor	*Poor*	*Average*	*Good*	*Very Good*	
Public Sector	Count	2	10	30	101	37	180
	% within	1.1%	5.6%	16.7%	56.1%	20.6%	100.0%
Private Sector	Count	6	11	48	88	27	180
	% within	3.3%	6.1%	26.7%	48.9%	15.0%	100.0%
Total	Count	8	21	78	189	64	360
	% within	2.2%	5.8%	21.7%	52.5%	17.8%	100.0%

Source: Primary data

Majority of the banking executives, i.e., 70 of them, have good or very good rating on overall self management skills. On a five point scale on the sub components of self management skills, all received above 3.38 rating; leading to a conclusion that majority of the executives in the banking sector are equipped with above average self management skills. Comparison of the Self Management Skills inventory between the sectors revealed no statistical evidences for a significant difference between public sector and private sector banking firms. However, comparison of *Skill inventory means* between sectors revealed some interesting information, two skills are found rated higher among public sector executives, they are *assertiveness* and *conformity to trends/norms.* It would be also worth noting that the skills *assertiveness* and *conformity to norms,* above a limit could be easily termed as aggressiveness and rigidity.

It can be observed from table 5.2 that in public sector banks, 15.6% of executives have very good Interpersonal skills; 3.4% are good, 31.1% have average Interpersonal skills ratings, 7.2% are poor and 6.7% is very poor in Interpersonal skills. In private sector organizations, 7.2% of executives are very good in Interpersonal skills, 32.8% have rated good Interpersonal skills, 37.8% have average rating in Interpersonal skills, 16.1% are poor, and 6.1% are very poor. It was found that, in comparison to the Self management skills, Interpersonal skills were rated lower among banking executives. The study revealed that less than half of the banking executives have above average interpersonal skills. Comparison of interpersonal skills inventory between the sectors revealed statistical evidences for a significant difference between public sector and private sector banking firms. Components of interpersonal skills that show significant difference between public sector and private sector organizations are: *appropriate use of power, conflict management, courtesy, empathy, forgiveness, generosity, promoting change, sensitivity to culture/gender.*

Table 5.2. Interpersonal Skills Ratings

Sector		*Interpersonal skills*					*Total*
		Very Poor	*Poor*	*Average*	*Good*	*Very Good*	
Public	Count	12	13	56	71	28	180
Sector	% within	6.7%	7.2%	31.1%	39.4%	15.6%	100.0%
Private	Count	11	29	68	59	13	180
Sector	% within	6.1%	16.1%	37.8%	32.8%	7.2%	100.0%
Total	Count	23	42	124	130	41	360
	% within	6.4%	11.7%	34.4%	36.1%	11.4%	100.0%

Source: Primary data

It can be observed from table 5.3 that in public sector banks, 34.4% of executives have very good technology skills; 35% have good, 18.9% have average, 8.3% have poor and 3.3% have very poor technology skills. In private sector, 36.1% of executives are very good in technology skills, 40.6% have good technology skills, 12.8% have average rating, 5.6% are poor, and 5% are very poor in technology skills. It can be further summarized that majority of the banking executives, almost three fourth of them, have above average rating on technology skills. This shows that majority of the executives, are equipped with sufficient technology skills, Comparison of the technology skills inventory between the sectors revealed no statistical evidences for a significant difference between public sector and private sector banking firms. However, comparison of technology *Skill Inventory Means* between sectors revealed couple of skills significantly rated higher among the private sector banking executives, they are *computer skills and mobile phone skill.*

Table 5.3. Technology Skills Ratings

Sector		*Technology skills*					*Total*
		Very Poor	*Poor*	*Average*	*Good*	*Very Good*	
Public	Count	6	15	34	63	62	180
Sector	% within	3.3%	8.3%	18.9%	35.0%	34.4%	100.0%
Private	Count	9	10	23	73	65	180
Sector	% within	5.0%	5.6%	12.8%	40.6%	36.1%	100.0%
Total	Count	15	25	57	136	127	360
	% within	4.2%	6.9%	15.8%	37.8%	35.3%	100.0%

Source: Primary data

HUMAN CAPITAL SKILL INVENTORY IN BANKING SECTOR: SECTOR COMPARISON

Below chi-square tests examines statistical evidences

of any significant difference in *human capital skill inventory* between private sector and public sector banking organizations. It can be inferred from table 6.1 that there is no significant difference in self management skills of executive workforce between public sector and private sector banking organizations. This leads to rejection of the hypothesis H.6.1, which states that there is significant difference in self management skills of executives between public sector and private sector organizations. It can be inferred from table 6.2 chi-square statistics that there is significant difference in people skills of executives between public sector and private sector organizations. This leads to acceptance of the hypothesis H.6.2 which states that there is significant difference in people skills of executives between public sector and private sector organizations. It can be inferred from table 6.3 chi-square statistics test that there is no significant difference in the technology skills of executives between public and private sector banks. This leads to the rejection of the hypothesis H.6.3. There is significant difference in technology skills of executives between public sector and private sector organizations.

Table 6.1. Self Management Skills Inventory: Sector Comparison- Chi-square Test

Chi-Square Tests

	Value	*df*	*Asymp. Sig. (2-sided)*
Pearson Chi-Square	8.658[a]	4	.070
Likelihood Ratio	8.796	4	.066
Linear-by-Linear Association	6.278	1	.012
N of Valid Cases	360		

a. 2 cells (20.0%) have expected count less than 5. The minimum expected count is 4.00.

Source: Primary data

Table 6.2. People skills Inventory: Sector Comparison-Chi-square Test

Chi-Square Tests	*Value*	*df*	*Asymp. Sig. (2-sided)*
Pearson Chi-Square	13.896[a]	4	.008
Likelihood Ratio	14.185	4	.007
Linear-by-Linear Association	8.117	1	.004
N of Valid Cases	360		

a. 0 cells (.0%) have expected count less than 5. The minimum expected count is 11.50.

Source: Primary data

Table 6.3. Technology skills Inventory: Sector Comparison- Chi-square Test

Chi-Square Tests	*Value*	*df*	*Asymp. Sig. (2-sided)*
Pearson Chi-Square	4.529[a]	4	.339
Likelihood Ratio	4.554	4	.336
Linear-by-Linear Association	.538	1	.463
N of Valid Cases	360		

a. 0 cells (.0%) have expected count less than 5. The minimum expected count is 7.50.

Source: Primary data

CONCLUSION

Referring to the above inferences, it can be concluded that human capital need to be given the prime role in determining the productivity of banking industry in particular and service industry in general. There are healthy indicators on the general executive profile of banking executives, however, finding of comparative analysis between public sector and private sector show signals for possible remedial measures.

FUTURE WORK

The results of this study are encouraging and we are extending our work to analyze the relationship between *Organizational skill inventory* and *Banking Service Quality, Role of training in developing organizational skill inventory,* and *Impact of organizational skill inventory on the customer satisfaction index.*

REFERENCES

1. Adler, P. S. and S-K. Kwon (2002): "Social Capital: Prospects for a New Concept." Academy of Management Review 27 (1): 17-40.
2. Aiken, L. S. and S. G. West (1991): Multiple Regression: Testing and Interpreting Interactions. Newbury Park, CA: Sage Publications.
3. Carpenter, M. A., W. G. Sanders and H. B. Gregersen (2001): "Bundling Human Capital with Organizational Context: The Impact of International Assignment Experience on Multinational Firm Performance and CEO Pay." Academy of Management Journal 44 (3): 493-512.
4. Collins, C. J. and K. D. Clark (2003): "Strategic Human Resource Practices, Top Management Team Social Networks, and Firm Performance: The Role of Human Resource Practices in Creating Organizational Competitive Advantage." Academy of Management Journal 46 (6): 740-751.
5. Danneels, E. (2003): "Tight-loose Coupling with Customers: The Enactment of Customer Orientation." Strategic Management Journal 24 (6): 559-576.
6. Delery, J. E. and D. H. Doty (1996): "Modes of Theorizing in Strategic Human Resource Management: Tests of Universalistic, Contingency, and Configurational Performance Predictions." Academy of Managment Journal 39 (4): 802-835.
7. Dyer, J. H. and H. Singh (1998): "The Relational View:

Cooperative Strategy and Sources of Inter-organizational Competitive Advantage." Academy of Management Review 23 (4): 660-679.

8. Dyer, L. and T. Reeves (1995): "Human Resource Strategies and Firm Performance: What do We Know and Where do We Need to Go?" International Journal of Human Resource Management 6: 656-670.

9. Edvinsson, L. and M. S. Malone (1997): Intellectual Capital: Realizing your Company's True Value by Finding its Hidden Brain Power. New York, NY: Harper Business (a division of Harper Collins Publishers).

10. Guest, D. E. (1997): "Human Resource Management and Performance: A Review and Research Agenda." The International Journal of Human Resource Management 8 (3): 263-276.

11. Herremans, I. M. and R. G. Isaac (2004): "The Intellectual Capital Realization Process (ICRP): An Application of the Resource-based View of the Firm." Journal of Managerial Issues 16 (2): 217-231.

12. Hitt, M. A., L. Bierman, K. Shimizu and R. Kochhar (2001): "Direct and Moderating Effects of Human Capital on Strategy and Performance in Professional Service Firms: A Resource-based Perspective." Academy of Management Journal 44 (1): 13-28.

13. Huselid, M. A. (1995): "The Impact of Human Resource Management Practices on Turnover, Productivity, and Corporate Financial Performance." Academyof Management Journal 38 (3): 635-672.

14. Jaccard, J. and C. K. Wan (1996): "LISREL Approaches to Interaction Effects in Multiple Regression." Chapter in Quantitative Applications in the Social Sciences, Vol. 114. Ed. M. S. Lewis-Beck. Thousand Oaks, CA: Sage.

15. Leana, C. R. and H. J. Van Buren, III. (1999): "Organizational Social Capital and Employment Practices." Academy of Management Review 24 (3): 538-555.

16. M. Subramaniam and S. A. Snell (2004): "Intellectual Capital Profiles: An Examination of Investments and Returns." Journal of Management Studies 41 (2): 335-361.

17. Nahapiet, J. and S. Ghoshal (1998): "Social Capital, Intellectual Capital, and the Organizational Advantage." Academy of Management Review 23 (2): 242-266.

18. Nelson, R. R. and S. G. Winter (1982): An Evolutionary Theory of Economic Change. Cambridge, MA: Belknap Press of Harvard University Press.

19. Pfeffer, J. (1994): "Competitive Advantage through People." California Management Review 36 (2): 9-28.

20. Priem, R. L. and J. E. Butler (2001): "Is the Resource-based 'View' a Useful Perspective for Strategic Management Research?" Academy of Management Review 26 (1): 22-40.

21. S. E. Jackson and R. S. Schuler (1997): "Technical and Strategic Human Resource Management Effectiveness as Determinants of Firm Performance." Academy of Management Journal 40 (1): 171-188.

22. Sirmon, D. G., M. A. Hitt and R. D. Ireland (2007): "Managing Firm Resources in Dynamic Environments to Create Value: Looking Inside the Black Box." Academy of Management Review 32 (1): 273-292.

23. Subramaniam, M. and M. A. Youndt (2005): "The Influence of Intellectual Capital on the Types of Innovative Capabilities." Academy of Management Journal 48 (3): 450-463.

24. Tsai, W. and S. Ghoshal (1998): "Social Capital and Value Creation: The Role of Intra-firm Networks." Academy of Management Journal 41 (4): 464-478.

25. Watson, A. and B. Wooldridge (2005): "Business Unit Manager Influence on Corporate-level Strategy Formulation." Journal of Managerial Issues 17 (2): 147- 161.

26. Xiao Li, S. and T. J. Rowley (2002): "Inertia and Evaluation Mechanisms in Inter-organizational Partner Selection: Syndicate Formation Among US Investment Banks." Academy of Management Journal 45 (6): 1104-1119.

27. Youndt, M. A. and S. A. Snell (2004): "Human Resource Configurations, Intellectual Capital, and Organizational Performance." Journal of Managerial Issues 16 (3): 337-360.

7

Role of Banks in Financing Higher Education Aspirants

K. Govindarajalu
S. Balamurugan

INTRODUCTION

One of the major concerns of the Government is to ensure that nobody is denied professional education because he or she is poor. The Indian Banks Association (IBA) had formulated a comprehensive model educational loan scheme for adoption by all Banks, aimed at providing financial support from the banking system to deserving/meritorious students for pursuing higher education in India and abroad. Government of India has now approved a Scheme to provide full interest subsidy during the period of moratorium on loans taken by students belonging to economically weaker sections from scheduled banks under the Educational Loan Scheme of the Indian Banks' Association, for pursuing any of the approved courses of studies in technical and professional streams, from recognized institutions in India.

However, it is necessary to oversee the performance of banks in financing higher education aspirants in order to identify the problems faced by banks as well as students who are in need of bank loans for their higher education.

OBJECTIVES OF THE STUDY

- To study the role of banks in providing education loan to higher education aspirants
- To analyze the performance of banks in providing education loan
- To examine the relationship between banks and education loan seeker

METHODOLOGY

For the purpose of the study, secondary data regarding the total number of beneficiaries through education loan, the amount of education loan given by the banks and the outstanding amounts have been collected and analyzed. Secondary data was collected from various web sources such as Reserve Bank of India, Indian Banks Association websites.

THE NEED FOR STUDENT LOANS

From the perspective of the student, the ability to borrow for at least some of the costs of their higher education gives young persons the ability to invest in their own futures. While many or most students might prefer all of the money to come either from parents or (preferably) from taxpayers, in light of the demonstrable private benefits from higher education that accrue to the student—including both monetary (i.e. higher future earnings) and non-monetary (e.g. higher status, access to generally more interesting and pleasant jobs, and more choices of occupations, mates, and places to live)—such an investment is perfectly reasonable. In fact, in light of the limits on both parental and governmental contributions as well as on part-time employment possibilities, borrowing, for some students, will be the difference between having and not having access to higher education.

FINANCIAL SUPPORT TO HIGHER EDUCATION ASPIRANTS

To offset the increase in fees, the Government of India announced a new education loan program, the Educational Loan Scheme, in April 2001. The scheme provides loans to "poor and needy" Indian citizens to undertake basic education and to "meritorious student" to pursue higher education at home or abroad. As compared to the bank-specific education loans scheme in the past, the new scheme is a) non-bank specific in nature as it can be adopted by all banks, b) wider in scope as it includes a large number of courses, and c) broader in scope as it covers both fee and non-fee expenditures which are related to study (Narayana, 2002). The program does not require collateral for the first Rs 400,000 loaned and the maximum amount awarded is Rs 750,000 for studies in India and Rs 1,500,000 for studies abroad. The interest rate is not compounded during the repayment holiday/moratorium (course period plus 1 year or 6 months after getting a job, whichever is earlier).

Reserve Bank of India and India Banks Association have stipulated conditions that for Education Loans upto 4 lakhs, collateral security, third party guarantee and margin money should not be obtained. Even the rate of interest is limited to BPLR rate, presently, around 12 percent. In spite of the immunity given, almost many Bank Managers insist on collateral security, guarantee, margin and charge higher rate of interest.

EDUCATIONAL LOAN SCHEME

Government of India in consultation with Reserve Bank of India (RBI) and Indian Banker's Association (IBA) has framed a Comprehensive Educational Loan Scheme to ensure that no deserving student in the Country is deprived of higher education for want of finances. The new scheme covers all type of courses including professional courses in schools and colleges in India and abroad.

The salient features of the scheme are as under :

- The scheme envisages loans up to Rs.7.5 lakh for studies in India and up to Rs. 15 lakh for studies abroad.
- For loans up to Rs. 4 lakh no collateral or margin is required and the interest rate is not to exceed the Prime Lending Rates (PLR). For loans above Rs. 4 lakh the interest rate will not exceed PLR plus 1 percent.
- The loans are to be repaid over a period of 5 to 7 years with provision of grace period of one year after completion of studies.

Objectives of the Education Loan Scheme

The Educational Loan Scheme aims at providing financial support from the banking system to deserving/ meritorious students for pursuing higher education in India and abroad. The main emphasis is that every meritorious student though poor is provided with an opportunity to pursue education with the financial support from the banking system with affordable terms and conditions. No deserving student is denied an opportunity to pursue higher education for want of financial support.

Benefits of Taking Education Loans

1. Financial support for professional courses such as MBA, BTech and MBBS
2. Available for higher education in India and abroad
3. Easy repayment only after job placement
4. Affordable Interest Rates
5. Lesser burden on parents

6. Loan cover upto as much as 20 lakhs available by various banks
7. Expenses such as tuition fees, travel expenses, hostel charges are included in education loan

Beneficiaries of higher education are not only the students, but also their families, the employers, the government and the society at large who benefit from higher education. The 'externalities' associated with higher education, including 'dynamic' externalities, are acknowledged to be huge.

PERFORMANCE OF BANKS UNDER EDUCATION LOANS

Table-1 shows the details of education loan given by public sector banks from the period 2005 to 2009. In 2005, total number of education loan provided is 468207 whereas 1603385 in 2009. Total amount outstanding was 6713.16 Crores in 2005 and 27645.58 Crores in 2009 which reveals that the level of students who availed education loan and the amount financed to them by banks have been increasing drastically.

Table 1. Education Loans Given by Public Sector Banks

(Rs. In Crores)

Year	*No. of Accounts*	*Amount Outstanding*
31.03.2005	468207	6713.16
31.03.2006	679945	10012.49
31.03.2007	944397	14282.56
31.03.2008	1246870	19816.54
31.03.2009	1603385	27645.58

Source: Indian Banks Association

Distribution of Outstanding Advances of Public Sector Banks to Education Loan

Table-2 gives the information of the outstanding advances under education loan and the total bank credit as of March 2009. All the PSU banks put together have given finance to 15.80 lakh students amounting to 26925 Crores. The total bank credit as at that day was 22.83 lakh Crores. The education loan constitutes only 1.18 percent of their total bank credit.

Table 2. Distribution of Outstanding Advances of Public Sector Banks to Education Loan (March 2009)

(No. of Accounts in lakh and Amount in Rs. crore)

Bank Group/Bank	*Education Loan*		*Total Bank credit*	
	No. of Accounts	*Amount Out-standing*	*Amount*	*% of Education loan*
A. State Bank Group	**5.28**	**9469**	**747871.48**	**1.27**
State Bank of India	3.14	6182	549296.81	1.13
State Bank of Bikaner & Jaipur	0.15	280	30088.10	0.93
State Bank of Hyderabad	0.46	836	43937.72	1.9
State Bank of Indore	0.10	165	21746.58	0.76
State Bank of Mysore	0.23	391	25869.88	1.51
State Bank of Patiala	0.21	245	43960.81	0.56
State Bank of Travancore	0.99	1370	32971.58	4.16
B. Nationalized Banks	**10.52**	**17457**	**1535601.92**	**1.14**
Allahabad Bank	0.30	638	59443.40	1.07
Andhra Bank	0.75	1391	44427.60	3.13
Bank of Baroda	0.60	1165	144844.87	0.8
Bank of India	0.75	1324	144731.56	0.91
Bank of Maharashtra	0.17	315	34817.28	0.9
Canara Bank	1.47	2301	139036.91	1.65
Central Bank of India	0.53	811	86740.27	0.93

Bank Group/Bank	*Education Loan*		*Total Bank credit*	
	No. of Accounts	*Amount Out-standing*	*Amount*	*% of Education loan*
Corporation Bank	0.32	664	48927.12	1.36
Dena Bank	0.13	241	29185.36	0.83
IDBI Bank Ltd.	0.03	52	103915.07	0.05
Indian Bank	1.28	1591	51830.64	3.07
Indian Overseas Bank	0.78	1033	75809.54	1.36
Oriental Bank of commerce	0.36	770	69064.72	1.11
Punjab National Bank	0.93	1611	156098.45	1.03
Punjab & Sind Bank	0.06	179	24698.10	0.11
Syndicate Bank	0.81	1150	82495.04	1.39
Union Bank of India	0.53	957	69669.05	1.37
United Bank of India	0.20	344	98264.85	0.35
UCO Bank	0.28	490	35727.45	1.37
Vijaya bank	0.24	431	35874.63	1.2
Public Sector Banks (A+B)	**15.80**	**26925**	**2283473.40**	**1.18**

Source: RBI

Note: Data are provisional

Performance of Banks under Education Loan in Tamilnadu

Table-3 reveals the education loan outstanding as on 30th Sep 2010 along with the total outstanding of advances of all banks in Tamilnadu. In Tamilnadu, all the Banks have an outstanding of Rs.8841 Crores under education loan. This constitutes 2.79 percent of their total advances. Public Sector Banks have an outstanding of Rs.8511 Crores, constituting 3.65 percent of their advances. Private Banks in Tamilnadu have done very poorly under education loan. They have given only 0.39 percent of their total advances. Excepting

Lakshmi Vilas Bank and Tamilnadu Mercantile Bank, other banks have not taken the education loan seriously. Axis Bank, ICICI Bank and IndusInd Bank have practically not contributed anything under education loan.

Table 3. Education Loan Outstanding as on 30th Sep 2010

Bank	*Advances*	*Education*	*% of Education loan*
Indian Bank	26073.28	1959.95	7.52
Indian Overseas Bank	26763.00	1234.28	4.61
Syndicate Bank	6189.72	269.73	4.36
Canara Bank	25615.65	1096.72	4.28
Union Bank of India	7134.85	275.77	3.87
State Bank of Travancore	4605.61	161.96	3.52
Bank of India	8897.00	302.45	3.40
Central Bank of India	8158.29	261.93	3.21
State Bank of India	58975.27	1847.70	3.13
State Bank of Mysore	2489.82	72.18	2.90
Corporation Bank	7071.49	187.11	2.65
Bank of Baroda	7728.95	204.36	2.64
UCO Bank	4529.73	119.42	2.64
Andhra Bank	3624.74	93.79	2.59
Vijaya Bank	2643.68	59.90	2.27
State Bank of Hyderabad	1679.77	33.10	1.97
State Bank of B & J	1013.88	19.67	1.94
Dena Bank	1303.69	24.69	1.89
Oriental Bank of Commerce	3132.59	52.96	1.69
Bank of Maharashtra	875.84	14.39	1.64
Allahabad Bank	2595.50	41.86	1.61
United Bank of India	1703.07	20.20	1.19
Punjab National Bank	15721.07	145.14	0.92
State Bank of Patiala	743.37	6.14	0.83

Bank	*Advances*	*Education*	*% of Education loan*
State Bank of Indore	529.06	2.60	0.49
Punjab & Sind Bank	1105.24	3.99	0.36
All Public Sector Banks	230904.16	8511.99	3.69
Lakshmi Vilas Bank Ltd.	3362.15	42.05	1.25
Tamilnad Mercantile Bank Ltd.	6408.64	78.67	1.23
Pallavan Grama Bank	700.05	7.70	1.10
City Union Bank Ltd.	5638.96	47.91	0.85
Karnataka Bank Ltd.	1400.43	11.12	0.79
Catholic Syrian Bank Ltd.	1570.21	11.17	0.71
Dhanalakshmi Bank Ltd.	815.10	5.43	0.67
Karur Vysya Bank Ltd.	6656.48	44.32	0.67
Pandiyan Grama Bank	2214.78	14.28	0.64
Federal Bank Ltd.	2758.71	9.72	0.35
HDFC Bank Ltd.	13619.68	31.74	0.23
Jammu & Kashmir Bank Ltd.	201.95	0.42	0.21
South Indian Bank Ltd.	5488.19	10.85	0.20
ING Vysya Bank	1495.11	2.22	0.15
IDBI Bank Ltd.	10384.12	6.59	0.06
Axis Bank Ltd.	7142.82	3.46	0.05
Bank of Rajasthan Ltd.	204.68	0.08	0.04
ICICI Bank Ltd.	13414.69	1.88	0.01
Indus Ind Bank Ltd.	1962.72	0.00	0.00
Private Banks	85439.47	329.61	0.39
All Banks in Tamilnadu	**316343.63**	**8841.60**	**2.79**

Source: State Level Bankers Committee, Tamilnadu

PUBLIC SECTOR BANKS

The total outstanding under Education Loan as at 30th Sep 2010 is Rs.8841 Crores (2.79% of total advances in TN). Public Sector Banks have contributed to the extent of Rs. 8512 Crores (3.7%). Indian Bank stands top with outstanding of Rs.1950 Crores (7.5 percent of the total advances in TN) and SBI has outstanding of Rs.1848 Crores (3.1% of total advances in TN). Very unfortunately, Public Sector Banks do not take much interest in creating proper awareness among students and parents about the education loan, while they take huge initiative for car loans, housing loans, etc. If they take initiative of proper awareness campaign, it would be easy for them to manage the portfolio.

PRIVATE BANKS

Performance of Private Sector Banks under education loan is very poor in Tamilnadu. The outstanding of all the private banks is only Rs.340 crores (0.39% of their total advances in Tamilnadu). Lakshmi Vilas Bank and Tamilnadu Mercantile Bank have done more than 1% of their advances.

Scant Respect by ICICI Bank towards Education Loan

Though ICICI Bank has the maximum credit disbursement (Rs. 13415 Crores) among the private banks, their contribution towards education loan is only Rs.1.8 Crores (0.01% of their advances in Tamilnadu). Axis Bank and Indus Ind Bank have also not contributed anything towards education loan.

RELATIONSHIP BETWEEN BANKS AND EDUCATION LOAN SEEKERS

In early Jan 2010, Editorial Team of an e-zine 'pr-e-sense' conducted an online survey to understand the various types of problems that the education loan seekers face from the Banks. Various general observations were made by the editorial team, covering all the public sector Banks. There is a lack of awareness about the Education Loans among the students, parents and even NGOs. Bankers take advantage of this lack of awareness.

- Bankers do not give application forms to the students in the first stage. Loan seekers are made to visit the Banks many times.
- Quota over, not in our area, we do not give education loan, come next year, degree course is not eligible, etc. are the common reasons given by the Bank Managers to the loan seekers. Due to lack of awareness, they also believe this and go away.
- Even if somebody takes up with Higher Authorities, the Bank Managers seek protection saying that 'no such application received'. (When Editorial Team of 'pr-e-sense' took up a Case Study with the concerned Zonal Office of the Bank, immediate reaction was 'No such application pending').

Some of the problems faced by the students from banks

- Students are asked to go to pillar to post by the Branch officials and they are not given proper response
- Demanding of collateral security / guarantee even for smaller amount
- Insisting on payment of interest every month, before completing the studies
- Branch officials not aware of education loan procedures and giving scant respect to the students with poor background, etc.

Some of the problems faced by the bankers

- Students from unauthorized colleges and unauthorized courses demand education loan
- Students demand loans for courses, which can not

provide employment (Eg. teachers training courses)

- Since banks are lending funds, some of the colleges inflate their estimates to get more money, which will ultimately make the students as heavy borrowers. Even many colleges send the estimates as Rs.3,99,500/- to avoid offering collateral security. Banks are unable to confirm the genuiness of the proposals
- Some of the students, who availed education loan from banks shift their places without informing the bank and do not even repay the loans. this causes lot of difficulties for the banks and the officials
- The colleges do not give estimates on admission. Without estimates, banks cannot process the loans

FINDINGS

- Need for financing higher education aspirants in the present scenario is highly notable and Banks play a vital role in financing higher education aspirants.
- Education loan scheme of Government of India is appreciable as it provides benefits not only to banks and education loan seekers but also to the development of the economy through fund mobilization.
- Performance of public sector banks in providing education loan is somewhat satisfactory whereas, the performance of private sector banks under education loan is very poor in Tamilnadu.
- Relationship between banks and education loan seekers is still not good enough due to the problems persist on borrowing education loan from the banks and repayment from the students who got education loan.

CONCLUSION

Though RBI and IBA have given strict guidelines,

almost all the Branches insist on collateral security, third party guarantee, margin money from the applicants, even if the loan is less than 4 lakhs. Even the Zonal Offices seem to be defending such violation. Higher education has become very important with advancing science and technology. Many youngsters today want to pursue higher education; some are very hard working and need to be supported. Insuring the loan and having an insurance company take the repaying responsibility, is one way of solving the problem. While emphasizing on higher education, one must also take into account primary and secondary education that develop children for a future higher education. This should be considered in totality. After all, when a student takes a loan to pursue higher education and becomes a scientist or technocrat, the money is an investment and not a liability.

Students should be a responsible Citizen by promptly repaying the Education loan availed from the Bank. Even though they shift their location, job, etc., they should keep updated with their financing banker. If students have any genuine problem, discussion should be made with Bank Manager, who can guide them. Confidence should be given to the bankers that students are trust worthy borrowers. Banks are great reservoir of finance. A trust worthy borrower can avail lot of support from the Banks in future.

REFERENCES

1. Bruce Chapman (2005), "Income Contingent Loans for Higher Education: International Reform", Discussion Paper Discussion paper NO. 491, Centre for Economic Policy Research, The Australian National University, June 2005.
2. Bruce Johnstone.D (2006), "Financing Higher Education: Cost Sharing in International Perspective", International Comparative Higher Education Finance and Accessibility Project (ICHEFAP), State University of New York, Buffalo, New York, March, 2006.

3. Carnoy, M. (1999), "Globalisation and Educational Reform: What Planners Need to Know", Report No.63, International Institute of Educational Planning, Paris.
4. Charlene Wear Simmons (2008), "Students Loan for Higher Education", California Research Bureau, Jan 2008.
5. Jandhyala B.G Tilak (1999) "Student Loans as the Answer to Lack of Resources for Higher Education", Economic and Political Weekly, January 9, 1999.
6. Geetha Rani.P, (2002), "Financing Higher Education in India during the Post Reform Period: Focus on Access and Equity", NIEPA Occasional Paper, No.31, NIEPA, New Delhi, September, 2002.
7. Hua Shen Adrian Ziderman (2008), "Student Loans Repayment and Recovery: International Comparisons" Discussion Paper No. 3588, IZA, Germany, July 2008.
8. Survey of Corporate ezine PR-e-Sense, (2010): http://www.primepointfoundation.org

Section II : Micro Finance and Financial Inclusion

8

New Dimensions of Micro Finance for Sustainable Development through Corporate Social Responsibility

K. M. George
Isabella George

INTRODUCTION

It is amazing to note that the literature on corporate social responsibility (CSR), micro finance and NGOs abunds. The advent of the term CSR can be traced back to the 1970s. But it became prominent after the mid 1980s. It is also known by different names like corporate responsibility, corporate conscience, corporate social performance and the like. CSR means that businesses would monitor and ensure its support to rules and regulations of the land where it operates, maintain ethical standards and the norms of consciousness. This means among others, businesses shall ensure responsibility for its likely influence on stakeholders, environment, and the community at large. It is a proactive approach to bringing in holistic growth by containing the ill effects on environment on the one hand, and bringing in a new deal in relation to mother earth vis-à-vis consumers, employees, environment, business profits, etc.

The theme of CSR is much debated and criticized the world over. Proponents of CSR argue that there is a very strong case for CSR. Critics argue that CSR distracts from the fundamental economic role of businesses. Many a critic argues that it is nothing more than superficial window dressing. Another argument is that it is an attempt to pre-empt the role of governments as a watchdog over powerful multinational corporations*. However, Corporate Social Responsibility has been redefined throughout the years. Therefore, the theme deserves great deal of thought in its approach and handling. The views of the corporate executives on NGOs and the deployment of micro credit through them are very important. At least five per cent of the sample respondents of the field study were corporate executives and to that extent the study has covered that lacuna, though not fully.

HYPOTHESIS

The major hypothesis of the empirical study was to

* Acknowledging the help received from others is a very difficult job. We are grateful to all our respondents who come from three continents for their time and commitment. We want to place on record our special gratitude to Prof Dr. Albert Schram, School of Business and Economics, Maastricht University; Dr. Michael Ashkenazi, Senior Researcher of Bonn International Centre for Conversion; Mr. K. Kannan, Director, Asian Development Bank, Manila and Mr. Kishore Menon of Bamco, Bahrain for editing an earlier version of this paper. They did contribute immensely. However, errors if any are solely attributable to the authors.

ascertain whether CSR of businesses adequately empower NGOs with micro finance for ensuring sustainable development.

MICRO FINANCE & MACRO CHALLENGES

Any discussion on the captioned theme becomes meaningful only if micro finance is touched up on at least thematically. As such, an effort is made in the following section to familiarize the readers with MFIs and the challenges of micro finance globally and particularly, in the Indian context. It is worth recalling that there is greater awareness at the international level after the demise of the Lehman Brothers, that the poor are better credit risks than the high flyers. This is one of the attractions of micro finance - the lending of tiny sums to those who are at the bottom of the economic pyramid. They range from farmers in rural areas, to shop keepers, artisans as well as very small businesses. The sums involved may be as little as USD 50. The beauty is that MFIs reach those areas through NGOs where banks shy away from, on account of connectivity problems, high risk and transaction costs. There is a word of caution that too much commercialism may ruin micro finance.

Taking a clue from the foregoing warning, it may be worth recalling the recent developments in the Indian micro finance market. With an estimated USD 6000 million lent to around 27 million active borrowers, the Indian micro finance business has entered the mainstream. It is no more a fringe financial activity by any imagination, calling for acts of good governance in place. MFIs have been very active even in the remotest villages of some selected South Indian states. Their slogan, "we are the last mile connectivity in rural finance" was considered as an amazing instrument of financial inclusion of the marginalized and the hitherto neglected by the organized banking system of the country. Default by a single borrower impairs the eligibility of the group to receive further credit, was a great repayment ensuring factor as well as proper end use of credit. Two questions arise here. One is the adequacy of the loan in relation to the purpose of the loan and the other question relates to the credit absorption capacity of the borrower in relation to the marketing arrangements of the marketable surpluses of the borrower. There is a danger of multiple borrowings from different MFIs and even village money lenders in the absence of principles of good governance in operation. Another related issue may be of transparency in the operations of the MFIs, particularly pertaining to the interest regime. It may be recalled that in any discussion on inclusion, at least in the short term, profitability and social justice cannot co-exist unless conscious policy interventions are effected by fiscal and monetary policy makers. It may be recalled that for financial inclusion, adequate preparations are required, both at the beneficiary and policy makers levels, so that the erstwhile bitter experiences of the chaotic rush for receiving the payments of wages of NREGP at the bank branches are not repeated.

It is worth recalling that micro finance has rapidly grown in many countries in the recent past. There are some 30 million clients of MFIs in India during 2010. India is one of the biggest markets of micro finance in the world today. But in India a new breed of MFIs has come to stay, namely pro-profit micro finance lenders. They have annoyed both the NGO sector and the government alike. In the Indian state of Andhra Pradesh, with the largest number of micro finance borrowers, local politicians have halted the MFIs by an executive order of the government. It is a truism that the poor often use micro loans to pay off far more expensive loans contracted from village money lenders. In Bangladesh the MFIs can charge only a maximum of 27 per cent as annual interest on micro loans. It seems the Indian authorities are also planning to cap micro finance interest rates. It may be worthwhile to permit MFIs to take deposits and to augment the introduction of the proposed unique identity number (UIN) (Aadhaar) to all, as it may help to track the clients' overall indebtedness, credit histories, etc., among others.

This is by way of some understanding of the micro finance and its current challenges. It is time to get back to the main hypothesis of the present paper and its detailed analysis.

SOURCES OF DATA & METHODOLOGY

Having seen the advent and background of CSR, the whole issue is examined with the help of some empirical data collected from a randomly selected international sample study of seven countries, spread over three continents. It was designed in such ways that both developed and developing countries represent the sample along with a mix of large and small economies as well. Data were collected on a pre-structured questionnaire electronically. Though it was proposed to collect data from some 300 respondents, in effect, only 100 respondents had returned the filled-in questionnaires. The sample respondents were well educated and had adequate exposure to CSR related subjects, to comment on it. Some of them were really practitioners of CSR regime themselves. Most of the respondents were personally known to the authors, owing to their professional erstwhile interactions with them.

The countries covered for the field work included Australia, UK and Italy as representatives of the developed world. The developing economies constituted India, Bahrain, Qatar and Afghanistan. The selection of these countries was mostly on account of the personal familiarity of the authors with the respondents. Nearly 10 sample respondents each had returned the filled questionnaires from these countries. In addition, around 30 filled-in questionnaires had come from other countries like Pakistan, Bangladesh, Nepal, Sri Lanka, PNG, Singapore, Philippines, etc. But the number of such questionnaires was less than five from any one country. For the purpose of data collection, the calendar year 2009-2010, (July 2009 to June 2010) was considered as the study period, while field work was done during July, Aug and Sept 2010.

LIMITATIONS OF THE STUDY

The major limitation of the study is that the sample constituted only 100 respondents. For a study of a global nature, seeking to come out with policy implications, this is a major limitation. Again, there were no face to face interviews with the respondents and as such the body language communications and observation techniques could not be profitably made use of. Respondents, it is assumed, were in the same wave length with the interviewer even in an online survey. In fact, it is not always correct to assume so.

FINDINGS & DATA ANALYSIS

As the Table1 is self explanatory, the following table examines the literacy details of the sample respondents. Nearly 86 per cent of the sample constituted highly educated respondents. They were reasonably well informed about CSR. Besides, they were competent to comment on CSR. Some of them were even representing business houses themselves and had practiced CSR (Table 2).It could be seen from the Table-3 that the sample had nearly 40 per cent of the respondents classified as senior citizens. They were all mature people capable of assessing the field realities.

Table 1. Shows the details of respondents, country wise distribution

Country	*Respondents*
India	10
Afghanistan	10
Australia	10
UK	10
Italy	10
Bahrain	10
Qatar	10
Others	30
All	100

Table 2. Level of Literacy of the respondents

Under graduates	14
Graduates	55
Post Graduates	31
All	100

Table 3. Shows the details of age distribution of the sample

Age group	*Respondent*
Less than 40 years	Nil
40 to 60 years	61
Above 60 years	39
All	100

While some 33 per cent of the sample had reported an average annual income of more than USD 20,000, 67 percent accounted for less than USD 20,000. In the international context of both developed and developing economies, this average income is a clear indication of the financial standing of the respondents(Table-4). It is very clearly brought to sharp focus by an overwhelming majority of the respondents that their perception of CSR is to plough back part of the profits of companies and businesses for sustainable development oriented activities of the community presented in Table 5. Another attempt was made to ascertain as to which would be the appropriate agency to channel the CSR funds. The summary findings are tabulated and presented in Table 6.

Table 4. Shows the details of the annual average income of the sample in U.S. Dollars.

Av income	*Respondent*
Less than 2000	Nil
2001 to 20,000	67
Above 20,000	33
All	100

Table 5. Shows the perception of the respondents about CSR. It was asked as to what they understood by CSR. The tabulated summary is presented in the table below.

Corporate entities ploughing back a part of their profits to sustainable development activities of the community	73 %
Organizations sharing their profit with the poor	20 %
Businesses helping society with funding	7 %

Table 6. Agency to channel CSR Funds: NGOs

Good to channel through NGOs	93
Not good to have NGOs	7
All	100

It is worthwhile to mention that a clear choice was offered to the respondents among NGOs, community organizations, local self government organizations, churches, temples and such other religious organizations. But the response was only confined mostly to NGOs. It is worth recalling that nearly 93 per cent of the respondents had favored NGOs as the right vehicle to channel CSR funds on account of their grass root level connections and transparency in their approach and out look. Of course, they were very vocal in their views about cowboy NGOs. They were voting only for NGOs which are above board and run on professional lines with credibility. A question was asked about the desirability of NGOs taking up micro finance activities on a larger scale, using CSR funds. In fact, there are some misgivings in the minds of many people. The results are presented in Table 7.

Table 7. NGOs to take up Micro Finance activities:

Agreeable	90
Disagreeable	7
Indifferent	3
All	100

It can be seen from the foregoing table that an overwhelming majority of the sample had opined that NGOs may take up micro finance activities by making use of CSR related funds for ensuring sustainable development in the community around them. Again, this is with a qualifying clause that it must be woven around those NGOs which have track operational record. As a logical corollary to the foregoing discussion, the cost effectiveness of NGOs in relation to micro finance was discussed with the sample respondents. The results are presented in Table 8.

Table 8. Micro Finance & NGOs: Cost Effectiveness:

Cost effective	97 %
Ineffective	3%
All	100

It is evident from the foregoing table that around 97 per cent of the sample respondents had voted in favour of cost effectiveness of micro finance operations by NGOs. May be the wisdom coming from the field is worth experimenting with location and regional refinements. It offers new challenges for policy makers and researchers around the globe. Asked about recovery performance as experienced by NGOs with regard to micro finance, the Table 9 presents the field realities across the sample countries. The better recovery performance of NGOs in relation to micro finance at 67 percent cannot be taken as a major suggestive indication. It may be noted that nearly 33 per cent of the respondents had opined that NGOs do not make any difference with regard to recovery of micro finance activities. However human rights violations related to MFIs must be the topic of debate and research as many a MFI is not for profit alone any more. Another hypothesis tested in the study was that micro finance may be disbursed through self help groups (SHGs). Again this was a debatable subject. The results are tabulated and presented in Table 10.

Table 9. Recovery Performance of NGOs in relation to Micro Finance:

Ensure better recovery	67 %
Does not make any difference	33%
All	100

Table 10. Micro Finance to be disbursed through SHGs:

Only through SHGs	63 %
Through others	37%
All	100

It may be noted that while 63 per cent of the sample respondents had favoured the exclusiveness of SHGs in indulging in the micro finance domain, some 33 per cent had voted for other agencies to do this job. This means no exclusiveness was voted for any one agency. Again, this may be a worthy topic for future researchers to be taken up. While responding to micro finance through the NGOs, the voice of the respondents was more discernible (Table 11). Respondents from almost all countries had favored the micro finance lending through NOGs. It may be worthwhile to experiment this approach to prove or disprove it on a larger scale by innovative CSR oriented businesses. Respondents were asked about their views regarding wider coverage in terms of deployment of funds of CSR through the medium of NGOs. The results are presented in Table 12.

Table 11. Deployment of CSR related funds by NGOs

Better to opt for NGOs	85 %
Look for other agencies	15 %
All	100

Table 12. Wider coverage of CSR related funds through NGOs:

Required	100
Not necessary	Nil
All	100

It is interesting to note that all the respondents had opined that wider coverage of CSR related fund deployment may be done only through NGOs. Whenever qualified and competent NGOs are not available, the corporate bodies in question may identify other organizations or do the job themselves. Obviously it is an excellent policy indication for those who are the movers and shakers of policy domain in the developing world and that too, particularly, in the context of the Millennium Development Goals of the United Nations.

HOW TO EMPOWER NGOs THROUGH CSR RELATED ACTIVITIES?

Much depends on our perception. It was pointed out by many a respondent from the developing countries that, lack of training is a major stumbling block withholding the NGOs from putting up a good performance. In order to overcome this inadequacy in training in financial management, targeted training programmes may be imparted. The local communities and NGOs are to be empowered by undertaking study tours. This would initiate them to several new things. According to conventional wisdom, it is said that seeing is believing. NGOs are to be trained on an ongoing basis, particularly with targeted training inside NGOs. The starting point is to empower the NGOs themselves. This is imperative for any activity to be undertaken by NGOs. As already mentioned elsewhere in this paper, select only those NGOs with impeccable integrity to channel the CSR funds for redeployment. Again, the selected NGOs must have undergone both financial and social audit and must be like role models.

It was suggested that NGOs must be strengthened with professional staff and competent advisors. It was felt that only those NGOs with sound monitoring and evaluation systems may be selected for channeling the CSR funds for redeployment. NGOs which resort to strong arm tactics in effecting recovery may be discriminated against, in channeling the CSR funds. In fact, intimidating methods in recovering dues of loans or outstanding amounts must be done away with. MFIs are to be subjected to strict and close scrutiny for human rights violations related to micro credit loan processing, sanction, disbursal and recovery.NGOs are to be assessed periodically to review their credibility and to ascertain whether they function as friend, philosopher and guide to their stakeholders and SHGs.

POLICY IMPLICATIONS

It may be clearly understood that the corporate bodies owe certain duties to the community and should be transparently responsible to them and to the society at large. First and foremost among them is strict compliance with laws of the land in relation to pollution, health, environment and concern for the society. This is all the more essential in the prevailing socio-economic milieu where the corporate bodies in several countries indulge in polluting the rivers and other water bodies including aquifers. It is high time to have an inclusive growth approach, rather than following an undeclared anti-social and anti-people approach on the one hand and a proclaimed CSR creed on the other. Corporate bodies everywhere, namely in production, trading, banking, etc., should not be doing any unethical operations for amassing instant profits by exploitations and manipulations. Basically good governance is the key word, preamble and post-script for CSR.

It may be perceived unambiguously that this paper is not an attempt to debate the pros and cons of CSR. But it is looking into CSR as and when it comes in the form of resources for redeployment. As such it is examining the desirability of channeling the CSR recourses through NGOs and dedicating it under the head of micro finance.It is very clearly brought to sharp focus by an overwhelming majority of the respondents that their perception of CSR is to plough back part of the profits of companies and businesses for sustainable development oriented activities. It is worth recalling that 93 per cent of the respondents had favored NGOs as the right vehicle to channel CSR funds on account of their grass root level connections and transparency in their approach and outlook. Of course, they were very vocal in their views about cowboy NGOs as well. They were voting only for NGOs which were above board and run on professional lines with credibility. An overwhelming majority had opined that NGOs may take up micro finance activities by making use of CSR related funds for ensuring sustainable development in the community around them. 97 per cent of the sample respondents had voted in favor of cost effectiveness of micro finance operations by NGOs. May be, the wisdom coming from the field is worth experimenting with location and regional refinements. The extent of recovery performance of NGOs in relation to micro finance at 67 percent as "better recovery" cannot be taken as a major suggestive policy indication. It may be noted that 33 per cent of the respondents had opined that NGOs do not make any difference with regard to recovery of micro finance activities. In contrast, the recovery performance of micro finance institutions in Bangladesh at 95 percent is laudable and even worth studying. MFIs are to be subjected to strict and close scrutiny for human rights violations related to micro credit loan processing, sanction, disbursal and recovery. But one important factor affecting the loan utilization and resultant repayment, is the general inequalities and asymmetries that are prevailing in the economy. Income inequality is the major factor to be reckoned with. It is a sad commentary of our developmental dynamics that those with resources are included and those without resources are excluded. In fact the policy thrust must be one of integrated and inclusive approach towards planning and development. The starting point for any meaningful policy intervention aimed at the poor is that micro studies are required to theorize and conceptualize many a hunch and that is possible, among others by engaging focus group discussions on an on going basis.

It is interesting to note that all the respondents had opined that wider coverage of CSR related funds deployment may be done only through NGOs. Obviously it is an excellent policy indication for those who are the movers and shakers of policy domain in the developing world and that too particularly, in the context of the Millennium Development Goals of the United Nations. The starting point is to empower the NGOs themselves. As already mentioned elsewhere in this paper, select only those NGOs with impeccable integrity, to channel the CSR funds for redeployment. Again the selected NGOs must have undergone both financial and social audit and must be role models. It was suggested that NGOs must be strengthened with professional staff and competent advisors. It was felt that only those NGOs with sound monitoring and evaluation systems may be selected for channeling the CSR funds for redeployment.

NGOs which resort to strong arm tactics in effecting recovery may be discriminated against in channeling the CSR funds. In fact, intimidating methods in recovering dues of loans or outstanding amounts must be done away with. NGOs are to be assessed periodically to review their credibility and to ascertain whether they function as friend, philosopher and guide to their stake holders and SHGs. Researchers are challenged the world over and particularly in Asia, Africa and Latin America to take up the CSR-NGO-Micro-credit-theme as the prime theme of investigation during the first half of the 21st century. It may be noted that out of the eight MDGs, at least eradication of poverty and hunger is directly related to the theme of this paper. Gender equality and women employment under the banner of SHGs and NGOs in relation to micro finance do find a prominent place in the modes operandi of the achievement of the MDGs of the UN. The future beckons, shall we falter?

9

Financial Inclusion in India: A Comparative Study of PSBs, RRBs, Foreign Banks, and Private Banks

Y. G. Baligatti
Shridevi V Patted

FINANCIAL INCLUSION : CONCEPTUAL FRAMEWORK AND SIGNIFICANCE

There is no universally accepted definition of financial inclusion. It varies across the countries, depending on the level of social and financial developments of the country under consideration. Generally it refers to the attempts made to reach the people who are excluded from mainstream of financial system. As a result, its referral masses include all types of people who make little or no use of financial services due to some of the potential problems encountered by them.

It is the process that prevents poor and disadvantaged social groups from gaining access to financial system. It may be related to the social aspects like poor and socially disadvantageous group or segments of population such as individuals, and households. The focus of exclusion may also be on a particular source of credit, or access to particular financial products/services like insurance, money transfer and savings. According to the World Bank, 'broad access to financial services implies an absence of price and non-price barriers in the use of financial services; it is difficult to define and measure because access has many dimensions.' In the views of Dr. Rangrajan (Chairman of Committee on Financial Inclusion), 'financial inclusion is the process of ensuring access to financial service and timely and adequate credit where needed by vulnerable groups such as weaker sections and low income groups at an affordable cost.' The process of financial inclusion consists of seeking each household and offering their inclusion in the banking system. Financial inclusion means the provision of affordable financial services, viz., access to payments and remittance facilities, savings, loan and insurance services by the formal financial system to those who tend to be excluded. For all practical considerations, financial inclusion refers access to financial products or services and the role of financial institutions in providing various financial products and services.

SIGNIFICANCE OF FINANCIAL INCLUSION

Financial inclusion is one of the major determinants of economic growth. But it is witnessed that there are glaring facts about financial exclusion that have hindered the economic growth. The Report on Financial Inclusion states that 51.4% of the farming households are financially excluded from all the sources of finance. It is a serious concern to note that a considerable section of the population are considered to be 'unbanked'. Hardly 10% of the villages have access to financial system, women are the biggest losers when it comes to access of financial services where only 15% of the women have financially included. Further, there is one branch catering to the banking needs of 16000 population and only 40% of the population across the country has bank account. The exclusion is more severe particularly among in small income groups, just 13% are availing loans from the bank in the income bracket of less than Rs 50000. This figure speaks of the urgent need for extending the financial services to achieve the objective of inclusive growth of the nation.

Financial exclusion will hinder the growth of the national economy and has a strong bearing on the savings and investment. Hence, financial inclusion is the pre-requisite for economic development of the nation that provides an opportunity to build savings, make investments and avail credit that promotes production and employment.

Absence of banking facilities has made the savers to incur the inherent risk in holding and storing the money that increases the vulnerability to loss or theft of cash. Lack of access to banking services compels the savers to deposit their savings in informal sources like money lenders which is highly risky and will not enjoy the tax benefits. It also increases the source of money supply of money lenders and may pose a challenge to the formal financial mechanism by charging abnormally high interest. Hence, access to financial services is imperative that provides an avenue to bring the savings of the poor into the formal financial system and channel them into productive investments.

It is proved beyond doubt, that the absence of banking facilities will compel the poor to obtain credit from informal sources like moneylenders having high cost of credit resulting to greater financial strain and unmanageable debt. Access to financial services helps the poor to insure themselves against income shocks and equip them to meet emergency. It protects the poor from the clutches of the moneylenders.

Financial inclusion serves as a tool in the hands of the government to alleviate the poverty. Absence of access to financial services makes exclusion of large chunk of socially disadvantaged people from the mainstream of the society. Ultimately, at the wider level of society and nation, it would be a cause of poverty leading to social exclusion. To prevent this situation, the government has adopted several social security measures. Such measures are to be implemented successfully only when there would be a provision for access to financial services.

One cannot deny the danger that the banks may loose the valuable business opportunities that will arise from extending financial services to the lower income groups. There is a lot of potential to increase the savings, deposits as well as credit needs of lower income groups implying profitable business for banks in medium term activities. Banks are benefited in the form of large number of savings bank deposits with low cost that enables the banks to reduce their dependence on bulk deposits involving high cost. Further, it also enables banks to expand credit delivery through banking technology and to meet the requirements of lower income groups leading to increase in their income and savings.

OBJECTIVES, SCOPE, SOURCES AND METHODOLOGY

The primary objective of this study is to make a comparative evaluation of financial inclusion as promoted by PSBs, RRBs, Foreign and Private sector banks. The various dimensions of financial inclusion identified for the purpose of the present inquiry include occupation-wise credit of scheduled commercial banks, population-wise share of deposits, credit and number of offices, gender-wise percentage distribution of outstanding credit, and region-wise distribution of deposits and credits. Accordingly, the study has the following objectives to fulfill:

1. To portray the occupation-wise credit flow by the selected banking segments
2. To trace the number of savings bank accounts and amount of savings deposit of banks.
3. To trace the number of credit accounts and outstanding credit as per size of credit limit of banks
4. To assess the gender-wise distribution of outstanding credit
5. To evaluate the region-wise distribution of deposits and credits.
6. To examine the population-wise shares of deposits and credit

The study is based on secondary data drawn from the *Basic Statistical Returns of Scheduled Commercial Banks in India and Statistical Tables relating to Banks in India.* The study covers half a decade period from 2006 to 2009. The data relating to PSBs consisted of aggregate data of State Bank group and other Nationalised banks taken on average basis. All other data relating to banks have been arrived on an average basis of five years from 2006 to 2009. Simple techniques such as percentages, averages, and trend ratios are used in evaluating the role of PSBs, RRBs Private and Foreign banks in promoting financial inclusion from the perspective of the dimensions chosen for the study. Appropriate recommendations for further enhancement of financial inclusion are proposed in the last section of the paper.

FINANCIAL INCLUSION : A COMPARATIVE ASSESSMENT

The literature on financial inclusion lacks comprehensive measure that can be used to indicate the extent of inclusion across countries. There is no single comprehensive measure that can be used to indicate the extent of financial inclusion across the economy. According to the Rangarajan Committee 'Report on Financial Inclusion in India', financial inclusion should include access to mainstream financial products such as bank accounts, credit, and remittance and payment services. Therefore, an assessment of financial inclusion of the scheduled commercial banks has been made hereunder from the point of view of the following indicators:

1. Occupation-wise distribution of credit
2. Number and amount of savings bank account
3. Number of credit accounts and credit amount outstanding as per size of credit limit
4. Gender-wise distribution of outstanding credit
5. Region-wise distribution of deposits and credit
6. Population-wise share of deposits, credits and rural offices

OCCUPATION-WISE DISTRIBUTION OF CREDIT

Farmers and other weaker sections of the society such as farmers, retailers, artisans and small scale industrialists etc are the vital components of the economy. Agriculture not only plays the pivotal role for achieving the high growth but also inclusive growth for the economy as a whole that contributes about 20% of the Indian GDP and provides employment to 2/3 Indian population. Rangarajan Committee 'Report on Financial Inclusion in India' has observed that, in India 51.4% of farmer households are financially excluded from both formal/informal sources and 73% of farmer households do not access formal source of credit. The Committee also viewed that ensuring timely and adequate credit to weaker sections and lower income groups at an affordable cost is necessary. Hence, it is necessary to examine the share of bank credit in agriculture and other occupations. The information relating to percentage distribution of credit of scheduled commercial banks according to occupations is given in Table 1. Table 1 reveals that there is a considerable gap in the distribution of bank credit to various occupations among the banks. The share of all the banks in credit to transport, retail and village artisans and SSI is negligible. But, RRBs are is way ahead of rest of the banks to all the sectors of the community particularly to agriculture (53.29%) followed by PSBs (11.43%) Private (5.98%) and Foreign banks (1%) respectively. This reflects the highest reach of RRBs to farmers. It is also evident that, there is no sizeable amount of PSBs resources distribution to farming community and the share of private and Foreign banks to farming community is negligible. This shall be attributed to better outreach of RRBs to farmers and other weaker sections of the society and indication of utter negligence of farming and other weaker sections of the community by the Private and Foreign banks.

Table 1. Percentage distribution of credit of scheduled commercial banks according to occupations (5 Years Average)

Occupation	*PSBs*	*FBs*	*RRBS*	*PVT Banks*
Agriculture	11.43	1	53.29	5.98
Transport	1.25	1.25	1.41	2.6
Retail	4.93	8.35	8.17	4.56
Village Artisans	0.33	0.18	1.3	0.09
SSI	2.73	1.01	0.6	1.18

NUMBER AND AMOUNT OF SAVINGS BANK ACCOUNT

Savings bank account is another indicator to measure the financial outreach of banks. This is particularly important for the people with low and irregular income where their capacity to earn is limited. Such type of account promotes thrift and develops the savings among the poor. Opening more number of such deposit accounts involving small amount is the reflection of better outreach of banks to the poor population in meeting their requirements of mobilization of savings. The information relating number and amount of savings bank account is given in Table 2. RRBs accounts dominant share both in terms of number of savings bank accounts (80.76%) and in amount (53.08%) signifying the highest outreach of small account holders with high degree of mobilisations of savings. The share of PSBs, Foreign banks and Private banks in terms of account is (71.5%), (68.72%) and (63.14%) respectively. But in terms of amount, there is a wide gap between RRBs(53.08%) and other banks, PSBs (28.32%) Private (17.84%) foreign banks(15.32%) implying lower degree of mobilization of savings by other group of banks. From the above, it is evident that RRBs are serving more number of small savers and mobilizing higher amount of deposits from them implying high degree of outreach of RRBs towards small savers.

Table 2. Number and amount of savings bank account (5 Years Average) (In Percentages)

Banks	*% of Savings bank accounts to total number of accounts*	*% Amount of savings deposits to total deposits*
PSBs	71.5	28.32
FB	68.72	15.52
RRBs	80.76	53.08
PVT	63.14	17.84

Source: Basic Statistical Returns of SCBs in India.

PSBs=Public Sector Banks, FBs= Foreign banks, RRBs=Regional Rural Bank

NUMBER OF CREDIT ACCOUNTS AND OUTSTANDING CREDIT AS PER SIZE OF CREDIT LIMIT

For the purpose of measuring financial inclusion, progress made by the banks in extending credit to small borrowers involving small amount is more relevant. Extending credits to more number of borrowers involving small amount is the indication of increased efforts of the banks to reach the poor population and meet their credit needs who are having meager source of income and are not affordable to provide security for their loan. The information relating number of credit accounts and outstanding credit as per size of credit limit of scheduled commercial banks is given in Table 3. There is a wide gap in providing credit to small borrowers among the banks both in terms of number of accounts and the amount of credit. The striking observation is that, RRBs are far ahead of the rest of the banks both in terms of number of accounts (63.29%) and in amount (26.16%). The other banks are lagging far behind in terms of number of accounts PSBs (39.95%) private (34.38%) and foreign banks (25.87%) respectively and in terms of amount,

Table 3. Number of credit accounts and credit amount outstanding as per size of credit limit of the scheduled commercial banks (In percentages) (5 Years Average)

Credit Limit up Rs. 25,000

Banks	*% of Number of small accounts to total accounts*	*% of credit to small accounts to total credit*
PSBs	39.95	2.10
FB	25.87	0.92
RRBs	63.29	26.16
PVT	34.38	1.47

Source: Basic Statistical Returns of SCBs in India

the share of PSBs (2.1%), Private (1.47%) and foreign banks (0.92%) is negligible. This is the reflection of the excellent performance of RRBs in reaching the small borrowers who are having meager source of income and in meeting their credit needs. It also reflects the utter negligence of such borrowers by the other banks.

GENDER-WISE DISTRIBUTION OF OUTSTANDING CREDIT

Gender base is also one of the yardsticks to measure the financial inclusion because access to credit is often limited for women who may not have assets such as land and property in their own name and are unable to provide collateral securities to obtain credit. Banks are required to play a critical role in women empowerment by meeting their credit needs. Higher share of credit to women is the reflection of more empowerment of women that enables them to reduce their dependence on men and contribute income to the family. The information relating percentage distribution of outstanding credit of scheduled commercial banks according to gender is given in Table 4. The overall share of credit to women in all the banks both in terms of number of accounts and amount of credit is significantly low. Number of credit accounts are in the range of (20.42% to 25.34%) and amount of credit is in the range (8.78% to 19.84%) which is significantly lower compared to their male counterparts who are having the dominant share of credit accounts ranging from (64.9% to 72.72%) and credit amount ranging from (26.84% to 70.38%). This indicates the fact that the women are the biggest losers when it comes to accessing financial services. It is the clear indication of inadequate efforts of the banks to reach the women in meeting their credit needs. But among the bank groups, RRBs are enjoying the dominant position in extending credit to women both in terms of account (25.34%) and in terms of amount (19.84%) followed by PSBs (11.6%) Private (9.96%) and foreign banks (6.78%) in terms of amount. From the above, it is evident that RRBs are playing a significant role in meeting the credit requirements of more number of women with higher amount of credit. This signifies a high degree of outreach towards women. It is also evident that the other banks are not making concrete efforts to reach the women in meeting their credit requirements.

Table 4. Gender-wise distribution of outstanding credit (In percentages) (5 Years Average)

	Percentage of credit to male & female			
	Male		*Female*	
Banks	*No. of A/c s*	*Amount*	*No. of A/c s*	*Amount*
PSBs	70.38	48.32	20.42	11.6
FB	64.9	26.84	24.58	8.78
RRBs	72.72	70.38	25.34	19.84
Pvt	67.52	28.3	23.2	9.96

Source: Basic Statistical Returns of SCBs in India.

REGION-WISE DISTRIBUTION OF DEPOSITS AND CREDITS

The objective of financial inclusion is to extend the scope of activities of the organized financial system to all the regions and to all the people residing in remote and rural areas across the country. Hence, it is necessary to assess the regional share of deposit and credit of banks to ensure that the banks are reaching every geographical part of the country and contributing for the equitable growth of all the regions. The information relating to region-wise distribution of deposits and credits of scheduled commercial banks is given in Table 5. The share of both deposits and credits of all the commercial banks in NER is significantly lower. The share of commercial banks in deposits is ranging from (0.14% to 4.62%) and the share of credit is in the range of (3.74%)

signifying the utter failure of banks in reaching the population of NER. But among the bank groups, RRBs are far ahead of rest of the banks both in terms of deposits (4.62%) and credits (3.74%) followed by PSBs, deposits (2.13%) and credit (1.14%). The striking observation is that the share of private and foreign banks is fractional. From the above, it is evident that, RRBs are making tremendous progress in reaching the remote and most backward areas of NER population. It also reflects the utter failure of private and foreign banks to reach the population of this region and their contribution in providing financial access to this region is zero.

Table 5. Region-wise percentage distribution of deposits and credits of Scheduled commercial banks (5 Years Average)

Region	*PSBs*		*FB*		*RRBs*		*PVT*	
	De.	*Cr.*	*De.*	*Cr.*	*De.*	*Cr.*	*De.*	*Cr.*
North	23.04	22.71	19.42	25.2	13.6	13.22	25.1	14.86
NER	2.13	1.14	0.14	00	4.62	3.74	0.32	0.14
Eastern	13.2	9.2	5.19	04	22.96	17.92	5.08	3.42
Central	13.96	9.11	0.96	0.24	32.88	26.28	3.58	1.9
Western	25.12	30.57	56.76	43.88	5.68	5.1	40.44	55.3
Southern	22.54	26.63	16.78	26.64	20.3	33.74	25.48	24.34

Source: Statistical Tables Relating to Banks

De. = Deposit; Cr. = Credit

POPULATION-WISE SHARE OF DEPOSITS, CREDITS AND NUMBER OF OFFICES

Financial inclusion means providing financial services to all the population residing in rural and remote areas. Major chunk of the population like farmers and their house holds, landless laborers and village artisans etc who are residing in remote and rural area forms major part of the financial exclusion. As per the NSSO survey report, overall 73% of farmer households have no access to formal sources of credit. Hence, it is necessary to examine the role of banks in providing financial service in rural areas. The analysis of progress made by the banks in reaching the rural people by the banks is made on the following parameters.

(A) Number of rural offices : It indicates the reach of banks to the unbanked areas and providing financial access to the disadvantaged population .

(B) Amount of rural deposits to total deposits : This indicates the progress made by the banks in mobilising the savings of rural population and to promote the savings and thrift habits among them.

(C) Amount of rural credit to total credit : This reflects the efforts made by the banks in meeting the credit needs of rural population.

The information relating to rural deposits, rural credit and rural office is given in Table 6.

It is evident from Table-6 that, RRBs are exhibiting a spectacular performance in serving the rural population. The percentage of rural office to total office is considerably high (78.09%) in comparison to PSBs(35.66%) and Private (14.2%). Again, in terms of rural deposits and rural credits, the RRBs are enjoying lion's share. The share of RRBs in rural deposits (67.72%) and rural credit (67.51%) is followed by PSBs with a the share of deposit at 10.25% and credit at 8.57%. The notable observation is negligible share of Private banks both in rural deposits and credits and the absence of foreign banks from rural areas. From the above, it is evident that RRBs demonstrated a tremendous progress in providing access to the rural masses and it reveals their serious concern in serving the rural population. It also reflects the least concern of foreign and private banks towards the rural people.

Table 6. Population-wise share of deposits, credits and offices of scheduled commercial banks (5 Years Average)

(In percentages)

Banks	*% of rural office to total office*	*% of rural deposits to total deposits*	*% of rural credit to total credit*
PSBs	35.66	10.25	8.57
FB	-	-	-
RRBs	78.09	67.72	67.51
PVT	14.2	2.65	2.21

Source: Basic Statistical Returns of SCBs in In

FINDINGS AND SUGGESTIONS

From the preceding discussion, the following observations are made:

1. It is found that RRBs are having a better outreach to farmers and other weaker sections of the community. There is no sizeable amount of PSBs resources being distributed to farming community. Hence, it is required to increase the size of lending of PSBs to the agriculture and other unorganized sectors. The study reveals that the share of private bank (5.6%) and foreign banks (1%) to farmers is negligible. Hence, there is a need to design their plan to allocate sizable amount of credit to such vulnerable group to promote the financial inclusion.
2. It is witnessed that the RRBs accounts have a dominant share both in terms of number and amount of savings bank accounts. This is indicative of serving more number of small savers implying a high degree of outreach. But in case of other group of banks there is no significant amount being mobilized implying lower degree of reach to small savers. Hence there is a need

to expand comprehensive financial services to the small savers by the other group of banks.

3. It is found that, there is wider gap in providing credit to small borrowers among the banks. RRBs are far ahead of rest of the banks and have exhibited excellent performance in reaching the small borrowers who are having meager source of income. But, it is observed that, the other banks are lagging far behind particularly the foreign and private banks. It speaks of their utter failures in providing credit to small borrowers. Hence there is a need on the part of the private and foreign banks to lend to low income groups and promote inclusive growth.

4. It is observed that, the overall share of credit to women in all the banks is significantly low. But among the bank the selected bank groups, RRBs are enjoying the dominant position in extending credit to women signifying high degree of outreach towards women. It is also pointed out that the other bank groups are not making concrete efforts to reach the women in meeting their credit requirements. Hence, private and foreign banks need to have business plans exclusively for financial inclusion for women.

5. It is pointed out that, the share of both deposits and credits of all the commercial banks in NER is significantly lower. But among the bank groups, RRBs are far ahead of rest of banks both in terms of deposits (4.62%) and credits (3.74%) implying tremendous progress in reaching the remote and most backward area of NER population. The foreign and private banks have exhibited their utter failure to reach the population of this region. Hence, it is imperative on the part of the private and foreign banks to evolve a special mechanism to expand their financial services to this remote areas.

6. It is traced that RRBs are exhibiting a spectacular performance in serving the rural population with their dominant share in rural offices, rural deposits and rural credit implying their serious concern in serving the rural population. The notable observation is the negligible share of Private banks both in rural deposits and credits and absence of foreign banks from rural areas reflecting least concern of foreign and private banks towards the rural people. Hence, it is more appropriate on the part of the foreign and private banks to concentrate on the mobilization of rural savings and deployment of credit to rural areas so as to fulfill the task of financial inclusion.

It is the need of the hour to adhere strictly to the suggestions of RBI to address the problem of financial exclusion. Some of the measures suggested by RBI are as under:

- No-frill accounts with low or minimum balance and charges, to expand the outreach of such accounts to all the sections of the population.
- Encouraging persons belonging to low income group to open bank account with simplified procedures of 'know your customer.'
- To set up credit counseling and financial centers by the banks that promotes the spread of financial literacy among the public.
- To utilize the services of NGOs/SHGs by the banks to promote micro-finance activities.

If these suggestions are implemented, it will go a long way in promoting financial inclusion in the country. The efforts of the scheduled banks in the country would bear fruits in bringing more and more people, especially the vulnerable sections under the umbrella of formal financial system.

REFERENCES

1. RBI, (2005-09) Basic Statistical Returns of SCBs in India. *RBI Publication,* Mumbai.
2. RBI,(2005-09) Statistical Tables Relating to Banks in India, *RBI publication, Mumbai.*
3. Chakrabarty. K.C.(2009) " Banking: key Driver for inclusive Growth" *RBI Monthly Bulletin,2009.*
4. Devaprakash,(2010) "Tackling Financial Exclusion". *The Indian Banker.* Vol. V Sept 2010.
5. *Duvvuri Subbarao (2009) "Financial Inclusion: Challenges and Opportunities, RBI Monthly Bulletin Jan, 2010.*
6. Financial inclusion rbi.org.in/scripts
7. Rangarajan Committee Report on Financial Inclusion rbi.org.in / scripts.
8. Sadakkadulla. J,(2009) "Financial Inclusion: The road ahead"., *Bank Quest.* Vol. 80 Jan / March 2009.
9. Tara. S. Nair., (2010) "Commercial Banks and Financial Inclusion in the North Eastern States". *Prajnan.* Vol. xxxix, 2010.

10
'Discredited Credits' Examining the Politics of Financial Exclusion in India

Sabu Thomas

INTRODUCTION

The idea of democracy stands for equality in status and opportunities. This equality is generally attained through state instrumentalities. However in larger democracies with multicultural constructive designs, top down model of regulative enforcements are to be highly supported with civil society interventions. In this aspect a democratic society is more or less hypothetical if the economic dimensions are discounted from the debate. In fact many of the political explanations of existing social order are founded on economic interpretations[1] .Consequently financial exclusion is highly disadvantageous to any democratic order.

The debate on financial exclusion is of tremendous

importance to developing and underdeveloped economies. Here the economic disparity is usually high, making the marginalized and inaccessible more and more vulnerable in practice. The disadvantageous classes were naturally classified as 'unbankable' (Sidarama 2010) in the developmental process. What follows is citizen discontent, riots and suicides. In the case of developing states agriculture being the major employer the society becomes a highly risk society (Beck 1998, Kausal 2011) and globalisation further weighed upon the risk. Historically, agriculture has driven economic performance in many countries, generating growth that has been shown to be at least twice as effective in reducing poverty as growth in other sectors. Investment in agricultural and rural development is therefore vital to food security and sustainable economic development. As such it is supportive to the functioning of a democracy[2] .In this context any developmental initiatives should address the rural and specifically the agricultural sector of economy. Even though financial sector makes significant improvements in all the areas relating to financial viability, profitability and competitiveness, there are concerns that banks have not been able to include vast segment of the population, especially the underprivileged sections of the society, into the fold of the industry. This grave issue of financial exclusion is a serious concern for policy and governing circles.

FINANCIAL EXCLUSION

The term financial exclusion refers to those processes that prevent poor and disadvantaged social groups from gaining access to the financial system. It results in uneven development or later to under development. In fact exclusionary principle is an inherent quality of any financial structure. Andrew (1995) observes;

> " ...The financial system has an inherent tendency
> to discriminate against poor and disadvantaged

> groups. In other words, the poorer and more disadvantaged an individual, the more likely it is that they will be excluded from the financial system. The reason for this is that the financial-services industry operates in a way that favors the socially powerful. Consider how the cost of money is calculated within the financial system. The cost of money is determined by the level of risk which a financial institution believes it incurs in lending money to a borrower. The perceived level of risk is inversely related to the likelihood of the borrower repaying. The higher the perceived level of risk, the more a financial institution will ask a borrower to pay; or, conversely, the more likely it is that the borrower will repay the loan, the less they will have to pay for it." [3]

From the part of the institutions there is evidently the financing risk. There are three variables in the risk calculation. Firstly the length of lending period, secondly purpose and finally credit worthiness of the individual. On a close analysis it is evident that all these factors highly conspire against the powerless and makes financial exclusion a viable proposition in economic terms. But in a political dimension it should be evaluated in terms of development and democracy. The compatibility of financial policies with democracy should be evaluated and restructured.

In any system financial structures largely depends on trust and consequently in social capital[4]. The linkage between social capital and finance (Luigi 2004) strengthens the democratic argument and claims for larger inclusions. It is argued that the financial exclusion inherently leads to further social exclusion and democratic declines. Strandberg (2007) examined the relevance of social models in promoting economic structures. The study brings out the relevance of a cohabitation model asserting financial inclusion as a political requisite of democratic success. Thus, an all-inclusive financial system enhances efficiency and welfare by providing avenues for secure and safe saving practices and by facilitating a whole range of efficient financial services. The importance of an inclusive financial system is widely recognized in the policy circles and recently financial inclusion has become a policy priority in many countries[5]. Coupled with autonomy and market arguments of neoliberalisation this policy goal is distant and becoming ever complex. Neo-liberal de-regulation of financial service markets and resultant restructuring has created new patterns of banking service provisions, questioning the social service paradigms (Midgley 2005)[6]. It is in this context exclusion studies becomes ever more relevant and significant.

GLOBALISATION AND EXCLUSION

The propaganda of post-fordism resulted in market oriented policy regimes and consumerist pattern of economy. It was further complicated with the deterritorialization (Barney 2004) arguments of globalisation whereas competition became the highest ideal and success the ultimate virtue. Financial globalisation redefined vulnerability as incapacity and made exclusions a global phenomenon. The emergence of multinational corporations and the popularisation of FDI Mantras enchanted the policy structures to disregard their social commitments and democratic contracts. At this point we come across financial exclusion as a rule in developmental process that should be addressed with a casual mood. Daniel (2010) addresses this concern and points to the need of political analysis in public finance management in developing societies. He establishes that he basic question is more political than financial[7].

As a result of globalisation, marginalisation became a rule of the game. Financial policies all thought governments aimed at growth and profit. Welfare activities were 'economic spills' in neo-liberalism. It is well agreed that globalisation resulted in better economic avenues and higher trade volume. Global trade has considerably increased. Global quality of life also improved. But on the other side the picture is becoming more and gloomier.

"During the period between September 2006 and June 2008, international food prices almost doubled. The Food and Agriculture Organization of the United Nations (FAO) price index for all major foods rose by 78 per cent, with the indices for cereals and edible oils more than doubling. The effects of the price surge reverberated globally – including in food-rich, wealthy countries. The worst hit, however, were low-income, food-deficit countries with meager stocks. For instance, from July 2007 the price of rice doubled in just one year in Senegal. In Eritrea, the price of wheat flour in Asmara more than doubled in the same period, while wheat prices grew by 60 per cent in The Sudan and in Sri Lanka. Rice prices rose 66 per cent in Bangladesh and doubled in Haiti between August 2007 and August 2008. Many other countries were similarly affected". (Nwanze, Rural Poverty Report 2011)[8].

The situation becomes more grave as the affected parties are the excluded and marginalised. Along with the jubilant growth of economies the numbers of hungry citizens also grown in unprecedented scale and dimension[9] .The Food and Agriculture Organisation estimated that the 2008 price hike added 100 million to the global number of hungry people. However prices are not the only factors that made the hunger issue so grave. It was coupled with low and declining public and private investments in agriculture, thin and uncompetitive local markets, weak rural infrastructure, inadequate production and financial services for farmers etc. The list should be incomplete if we omit the impact of industrial approach to boosting crop yields. It stripped many farmers of their self sufficiency. The world wide incidents of farmer suicides are a direct consequence of this level of industrialization and neglect of small scale farming sector.

Thus an anti-hunger mission should target the agriculture sector, specifically rural agriculture sector. Financial Inclusion is the first and foremost vaccine to fight this epidemic.

THE INDIAN SCENARIO

"...Yet every third human being in the world without safe and adequate water supply is an Indian. Every fourth child on the globe who dies of diarrhea is an Indian. Every third person in the world with leprosy is an Indian. Every fourth being on the planet dying of water-borne or water related diseases is an Indian. Of the over sixteen million tuberculosis cases that exist at any time world wide, 12.7 million are Indian..." (Sainath 1996)[10]

In many of the recent financial forecasts India is evaluated as a potential power in the global market. Amidst the hues and cries of global recession Indian economy attracted attention and won appreciation[11]. (Alexander 2010, Singh 2010, Thushar 2007). However these claims and achievements are peripheral to the social structure and development penetration is still the lowest in the continent. The rural villages in India are still deprived of the benefits of economic development. The extreme Financial exclusion levels deepens the wounds. The Reserve Bank 'Report on Trend and Progress of Banking in India 2009-10' reports that even though per person bank branch ratio in India is satisfactory all other indicators are highly disadvantageous to financial inclusion in India. Further, the size and depth of the banking sector when measured taking private credit to GDP ratio also works out to be much lower for India than many of its Asian peer group countries. Thus the exclusion figures lower the prestige and position that the country acquired in the financial sector.

The national policy makers were concerned about the gravity of the issue from the earlier days itself. There were a number of policy initiatives from the part of government to address financial exclusion. Bank nationalisation can be considered as the jumping board. Later there were various initiatives like Rural Banks[12], NO-Frills Accounts, Co-operatives, Kissan Credit Cards[13] and the like. But in practice all these initiatives appear as a kind of 'whitewash' over the cashless, hopeless rural folks. The working of Rural Banks were below satisfaction levels, credit card are still in 'agenda' and NO-frills are non reachable. The basic issue is about the very definition of exclusion offered by Reserve Bank and other policy circles. To them it is a matter of credit and accounts. Thus an RBI report speaks enthusiastically about inclusion measures.

"Financial inclusion in the Indian context has been defined as the provision of affordable financial services, viz., access to payments and remittance facilities, savings, loans and insurance services by the formal financial system to those who tend to be excluded. The Indian policy approach towards financial inclusion, since early 2000s has been focused on ensuring inclusion at the individual and household level"[14].

In the Indian scenario exclusion should be addressed beyond credits. It is largely a matter of financial management and self sustainability. It is difficult to agree with the argument on credit empowerment. (Sainath 1996). In many developed states there are strict legislative measures to enforce financial inclusion. In the case of America, a civil rights law, namely Community Reinvestment Act (CRA) prohibits discrimination by banks against low and moderate income neighborhoods. In Britain a Financial Inclusion Fund to promote financial inclusion was established and banks were legally assigned responsibility in removing financial exclusion. But in India there are only guidelines and directives and no more strict regulations.

DISCREDITED CREDITS

The social responsibility of banking sector was the logic of bank nationalisation in India. Governments tried to line the banks in tune with the socialistic pattern of society envisioned in the preamble of the constitution. Banks were asked to come out of the 'cash box' and to get involved in the democratic society. This policy shift was further smoothened by omitting property right from the divine area of fundamental rights in the constitutional scheme. The nationalisation resulted in a new philosophy and methodology in Indian financial sector. But the results were far beyond policy expectations. The wave of neo-liberalism put the last nail on the philosophy. With the advent of new economic order the Liberalisation-Privatisation-Globalisation wave overtook the inclusion initiatives. Private Banks and foreign banks were given a free-to-go license with minimum inclusion costs. This is well evidenced with the ATM location analysis provided by reserve bank report. Out of the 1026 ATMs of Foreign banks only 6 is located in rural areas. It makes only 0.6% of ATMs. For the new private sector banks the figure is 4.2 and for State Bank Group the figure is 12.5. As per the RBI data the number of ATM users in a rural centre is 43500 in 2010 and for an urban centre the figure is 8100. The average figure stands at 19700.This is a sample from a wide universe of neo-liberal banking which discredits national inclusion exercises.

The question is how the so called credits will reach the excluded with no ATMs and no banks. Further the credit disbursement pattern is a matter of discussion. As per 2010 statistics Rural Banks are more interested in short term loans. Naturally these loans are given to the easy-pay group. A long term investment in agriculture seems to be risky by the financier. Large shares of RRB loans were distributed under the head 'other purposes'. Another irony of the credit pattern is that whereas more than 90% of the rural population engages in agriculture production, credit allotted to this sector is only 54.8% of the total credit disbursed. Here also the credit credibility question arises.

Despite the inclusion figures the rural poor in India is in a dilemma. It is simply about survival or vanishing. The number of farmer suicides reached alarming numbers. Many studies revealed that these suicides were associated with loan repayments. The suicide however does not make any solution but makes further burden on inclusion targets. Many a times, headless families were to manage agricultural production in different psychological context in a post suicide scenario. Here no number of ATM's and cards will save them. Basically what required is entitlement (Manjin 2010). The formalization of land title and access to credit are intricately to be connected in development policy prescriptions. The concept of financial inclusion should take account of this task. Credit disbursement should target entitlement measures in a deeper way.

Financial exclusion can be better fought with new technologies. The planning commission of India advises the m-governance mode for inclusion moves. The mid-term appraisal report on 11th plan notes,

"One of the major innovations in Financial Inclusion can be through the use of Mobile Technology for delivering basic financial services. The proposal assumes significance considering the growing number of mobile subscribers among the rural population and the disadvantaged sections. With mobile subscribers in rural areas far outnumbering bank account holders, a large section of rural population now has access to mobile telephony but not to financial services through banks. With the rural mobile subscriber base expected to grow significantly over the next few years, a delivery mechanism that enables provision of basic financial services on the individual's mobile would be a major step in the direction of reaching out to the "unbanked" population of the country"[15].

The planning commission suggests that the rural people can be better connected through new technologies. From the side of the financial institutions it will offer cheaper solutions also (Rajnish Tiwari et.al 2007). In this connection the credit rating of the farmers can be audited and accounted in an easy manner. The 'credit over-burden' of micro financing can be reduced to safer levels, thus benefitting farmers and institutions alike. However there are security concerns that should be well addressed immediately. An illiterate population is in the danger of becoming easy prey for 'phishers' and the like. It is observed that this possibility is not well considered by policy circles. A strong and efficient cyber regulation and execution system will have to be built upon. In the case of regional rural banks, which are created for the excluded, technology adoption is still lagging far behind.

CONCLUSION

Financial exclusion is one of the major reasons of poverty in India. The rural poor are the real victims of poverty and in the sense of financial management they are the most risky customers. The report of task force on Credit Related Issues of Farmers, appointed by Ministry of agriculture (2010) observes,

"The farmer is a risk-taking entrepreneur who faces uncertainties from weather, spurious inputs, pests and diseases, and market shocks among other risks. Inadequate and untimely credit along with procedural hassles from formal institutions add to his/her burden. In recent years, policy interventions have led to doubling of agricultural credit, but the limited access of small and marginal farmers to institutional credit continues to be a matter of concern. What is worrying is that the proportion of such farmers is increasing and they form more than four-fifths of the operational holdings"[16].

Governments have introduced many measures including large scale debt waiving. But the situation is becoming grave day by day. The credit taskforce report is of the view that the benefit of inclusion measures reaches the targets only through filters. There are money lenders, officials, absentee-landlords and lot more to avail governmental subsidiaries. In fact it is high time to rethink about the priorities in our financial management. Easy credit is an escapist solution. It should be replaced with grass-root level empowerment measures. In the case of a small scale rural farmer his first priority is not an ATM at his neighborhood but a clear title deed. Financial exclusion instruments should start from this level. It is worthy to note the contributions of Self Help Groups in strengthening and empowering local communities. Instead of placing credit at the hands of a selected and 'trustworthy repayers', financial institutions should focus on the SHG's. These groups can better identify public needs and assure better repayments. The community level intervention is an alternative to the outdated institutional models. It also assures the social capital support in banking.

In practical terms financial inclusion is a risky business for profit motivated business concern. More rural branches mean more and more loss. It should be noted that the Reserve Bank of India itself is seriously discussing about freeing the public banks from running the rural banks[17]. But social welfare is the dividend and profit of democracy. A democratic system by principle is designed to attend the issues of its excluded members first. In the Indian context it is suggested that financial inclusion should become a corner stone of our financial policies. Such policies should focus the remote and inaccessible centers of populations. They are no more any non performing assets of policy but life lines of political order.

ENDNOTES

1. The Marxian analysis of state provides the best example. Accordingly state is a product of economic relations. Even the individual identity is closely connected with the class and incidentally any class is a derivative of existing economic division. This argument is dominant in many of the theories of liberal democracy also. For a discussion see, Abbinnett Ross (2006) Marxism after Modernity, New York, Palgrave
2. According to Nwanze (2010) the vast majority of today's developed countries grew from strong agricultural foundations, where surplus production generated wealth and prosperity. The author points that Poverty is predominantly rural. Globally, three quarters of people living in extreme poverty are in rural areas and depend on agriculture and related activities for their livelihoods. See, Nwanze Kanayo F(2010). "IFAD Ocassional Paper." Change Africa from Within,Rome, Project Syndicate
3. Andrew Leyshon and Nigel Thrift (1995). "Geographies of financial exclusion: financial abandonment in Britain and the United States." Transactions of the Institute of British Geographers, 20,3: P-314
4. Luigi Guiso (2004) observes, "Since financial contracts are the ultimate trust-intensive contracts, social capital should have major effects on the development of financial markets. Financing is nothing but an exchange of a sum of money today for a promise to return more money in the future. Whether such an exchange can take place depends not only on the legal enforceability of contracts, but also on the extent to which the financier trusts the finance." See Luigi Guisoet.al (2004). *"The Role of Social Capital in Financial Development."* The American Economic Review, 94,3: P-527
5. Financial inclusion also gains a prominent place in Bankers agenda all over the world. The German Bankers' Association introduced a voluntary code in 1996 providing for an 'everyman' current banking account that facilitates basic banking transactions. In South Africa, a low cost bank account called 'Mzansi' was launched for financially excluded people. In India, the Reserve Bank of India has

initiated measures like Rural Banking, no-frills account, micro financing, kissan credit cards etc.

6. The relevance of financial inclusion is well evidenced by Midgley (2005). Accordingly, "Financial product ownership would be a prerequisite for individuals, as responsible citizens, to provide for their own financial security, with the state providing welfare support as a last resort. Second, the means to inclusion would be achieved through the market (financial industry) rather than through direct state provision. Additionally, modernization would be achieved by introducing automated credit transfers of welfare payments to reduce the costs of administration and fraudulent claims". Refer MidgleyJ (2005). "Financial inclusion, universal banking and post offices in Britain." *Area*, 37,) : P-278

7. Daniel (2010) points that political approach to public finance is heavily supported by many donor agencies. PFM specialists are convinced that having the politicians on board is a critical success factor for sustainable reforms. For discussion see Daniel Bietenhader and Andreas Bergmann (2010) "Principles For Sequencing Public Financial Reforms in Developing Countries." International Public Management Review ,11,1: pp,52-66.

8. Nwanze, Kanayo F(2010) *Rural Poverty Report 2011.* International Fund for Agricultural Development, Rome,P-30

9. Secretary of State for International Development, United Kingdom, Alexander Douglas in a recent article observed the impact of economic crisis and new policies on the marginalized. He observes, "Many more families are now being faced with the toughest decisions of extreme poverty: pulling children out of school to help provide for the family; forgoing medicines; and even choosing which of their children to feed. Indeed lives are threatened - infant mortality rates are set to rise by an additional 200,000 to 400,000 deaths each year from now to 2015 if the crisis continues" See Alexander, Douglas , (2010) "The Impact of the Economic Crisis on the World's Poorest Countries."

Global Policy,1,1: P-118.

10. See Sainath P (1996) Everybody Loves a Good Drought. New Delhi, Penguin, pp,24-25

11. According to the International Monetary Fund statistics India is the eleventh largest economy in terms of GDP and fourth largest economy in terms of purchasing power parity. Moreover the 2008 indicators identify India as world's second fastest growing major economy. As such it becomes a preferred investment spot for foreign investors. In this connection U.S stands as the third largest investor in India with 37,991.25 core rupees in investment from April 2000 to May 2010. See http://www.imf.org/external/pubs/ft/weo/2010/01. Accessed on 08-01-2011, Also refer Department of Industrial Policy & Promotion, Ministry of Commerce and Industry, http://dipp.nic.in/fdi_statistics/india_FDI_May2010.pdf Accessed on 09-01-2011

12. Regional Rural Banks (RRBs) were established in 1975 with a view to developing the rural economy as well as to create an alternative channel to the 'cooperative credit structure' so as to ensure sufficient institutional credit for the rural and agriculture sector. RRBs are jointly owned by Government of India, the concerned State Government and Sponsor Banks. There are 15155 branches of RRBs as on 31st March, 2009 in 615 districts in the country.

13. The KCC came into existence in 1998-99 as a credit product that allowed farmers the required financial liquidity and avail credit when it was absolutely needed, providing in the process flexibility, timeliness, cost effectiveness and hassle free services to the farmers.

14. Reserve Bank of India. *Report on Trend and Progress of Banking in India 2009-10*. Mumbai: Reserve Bank of India, 2010,P-111

15. Mid-term Appraisal Report of 11th plan, Planning Commission, Government of India, P-56

16. Report of the Task Force on Credit Related issues of Farmers, Ministry of agriculture, Government of India, June 2010, P-3

17. The idea gained momentum during the deliberations on KC

Chakrabarthi Committee report measures on strengthening RRB's. See. *Public Banks may get to exit RRB's,* Dheeraj Tiwari (2011), The Economic Times, January 19, P-11

REFERENCES

1. Abbinnett Ross (2006). *Marxism after Modernity,* New York, Palgrave
2. Alexander Douglas (2010) "The Impact of the Economic Crisis on the World's Poorest Countries." *Global Policy,* 1,1:118-120
3. Andrew Leyshon and Nigel Thrift (1995) "Geographies of financial exclusion: financial abandonment in Britain and the United States." *Transactions of the Institute of British Geographers,* 20,3: 312-341.
4. Barney Darin (2004). *The Network Society.* Cambridge ,Polity Press
5. Beck Ulrich(1998) "The Risk Society." In *The Politics of Risk Society,* Jane Franklin(ed), pp.9-22. Cambridge: Polity Press
6. Daniel Bietenhader and Andreas Bergmann(2010). "Principles For Sequencing Public Financial Reforms in Developing Countries." *International Public Management Review,* ,11,1:52-66.
7. G. Sidarama Reddy, N.V.Gudagaganavar(2010) "Banks and the rural poor-Bridging the gap through SHG bank linkage." *Banking Finance,*23,7:13-17.
8. Reserve Bank of India (2010) . *Report on Trend and Progress of Banking in India 2009-10.* Mumbai, Reserve Bank of India
9. Kausal, Neeraj (2011) "Farmers and their sisyphen task." *Economic Times,* January 13, p- 10.
10. Luigi Guiso, Paola Sapienza and Luigi Zingales (2004) "The Role of Social Capital in Financial Development." *The American Economic Review,* 3,94: 526-556.
11. Manjin Ambreena (2010) "Eliminating Poverty? 'Financial Inclusion', Access to Land,and Gender Equality in International Development." *The Modern Law Review,* 6,73: 985-1025.

12. Midgley J (2005). "Financial inclusion, universal banking and post offices in Britain." *Area* 3,27:277–285.

13. Nwanze Kanayo F(2010). "IFAD Ocassional Paper." *Change Africa from Within.* Rome, Project Syndicate

14. Nwanze Kanayo F (2010)*Rural Poverty Report 2011.* International Fund for Agricultural Development, Rome: Quintily, Rome

15. P. Sainath (1996),*Everybody Loves a Good Drought,* New Delhi, Penguin

16. Rajnish Tiwari, Stephan Buse and Cornelius Herstatt (2007) ""Mobile Services in Banking Sector: The Role of Innovative Business Solutions in Generating Competitive Advantage." *Proceedings of the International Research Conference on Quality, Innovation and Knowledge Management.* New Delhi, pp. 886-894.

17. Singh Anoop(2010) "Asia leading the Way." *Finance & Development,June:* 4-6.

18. Strandberg Urban (2007) "Striving for economic prosperity, requiring political legitimacy." *European Review* 3, 15: 321-333.

11
Promotion Strategies for Banking Services

Joseph Sebastian Thekedam

INTRODUCTION

Promotion is the direct way an organization tries to reach its publics. With the growing importance of the financial sector, pressures are escalating for more effective marketing management of the financial services. In spite of major changes on the market of financial institutions, there are indications that banks have not yet successfully embraced the marketing philosophy or achieved levels of its implementation consistent with satisfied customers. Financial institutions are realizing that their established promotion practices are inadequate for new market conditions as levels of customer defection in the sector grow. Traditionally, banks have tried to reach out to everyone in the community, but recent research studies propose that banks should aim to identify and serve micro-segments. (Dawes & Brown, 2000)

Banks have been encountering numerous challenges including competition, recessions and image problems.

Additionally, many banks have been facing mature domestic markets with limited future growth potential. The issues of marketing are becoming more complicated as internationalization of financial services continues to increase. Under these circumstances effective promotion of financial services is crucial for the survival, growth and development of the banks. Promotion of financial services is an understudied area. Much of the bank marketing literature has concentrated on marketing theory more than promotion practice. The main motive for conducting this study is due to the fact that limited research is available within this area.

OBJECTIVES OF THE STUDY

The main purpose of this research study is to gain a better understanding of the new generation banks' promotion strategies in the new scenario of globalization and internationalization. The other important objectives of the study are the following:

- To study how the banks tries to reach its publics through the five elements of the promotion mix, i.e. advertising, sales promotion, personal selling, public relations, and direct marketing.
- To analyze how the external factors are influencing the choice of promotion strategy for banking services.
- To investigate whether the banks use a pure adaptation or a pure standardization strategy or a contingency approach of the promotion strategy.

THEORETICAL FRAMEWORK

Promotion is the direct way in which an organization communicates the product or service to its target audiences. Within the financial services industry, promotion is used in many different ways. The promotional tools can be categorized into five main elements: Advertising, Sales

Promotion, Public Relations, Personal Selling, and Direct Marketing

Advertising

A bank attempting to generate a long term build-up of its name would use institutional advertising, while a bank interested in promoting its brand name and its different services would use a brand advertising policy (Brassington & Pettitt, 2000). There are two types of advertising channels appropriate for financial advertising. That is "above-the-line" and "under-the-line" advertising. *Above-the-line* advertising contains different channels of communication, such as television, radio, posters, magazines and newspapers. *Under-the-line* advertising is the invisible advertising of the bank's services, including leaflets, pamphlets, explanatory guides and manuals that can be used to support selling of a specific service (Meidan, 1996).

Sales Promotion

Special offers, coupons, and other forms of price manipulation are the dominant forms of sales promotion techniques used by banks. The primary objectives with sales promotion within financial services are to attract new customers; to increase the level of deposit accounts, thereby increasing the banks share of savings; to increase market share in selected market segments; and to lower the cost of acquiring new customers by seeking to avoid direct price competition with other financial institutions. (Meidan, 1996)

Public Relations

The essence of public relations is to look after the nature and quality of the relationship between the organization and its different publics, and to create a mutual understanding. Public relations cover a range of activities, for example the creation and maintenance of corporate identity and image; charitable involvement, such as sponsorship, and community initiatives; media relation for the spreading of good news, as well as for crisis management, such as damage limitation. (Brassington & Pettitt, 2000)

Personal Selling

Personal selling can be performed either face-to-face or through technological aids such as the Internet. The relationship between the salesperson and the customer is perceived as being of great importance for the marketing of a bank. Hence, the sales force within the financial services industry needs not only to be trained in the art of selling, but also to be aware of all the services available and be able to clearly explain what each service offers. Since customers' needs and motivation are likely to be complex, and their ability to assess alternative courses of action without professional assistance is likely to be limited, it is of great significance for the sales force to know their customers, as well as their products. (Julian & Ramaseshan, 1994)

Direct Marketing

The financial sector can extend its "face-to-face" selling towards direct marketing of products and services in the form of phone, mail, or computer transactions.

Adaptation and Standardization of the Promotion Strategy

It is not possible to use either total standardization or complete adaptation in promotion strategy (O.Donnell & Jeong, 2000). The degree to which these are used depends on a number of internal factors, for example organizational structure and managerial orientation, and external factors, such as target market and environment. Cavusgil *et al.* (1993) states that standardization and adaptation should be seen as two extremes, and choosing one of these approaches without adjusting it will not be successful.

Relationship Banking

Relationship banking is part of Relationship Marketing (RM), which aims to create a client relationship from the start to satisfy and keep existing customers (Lindgreen, Davis, Brodie & Buchanan-Oliver, 2000). Banks moved into relationship banking, because they operate in an intensively competitive environment and offer a wide variety of new services to customers (Zineldin, 1996). According to Heffernan, O'Neill, Travaglione and Droulers (2008) one of the reasons why banks operate in a very competitive market, is because they provide homogenous products and services. Therefore, they need to seek differentiation and they can achieve that through developing good relationships with their customers. The key elements of relationship banking are promise, trust, technology, customer satisfaction, price, loyalty, role of the branch manager or relationship manager, and quality of the service.

METHODOLOGY

This research study is mainly descriptive in nature with both explorative and some explanatory influences. In order to gain a better understanding of banks' promotion strategies the researcher has chosen a qualitative approach that enables to obtain more in-depth information. A case study strategy is used to get an in-depth situational picture. A case study is the preferred strategy when the investigator has little control over events and when the focus is on a contemporary phenomenon within some real-life context. Due to the fact that we draw the conclusions in this research study from the information gathered during the interviews and since the data is full of perceptions and beliefs, the data is non-quantifiable.

Sample Selection

The choice of sample technique is dependent on the

feasibility and sensibility of collecting data to address the objectives. The researcher has chosen seven new generation banks, Bank of Punjab, Centurion Bank, HDFC Bank, ICICI Bank, IDBI Bank, IndusInd Bank, and UTI Bank. The researcher selected these banks, which operate on the same level to be able to have a better understanding of banks' promotion strategies in the new scenario of globalization and internationalization.

Data Collection Method

For this study, the researcher regard that the personal interview is a suitable approach due to the fact that selected people will be interviewed within a time limit and with a protocol of questions. This research study has a qualitative approach, due to the fact that the researcher is going to interview selected people from the bank sector and therefore it is not necessary to have a quantitative approach. To get accurate information about the banks' promotion strategies the bank authorities were requested to provide appropriate interview respondents. The researcher decided to interview two respondents each from the seven new generation banks selected for this study. In order to collect secondary data, the researcher visited the different websites of the new generation banks and found general information about them.

Data Analysis

In order to analyze the data collected, the researcher performed a within-case and cross-case analysis. Applying these two analyzing methods facilitate comprehending the data and relating it to the theory. Within-case analysis is known as comparing the data against the theory applied, while cross-case analysis is comparing data between cases. To increase the reliability a structured interview guide was prepared. In order to increase validity, the structured interview guide was reviewed by the experts in the field and collected feedback from them before conducting the interview. Additionally, during the interviews the researcher further explained some of the questions from the interview guide to avoid confusion.

ANALYSIS

The Promotion Mix for Banking Services

The promotion tools analyzed are advertising, sales promotion, public relations, personal selling and direct marketing.

Advertising

The new generation banks use both institutional and brand advertising to promote their banking services. This is in accordance with the theoretical concept that a financial organization can use both institutional and brand advertising activities and often in combination with each other. Institutional advertising is currently the most frequent form of advertising used by new generation banks in India. Institutional advertising is mostly exposed through television or outside media, such as ad-pillars and posters. Furthermore, television commercials are mainly used for the purpose of building the brand name and brand recognition. However, since the market became aware of new generation banks, advertising in magazines and radio also become significant. In addition, brand advertising, which is concentrated mostly on specific services, is also of great importance. It focuses on reaching the customers who are most likely to be interested in the service, and on being cost efficient. It is performed in order to reach short-term goals such as selling a specific amount of home loans or credit cards within a certain period of time. In order to conduct brand advertising, the target segment is defined, since the aim is to advertise specific services to specific customer segments. Therefore the type of media is chosen. The circulars and magazines are the most commonly used distribution channels whereas television is most widely used media channel.

The new generation banks have divided their advertising into "under-the-line" and "above-the-line" advertising. Over-the line advertising is frequently used through poster, magazine and news paper advertising. However, the usages of banners on websites of other companies are also an important way to promote new generation banks services. Under-the -line advertising is commonly used at the offices and sales points. Leaflets, pamphlets, explanatory guides and manuals are made available, either in combination with personal selling or for customer self-service. Normally, the new generation banks have a number of advertising campaigns in an year; however this depends on the economical and competitive situation on the market. The individual brand advertising campaigns follow the image the bank has created through its institutional advertising in form of having the same color scheme and always using the new generation banks logotypes. Advertising is the second most important promotional tool after personal selling, since it effectively creates awareness of the brand and helps to create a brand image.

Sales Promotion

The new generation banks use sales promotion to some extent in the form of special offerings and giveaways. New generation banks like IDBI bank is offering for their clients special favours like "free any where banking", attractive rates for home loans, ASBA facilities, free cheque collections and free DD/Pay orders, RTGS and lots more. However, special offerings are not commonly used by the new generation banks and only when the market conditions are favourable. Giveaways are mostly offered to corporate customers and private customers in the upper segment. Examples of giveaways include the new generation banks branded gifts, such as pens, calendars and diaries. These are handed at meetings with the corporate or private customers.

Public Relations

Public relations are handled by the new generation banks through a number of media and ways, with varying objectives. In order to inform the public about the new generation banks and its products, the company tries to appear in news television programmes to write articles in financial magazines. For the creation of goodwill, the new generation banks are sponsoring a number of social projects, where the main fields include culture, sports and social affairs. The sponsorship principles are based on the objectives established by the new generation banks, as well as the local circumstances, relevance and significance of the supported projects to the whole society or certain social groups. First and foremost integrity, cultural value and social background of the projects are evaluated. The budget and significance of the project as well as the banks' current resources also influence the volume of the sponsorship and the choice of projects.

Personal Selling

Personal selling is performed by the new generation banks through the telephone, internet and interaction at the offices. Services such as accounts, credit cards, loans, investment funds and insurance are offered to the customers. In order to effectively manage the personal selling activities, the new generation banks have segmented their customer groups. Customers in the upper segment have their personal banking advisor, as well as corporate customers with a turnover above a certain level also have their own contact person. Additionally, the telephone bank calls customers, mostly from the upper segment, to inform about offerings and new products. Less profitable customers are mostly informed about their offerings via mail. This concept is called one-to-one and one-to-many, and was developed in order to be most cost efficient. Customer relations are also handled on commission by telemarketing companies who contact the new generation banks customers to inform about offerings or new products. Customers of competing banks are also contacted and provided with information in order to convince them to choose the new generation banks over other banks. Most of the personal selling is performed in the everyday work at the offices. It is commonly used in order to reach customers "right on the spot", for example by promoting the new generation banks services to employees of a firm that is already a customer of the bank. Making "right on the spot" selling is a very central part of the promotion strategy. This is sometimes performed when the customer visits the office for another cause than actually buying a service. However, personal selling is also often performed on request of the customer. The employees working with personal selling annually acquire additional education in order to increase their competence.

Direct Marketing

The new generation banks normally uses direct marketing in connection with new product launches and special offers. It is mostly conducted through post circulars, but also through telemarketing companies contacting existing and potential customers. The new generation banks have a data base with customer information in order to perform segmentation and targeting efficiently. Firstly, the already existing customers are targeted and thereafter potential customers within the new generation banks' target segment. After deciding which target segment to focus on, the choice of media is made. The new generation banks have extended their "face-to-face" selling towards direct marketing of products and services in the form of telephone, mail and computer transactions.

External Factors Influencing the Choice of Promotion Strategy

With regard to the **external factors** influencing the choice of promotion strategy for banking services, the external factors like cultural aspects, competition of the market, economic factors and technology orientation of the industry are of great importance when making a decision about new generation banks promotion strategy.

Adaptation and Standardization of the Promotion Strategy

The analysis of the empirical data reveals that the arguments pro **adaptation** are the differences in the media scene, the nature of the competition, and the service is at different stages of its life-cycle. The arguments for **standardization** are cost reduction and economies of scale

Relationship Banking

The findings from the empirical data collected substantiate the view that for establishing a long term relationship requires several factors to take into consideration. First of all there is the trust between the branch manager and the customer. For the new generation banks this is a factor of high importance. The trust is an essential part of relationship banking due to the fact that there is a high similarity in the products and services offered in the bank sector. It is not difficult for a customer to switch banks, but once trust is built they will more likely to stay. Therefore, the data collected supports the theory that trust is an essential part of relationship banking. The technology is not as vital as the trust because banking about human contact and interaction. Therefore, the technology does not have a high level of importance. However it will facilitate in some aspects such as: finding new potential customers, helps the branch managers with recommendations for the customer and virtual banking. Customers are more price sensitive and they would switch bank because of the price difference. In new generation banks the price varied depending on the service the customer utilized. Loyalty is an aspect the new generation banks focus on. Along with trust, loyalty is an essential factor that will be an outcome of a strong and close relationship. Satisfying the customer is the main target for the new generation banks. A satisfied customer is a customer who will return and use more services. If the customer is not satisfied and happy with the banking, they will most likely find another bank for further transactions in the future. The branch manager has a significant and important role in banking. They are the key factor in relationship banking, due to the fact that they are the first with whom the customers contact. Their task is to establish a strong relationship and have a responsibility to assure that the customer's needs and preferences are met and fulfilled. Lastly, the quality is certainly an important factor. As mentioned earlier, the bank's services and products are homogeneous which makes them very competitive. For that reason, the quality has a large impact on if the customer returns or not.

CONCLUSIONS

The research study shows that all parts of the promotion mix are used to some extent for promotion of banking services. **Personal selling** is considered to be the most important promotional tool, as it aims to build relationships between the customer and the bank. Relationships are crucial, since they make the customer loyal to the brand and enable the bank to reach its long-term goals. Concerning **advertising** banks use both institutional and brand advertising. Institutional advertising is conducted for brand building, which is vital due to the fact that all banks offer similar products. It is of great importance to have a strong brand in order to attract customers. Institutional advertising is conducted through television, magazines and outdoor media, in order to combine a strategy that reaches a broad crowd and that is somewhat cost efficient. Thereby less profitable and potential customers are also targeted. The brand advertising aims specific services towards specific customer segments. Banks tend to be selective when it comes to promoting specific services and they focus on their primary customers. Brand advertising is primarily used in order to reach short term goals. Above-the-line and under-the-line advertising are both of importance for banks. A combination of the two in their promotion strategy is preferable, as they are a great complement to one and other. Furthermore, under-the-line promotion is an essential complement for personal selling, since it provides the customer with information regarding the different services that are offered. Banks are careful in their use of **sales promotion**. However, special offerings and other forms of price manipulation are used to some extent. **Public relations** are performed in order to create goodwill and to spread information. This is done through participation in business magazines as well as via sponsoring of social projects. The aim of **direct marketing** is to inform as well as to promote. It is commonly used through post circulars, but the use of internet is also considered to be of importance.

From the case analysis the following conclusions are drawn:

- All promotion tools in the promotion mix are used to some extent for the promotion of banking services.
- Personal selling is the most important promotion tool when promoting banking services.
- Segmentation of customers is an essential part of the promotion for banking services.
- A strong brand is crucial in order to attract customers.

Concerning the external factors influencing the choice of promotion strategy, the researcher found that theory and empirical findings to a great extent corresponded. The cultural aspects factor is the most important external factor influencing the choice of promotion strategy. The other external factors that influence the choice of promotion strategy are the technology orientation of the industry, the competitiveness of the market and the economic factors.

Banks use neither a pure adaptation nor a pure standardization strategy and therefore the conclusion is that a contingency approach of the promotion strategy is applied. The most important reason for adapting is the different customer preferences and expectations. Adaptation is carried out with regard to media, language, competition and stage in the life cycle of the bank as a brand. The most important reason for standardizing is cost-reduction and economies of scale. Our empirical findings points out that a lot of material, especially connected to personal selling should be standardized. Another important reason for standardizing is the creation of a consistent and uniform brand image.

IMPLICATIONS

- Managers who wish to conduct promotion should focus on personal selling, since it is the most important promotion tool and it involves establishment of relationships with individual customers. It is of great importance to provide specific education for the sales personnel, since they are the ones interacting with customers, and thereby affecting customer perception of the bank. Advertising should also be emphasized due to its ability to reach a broader public and create awareness and interest among potential customers. The remaining three promotion tools are also applicable, and should be used as a complement to personal selling and advertising.
- The factors that are most influential on the choice of promotion strategy, and therefore should be taken into extra consideration, are the cultural aspects, the

technology intensity of the industry, the competitive environment of the market and the economic factors involved.

- Managers should attempt to standardize their promotion to the extent possible, in order to diminish expenses and achieve economies of scale. However due to differing preferences and expectations of the customers, a great deal of the promotion must be adapted.

Implications for Further Research

- Since our study only focuses on one element of the marketing mix, namely promotion, it would be of interest to conduct a study of the other three elements, i.e. price, place and product.
- Another interesting field of study is brand management within the banking industry.
- It should also be of interest to study how the Internet should be used as a marketing tool for banks in the most efficient way.

REFERENCES

1. Albers-Miller, N.D. & Straughan R.D. (2000). Financial Services Advertising in Eight non-English Speaking Countries, *International Journal of Bank Marketing*, Vol. 18 No. 7, pp. 347-358.
2. Brassington, F. & Pettitt, S (2000). *Principles of Marketing*, 2nd Edition, Harlow: Pearson Education Limited.
3. Cavusgil, S.T., Zou, S. & Naidou, G.M. (1993). Product and Promotion Adaptation in Export Ventures: An empirical Investigation, *Journal of International Business Studies*, Vol.24, No. 3.
4. Dawes, J. & Brown, R.B. (2000). Postmodern Marketing: Research Issues for Retail Financial Services. *Qualitative Market Research: An International Journal*, Volume 3, No. 2, pp. 90-98.

5. De Mooij, M. (1994). *Advertising Worldwide*. 2nd Edition, Trowbridge: Prentice Hall

6. Heffernan, O'Neill, Travaglione and Droulers (2008). Relationship marketing. The impact of emotional intelligence and trust on bank performance. *International Journal of Bank Marketing*,Vol. 26 (3), pp. 183-199.

7. Joseph, B., Joseph, M. & McClure, C. (1999). Service Quality in the Banking Sector: the Impact of Technology on Service Delivery, *International Journal of Bank Marketing*, Vol. 17 No. 4, pp. 182-193.

8. Julian, C.C. & Ramaseshan, B. (1994). The Role of Customer-contact Personnel in the Marketing of a Retail Bank's Services. *International Journal of Retail & Distribution Management, Vol. 22No. 5, pp. 29-34.*

9. Lee, J. (2002). A Key to Marketing Financial Services: the Right Mix of Products, Services, Channels and Customers. *Journal of Services Marketing*, Vol. 16 No. 3, pp. 238-258.

10. Lindgreen, A., Davis, R., Brodie, R.J., & Oliver, M.B. (2000). Pluralism in contemporary marketing practices. *International Journal of Bank Marketing*, Vol. 18 (6), pp. 294-308.

11. McLaughlin, C. P. & Fitzsimmons, J.A. (1996). Strategies for Globalizing Service Operations. *International Journal of Service Industry Management*, Vol. 7 No. 4, pp. 43-57.

12. Meidan, A. (1996). *Marketing Financial Services*, Hampshire and London: Macmillan Press Ltd.

13. Mortimer, K., (2001). Services Advertising: the Agency Viewpoint. *Journal of Services Marketing*, Vol. 15 No. 2, pp. 131-146.

14. O'Donnell, S. & Jeong, I. (2000) Marketing Standardization within Global Industries. *International Marketing Review*, Vol. 17, No. 1, pp. 9-33.

15. Papavassiliou, N. & Stathakopoulus, V. (1997). Standardization vs. Adaptation of International Advertising Strategies: Towards a Framework. *European Journal of Marketing*, Vol. 32, No. 7, pp. 504-527.

16. Van Mesdag, M. (2000). Culture-Sensitive Adaptation or

Global Standardization-the Duration of Usage Hypothesis, *International Marketing Review*, Vol. 17, No. 1, pp. 74-84.

17. Yin, R.K. (1994), *Case Study Research, Design and Methods*, 2nd Edition, Thousand Oaks: Sage Publications, Inc.
18. Zineldin, M., (1996). Bank-corporate client "partnership" relationship: benefits and life cycle. *International Journal of Bank Marketing*, Vol. 14 (3), pp. 14-22.

12
Designing a Methodology to Investigate Accessibility and Impact of Financial Inclusion

Manohar V. Serrao
A. H. Sequeira
V. Basil Hans

INTRODUCTION

'Inclusive growth' - with interchangeable terms like 'broad based growth', 'shared growth', 'pro poor growth' etc. - is the buzz topic in modern times particularly with reference to emerging economies of the world. This is nothing but the participation of all sections and regions of society in the growth of the economy and their reaping the benefits of growth. This is imperative for achieving the equity objective in growth. The challenges of achieving more inclusive

growth. This is imperative for achieving the equity objective in growth. The challenges of achieving more inclusive growth can be met by policies that encourage more and more social, political and financial inclusion. Financial inclusion, in a broader sense refers to delivery by the financial system of the economy to its members. Poignantly it is the easier, timely and affordable access to financial services to the vast sections of disadvantaged and low income groups who tend to be 'excluded' from the formal banking channels. According to the RBI it is 'connecting people' with the banking system and not just the delivery of credit. Micro finance is micro credit *plus*.

In India poverty alleviation has perennially been the central theme of planning and governance. The Eleventh Five Year Plan (2007-12) has specifically underlined the need for "more inclusive growth". To have an effective policy towards poverty alleviation financial inclusion of the poor and marginalized class is a crucial and pragmatic measure. To achieve this empirical evidence that links access to financial services to development outcomes will have to be conditioned. This has made the area of financial inclusion a challenging one in view of the policy planning for effective financial development.

A well developed financial system is essential for a faster and broad-based economic growth. It is highly important for economic development and human well-being. It brings poor people in to the mainstream of the economy and allows them to contribute more actively to their personal economic development (UN 2006). These groups constitute a significant part of the beneficiaries. But access to finance by the poor, weaker sections and the marginalized is woefully limited due to several reasons. This necessitates a good mechanism to operationalize financial inclusion. Literature on financial inclusion shows that there is a need for the research and data to be conditioned on implementing financial inclusion and determining its effectiveness in India. This paper, therefore, is an attempt to analyze the various steps in collecting financial inclusion data so as to provide a means of monitoring and promoting financial inclusion on the one hand, and to measure the impact of access to finance to strengthen the policy formulation, on the other. We have come out with a systematic approach to determine the appropriate research strategy to measure the access to formal financial network and its impact. The objectives of the paper are:

1. To evolve a measurable definition of financial inclusion;
2. To discuss the type of data and their collection needed with regard to developing appropriate and relevant policy; and
3. To explore a reasonable methodology that incorporates all the aspects of impact of financial inclusion

THEORETICAL BACKGROUND

Theories of development advocate that financial development creates enabling conditions for growth through 'supply-leading' or 'demand-following' channel. Theories also perceive the lack of access to finance as a critical factor responsible for persistent income inequality as well as slower growth. Therefore, access to safe, easy and affordable source of finance is recognized as a pre-condition for accelerating growth and reducing income disparities and poverty which creates equal opportunities, enables economically and socially excluded people to integrate better into the economy and actively contribute to development and protect themselves against economic shocks.

Modern development theory says that the evolution of financial development, growth, and intergenerational income dynamics are closely intertwined. Finance influences not only the efficiency of resource allocation throughout the economy but also the comparative economic opportunities of individuals – the relatively rich vis-à-vis the relatively poor households.[1] This crucial focus on the financial sector in economic modeling has also been strengthened with the historical development of views on the links between economic growth and income inequality. It was long believed that the early stages of economic development would inevitably be accompanied by inequality and concentrations of wealth. Kuznets (1955, 1963) reasoned that this trade-off meant that inequality would increase in the early stages of development until the benefits of growth spread throughout the economy.

In the model of Galor and Zeira (1993), it is because of financial market frictions that poor people cannot invest in their education despite their high marginal productivity of investment. In Banerjee and Newman's model (1993), individual's occupational choices are limited by their initial endowments. Demirguc Kunt and Levine (2007) argue that reducing financial market imperfections to expand individual opportunities creates positive, not negative, incentive effects. These models show that lack of access to finance can be the critical mechanism for generating persistent income inequality or poverty traps, as well as lower growth.

ROUTES OF FINANCIAL INCLUSION IN INDIA

By and large, financial inclusion is meant to be banking inclusion. Historically, the RBI and the Government of India (GOI) have been making efforts to increase banking penetration in the country. Some of these measures include the creation of an extensive network of rural cooperative banks in 1950s, nationalization of banks by the RBI in 1969 and 1980, the creation of State Bank of India in 1955, lead bank scheme in 1970, establishment of Regional Rural Banks in 1975, introduction of Self Help Group-Bank Linkage program in 1992 (a landmark in the field of micro financing), formulating Kisan Credit Card in 2001, creation of 'no-frill' or 'zero balance savings account' for the common man (2005), simplification of Know Your Customer (KYC) norms, permission to utilize the non-governmental organizations, micro finance institutions and other civil society organizations as financial intermediaries, General Credit Cards etc. The emergence of financial inclusion in general and micro finance in particular, is therefore, to be seen in the genesis and sustenance of banks in India, as also their diversities.[2]

More recently, in January 2006, banks were permitted to utilize the services of non-governmental organizations (NGOs/SHGs), micro-finance institutions and other civil society organizations as intermediaries in providing financial and banking services through the use of business facilitator and business correspondent models. To extend hassle-free credit to bank customers in rural areas, the guidelines on General Credit Card (GCC) schemes were simplified. With a view of providing hassle free credit to customers, banks were allowed to issue general credit cards akin to Kisan Credit Cards (KCC).

A simplified mechanism for one-time settlement of loans was suggested for adoption by RBI. The Reserve Bank has also been periodically issuing guidelines on public grievance redressal mechanism in banks, including constitution of Customer Service Centers for ensuring improvements in quality of service rendered. Along with this Government of India in its various initiatives of development process expressed its explicit concern of promoting overall inclusion. Some of its initiatives are the Rural Employment Guarantee Scheme, the Bharat Nirman programme, the Sarva Shiksha Abhiyan, etc. A Committee on Financial Inclusion (Chairman: Dr. C. Rangarajan) had also been constituted by the Government of India in June

2006, to recommend a strategy to achieve higher financial inclusion in the country.

CURRENT STATUS OF FINANCIAL INCLUSION IN INDIA

Just as financial inclusion or the opposite of it is experienced by both developing and developed economies, even in India it is experienced by all in various degrees. The RBI informs that as many as 139 districts suffer from massive financial exclusion, with the adult population per branch in these districts being above 20,000 and only 3 per cent with borrowings from banks. The average number accounts in every region of India are below the All India average of 39 per 100 of population (Table1). The north-east region is poorly served (19 persons holding account). The criticality of the issue become more when we note that even though 40 per cent of overall branch network are in rural India, only 5.2 per cent of India's villages have bank branches, with population covered by each branch coming down from 63,000 in 1969 to 16,000 in 2007. Very few people in the low income bracket have access to formal banking channels. 51.4 per cent of farm households have no financial access, formal or informal in India. In urban India the picture is not bright either: only 34 per cent of people with annual earnings less than Rs.50, 000 had a bank account in 2007 (rural: 26.8 per cent).

There are also variations within regions with regards to access to services and nature of services. Many have Savings Bank Accounts but not Fixed Deposit Accounts. One may be tempted to think that after the introduction of no-frills account the scenario has entirely changed. On the contrary, a consultancy based study says that only 11 per cent of 25.1 million of such accounts opened between April 2007 and May 2009 are operational. This means the hyped (?) Business Correspondent model of banking has failed. The added concern is that unorganized sector's share in rural lending has been rising.

Table 1. Financial Inclusion in India: Coverage of Banking Services

Region	*Current Accounts*	*Savings Accounts*	*Total Population*	*Total No. of Accounts*	*Number of Accounts per 100 population*
North	42155701	52416125	13267462	56631826	43
North East	476603	6891081	38495089	7367684	19
East	1814219	47876140	227613073	49690359	22
Central	2202217	64254189	255713495	66456406	26
West	3178102	49525101	149071747	52703203	35
South	466014	83386898	223445391	88052912	39
All India	16552856	304349534	102705247	320902390	31

Source: Situation Assessment Survey 59th Round, NSSO, 2003.

SUPPLY AND DEMAND SIDE OF FINANCIAL INCLUSION

We can also analyze the process of financial inclusion by considering its supply side and demand side. Supply side includes the providers and regulators of financial services. In India we have Government of India/ Finance ministry/ RBI as regulators. Government of India/RBI along with the network of various financial intermediaries like NABARD, commercial banks, both public and private sector, Regional Rural Bank's, cooperative banks, micro finance institutions, SHG-bank linkage network, micro insurance, control the process of financial inclusion. This network provides access to loans and other financial services to the poor for their business and livelihood. Its success depends on rural infrastructure, literacy rates and the linkages between banks and micro finance institutions and voluntary groups. The type of technology used for financial inclusion also plays a dominant role.

On the demand side of the financial inclusion we have customers of banking services especially common man who belong to weaker sections of the society. Their inclusion to the banking facilitates depends on issues like human development, access to land, infrastructure support, access to work etc. and the network of regulators of financial inclusion. Common man belong to vulnerable sections of the society needs access to finance for the several purposes. The most important is contingency planning and risk mitigation. Households build buffer savings, allocate savings for retirement and purchase insurance and hedging products for insurable contingencies. Once these needs are met, households typically need access to credit for livelihood creation as well as consumption and emergencies. Finally, wealth creation is another area where financial services are required. Households require a range of savings and investment products for the purpose of wealth creation depending on their level of financial literacy as well as their risk mitigation.

METHODOLOGY TO MEASURE THE ACCESSIBILITY AND IMPACT OF FINANCIAL SERVICES

Definition of Financial inclusion and measuring financial access

To condition the empirical evidence that links access to financial services to development outcomes, developing a contextually relevant definition of financial inclusion and analyzing its components will be critical which can provide helpful direction not only by guiding what variables to measure, also in identifying the benchmarks of aspects and impact of financial inclusion.

Financial inclusion is timely delivery of financial

services at an affordable cost to the vast sections of the disadvantaged and low-income groups. The various financial services include credit, savings, insurance and payments and remittance facilities. The objective here is to extend the scope of activities of the organized financial system to include within its ambit people with low incomes. This is an attempt to lift the poor from one level to another so that they come out of poverty. This can be achieved through state driven intervention or through voluntary effort by the banking community to bring within the ambit of the banking sector the large strata of society.

The above definition encompasses the two dimensions of financial inclusion, viz., access to a range of formal financial services and availability of competitive options. This also indicates the obstacles that could lead to financial exclusion like topography and distance, regulations, psychology, information asymmetry and low financial acumen among others (United Nations, 2006).

In the Indian context, financial inclusion, according to the Finance Minister's 2006-07 budget speech, was defined as "the process of ensuring access to timely and adequate credit and financial services by vulnerable groups at an affordable cost" (Union Budget, 2007-2008). In a similar vein, the Committee on Financial Inclusion defines financial inclusion as "...the process of ensuring access to financial services and timely, adequate credit where needed, to vulnerable groups such as weaker sections and low income groups, at an affordable cost".[3]

Parameters of financial inclusion

Access to formal financial services: Access – full or partial – is nothing but the ability to use available financial services and products from formal institutions. This requires an insight and analysis of potential barriers to opening and using a bank account such as cost, physical proximity of bank branches etc., proportion of the population with an account can be a proxy for measuring the access component and data can be extracted through the information provided by financial institutions. Partial and full access, in turn is determined by factors such as scope, institutional structure, quantity, price, quality gender, age etc.

Quality of financial services: This is a measure of the relevance of the financial service to the lifestyle needs of the consumer. This component encompasses the experience of the consumer, his attitudes and opinion towards the financial products available etc. This measure would be used to gauge the nature and depth of the relationship between the financial service provider and the consumer as well as the choices available and their implications. Data will be gathered through demand side survey. Quality dimension becomes crucial in cases where disparity in service deliver is sharp and exact feedback from users is difficult to obtain.

Usage of financial services: This component will focus on the depth and extent of financial service or product. This is about the regularity, frequency and duration of use over time which also involves measuring what combination of financial products is used by household. Data will be gathered through demand side survey.

Welfare component: This component will measure the impact of a financial service which had on the lives of the consumers. This will focus on the changes in consumption, total assets of the household, household expenditure, empowerment of women etc. This is nothing but capturing an improvement in wellbeing resulting from financial inclusion. Data can be gathered through demand side survey.

Data required for the measurement of access to financial services and its impact

Researcher has to understand the design, sources of information and variables needed to measure the access and impact of financial services on the households of vulnerable sections of the society. Relevant and meaningful data on poverty levels, population-BPL, bankable activities and their financial size, the excluded-included segments of population, the clientele who still face various constraints in access of financial services (say, infrastructural, technological etc), have to be gathered and analyzed. Both quantitative and qualitative data (e.g. psychology of the borrower) are necessary to gauge the reach and impact of financial inclusion. Data should be put to rigorous tests before they are considered as results or findings fit for policy action.

A study of financial inclusion has to be multivariate. Financial inclusion by its very nature is multi-dimensional in objectives, types and functions: credit, money-advice, investment, insurance etc. Among experts there seems to be no consensus as to which set of attributes/variables are important to measure financial inclusion. While measuring access to credit from banks, for instance, there are a number of indicators available to a researcher, viz geographic-branch penetration, demographic-branch penetration, geographic-ATM penetration, demographic-ATM penetration, credit accounts per capita, credit-income ratio, etc. The indicators broadly fall into two categories – those measure the outreach of the financial sector in terms of access to banks' physical outlets, and those that measure the use of banking services. If take into account the occupational pattern or nature of activities of the beneficiaries some more indicators can be added. Similarly, taking into account the political/ democratic dimensions of financial development via governments and NGOs (e.g. SHGs) additional indicators may find place – autonomy, ownership, distribution, etc – which however may vary across countries, across states within a country, across districts within a state and so on. Heterogeneous elements may then pose problems, both statistical and non statistical. It is with these constraints, nay challenges that researchers in recent times are engaged in devising indices of financial inclusion.

In a recent article Chakravarty and Pal (2010) have demonstrated that the axiomatic measurement approach developed in the human development literature can be usefully applied to the measurement of financial inclusion. They have developed a conceptual framework for aggregating data on financial services in different dimensions. The suggested index of financial inclusion allows calculation of percentage contributions of different dimensions to the overall achievement. This in turn enables the researchers to identify the dimensions of inclusion that are more/less susceptible to overall inclusion and hence to isolate the dimensions that deserve attention from a policy perspective.

The actual research problem we face here is that certain parts of the population are systematically excluded from the reach of formal financial sector or some parts of the population are over included. This problem may be confounded when time dimension is added: as Hulme opines, in studies of financial inclusion, fungibility and casuality are also to be taken into account; as income data alone may not resolve the problem, rigorous data collection over a long period becomes important. The corollary is that one should spell clearly if the study is meant to understand the economic and social 'benefits; of the inclusion program or 'impact'. The latter requires rigorous study.

Thus, appropriate policy response which is based on the data that is available in various primary and secondary sources is pertinent. After analyzing this data the inference that is arrived at will play a deciding role in designing the policy of financial inclusion. In this regard researcher has to explore different levels of investigative research questions which are critical in designing different survey designs which will be used in the process of measuring the access and impact of financial services.

The first level of questions will focus on to explore the current status of financial inclusion. A one time cross-sectional survey designed could be used in this direction. The second level of questions will focus on the level of improvement in financial inclusion. A repeated cross section survey design would provide necessary input in this direction. Level third questions are designed to measure impact of financial inclusion which has complex sampling considerations. Surveys need to be conducted over time, at the same time having a control group which is not affected by the policy required in this regard.

Sources of data on financial inclusion

Financial inclusion data may be distinguished based on data source, namely: supply-side and demand side. Both play important roles in measuring extent and impact of financial inclusion (Honohan, 2005). The roles, in turn depend on the nature and magnitude (value) of the ascribed variables (Table 2).

In a methodological survey of financial inclusion the impact of inclusion can be best captured by following certain rules: one is to identify the variables suitable for the objectives of the study; second is to break them in to broad categories to be integrated to the various dimensions of financial inclusion like access, quality etc. (A comprehensive and preliminary literature survey comes in handy in this regard) and third the extent of impact in terms of inclusion or exclusion should be measured in terms of both demand and supply of financial services.

Supply side surveys typically capture information, such as number of accounts and product specifications, from financial service providers in order to estimate the percentage of the population that uses financial services. This data can

Table 2. Variables Identified

Core topics	*Demand-side variables*	*Supply side variables*
Nature of financial inclusion	• Population in regions • Recent and past usage patterns	• Type of financial network • Number of branches of various financial institutions / insurance companies/ SHGs/BC/BF, FSC etc
Extent of financial inclusion	• Level of income • Members having access to financial services in Household • Source of Income • Household particulars like caste, education, gender, head of household etc	• Number of accounts • Geographic distribution of banks, branches and other banking facilities into different regions of the economy • Population per bank branch • Number, type of various financial products
Socio-Economic Impact of access to financial services	• Household income • Employment • Household assets • Housing pattern • Expenditure • Education • Health facilities • Confidence level • Skills and empowerment of members • Mobility of members	• Product features • Summary of loan accounts • History of loan accounts

be used as a proxy for determining the level of access to financial services. For instance, Beck, Demirguc-Kunt and Martinez (2007) use supply side indicators to determine the level of financial access in 99 countries. The World Bank (2008) published reports on potential barriers to financial access based on supply side data. In the year 2009, the IMF in its annual International Financial Statistics publications announced an effort to include eight financial inclusiveness indicators collected based on the supply side data from regulators of financial services. Supply side data is the easiest and least expensive source to collect financial access data. Aggregation of data is the only required step in this direction.

But it will have limitations like double counting, segmentation, and aggregation.

Demand side survey gives a clear picture of financial inclusion from customers. These survey based on samples of households which collects the information about the respondent which focuses on the fact that who is being served by the formal financial setup. However, demand side information has been lacking in most countries because it is not collected by regulators of financial inclusion. There are two examples of national demand side surveys of financial access, FinScope Survey and the World Bank's Financial Access Survey.

The important key issues to be considered when designing household level survey are sampling, sampling unit, survey instrument and survey design. Sufficient sample size which is carefully collected, drawn from an appropriate sampling frame, such as population census, random selection of respondents will improve the quality of data from demand side surveys.

As far as the sampling unit is concerned researcher can select the household or an individual in the household. Using the household as the unit of analysis may provide a robust data across the household. The scope of the study (rural and urban) will play the deciding role in this regard.

Since the objective of measurement is not only to attain an overall picture of financial inclusion, but also to measure impact of financial inclusion in the research area(across rural and urban), it is important to gather data such as income, age, education and household composition. Covariates which can be considered in this direction are income (amount and source), education level, employment status, socioeconomic characteristics and household composition.

TECHNOLOGICAL AND HUMAN APPROACH TO STRENGTHEN FINANCIAL INCLUSION

A unique characteristic of the financial inclusion program is the combination of human and technological aspects of it. This is inevitable. Therefore, while scoping a study on accessibility and impact of financial inclusion, researcher has to examine the existing modes and modalities of techno-human inputs of inclusion as well as the outcomes, and be able to suggest alternatives to any model that is either heavily techno-centric or techno-poor. This need becomes all the more significant when financial services in general and banking in particular is becoming increasingly technology-oriented. User friendly techniques need to be adopted while also making people computer savvy. This is quite a challenge in rural India. The Gen-next technology has to provide/transfer not merely digital cash faster but also other face-to-face services such like money advice. While merchant banking has already gone 'digital', it is to be seen how technology would cope with the upcoming challenges. As for instance what about technology for social intermediation? Out-of-the box solutions are required not to keep the poor out in the cold. Knowledge-based financial inclusion can be broad based provided ethical issues (including the ethics of repayment) are also resolved. Economics, sociology and anthropology need to be consulted, together. There is ethical and economic justification for looking beyond income poverty, that is, to move from financial intermediation to social intermediation. So today we need to not only evolve new products or services under the gamut of financial services but also explore new frontiers of development, social and economic. This hinges on human development in terms of infrastructure for health, education, skill and enterprise. This is also in-keeping with the Millennium Development Goals (MDGs).

CONCLUSION

Based on our study the conclusion is that accessibility and impact of financial inclusion offer the researcher a broad spectrum of methodological investigation. The techniques of survey, choice of variables, methods of data collection and analysis have to take into account the critical conceptual and practical aspects therein. There is no single route to financial inclusion. Further the study also finds that methodological approach keeps evolving with the changing functional, technological and human perspectives of inclusive growth in general and financial inclusion in particular. Therefore, suggestion is to blend technological and human approaches that strengthens the enabling and evaluatory mechanisms of financial inclusion.

REFERENCES

1. Anderson, Sweeney, Williams, (2002), *Statistics for Business and Economics*, Thomson Businesses Information India Pvt. Ltd., India.
2. Basu, Priya (2005). "A Financial System for India's Poor", *Economic and Political weekly*, September, 10-15, pp. 4008-401.
3. Beri, G. C., (2008). *Marketing Research*, Tata McGraw-Hill Publishing Company Limited, New Delhi.
4. Chakravarty, Satya R., and Rupayan Pal (2010) "Measuring Financial Inclusion: An Axiomatic Approach", Working Paper - 2010-003, Indira Gandhi Institute of Development Research, Mumbai, March. *http://www.igidr.ac.in/pdf/publication/WP-2010-003.pdf*
5. Dev, Mahendra (2006). "Financial Inclusion Issues and Challenges", *Economic and Political weekly*, October 14 pp. 4310-4313.
6. EPW Research Foundation (2006). 'Financial Inclusion in a Deregulated Regime', Economic and Political Weekly, May 20, pp. 1940-1946.
7. Gopinath, Shyamala (2006). "Inclusive Growth: Role of Financial Education", *RBI Bulletin*, December, pp. 1517-1521.

8. Government of India (2008). Report of the Committee on Financial Inclusion, 2008, January.

9. Government of Karnataka (2005). *Karnataka Human Development Report, 2005.*

10. Hans, V. Basil (2008). "Innovations in Microfinance – Looking Beyond IncomePoverty".Available at *http://papers.ssrn.com/* (accessed January 19, 2011).

11. Hans, V. Basil (2010). Inclusive Growth in India: Dimensions and Directions. In Rasure, K A. (ed.), *Incluisve Growth – Challenges and Opportunituies,* Vol. I, Oxford Book Company, Jaipur.

12. Jayasheela, Dinesha P.T. and V. Basil Hans. (2008). Financial Inclusion in India: An Overview. In Sohani, A K (ed.), *Financial Inclsuion – Perrwectives and Country Experiences,* Icfai University Pres, Hyderabad.

13. Joshi, Kumar Manoj (2008). "Financial Inclusion Need for No-Frills Account", *Professional Banker,* April, pp. 14-18.

14. Kamath, Rajalaxmi (2007). "Financial Inclusion vis-à-vis Social Banking", *Economic and Political Weekly,* April 14, pp. 1334-1335.

15. Krishnan, Rajeshwari and Vasan, Uma (2008). "Financial Inclusion Changing Paradigms", *Professional Banker,* January, pp. 14-18.

16. Leeladhar, V., (2006). "Taking Banking Services to the Common Man – Financial Inclusion", *RBI Bulletin,* January, pp. 73-77.

17. Mohan, Jagan V., (2008). "A Stock-taking on Financial Inclusion", *Professional Banker,* February, pp. 57-59.

18. Mohan, Rakesh (2006). "Economic Growth, Financial Deepening and Financial Inclusion", *RBI Bulletin,* November, pp. 1305-1319.

19. Murthy, GRK (2009). "Rural Credit: A New Model of Credit Delivery for 'Inclusive Growth'", *Karapuramanjari,* Thursday, December 10. *http://karpuramanjari.blogspot.com/2009/12/rural-credit-new-model-of-credit.html*

20. P.T. Dinesha and Jayasheela (2010).Inclusion through SHG

Micro-fiance: A Macro Perspectiev. In In Rasure, K A. (ed.), *Incluisve Growth – Challenges and Opportunituies*, Vol. I, Oxford Book Company, Jaipur.

21. P. VasanthaKumari (2009). "Sustainable Development through Women Empowerment: A Study of Performance and Possibilities of SHGs in India", *Nitte Management Review*, Vol.3, No. 1, July, pp. 29-38.

22. Prasad, Chowdari and B. Yerram Raju, (2009). "Financial Inclusion in India - Yet another Ritual or an Integrated Tool for Poverty Alleviation", *Nitte Management Review*, Vol, 3, No. 1, July, pp. 17-28.

23. Rao, Subba K. G. K., (2007). "Financial Inclusion an Introspection", *Economic and Political Weekly*, February 3-, pp. 355-360.

24. Sarangapani, A. and Mamatha T., (2008). "Self-Help Groups-Bank Linkage-Impact Assessment, Empowerment and Sustainability of Microfinance A study", Professional Banker, August, pp. 43-51.

25. Satish, D. (2006). "Financial Inclusion Taking Banking to the Masses", *Professional Banker*, pp. 41-43.

26. Shah, Mihir, Rao, Ranga and Shankar, Vijay P. S. (2007), "Rural credit in 20th Century India - Overview of History and Perspectives", *Economic and Political Weekly*, April 14, pp 1351-136.1

27. Srinivasan, N., (2007). "Policy Issues and Role of Banking system in Financial Inclusion", *Economic and Political Weekly*, July 28, pp 3091-3098.

28. Thorat, Usha, (2006). 'Financial Inclusion and Millennium Development Goals', *RBI Bulletin*, February, pp. 239-243.

29. Thorat, Usha, (2006). "Financial Inclusion for Sustainable Development Role of IT and Intermediaries", *RBI Bulletin*, December, pp. 1523-1526.

30. Thorat, Usha, (2007). "Financial Inclusion- the India experience", *BIS Review*, pp. 1-8.

31. Thorat, Usha, 2008, "Inclusive Growth- The Role of Banks in Emerging Economies", *RBI Bulletin*, March, pp. 411-424.

32. United Nations Organization (2006). *Building Inclusive Financial Sectors for Development*, Blue Book, UN New York

33. World Bank (2008). *Finance for all?* , A world Bank Policy Research Report, Washington D.C

FOOTNOTES

1. A World Bank Policy Research Report, 'Finance for All? - Policies and Pitfalls in Expanding Access', (2008).
2. See for instance, N.K. Thingalaya, Banks in the South: Past, Present and their Future, Justice K S Hegde Institute of Management, Nitte, 2009.
3. Report of the Committee for Financial Inclusion, RBI India 2008

13

RRB's Potential Role in Financial Inclusion in India: The Challenges Ahead

U. Arabi

INTRODUCTION

The Indian rural banking industry has shown tremendous growth in volume and complexity in the rural areas during the last few decades. The recent developments in banking technology have transformed banking staffed branches to a system supplemented by channels like automated teller machines (ATM), credit/debit cards, internet banking, online money transfers, etc. However, currently, only 37 per cent of branches of Scheduled Commercial Banks (SCB) are in the rural areas and only about 40 per cent of the country's population has bank accounts. This shows that, despite making significant improvements in all the areas of financial viability, profitability and competitiveness, the banks have not been able to include vast segment of the population especially the underprivileged sections of the society into the fold of basic banking services. In this context, although several efforts are being made to study the causes of financial exclusion and designing strategies to ensure financial inclusion of the poor and disadvantaged in the Indian rural context, these efforts are not able to truly lift the financial condition and standards of life of the poor and the disadvantaged through access to banking services.

Recently, access to finance by the poor and vulnerable groups is regarded as a prerequisite for poverty reduction and social cohesion, which has also become an integral part of efforts to promote inclusive growth. Thus, the financial inclusion is recognized as a priority agenda in growth strategy of the Government in India. Undoubtedly financial inclusion is stepping stone for inclusive growth and its essence is to ensure that a range of appropriate financial services is available to every individual and enabling them to understand and access those services. Financial inclusion denotes delivery of financial services at an affordable cost to the vast sections of the disadvantaged and low -income groups. The various financial services include credit, savings, insurance and payments and remittance facilities. Hence, the objective of financial inclusion is to extend the scope of activities of the organized financial system to include within its ambit people with low incomes. Apart from the regular form of financial intermediation, it include a basic no frills banking account for making and receiving payments, a savings product suited to the pattern of cash flows of a poor household, money transfer facilities, small loans and overdrafts for productive, personal and other purposes, insurance (life and non-life), etc. In view of these, a broad working definition of financial inclusion may be formed thus, 'as the process of ensuring access to financial services and timely and adequate credit where needed by vulnerable groups such as weaker sections and low income groups at an affordable cost'.

Financial inclusion is delivery of banking services at an affordable cost to the vast sections of disadvantaged and low income groups. As banking services are in the nature of public good, the scope of financial inclusion can be expanded either through state-driven intervention by way of statutory enactments or through voluntary effort by the banking community itself for evolving various strategies to bring within the ambit of the banking sector the large strata of society. But, when bankers do not give the desired attention to certain areas the Reserve Bank of India place a lot of emphasis on financial inclusion. Presently in India financial inclusion is confined to ensuring a bare minimum access to a savings bank account without frills to all.

This paper is organised in to five sections:

1. Potential Role of RRBs in Financial Inclusion
2. The rationale of RRBs and its contributions towards the financial inclusion in the India
3. The overall performance of RRBs in India
4. Challenges of RRBs and Financial Inclusion in India
5. Conclusion.

POTENTIAL ROLE OF RRBs IN FINANCIAL INCLUSION

The financial system in India has grown rapidly in the last 35 years and its functional and geographical coverage is truly impressive. But, there is exclusion of the poorer sections of the society; still they have not been able to access adequately financial services from the organized financial system. While banks and other financial institutions can also take some efforts on their own to improve the absorptive capacity of the clients, it is equally important for Government at various levels to initiate actions to enhance the earnings capacity of the poorer sections of the society. The two together can bring about the desired change of greater inclusion quickly.

With merger infusing the much needed financial strength in RRBs coupled with the local feel and familiarity they command, RRBs are in a unique position to play a decisive role in financial inclusion. In rural areas, RRBs account for a substantial 37% of total offices of all scheduled commercial banks. In semi-urban areas, their share comes to 15%. It goes without saying that exclusion is more severe in rural areas. Post-merger RRBs represent a powerful instrument for financial inclusion. Their outreach vis-à-vis other scheduled commercial banks particularly in regions and across population groups facing the brunt of financial exclusion is impressive. With merger infusing the much needed financial strength in RRBs coupled with the local feel and familiarity they command, RRBs are well positioned to play a major role in financial inclusion particularly in areas / regions with high rates of financial exclusion. RRBs were originally created to cater to neglected sections / areas as they were expected to have sound financial management combined with local feel and familiarity. With the amalgamation of RRBs, they have acquired the critical mass in terms of financial strength to widen and deepen their outreach. With the requisite strength having been developed, RRBs are the best suited vehicles to widen and deepen the process of financial inclusion.

Scaling-up access to finance for India's rural poor, to meet their diverse financial needs (savings, credit, insurance, etc.) through flexible products at competitive prices, presents a formidable developmental challenge in a country as vast and varied as India. But the opportunities too are plentiful, and the government has an important role to play in creating space and a flexible architecture for innovations. Financial inclusion is, and needs to be seen as, crucial in achieving pro-poor growth and poverty reduction goals. With merger infusing the much needed financial strength in RRBs coupled with the local feel and familiarity they command, RRBs are in a unique position to play a decisive role in financial inclusion. RRBs are well positioned to play a major role in financial inclusion particularly in areas / regions with high rates of financial exclusion. RRBs were originally created to cater to neglected sections / areas as they were expected to have sound financial management combined with local feel and familiarity. With the amalgamation of RRBs, they have acquired the critical mass in terms of financial strength to widen and deepen their outreach. With the requisite strength having been developed, RRBs are the best suited vehicles to widen and deepen the process of financial inclusion. However, utmost care must be taken to ensure that in the process of fulfilling the socio-economic objective of financial inclusion, RRBs' do not again fall into the vicious circle of deteriorating financial performance and deviation from their mandate. RRBs may be provided adequate promotional and developmental assistance to contribute substantially to financial inclusion in a way that the business generated out of inclusion efforts add positively to their performance.

In the context of initiatives taken for extending banking services to the small man, the mode of financial sector development until 1980's was characterized by; a hugely expanded bank branch and cooperative network and new organizational forms like RRBs; a greater focus on credit rather than other financial services like savings and insurance, although the banks and cooperatives did provide deposit facilities; lending targets directed at a range of 'priority sectors' such as agriculture, weaker sections of the population, etc; interest rate ceilings; significant government subsidies channeled through the banks and cooperatives, as well as through related government programmes; a dominant perspective that finance for rural and poor people was a social obligation and not a potential business opportunity. It is absolutely beyond any doubt that the financial access to masses has significantly improved in the last three and a half decades. But the basic question of the quantum of deposit accounts (current and savings) held as a ratio to the adult population has not been uniformly encouraging. There is a tremendous scope for financial coverage if we have to improve the standards of life of those deprived people.

With a view to enhancing the financial inclusion, as a proactive measure, the RBI in its Annual Policy Statement for the year 2005-06, while recognizing the concerns in regard to the banking practices that tend to exclude rather than attract vast sections of population, urged banks to review their existing practices to align them with the objective of financial inclusion. In the Mid Term Review of the Policy (2005-06), RBI exhorted the banks, with a view to achieving greater financial inclusion, to make available a *basic banking* 'no frills' account either with nil or very minimum balances as well as charges that would make such accounts accessible to vast sections of the population. The nature and number of transactions in such accounts would be restricted and made known to customers in advance in a transparent manner. All banks are urged to give wide publicity to the facility of such no frills account so as to ensure greater financial inclusion. Further, in order to ensure that persons belonging to low income group both in urban and rural areas do not face difficulty in opening the bank accounts due to the procedural hassles, the KYC procedure for opening accounts has been simplified for those persons who intend to keep balances not exceeding rupees fifty thousand (Rs. 50,000/-) in all their accounts taken together and the total credit in all the accounts taken together is not expected to exceed rupees one lakh (Rs.1,00,000/-) in a year.

ESTABLISHMENT OF RRBs AND ITS RATIONALE IN INDIA

The Banking Commission of 1972 recommended establishing an alternative institution for rural credit and ultimately Government of India established RRBs; a separate institution basically for rural credit on the basis of the recommendation of the Narashimham Working Group. The RRBs have been identified as scheduled commercial banks under the Reserve Bank of India Act-1934 and are authorized to transact banking business as defined in the Banking Regulation Act-1949. The RRBs were required, in particular, to under the business of providing credit facilities to the poorer sections of rural society, generally referred to as the Target Group. The underlying objectives as given in the preamble of RRBs Act of 1976, ".....to develop the rural economy in providing for the purpose of development of agriculture, trade, commerce, industry, and other productive activities in the rural areas, credit and other facilities particularly to the small and marginal farmers, agricultural labourers, artisan and small entrepreneurs and for matter connected therewith and incidental thereto." In other words, the Regional Rural Banks (RRBs) was created to meet the excess demand for institutional credit in the rural areas, particularly among the economically and socially marginalised sections.

Although the cooperative banks and the commercial banks had reasonable records in terms of geographical coverage and disbursement of credit, in terms of population groups the cooperative banks were dominated by the rural rich, while the commercial banks had a clear urban bias. In order to provide access to low-cost banking facilities to the poor, as institutions which "combine the local feel and the familiarity with rural problems which the cooperatives possess and the degree of business organization, ability to mobilize deposits, access to central money markets and modernized outlook which the commercial banks have". The multi-agency approach to rural credit was also to sub serve the needs of the input-intensive agricultural strategy (Green Revolution) which had initially focused on `betting on the strong' but by the mid-seventies was ready to spread more widely through the Indian countryside. In addition, the potential and the need for diversification of economic activities in the rural areas had begun to be recognized, and this was a sector where the RRBs could play a meaningful role. Regional Rural Banks were established under the provisions of an Ordinance promulgated on the 26th September 1975 and the RRB Act, 1976 with an objective to ensure sufficient institutional credit for agriculture and other rural sectors. The RRBs Act, 1976 succinctly sums up this overall vision to sub-serve both the developmental and the redistributive objectives: The RRBs were established "with a view to developing the rural economy by providing, for the purpose of development of agriculture, trade, commerce, industry and other productive activities in the rural areas, credit and other facilities, particularly to small and marginal farmers, agricultural labourers, artisans and small entrepreneurs, and for matters connected therewith and incidental thereto".

The RRBs mobilize financial resources from rural / semi-urban areas and grant loans and advances mostly to small and marginal farmers, agricultural labourers and rural artisans. The area of operation of RRBs is limited to the area as notified by GoI covering one or more districts in the State. RRBs are jointly owned by GoI, the concerned State Government and Sponsor Banks (27 scheduled commercial banks and one State Cooperative Bank); the issued capital of a RRB is shared by the owners in the proportion of 50%, 15% and 35% respectively.

Way back in 1975, RRBs were thought of as State sponsored, region-based, and rural oriented commercial banks which would blend the rural touch, local feel and familiarity with rural problems as also the low cost profile as possessed by co-operatives with the professional discipline and ability to mobilize resources of the commercial banks. RRBs were originally conceived as low cost institutions having a rural ethos, local feel and pro poor focus. However, within a very short time, most banks were making losses. The original assumptions as to the low cost nature of these institutions were belied. When the reform process in the banking sector was initiated, RRBs were taken up for a close look. The GoI in consultation with RBI and NABARD started the reform process thru' a comprehensive package for RRBs including cleansing their balance sheets and recapitalising them. Extant lending restrictions were removed and space and variety available for investment of their surplus funds was expanded. Simultaneously, a number of human resource development and Organisational Development Initiatives (ODI) were taken up by NABARD with funding support of the Swiss Development Corporation (SDC) and with the tools of training and exposure visits, ODI, technology support, computerization and use of IT, system development, etc. for business development and productivity improvement.

RECENT PERFORMANCE OF RRBs

Regional Rural Banks (RRBs) were created with the objective of combining the good features of cooperatives and commercial banks to provide regionally oriented institutions that could direct credit to the under-privileged sections of the rural population. Thus, RRBs can be regarded as an ideal institution for achieving financial inclusion in rural areas. With the onset of financial sector reforms, a number of changes were brought about in the policy framework relating to RRBs to impart operational freedom to these institutions and improve their weakening financial health. These changes were primarily reflected in the restructuring and amalgamation, recapitalisation of RRBs along with the application of prudential regulatory framework to these institutions. Regional Rural Banks (RRBs) form an integral part of the Indian banking system with focus on service to rural areas. The process of amalgamation of the RRBs was initiated by Government of India in September 2005 in a phased manner. Prior to the process of amalgamation, 196 RRBs sponsored by 27 SCBs and one State Cooperative Bank were operating in the country with a network of 14,484 branches spread over 523 districts as on March 31, 2005. Consequent upon the amalgamation, the number of RRBs declined to 82 operating in 26 States and in one Union Territory covering 619 districts with a network of 15,475 branches as on March 31, 2010.

Key Performance Indicators

Reforms introduced in RRBs by Government of India in consultation with RBI and NABARD have yielded positive results in respect of key performance indicators, as indicated in the Table 1.

Out of 82 RRBs, 79 RRBs were in profits during 2009-10 indicating an increase in the share of profit-making RRBs to 96.3 per cent during this year as compared to 93.0 per cent in the previous year. On the whole, all RRBs taken together reported a net profit of '1,884 crore showing a growth of 41.1 per cent in 2009-10. As a result, there was a marginal rise in the Return on Assets (RoA) of RRBs from 1.0 per cent in 2008-09 to 1.1 per cent in 2009-10. The RoA of RRBs in 2009-10 thus worked out to be relatively higher than that of SCBs. In 2009-10, the consolidated balance sheet of RRBs showed accelerated growth of 22.2 per cent as compared to 16.5 per cent during the previous year. On the liabilities side, deposits propelled the growth in balance sheets of RRBs, while on the assets side, the growth was mainly on account of investments. It may be noted that the credit-deposit ratio of

Table 1. Important Banking Indicators- Regional Rural Banks- Outstanding

Year	*Demand Dep. (DD)*	*Time Dep. (TD)*	*Total (DD + TD)*	*Bank Credit*	*Govt. securities*	*Other securities*	*Total*	*Cash in hand (Rs Cr)*
1981-82	90	262	352	439	0	0	0	11
1982-83	135	359	494	606	0	0	0	13
1983-84	194	494	689	813	0	0	0	18
1984-85	258	715	973	1134	0	0	0	24
1985-86	324	990	1314	1465	0	0	1	27
1986-87	417	1337	1754	1852	2	1	3	31
1987-88	536	1735	2271	2328	5	1	6	34
1988-89	645	2282	2927	2858	5	1	6	40
1989-90	817	2998	3815	3409	5	1	6	46
1990-91	941	3619	4560	3497	9	6	15	56
1991-92	1044	4227	5271	3951	8	17	25	64
1992-93	1093	5277	6370	4451	10	37	47	74
1993-94	1344	6651	8045	5024	39	52	91	86
1994-95	2115	8733	10848	6201	459	375	834	216
1995-96	2475	10895	13370	7289	842	983	1826	177
1996-97	2947	14025	16971	8544	723	1765	2488	226
1997-98	3805	17173	20977	9687	1011	2517	3528	253
1998-99	4688	20740	25428	11016	1191	3816	5007	300
1999-00	5105	24946	30051	12663	1224	4786	6009	343
2000-01	6098	29897	35995	15211	1642	5847	7489	357
2001-02	7305	35189	42494	18033	1970	4901	6871	400
2002-03	8513	39131	47644	21359	7673	4336	12009	471
2003-04	10727	42663	53390	25057	13324	4208	17532	547
2004-05	12757	45629	58286	31651	16970	3242	20212	598

Year	*Demand Dep. (DD)*	*Time Dep. (TD)*	*Total (DD + TD)*	*Bank Credit*	*Govt. securities*	*Other securities*	*Total*	*Cash in hand (Rs Cr)*
2005-06	17355	46840	64195	36050	16787	2263	19050	1155
2006-07	20003	61617	81620	48420	20249	2175	22424	1110
2007-08	21022	73390	94412	57417	23411	1976	25387	1104
2008-09	24353	89475	113828	64011	27118	2296	29414	1226
2009-10	28710	107104	135814	79086	38201	1029	39229	1434

Source: NABARD

Note : Dep. = Deposits

RRBs in 2009-10 stood at 57.6 per cent, a level far lower than that of SCBs.

In line with their role in furthering financial inclusion, priority sectors, which have generally constituted a major portion of the total advances of RRBs, occupied a share of about 82 per cent in their total advances at end-March 2010. Importantly, however, the share of agricultural credit in total credit from RRBs was on a declining trend in the recent years.

Over the past five years, RRBs transformation has resulted in a 200 per cent-plus increase in net profits, a 100 per cent increase in business, a gradual reduction in the number of loss-making banks and addition of 1,000 outlets. All this has been because of consolidation among RRBs. The Central Government initiated the process of amalgamating RRBs in September, 2005. Then, there were 196 RRBs. At the end of March 2006, the number came down to 133, and it consolidated to 82 by the end of March 2010. Though the number of RRBs has come down by more than half, their branch network has seen modest growth of about 6 per cent. At the end of the last fiscal, the number of branches reached 15,475 as against 14,489 in 2005-06. Obviously, the amalgamation and reduction of number resulted in rationalisation of RRBs to a great extent. This helped merge the weak RRBs with the stronger ones. For the strong RRBs, amalgamation gave the benefit of extending business operations to newer areas without much cost. It helped to increase customer base, reduce credit concentration risks by spreading the risk to more sectors and more agricultural crops in rural economies.

Table 2. Consolidated Balance Sheet of Regional Rural Banks (Amount in crores)

Item	*2008-09*	*2009-10*	*Percentage variation*
Share Capital	197	197	-
Reserves	6,754	8,065	19.4
Share Capital Deposits	3,959	3,985	0.7
Deposits	1,20,189	1,45,035	20.7
Current	6,432	8,065	25.4
Savings	63,675	75,906	19.2
Term	50,082	61,064	21.9
Borrowings from	12,735	18,770	47.4
NABARD	8,690	12,521	44.1
Sponsor Bank	3,931	6,165	56.8
Others	114	84	-26.3
Other Liabilities	6,820	8,041	17.9
Total Liabilities/Assets	1,50,654	1,84,093	22.2
Cash in Hand	1,587	1,784	12.4
Balances with RBI	5,882	8,145	38.5
Other Bank Balances	31,865	39,102	22.7
Investments	37,984	47,289	24.5
Loans and Advances (net)	65,609	79,157	20.6
Fixed Assets	278	379	36.3

Item	*2008-09*	*2009-10*	*Percentage variation*
Other Assets#	7,449	8,237	10.6
Credit -Deposit Ratio	56.4	57.6	
Investment - Deposit Ratio	54.8	50.2	
(Credit + Investment)- Deposit Ratio		111.3	107.8

Source: NABARD

Table 3. Financial Performance of Regional Rural Banks (Amount in crores)

Item	*2008-09*	*2009-10*	*%age variation*
A. Income (i + ii)	11,388	13,835	21.5
Interest income	10,579	12,945	22.4
Other income	810	890	9.9
B. Expenditure (i+ii+iii)	10,053	11,951	18.9
Interest expended	6,100	7,375	20.9
Operating expenses of which,	3,165	3,547	12.1
Wage bill	2,291	2,676	16.8
Provisions and contingencies	788	1,029	30.6
C. Profit			
Operating profit	2,123	2,913	37.2
Net profit	1,335	1,884	41.1
D. Total assets	1,50,654	1,84,093	22.2
E. Financial ratios#			
Operating profit	1.5	1.7	-
Net profit	1.0	1.1	-
Income (a + b)	8.3	8.3	-
(a) Interest income	7.7	7.7	-
(b) Other income	0.6	0.5	-
Expenditure (a+b+c)	7.3	7.1	-
(a) Interest expended	4.4	4.4	-

Item	*2008-09*	*2009-10*	*%age variation*
(b) Operating expenses	2.3	2.1	-
of which, Wage Bill	1.7	1.6	-
(c) Provisions and contingencies	0.6	0.6	-

Source: NABARD

Table 4. Purpose-wise Distribution of Credit from Regional Rural Banks (Amount in crores)

Purpose		*2008-09*	*2009-10*
I.	Agriculture (i to ii)	37,367 (55.1)	45,829(54.8)
	i. Short-term credit (crop loans)	26,652	33,208
	ii.Term credit (for agriculture and allied activities)	10,715	12,621
II.	Non-agriculture (i to iv)	30,435(44.8)	37,733(45.1)
	i.Rural artisans	772	857
	ii.Other industries	1,656	1,694
	iii.Retail trade	4,690	5,285
	iv.Other purposes	23,317	29,897
	Total (I+II)	67,802	83,562
Memo item :			
a.	Priority sector	56,555	68,660
b.	Non-Priority sector	11,247	14,902
c.	Percentage share of priority sector in total credit	83.4	82.2

Figures in parentheses indicate percentage share in total credit

Source: NABARD.

Table 5. Recent Performance Trends of the RRBs

Items	2005-06	2006-07	2007-08	2008-09	2009-10
Net Profits (Rs. In Crores)	617	625	1027	1335	1884
No. of RRBs	133	625	90	86	82
(profit/ loss making)	111/22	81/15	82/8	80/6	19/3
No. of branches	14,489	14,563	14,790	15,524	15,475
Deposits	71329	83144	99093	120189	145035
Loans & Advances	38520	47326	57568	66609	79157
NII	2852	3407	3982	4479	5570
Other Income	433	540	667	810	890
Wage Bill	1848	2051	2054	2291	2676
CD ratio (in %)	55.7	58.3	59.5	56.4	57.6
Share of CASA in deposits (in %)	59.14	61.21	59.63	58.35	57.9
Share of priority sector advances in total advances (in %)	81	82.2	82.9	83.4	82.2
Share of agricultural advances to total (in %)	54.2	56.6	56.3	55.1	54.8
Gross NPA (in %)	7.3	6.55	6.1	4.2	NA
Net NPA	3.96	3.46	3.4	1.8	NA

Source: RBI Reports on Trend and Progress of Banking in India

Net Profits Rise

From the tables presented above the over all performance of the RRBs is discussed as below:

There were as many as 133 RRBs that posted a profit

of Rs 617 crore in 2005-06 with 22 making loss that year. However with consolidation in the subsequent years, the net profit jumped to Rs 1,884 crore in 2009-10 with the number of RRBs being reduced to 82. Of them, only three incurred a loss (Table.1). By 2009-10, all RRBs taken together achieved a net profit of Rs 1,884 crore showing a growth of 41.1 per cent in 2009-10. As a result, there was a marginal rise in the return on assets (RoA) of RRBs from 1 per cent in 2008-09 to 1.1 per cent in 2009-10. The RoA of RRBs in 2009-10 thus worked out to be relatively higher than that of scheduled commercial banks. The expansion of service area after amalgamation of RRBs has helped to increase net profits. Earlier, RRBs were confined to one or two districts. The amalgamation of different RRBs of the same sponsor bank in a State helped the combined entity increase business and profits. Besides, RRBs were permitted to open branches at taluk headquarters also. Further, increase in competency of the staff, management quality, support from sponsor banks and National Bank for Agriculture and Rural Development through refinance at reasonable rates, comparatively large share of low cost deposits (current accounts, savings accounts, or CASA), lower operational costs, expertise acquired in asset management over time, effective investment management, etc., were instrumental in the growth in net profit. RRBs are now allowed to do para-banking activities such as life and non-life insurance businesses, helping them increase their non-interest income. Additionally, increased computerisation of RRBs, including introduction of core banking solution in some RRBs, has resulted in reduced operational expenses. The total business of KVGB, which was around Rs 3,000 crore during its formation in 2005, crossed Rs 8,000 crore in 2009-10. The bank recorded a net profit of Rs 72.14 crore in 2009-10.

Better Management of NPAs

RRBs seem to have better non-performing assets (NPA)

management with net NPA coming down every year after the amalgamation. In 2005-06, the net NPA stood at 3.96 per cent. It declined to 1.98 per cent in 2008-09. For better NPA management, RRBs are concentrating on rural credit and the major portion of the agricultural credit. The average size of a loan account is low and in certain RRBs, it is as low as Rs 50,000. Credit risk is thus well spread over several accounts, unlike commercial banks where the size of the loan account is much bigger and risk is more. Added to this, RRBs keep good rapport and liaison with rural borrowers and the follow-up of advances is effective. Problems of the borrowers are addressed promptly and remedial steps are taken timely. Rural borrowers are more amicable, and they accept RRBs as 'friend, philosopher and guide'.

CASA Performance

For RRBs, the ratio of low-cost deposits to the total deposits continues to remain above their big brothers. However, the share of CASA has also witnessed gradual decline in the recent years. RRBs that managed to mobilize 61.21 per cent of CASA of the total deposits in 2006-07 could not continue that further. In 2009-10, the share of CASA was at 57.9 per cent. They can take solace in the fact that their CASA share is more than that of their sponsoring public sector banks. The RRBs that managed to mobilise around Rs 38,233 crore in their savings accounts in 2005-06 took it to the level of Rs 75,906 crore in 2009-10. Experts felt that being the bankers for the villagers has helped RRBs garner more CASA than the commercial banks.

AGRI Advances Ratio

The Report on Trend and Progress of Banking in India 2009-10 is concerned the share of agricultural credit from RRBs was on a decline in the recent years. While agriculture credit to total credit was 54.2 per cent in 2005-06, it increased to just 54.8 per cent in 2009-10. Considering the increase in the volume of business over the years, this appears to be a bit low. Although, RRBs managed to take this share to 56.6 per cent in 2006-07, that did not continue for long. RRBs are also extending loans to non-agricultural sector in rural areas also. They are broad-basing their credit pattern. RRBs went ahead to finance vehicles for rural transport system. Financing of vehicles for rural transportation helped villagers, as they sold their produce in urban areas. On the return journey, they would bring items required by the villagers and sell them at their door steps.

Top performers

With an 858-branch network in 18 districts, the Central Bank of India-sponsored Uttar Bihar Gramin Bank had done a total business of Rs 8,377 crore and achieved a net profit of Rs 104.19 crore in 2008-09. The Syndicate Bank-sponsored Andhra Pragathi Grameena Bank, which covers five districts of the State, managed to do a business of Rs 6,120 crore and earn a net profit of Rs 75.96 crore from 356 branches. In terms of business per branch, one of the branches of the Canara Bank-sponsored Pragathi Grameen Bank in Bellary is reported to have done more than Rs 200 crore businesses. The Korrah rural branch of the Bank of India-sponsored Jharkhand Grameen Bank earned a net profit of Rs 1 crore, whereas Bank of India's Ranchi branch earned a net profit of only Rs 57.88 lakh. For instance, an RRB in Bihar recorded a net profit of Rs 104 crore during 2008-09, which is more than some of the old-generation private banks. In short, out of 84 RRBs in the country only six are in the red and the process of mergers implemented by the Union Government since 2005 has enhanced the viability of many of the RRBs.

Low-cost deposits

It is quite interesting to note that RRBs have more low-cost deposit accounts. Of the 9.35 crore deposit accounts with RRBs, the number of low-cost deposits stood at 7.47 crore.

The share of low-cost deposits among the total deposits of the Allahabad Bank-sponsored Lucknow Kshetriya Gramin Bank is 73.32 per cent. It is 71.64 per cent for the Punjab National Bank-sponsored Sarva UP Gramin Bank, and 71.25 per cent for Uttar Bihar Gramin Bank. The number of borrowing accounts remained at 1.7 crore at the end of March 2009. Of these, the share of small and marginal farmers was 89.08 lakh. An overwhelming percentage of these accounts were in the advance group of less than Rs 25,000 each. There were 15,181 branches of rural banks at the end of March 2009. Of these, Uttar Pradesh led with 2,962 branches, followed by Bihar with 1,479 branches and Karnataka 1,172 branches. Madhya Pradesh had 1,070 branches and Rajasthan 1,040 branches. The North-Eastern States had very few branches. For instance, Nagaland had just 10, while Arunachal Pradesh had 22 and Manipur 27 branches. Hence, it is suggested that, further consolidation in the number of RRBs, especially where they are confined to narrow operational areas with little scope for expansion. In the case of larger RRBs which have emerged bigger than some of the old generation private banks, there is scope for scaling up operations. Importantly, the sponsoring banks can expand their RRBs by merging rural branches with the RRBs at the State level. Hence, RRBs have to be equipped to undertake all types of businesses that commercial bank branches do.

RECOMMENDATION OF THE COMMITTEE ON FINANCIAL INCLUSION (2008)

Post-merger, RRBs, with 14494 branches, represent a powerful instrument for financial inclusion. Their role and relevance in financial inclusion is crucial as pointed as below:

In rural areas, they account for 37% of total offices of all Scheduled ?Commercial Banks.91% of the total workforce in RRBs is posted in rural and semi-urban areas as compared to 38% for other Scheduled Commercial Banks. In rural areas,

RRBs account for 31% of deposit accounts and 19% of deposit amount of all Scheduled Commercial Banks. Lower average deposit amount per account in RRBs as compared with commercial banks implies their better reach to small depositors. Share of RRBs in loan accounts is an impressive 37% in rural areas. Of all the scheduled commercial banks, RRBs account for 34% of branches in NE, 30% in Eastern and 32% in Central regions. Incidentally, these regions manifest financial exclusion of a high order.Of the total 29.25 lakh SHGs credit linked by the banking system (as on 31 March 2007), 31% linkage is done by RRBs. More significantly, the more backward a region, greater is the share of RRBs. In North Eastern Region, it is 56%, Central region 48% and Eastern region 40%. RRBs have also played a significant role as Self Help Promoting Institutions (SHPIs). As many as 104 RRBs (31 March 2006) are functioning as SHPIs with grant assistance from NABARD.

Keeping the above in view, the following recommendations are made for RRBs.

RRBs should extend their services to unbanked areas and increase their credit to deposit (CD) ratio. The post-merger scenario of RRBs poses a series of challenges for them and these are to be addressed. The following areas would require attention from the point of view of financial inclusion:Setting exclusive targets for microfinance and financial inclusion and Providing funding support & providing technology support

No further merger of RRBs

Further merger of all RRBs at State-level across sponsor banks is not required It may not also be desirable if there has to be a firm reinforcement of their rural orientation with a specific mandate on financial inclusion. Therefore, the process of merger should not proceed beyond the level of sponsor bank in each State.

Recapitalisation of RRBs with negative Net Worth

Recapitalisation of RRBs with negative net worth has to be given a serious consideration as it would facilitate their growth, provide lenders a level of comfort and enable their achieving standard capital adequacy ratio.

Strategic microfinance plan with NABARD support

RRBs have the potential and capability to emerge as niche operators in microfinance. They are playing a major role in the SHG - Bank Linkage Programme especially also as SHPIs. Their dual role has special meaning in areas which face severe financial exclusion and which do not have a sufficient presence of well performing NGOs. However, to upscale the programme to a level where it can really make a visible impact, RRBs need handholding particularly in the areas of training, promotion and development. NABARD may provide required assistance. NABARD should prepare a strategic action plan RRB-wise, for promotion and credit linkage of SHGs. RRBs may be asked to form, nurture and credit link at least 3,000 SHGs in districts covered by them in North-Eastern, Eastern and Central Regions. A Memorandum of Understanding (MoU) may be signed by RRBs with NABARD for a period of 5 years - with NABARD providing the promotional and development assistance out of the "Financial Inclusion Promotion and Development Fund" and RRBs forming, nurturing and providing financial services to SHGs. RRBs may accomplish the task with the support of individual rural volunteers, BFs, their staff members, etc. NABARD may closely monitor the programme - with focus on qualitative aspects.

NRFIP for RRBs

The strategy recommended for NRFIP for commercial banks would be equally applicable for RRBs. They would require promotional, funding and technology support in different areas as outlined below. RRBs may endeavour to cover a large part of their incremental lending through the group mode (SHGs/JLGs) as it will enhance their outreach to financially exclude. Lending through group mode would also keep NPAs at low level.

Pilot testing of BF / BC Model by RRBs

RRBs should adopt the BF and BC models as a major strategy of financial inclusion. NABARD should extend the required support including running pilots in selected banks. The proposal for a technology based intervention under the BC model would be equally relevant for RRBs. However, RRBs would require some handholding in implementing the proposal. NABARD may identify 10 RRBs across the country, giving greater weightage to regions manifesting higher levels of financial exclusion and work in strategic alliance with these RRBs and their sponsor banks in implementing the proposal. The RRBs identified by NABARD for the project will require developing a core banking software for proper integration of the technology model proposed. NABARD should enter into a MoU with identified sponsor banks and RRBs and provide initial funding and technology support.

Separate credit plan for excluded regions

The RRBs operating in predominantly tribal areas and having high levels of exclusion may prepare annual credit plans having a separate component for excluded

CHALLENGES AHEAD

Bank nationalization in India marked a paradigm shift in the focus of banking as it was intended to shift the focus from class banking to mass banking. The rationale for creating Regional Rural Banks was also to take the banking services to poor people. The branches of commercial banks and the RRBs have increased from 8321 in the year 1969 to 68,282 branches as at the end of March 2005. The average population per branch office has decreased from 64,000 to

16,000 during the same period. Financial inclusion and implementation of the Financial Inclusion Fund (FIF) and Financial Inclusion Technology Fund (FITF), Core Banking Solution (CBS) system, credit flow to agriculture, net non-performing assets, capital adequacy ratio and human resources development of the RRBs would be some of the key areas of focus. The working group on Information and Communication Technology through FIF and FITF had recommended "technology upgradation" interest-free loan with a moratorium period of three years, with repayment not exceeding 5 per cent of the profit. However, the recommendation is yet to be implemented, the release pointed out. "The RRBs are not in a position to use ICT-based solution, and, moreover, the timeframe for financial inclusion and migration to CBS is almost the same which gives rise to this conflict. Apart from CBS, a huge cost is involved for financial inclusion with ICT. If the bank has to bear both the cost, it may become unviable again," The existing infrastructure available with the RRBs was not adequate to handle the financial inclusion programme effectively. "Acute shortage of manpower, low level of technological up gradation, non-feasibility of business correspondent model due to geographical locations, particularly in the north east region, are working as deterrents in the financial inclusion programme.

The committee headed by Mr A.K. Khandelwal, former Chairman and Managing Director, Bank of Baroda, had recommended that each public sector bank should be allowed to settle salaries for its employees in accordance to their specific skill sets and the banks overall performance. The Chakrabarty committee which examined the financials of Regional Rural Banks (RRBs) recommended that, 40 of the 82 RRBs need to be recapitalized and the amount of recapitalisation is assessed at Rs 2,200 crore and is sought to be released in two instalments; Rs 1,337.50 crore in 2010-11 and Rs 862.50 crore in 2011-12 and also added the need for an additional Rs 700 crore for North-Eastern and Eastern Region RRBs, if they are not able to achieve the required minimum Capital to Risk Weighted Assets Ratio (CRAR) despite infusion of the assessed amount.The banks should come out of inhibited feeling that very aggressive competition policy and social inclusion are mutually exclusive. As demonstrated elsewhere, the mass banking with no-frills etc. can become a win-win situation for both. Basically banking services need to be "marketed" to connect with large population segments and these may be justifiable promotional costs. The opportunities are plenty.

- In the context of India becoming one of the largest micro finance markets in the world especially in the growth of women's savings and credit groups (SHGs) and the sustaining success of such institutions which has been demonstrated by the success of SEWA bank in Gujarat, low cost banking is not necessarily an unviable venture/proposition.
- The IBA may explore the possibility of a survey about the coverage in respect of financial inclusion keeping in view the geographical spread of the banks and extent of financial services available to the population so as to assess the constraints in extension of financial services to hitherto unbanked sections and for initiating appropriate policy measures.
- It may be useful for banks to consider franchising with other segments of financial sector such as cooperatives, RRBs etc. so as to extend the scope of financial inclusion with minimal intermediation cost.
- Since large sections of low income groups transactions are related to deposits and withdrawals, with a view to containing transaction costs, 'simple to use' cash dispensing and collecting machines akin to ATMs, with

operating instructions and commands in vernacular would greatly facilitate financial inclusion of the semi urban and rural populace. In this regard, it is worthwhile to emulate the example of 'e-Choupal' project brought forth through private sector initiative.

Some of the issues which could be on the agenda for future, are (i) expansion of RRBs into uncovered districts allotted to them. (ii) providing a range of products for all financial needs and focus on financial inclusion through progressive use of technologies and low cost alternative delivery channels, (iii) building a healthy and synergetic relationship between sponsor bank and RRBs, (iv) providing training to identified officers of RRBs to handle the portfolio of Investment and risk evaluation system, (v) focusing for enhancing non interest income, like bank guarantees, lending under consortium, remittance services, life and non life insurance, mutual funds, opening of capital gains deposit accounts, collection of taxes and conducting Govt. business, etc., (vi) increasing CD ratio, (vii) formulating loan scheme for supply chain, including storage, processing transportation, marketing and retailing, (viii) arranging both technical and commercial extension services for farmers with the help of professional agencies and technological platforms, (ix) building up rural banking skills and recognize acceptable banking risks so as mitigating them in lending decisions, (x) reviewing organizational structure, and (xi) setting up Computerized Data Processing Systems to handle the increased and diversified loan/investment portfolio and introduction of new banking products/financial services, etc.

CONCLUSION

Role of regional rural banks (RRBs) is very important in the real last mile financial inclusion. They are playing a greater role than scheduled commercial banks (SCBs) in achieving the goals of financial inclusion. However, RRBs needs to be technologically upgraded and other requirements are met by the government as well as banks sponsoring them. But the financial support to all RRBs is required so as to help them participate actively in the financial inclusion programmes. RRBs are, thus, the best suited vehicles to widen and deepen the process of financial inclusion.

Regulation and supervision of the RRBs needs to be urgently strengthened. Prudential regulation standards related to capital adequacy, asset classification, income recognition and provisioning need to be upgraded and introduced in a phased manner, and the supervisory enforcement improved. At the same time, this would need to be accompanied by operational restructuring, involving improvements in governance to reduce state interference, better management, staffing policies that allow banks to employ local staff who are familiar with the community and thereby better able to address the needs of their client, and the introduction of new products, such as loans with flexible repayment terms, and better services, such as door-step banking that can help better meet the needs of rural clients and minimise risk.

The RRBs would have to evolve specific strategies to expand the outreach of their services in order to promote financial inclusion. One of the ways in which this can be achieved in a cost-effective manner is through forging linkages with microfinance institutions and local communities. Banks should give wide publicity to the facility of no frills account. Technology can be a very valuable tool in providing access to banking products in remote areas. ATMs cash dispensing machines can be modified suitably to make them user friendly for people who are illiterate, less educated or do not know English. Thus, these banks need to redesign their business strategies to incorporate specific plans to promote financial inclusion of low income group treating it both a business opportunity as well as a corporate social responsibility. They have to make use of all available resources including technology and expertise available with them as well as the MFIs and NGOs. It may appear in the first instance that taking banking to the sections constituting "the bottom of the pyramid", may not be profitable but it should always be remembered that even the relatively low margins on high volumes can be a very profitable proposition. Financial inclusion can emerge as commercial profitable business; only the banks should be prepared to think outside the box.

The financial system in India has grown rapidly in the last 35 years and its functional and geographical coverage is truly impressive. But, there is exclusion of the poorer sections of the society; still they have not been able to access adequately financial services from the organized financial system. Hence, there is an imperative need to modify the credit and financial services delivery system to achieve greater inclusion. The implementation of the recommendations made in the Rangarajan Committee Report could go a long way to modify particularly the credit delivery system of the banks and other related institutions to meet the credit requirements of marginal and sub-marginal farmers in the rural areas in a fuller measure. However, creating an appropriate credit delivery system is only a necessary condition. This needs to be supplemented by efforts to improve the productivity of small and marginal farmers and other entrepreneurs so that the credit made available can be productively employed. While banks and other financial institutions can also take some efforts on their own to improve the absorptive capacity of the clients, it is equally important for Government at various levels to initiate actions to enhance the earnings capacity of the poorer sections of the society. The two together can bring about the desired change of greater inclusion quickly. Finally, all the recent circulars relating to financial inclusion, viz., no frills accounts, GCC, One Time Settlement (OTS) for loans up to Rs. 25,000, use of intermediaries, etc., should be implemented by RRBs.

REFERENCES

1. Agarwal, R.K. (1991) Evaluation of Working of Regional Rural Banks, Mittal Publications, New Delhi.
2. Ahmed, R. (1998) Rural Banking and Economic Development, Mittal Publications, New Delhi.
3. Ansari, Md. A. (1988) Working of RRBs in Eastern UP, Anmol Publication, New Delhi.
4. Basu, P. (2006), Improving Access to Finance for India's Rural Poor. Washington: The World Bank.
5. Bell, C. (1993), Interactions between Institutional and Informal Credit Agencies in Rural India, in Hoff, K; A. Braverman and J.E. Stiglitz (Eds.) The Economics of Rural Organisation. Theory, Practice and Policy, pp. 186-213 (New York: Oxford University Press).
6. Desai, B M and N V Namboodiri (2001), Organization and Management of Rural Financial Sector: Text, Cases and Exercises, Oxford Publishing House, New Delhi.
7. Karam Pal and Jasvir S Sura (2006), Efficacy of Regional Rural Banks (RRBs) in India: A Conventional Analysis JIMS-8M, The Journal of Indian Management and Strategy, Vol-11(4), Oct. - Dec.2006, pp. 4-12
8. Kalkundrickars, A.B. (1990), Regional Rural Banks and Economic Development (Delhi) Daya Publishing House.
9. Kumar Raj(1993)" Growth and Performance of RRBs in Haryana", Anmol Publications, New Delhi.
10. NABARD (2000) Task Force on Supportive Policy and Regulatory framework for Micro Finance in India, summary and Recommendations'.
11. National Bank for Agriculture and Rural Development (2004), Annual Report 2003-04, NABARD, Mumbai.
12. National Bank for Agriculture and Rural Development (2003), "Report of the Committee to suggest Amendments

in RRB Act" (Chairman : Shri M V S Chalapathi Rao), NABARD, Mumbai.

13. N.K.Thingalaya (2010) Regional rural banks can be viable business' Business Line Apr 06, 2010 *http://www.thehindubusinessline.com*
14. RBI (1989), "Report of the Agricultural Credit Review Committee: A Review of the Agriculture Credit System in India" , RBI, Mumbai.
15. RBI (2010) Report on Trend and Progress of Banking in India 2009-10
16. RBI (2009) Report on Trend and Progress of Banking in India 2008-09
17. RBI (2010) Handbook of Monetary Statistics of India 2010
18. RBI (2008) Report of the Committee on Financial Inclusion
19. Patel K.V. and Shete, NB(1980) "RRB performance and prospectus, " Prajanan, Jan-March pp. 1-40.

14

Micro-finance for Poor Women : A Study of Self Help Groups in Kerala

A. V. Hemalatha

INTRODUCTION

Women are generally the victims of any evil prevalent in the society. Even though women in Kerala show a better position in terms of positive indicators like high literacy, low infant mortality, and high level of life expectancy, none of these factors could transform the life situation of women even today, especially of rural women. Inherited handicaps pursue them and they continue to be in a state of deprivation. Hence it is high time that the need for making poor women, competent and self reliant by acquiring economic independence is felt as a necessity.

Banks and financial institutions undertake various welfare programmes for the benefit of rural poor, but women were often outside the ambit of many such programmes. Hence, the need for a supplementary credit delivery system which could provide required credit on cordial terms to women was identified as a prerequisite to involve them in income earning processes. Micro credit movement in the state through the formation of Self Help Groups (SHGs) that work with the principle of self help and mutual help was emerged as a way out in providing credit on easy terms. Apart from finance, working in group provides a forum for women in identifying their potential and for developing preparedness to accept challenges and to work with confidence.

Micro finance programme has gained momentum since its inception as it emerged from a crucial situation where the rural institutional finance system failed to discharge the expected benefits to the poor. The system provides finance to the poor and neglected section of population who were outside the reach of formal financial institutions. The relevance of micro finance as a tool of poverty alleviation, employment generation and women empowerment is rightly reflected in the increasing number of SHGs which has reached to 69.5 lakh savings linked SHGs and 48.5 lakh credit linked SHGs covering a household of about 9.7 crore. (Status of Micro finance in India 2009-10)

Provision of micro finance facilitates the poor and neglected section of population, in fulfilling their consumption and production needs. Credit being the most crucial ingredient for engaging in any economic endeavour, a need for awareness and knowledge of its availability and proper utilisation is essential. For imparting knowledge and awareness to the rural women, the organisations set up at the community level play a significant role. Participation of women in all development activities of the state and creation of a situation where the fruits of development can be shared and enjoyed by men and women alike should be spawn in the state.

OBJECTIVES OF THE STUDY

The study is carried out with the following objectives.

1. To examine the nature and working of Self Help Groups in Kerala.
2. To study the impact of SHGs on rural women.
3. To make suggestions for the improved performance of the Groups based on the findings of the study.

METHODOLOGY AND SAMPLE DESIGN

The study is designed as descriptive cum analytical. Both primary and secondary data are used in the study. Six districts are selected for the study, two districts from each of the three regions, namely, Southern, Central and Northern. Thiruvananthapuram and Alapuzha from Southern region, Idukki and Trissur from Central region and Wayanad and Kannur from Northern region. A schedule of Non Government Organisations that facilitate the formation of SHGs and the number of SHGs promoted by them are obtained from the reports published by NABARD. From the list of SHGs maintained by the NGOs in various districts, groups with more than 3 years of existence are taken for the study. Thus 25 SHGs are selected from each of the six districts constituting a sample of 150 SHGs.

A well structured questionnaire is used for collecting data. Secondary data is collected from the records maintained by the group for securing qualitative data and from the reports of NABARD. The collected data are processed and analysed by using statistical tools like percentages, weighted average and Chi-square test.

NATURE AND WORKING OF SELF HELP GROUPS

Self help groups are informal organisations formed voluntarily by poor people at the grassroots level for the purpose of reaping economic benefits out of mutual help, solidarity and joint responsibility. Savings and credit is the basis of the SHG concept. It is based on the philosophy of people's participation in the strategy and execution of all schemes and activities meant for them.

Various NGOs in the state assist women in forming groups and provide them necessary guidance for subsequent activities. The groups promoted by NGO have common bye law with specific rules and regulations regarding the formation, administration and functioning of the group. After the formation of a group an account is opened in the name of the group with a nearby bank.

The management of group vests with elected office bearers, normally a President, Secretary and a Treasurer. The secretary assumes the role of treasurer also for certain groups. The term of office of the managerial body is limited for a period of one to three years, with an intention to have rotation of leadership among all the members. However there are many cases where a few leaders continue in office and others either shy away from taking up office, or do not get an opportunity.

The groups meet at regular intervals at places decided by the members usually in the house of each member on a rotation basis. The savings of members are collected in the course of meeting. Applications for loans are also taken up for disposal at the meetings. Availability of funds and urgency of the need are normally the factors that influence decision on loan applications.

The Groups maintain a systematic record of activities in the minute books, accounts and day book, register of members, pass book etc, usually audited by the officials of NGOs, coordinators or chartered accountants. Also some of the members undertake audit who are trained by the coordinators of NGOs for the purpose.

SHGs get support and assistance from NGOs in facilitating smooth functioning. They arrange for finance from banks or other institutions, motivate them to start micro enterprises, impart training in leadership, accounting and

Entrepreneurial Development Programme. Proper supervision and monitoring is also executed by the coordinators of NGOs, expediting sustainable working of the group.

For examining the objectives of the study, 150 Self Help Groups are selected from six districts (25x6) of the state. The intention is to examine the nature and working of the groups and to assess the performance of group activities. A detailed exhibit of the discussions and results of the study brings into light the status of the SHGs in the study area.

LOCATION WISE DISTRIBUTION

SHGs mostly concentrate in rural areas and are designed to benefit poor women of weak socio economic condition. Women residing in rural areas are in dire need of support and assistance from others. Table 1 shows the area wise distribution of sample groups shows that the groups are formed mainly in rural and backward areas. Out of the total groups, 142 groups (94.6 %) are in panchayat whereas 8 groups (5.4%) are in municipality.

Table 1. Location wise Distribution of Sample SHGs

Region	*No. of units in Panchayat*		*No. of units in Municipality*		*Total no. of units*	
	No.	*Percent*	*No.*	*Percent*	*No.*	*Percent*
North	48	96	2	4	50	100
Central	47	94	3	6	50	100
South	47	94	3	6	50	100
Total	142	94.6	8	5.4	150	100

Source: Survey data

AUTHORITY THAT MOTIVATES GROUP FORMATION

The idea of forming groups and thereby creating an

economic security for poor women was disseminated by conducting meetings and campaigns by agencies like banks and NGOs at the local level. Prospective members were informed about the advantages of Group formation in tackling their personal problems. Table 2 shows that NGOs constitute the major motivators for women in all regions to start SHG with support and assistance in 89.3 per cent of cases. A minority (7.4%) is self motivated and banks motivate a few (3.3%).

Table 2. Authority that Gave Motivation to Start the Group

Region	*Motivating agencies*			*Totals*
	Bank	*NGO*	*Self*	
North	3(6)	45(90)	2(4)	50(100)
Central	2(4)	43(86)	5(10)	50(100)
South	0(0)	46(92)	4(8)	50(100)
Total	5(3.3)	134(89.3)	11(7.4)	150(100)

Source: Survey data (Values in parentheses denote percentages

FACTORS THAT MOTIVATE GROUP FORMATION

With the inspiration obtained from the agencies rural women prefer to join together in groups so that they could enjoy the benefit of collective effort. Rather than individual voice, group attempt will have more impact when addressing a common issue. Members turned out with varying response for their becoming a part and beneficiary of the group approach. Table 3 shows the prime motivation factor for starting the group as the consideration of members to the principle of self help and mutual help, showing the highest weighted score of 631. Maintaining a healthy relation with neighbours occupies the next highest score of 522. Preference to develop saving habit, acquiring economic independence and use of locally available resources are the other factors

Table 3. Scores of the Motivation to Start the Group

Reason	*Rank*					*Total*	*Weighted score*
	I	*II*	*III*	*IV*	*V*		
Self help and mutual help	85(56.67)	29(19.33)	21(14.00)	12(8.00)	3(2.00)	150(100.00)	631
Good relation with neighbors	20(13.33)	67(44.67)	35(23.33)	21(14.00)	7(4.67)	150(100.00)	522
Use of locally available resources	0(0.00)	3(2.00)	25(16.67)	35(23.33)	87(58.00)	150(100.00)	244
Economic independence	19(12.67)	24(16.00)	40(26.67)	40(26.67)	27(18.00)	150(100.00)	418
To develop saving habit	26(17.33)	27(18.00)	29(19.33)	42(28.00)	26(17.33)	150(100.00)	435

Source: Survey data (Values in parentheses denote percentage)

that stand in preferential order. The enthusiasm and initiative of women to experiment a new system for a common benefit is well reflected in the data.

PARTICIPATION IN GROUP MEETING

Groups conduct meetings at regular intervals. Attendance in meeting is made compulsory for ensuring representation of all members in financial dealings and in discussions involving common matters. Absence of members happens in exceptional cases on genuine reasons. Table 4 shows the status of participation in meeting. Participation of entire members is happening in the case of 86 groups (57.3 %) and majority of the members attend the meeting in the case of 64 groups (42.7%). Group meetings act as the forum for members to communicate and exchange ideas and information on matters of common interest and ensure transparency in financial dealings.

Table 4. Nature of Participation in Group Meeting

Nature of participation	*North*	*Central*	*South*	*Total*
Full participation	20(40)	29(58)	37(74)	86(57.3)
Majority participation	30(60)	21(42)	13(26)	64(42.7)
Total	50 (100.00)	50 (100.00)	50 (100.00)	150 (100.00)

Source: Survey data (Values in parentheses denote percentages)

ANNUAL SAVINGS OF THE GROUP

Thrift collected from members of the group is deposited in a bank account opened in the name of the group. Secretary of the group holds the charge of the bank dealings and maintains the pass book and other account books of the group, recording all financial dealings. The balance left after appropriating for group needs is deposited in the bank. Table 5 shows the annual savings of the SHGs, the highest position is in Northern region Rs.16,735.35 with a standard deviation 11,076.22. Southern region shows the mean value Rs.12,740.39 with standard deviation 10,823.9 and the lowest is found in central region showing mean value Rs.11,945.36 with standard deviation 10,843.9. Since the p-value (0.03002) is less than 0.05 there is significant difference in the saving pattern of the group among regions. The financial performance of SHG cannot be assessed on the basis of group fund deposited in the bank, as the amount when accumulated in to large sum is divided among the members and a fresh account will be started.

Table 5. Annual Savings of the Group

Region	*Number*	*Mean (Rs)*	*SD*	*F*	*p-level*
North	50	16735.35	11076.22	3.575082	0.03002
Central	50	11945.36	10843.08		
South	50	12740.39	10823.9		
Total	150	14304.36	11093.39		

Source: survey data

ASSET HOLDINGS OF THE GROUP

Groups possess assets like furniture and office equipments, buildings and machinery purchased for the conduct of their group activities, in addition to bank balance maintained with the common fund and interest collected from members. Table 6 shows the mean value of asset holdings of SHG being the highest in Northern region, with mean 56,777.19 and standard deviation 28,243.38. Southern region shows the mean value as 54,078.34 with standard deviation 28,600.09 and the lowest is found in central region 45,084.17 with standard deviation 26,714.61. Since the p-value (0.089769) is more than 0.05 there is no significant difference in the value of asset held by the group among regions.

Table 6. Value of Assets Held by the Group

Region	*Number*	*Mean (Rs)*	*SD*	*F*	*p-level*
North	50	56777.19	28243.38	2.443086	0.089769
Central	50	45084.17	26714.61		
South	50	54078.34	28600.09		
Total	150	53193.93	28244.7		

Source: Survey data

REPAYMENT PERFORMANCE OF MEMBERS

Assurance about repayment renders the key consideration while granting loan to members. The application for loan clearly specifies the purpose of loan taken. Pressure from group members acts as the measure to repay the loan in time. Banks having linkage with SHG admit that women are so prompt in the repayment of loan. Table 7 shows that in the case of 123 (82%) groups repayment of loan is always in time, a default is caused occasionally in 23 groups (15.3 %) and 4 groups (2.7%) experience irregularity in repayment. Co operation among group members, capability of group leader and good system of monitoring by NGOs are reported as the factors that contribute towards a systematic and effective system in the repayment behaviour of members.

Table 7. Repayment Performance of Members

Region	*Always regular*	*Mostly regular*	*Irregular*	*Total*
North	41(82)	8(16)	1(2)	50(100)
Central	39(78)	9(18)	2(4)	50(100)
South	43(86)	6(12)	1(2)	50(100)
Total	123(82)	23(15.3)	4(2.7)	150(100)

Source: Survey data (Values in parentheses denote percentages)

PROBLEMS FACED BY THE GROUP

Groups consisting of women with diverse nature and habits face difficulty in organising and managing the affairs for the common benefit. They sometimes disagree with matters in one way or other. Table 8 shows that majority groups (63.3%) experience no problem in the conduct of group activities. Rest of the groups confront with problems like passive attitude of members, difference of opinion among members, irregular loan repayment and 14 groups (9.3%) face all such problems. Groups with capable leaders to coordinate and control activities with the cooperation, mutual understanding and financial discipline of the members help to conduct group activities without encountering problems. The need for convincing members about the significance of group approach and properly orienting the group leaders for lenient dealings with members are identified as solution. The role of NGOs in this regard is highly emphasized in this context.

Table 8. Problems Encountered in the Conduct of Group Activity

Problems	*Passive attitude of members*	*Diff. of opinion among members*	*Irregular Repay-ment of loan*	*Comb ination of all*	*No problems*	*Total*
North	9(18)	4(8)	1(2)	6(12)	30(60)	50(100)
Central	10(20)	7(14)	2(4)	5(10)	26(52)	50(100)
South	3(6)	4(8)	1(2)	3(6)	39(78)	50(100)
Total	22(14.7)	15(10)	4(2.7)	14(9.3)	95(63.3)	150(100)

Source: Survey data (Values in parentheses denote percentages)

OTHER GROUP ACTIVITIES

Groups aiming at economic progress of the members are not confined to monetary dealings alone but do take up community development programmes also. Involvement in social activities demonstrates the social commitment that the groups could develop and adds to their visibility as a social organization in the society. A variety of programmes are conducted by the group, viz., village cleaning process, road construction work, conducting awareness seminar in women related subjects, involvement in anti-drug campaign and various women development programmes. A change in the attitude of women is reflected as they actively participate in several welfare measures of the society.

Reaching a level of maturity in its financial dealings and acquiring skill and competence induce certain groups to take up economic activities. They invest owned and borrowed funds with the confidence to carry out profitable enterprises. Tasting success by such groups in their venture attracts other groups in the nearby area to take up the same line of activity. As a consequence surplus of some product or service appears in the local market, creating problem to all in the field. Competition comes in the form of reduced price for quality products or production of same variety of products. Number of groups facing competition is more in southern region compared to other regions. Awareness about the imperilment of competition among the groups should be created. Motivation for initiating new line of activities needs to be imparted to them instead of one group imitating the other.

SUGGESTIONS

- The practice of dividing the common fund when accumulated into a larger amount by some of the groups should be discouraged. In fact the amount should be channelised for productive investment.

- Members should be properly advised to sort out minute issues in the conduct of group activities and to look for compromise within the group.
- Effective monitoring system is essential for any group activity and hence frequent interaction and monthly review of performance should be made by the NGOs for the growth and sustainability of SHGs.
- NGOs should take initiative to convene meetings of all groups together and discourage unhealthy competition posed by similar type of enterprises taken up by neighboring groups.
- A good data base on micro finance and the working of SHGs in each district should be maintained by NABARD, collecting information from various NGOs and banks. Success stories, if published may motivate others for better performance. NABARD should take initiative to exercise proper supervision of such work done.

CONCLUSION

SHGs have made a mark in the social life of rural economy in the state of Kerala, catalyzing flow of rural credit especially to women. The system is accepted as a vibrant tool for attaining economic independence and thereby to improve social status for women in rural household. However the goal set forth by the SHGs continues to be within the limits of easy access to micro-credit and to the maximum of setting up small enterprises. Being rated as an effective intervention to address the problems related to rural women, and poor households, the system has a place in the society, which shall be continued for a bright future.

REFERENCES

1. Karmarkar. K.G. (1999): Rural Credit and Self Help Groups, Micro-finance Needs and Concepts in India, New Delhi: Sage Publications.
2. State Focus Paper.(2009-10): Kerala, National Bank for Agriculture and Rural Development
3. Progress under Micro finance-Highlight., Status of Micro Finance in India. (2009-10): www.nabard.org/pdf

15

Questions on Financial Inclusion: Credit Requirements and Credit Sources of Low Income Groups - Need for New Credit Facility Models and Products

K. Sajan
M. A. Joseph

INTRODUCTION - FINANCIAL INCLUSION AND CREDIT SUPPLY

Financial inclusion- which means the provision of affordable financial services, including credit facility- of the disadvantaged and low income groups is a financial approach discussed extensively in India. Though its history can be traced from the objectives of creation of State Bank of India in 1955, nationalization of banks in 1969 and 1980 with sole objective of making banking accessible to every Indian, Lead District approach started in 1970 in which a bank in a district is given the responsibility of all round development of that district; establishment of Regional Rural Banks in 1975, Bank Linkage Programme (with Self Help Group- initially through savings and later through loan products) in 1992 and introduction of the *Kisan* Credit Card[1] scheme of 2001; the term financial inclusion got a place in the policy documents only in 2004. Through the Annual Policy Statement of the RBI for 2004-05, the then Governor, Dr. Y V Reddy stated, "... *While commercial considerations are no doubt important, the banks have been bestowed with several privileges, especially of seeking public deposits on a highly leveraged basis, and consequently they should be obliged to provide banking services to all segments of the population, on equitable basis.*"

As a positive measure, Reserve Bank through its Annual Policy Statement 2005-06 and in the Mid Term Review of the Policy 2005-06 had urged banks to review their existing practices so as to support the objectives of financial inclusion. Thus a number of measures were undertaken to attract the financially excluded population into the structured financial system from November 2005. Important among them were, 'no-frills' bank account with low or nil minimum balances and changes in the procedures like Know Your Customer for opening an account. Further, banks were permitted to utilise the services of NGOs, Micro-Finance Institutions and Self Help Groups as intermediaries in providing financial and banking services in Business Facilitator and Business Correspondent models.

In order to extend hassle-free credit to rural customers; the terms, conditions and guidelines on credit schemes were simplified. To enable rural customers' access on credit, *Kisan* Credit Cards - credit cards without insistence on security, purpose or end-use of credit - were made popular. Banks were advised to frame separate guidelines for each states, for a state-specific approach, to be evolved by the State-Level Bankers' Committee. For effective reach and to meet the challenges of financial inclusion such as; lack of adequate infrastructure, higher transaction costs and low volumes of transactions, IT-enabled services were used. More over new bank branches were opened in rural areas.

Outcome of these efforts were a massive increase in 'no frills' bank accounts. Kochhar, Sameer (2009) says that, between 2006 - 2007 financial year, 6 million new 'no frills' bank accounts were opened and from April 2007 to May 2009 it was 25.1 million. At the same time the Report on Trend and Progress of Banking in India 2006-07, of the RBI estimated that the credit support to the rural poor households was only of Rupees 223 billion, while the estimated requirements were of Rupees 4500 billion. The question is whether this massive opening of the accounts had a positive effect on the financial inclusion and financial needs of the disadvantaged and low income groups? This is a question to be answered. This study is an attempt made to answer certain selected segments of this problem.

REVIEW OF RELATED LITERATURE

There had been a few studies in India in the field of financial inclusion and non-institutional source of credit. But it is surprising that while Money Lenders exist in all parts of the country and have considerable share in the informal credit, there is only a little research on their operations. Important studies, essays and other relevant literatures related to present study ware reviewed and summarised.

Subbarao[2](2009) stated the importance, reasons and the extent of financial exclusion in India and various measures taken by the Central Bank to tackle this problem. He concluded that financial inclusion can be a win-win opportunity for the poor, for the banks and for the nation because of growing incomes, improving awareness levels and rising aspirations of the poor.

Chakrabarty[3] (2009) affirmed, '*...the belief that Credit is a Human Right as advocated by Nobel Laureate Professor Muhammad Yunus, and the poor can overcome poverty by generating their own employment and income, we have to develop a financial system which takes care of the needs of the poor on an urgent basis. Access to affordable financial services - especially credit and insurance - enlarges livelihood opportunities and empowers the poor to take charge of their lives.*' He believes that financial inclusion can help both in social and in sustainable economic growth.

Kochhar, Sameer (2009) studied the financial inclusion programmes in India and stated that, improving financial access in a way that benefits the poor requires a strategy for inclusion that goes well beyond credit for poor households. There is need for the 'Credit Plus' approach. Even in developed economies expanding access is an important challenge. He also pointed that, it is not enough to say that the market will provide, but it requires staff skills and systems that are different from those required by organisations engaged only in lending. The study also recommended that financial inclusion should be declared a national priority. It also gives lights on present state of financial inclusion in the country.

Salagrama, Venkatesh and Thaddeus, Koriya (2008) found that:

> *"... partly because of existing rules and partly because of a woman's savings record, the money she can get as loan from a self-help group is limited. It limits her ability to invest in business to capitalize on an opportunity. Private moneylenders give credit based on opportunities. ... In other words, credit from banks*

> *and self-help groups programmes still remain largely in the development mode and not in the commercial mode. The opposite is true with private moneylenders. There are other points about self-help groups credit, which reduces its effectiveness in meeting women's credit needs. ....Another advantage is that private moneylenders have over formal systems is that they share in the risk. When a fisher loses his or her investment for any reason, the private moneylender quickly helps him to restart operations in order to get his original investment back. In formal streams, a loan must be repaid irrespective of how it is performing. ...Fishers fail to get credit when they need it the most. In the self-help groups, largely artificial distinctions are made between consumption and production needs to assess the need for credit. This is a handicap when credit is a livelihood strategy for parts of the year. Lack of access to credit for consumption has a direct impact on the productive capacity of the household."*

Agrawal (2008) pointed the importance of financial inclusion and highlighted various policies adopted in India. He was of the opinion that the financial inclusion can help people to come out of abject poverty conditions. He also cautions that the financial markets must act responsibly and ensure that the spirit of financial inclusion is not breached in the future.

Committee on Financial Inclusion (2008) outlined the basic strategy for building an inclusive financial sector and recommended, effecting improvements within the existing formal credit delivery mechanism and suggested measures for improving credit absorption capacity, especially amongst marginal and sub-marginal farmers and poor non-cultivator households. It also stressed the importance of using technology and *evolving new models* for effective outreach.

Rangarajan[4] (2007) stated in a lecturer on financial

inclusion that, "*There is need for an attitudinal change, there is need for a change in organisational structure and there is need for innovative models of delivery at the doorstep. Financial inclusion is no longer an option, it is a compulsion.*"

Rao, Preethi (2007) had studied the working of *Chit funds* and the difficulties they face in their business. Questionnaire based interview technique was used to collect data from samples of *Chit fund* managers in Chennai. Main findings were that the *Chit funds* are a very good tool for financing the activities of small businesses and the regulatory hurdles that the *Chit* companies' face due to the stringent rules proposed by the Government had been a setback to the growth of the industry. The recommendation was to promote this concept and to conduct more rigorous research on the issues they face.

Jeromi, P. D. (2007) had analysed the working of money lenders in Kerala based on primary data. He attempted to critically review legal provisions, existing regulatory framework and supervision of money lenders. Suggestions of the study were to amend the provisions of Kerala Money Lenders Act 1958, to effectively control and supervise the working of money lenders and to enact a new legislation to protect the interests of depositors. He also recommended the Government to set up a separate wing for policy formulation, monitoring and supervision of money lenders.

Leeladhar[5] (2005) in a speech detailed the need, importance, present Indian scenario of financial inclusion and various steps towards financial inclusion. He is of the view that, '*...banks need to redesign their business strategies to incorporate specific plans to promote financial inclusion of low income group treating it both a business opportunity as well as a corporate social responsibility. They have to make use of all available resources including technology and expertise available with them as well as the MFIs and NGOs..... Financial inclusion can emerge as commercial profitable business. Only the banks should be* *prepared to think outside the box!'*

NEED AND SIGNIFICANCE OF THE STUDY

A recent study by *SKOCH* Development Foundation[6] shows only 11% of 25.1 Million *'No-Frill'* bank accounts opened between April 2007 and May 2009 are operational. It shows that the *Business Facilitator* and *Business Correspondent* models suggested by RBI to spread banking services across the country have failed. In March 2010, in an interview with CNBC-TV18, K.C. Chakrabarty, Deputy Governor, Reserve Bank of India, stated, "*Bank account will not give anything. When the transaction happens in the bank account and that is why we say no frill account is not financial inclusion, when the transaction takes place in that no frill account then the financial inclusion takes place*".

RBI's Report on Currency and Finance 2006-08, reviles that the percentage of people having bank accounts goes on reeducating as their annual income reduces (Table 1). This trend is same both in rural and urban areas. Only 34.1% of the urban and 26.8% of the rural population, whose total earnings in a year is less than Rupees 50,000, has a bank account.

Table 1. Earners Having a Bank Account-2007

(Percent of Total Earners)

Annual Income	*Urban*	*Rural*	*Total*
< 50,000	34.1	26.8	28.3
50,000 – 100,000	75.5	71.2	73.0
100,000 – 200,000	91.8	87.4	89.9
200,000 – 400,000	95.5	93.6	94.9
> 400,000	98.0	96.3	97.6
All	61.7	38.0	44.9

Source: Report on Currency and Finance 2006-08.

The All India Debt and Investment Survey (2003) has revealed that share of institutional agencies in the total cash dues of urban households had increased from 72% in 1991to 75.1% in 2002 and that of moneylenders had also increased during the period from 10.2% to 14.1%. In the case of rural households, the share of institutional agencies had declined from 64% in 1991 to 57.1% in 2002. And more significantly, the share of moneylenders had increased in the same period from 17.5% to 29.6% in the case of rural households. The survey reveals that out of every Rupees 1,000 outstanding of farmer households in the country, Rupees 257 was sourced from moneylenders in the country and it is Rupees 74 in Kerala.

Report on Currency and Finance 2006-08, evidences that the percentage of indebted earners who depends money lenders for credit requirements is inversely correlated with their income (Table 2). While 34.9% of indebted earners having annual income less than Rupees 50,000 bracket depend on Money Lenders for credit; it is only 5.5% for persons having an income above Rupees 400,000. But the Bank credit use shows a positive relationship with the annual income. Only 13.0% of the indebted earners having annual income less than Rupees 50,000 use bank credit. At the same time 62.8% persons having an income above Rupees 400,000 are using bank credit.

The tables 3, 4 and 5 were adapted from RBI's Report on Currency and Finance 2006-08. It shows that 26.3% of the total loan taken by the earning population is for meeting financial emergency in rural area and it is 31.0% in urban area. Meeting financial emergency is the single largest item among the various purposes of taking loan both in rural and urban areas. From the table 4 and 5 it is clear that, for the emergency financial requirements people approach non-institutional sources (29.4%) rather than the institutional sources (19.6%).

Table 2. Sources of Loans

(Percent of Indebted Earners)

Annual Income	*Banks*	*Money Lenders*	*Other Institutional & Non-Institutional Sources*	*Total*
< 50,000	13.0	34.9	52.1	100
50,000 – 100,000	34.5	19.6	45.9	100
100,000 – 200,000	49.3	12.0	38.7	100
200,000 – 400,000	51.6	11.8	36.6	100
> 400,000	62.8	5.5	31.7	100

Source: Report on Currency and Finance 2006-08.

Table 3. Purpose of Loan

No. of Loan Taking Earners in million (Percentage to Total)

Purpose of Loan (All Sources)	*Rural*	*Urban*
Meeting Financial Emergency	20.2 (26.3)	4.7 (31.0)
Medical Emergency	12.5 (16.3)	1.8 (11.7)
Business Needs	7.1 (9.3)	2.1 (14.0)
Others	36.8 (47.1)	6.5 (43.3)
Total	76.6 (100)	15.1 (100)

Source: Report on Currency and Finance 2006-08.

Table 4. Purpose of Loan

No. of Loan Taking Earners in million (Percentage to Total)

From Non-Institutional Sources	*Rural*	*Urban*
Meeting Financial Emergency	15.4 (29.4)	3.4 (34.3)
Medical Emergency	10.5 (20.1)	1.5 (14.8)
Business Needs	3.9 (7.5)	1.2 (12.3)
Others	22.6 (43.0)	3.8 (38.6)
Total	52.4 (100)	9.9 (100)

Source: Report on Currency and Finance 2006-08.

Analysing data and related literature, we found that merely having a bank account cannot solve the financial needs of the low income groups. There are some specific reasons due to which Money Lenders and other non-institutional credit source were largely used by the low income groups in rural and urban area than the Bank finance. Thus we conducted a study with the below given objectives.

Table 5. Purpose of Loan

No. of Loan Taking Earners in million (Percentage to Total)

From Institutional Sources	*Rural*	*Urban*
Meeting Financial Emergency	4.8 (19.6)	1.3 (24.9)
Medical Emergency	2.0 (8.1)	0.3 (6.0)
Business Needs	3.2 (13.0)	0.9 (17.1)
Others	14.3 (59.3)	2.8 (52.0)
Total	24.2 (100)	5.3 (100)

Source: Report on Currency and Finance 2006-08.

OBJECTIVES OF THE STUDY

The study was designed to answer a part of the felt problem - whether the various measures taken by the Reserve Bank of India and other related agencies for financial inclusion of the disadvantaged and low income groups were effective in the sense of their credit requirements? What are the specific reasons due to which Money Lenders and non-institutional source are largely used by the low income groups than the Bank finance? Thus the specific objectives of the study were:

- What is the most important financial need of the low income groups?
- What was/is the important source of credit to these low income groups?
- How the Non-institutional source of credit used by the

low income groups works?

- What is the rate at which the non-institutional source and Money Lenders lend?
- To put forward suggestions and commend on the findings.

STUDY LIMITATIONS

The study was carried out in a limited time and on limited sample size; thus the time factor and sample size were the important constraints of the study. Due to the peculiarities of the topic of the study, a few subjects – like Money lenders - were reluctant to be a direct participant in the data collection process. Data from such segments were collected indirectly and it is a limitation. Samples collected were based on convenient sampling technique thus all the limitations of such sampling applies here also. But the researchers had made all the efforts to overcome these limitations and the study results were capable of generalization.

SAMPLE AND METHODOLOGY

The study was carried out in Kasaragod and Kannur districts of Kerala State. The data were collected from the sample through direct personal interview with unstructured questions. In the case of samples coming under Money Lenders category, data were collected through indirect interview over telephone and in a few cases third party interviews were done. It was due to fear of the local Money Lenders in revealing their identity.

While studying the Unregistered *Chitty Fund Organizers* and *Kurri Runners,* the *Chitty Funds* operated by the co-operative societies and co-operative banks were kept out of the preview of the present study. Similarly all the *Chitty Funds* operated by the Governmental agencies such as Kerala State Financial Enterprise Ltd were also not studied.

Table - 6 gives the summary of samples from whom the data were collected, in order to study the low income groups, who use informal credit sources and Table -7 gives the summary of the samples of informal credit sources from which the data were collected for the study.

Table 6. Sample of the Low Income Groups Who Use Informal Credit Sources

Categories of Low Income Groups Studied	*Kasaragod*	*Kannur*	*Total*
Small Income Earning Persons	12	08	20
Small Fixed Shop Traders	11	07	18
Hawkers & Peddlers (Fish, Vegetable &Small Tea Shops)	10	09	19
Total	**33**	**24**	**57**

Table 7. Sample of the Informal Credit Sources

Categories of the Credit Sources Studied	*Kasaragod*	*Kannur*	*Total*
Unregistered *Kurri Runners*	06	05	11
Unregistered *Chitty Fund Organizers*	05	03	08
Local Money Lenders	03	02	05
Total	**14**	**10**	**24**

Data collected were qualitative and elaborative in nature. The outcome of the interviews were analysed, summarized and presented in accordance with the objectives of the study. While summarising the data, a few negligible differences in the interview documents were overlooked. For example, the time interval for receiving interest payments from creditors by local Money Lenders differ from 28 days, 30 days or one calendar month; while summarising it is taken as 28 days because of high frequency.

SUMMARY OF FINDINGS

The summary of findings is divided into two - findings relating to the working of informal credit sources and findings relating to credit needs, problems and significance of informal credit sources used by low income groups.

Summary of the Interviews with Various Informal Credit Sources

Informal credit sources used by the low income groups of the studied area differ widely from individual Money Lenders to informal association of persons like *Pana Payatt*[7]. In this study we have selected only three important informal credit sources such as unregistered *Chitty Fund* organizers, unregistered *Kurri Runners* and local Money Lenders.

Working of an unregistered *Chitty Fund.*

Workings of unregistered *Chitty Funds* are same as of registered *Chit* schemes which generally have a pre-fixed value and duration. Working of a registered *Chit fund* is detailed and then the main differences of unregistered *Chit fund* are compared.

A registered *Chit* scheme is a contract between the foreman and the subscribers where in subscriber agrees to remit a fixed amount of money every month for a pre fixed number of months. The total of the periodic subscription (*Installment Amount*) is called as the *Chitty Amount* (*Sala*) which is also pre fixed. The foreman admits members (*Tickets*) equal to the duration of the scheme who contributes the subscription every month to the *Chit Amount*. Then the *Chit Amount* is auctioned. The highest bidder wins the *Chit Amount* for that month. The maximum reduction (bid) possible is 25% as per the prevailing *Chitty* Act and if there is more than one subscriber interested in bidding at 25% reduction, the numbers of such bidders will be put to a 'lucky draw'. The bid amount is the discount which is reduced from the *Chit Amount* and the balance only is paid to the auction winner. Then the discount money is divided among the members as *'Profit'* and in the next month, the contribution is brought down by the amount of *'Profit'*. The foreman is entitled to a certain percentage of the *Chitty* amount, not more than 5% as per *Chitty* Act, as his commission from each member.

Example

Chitty Amount (*Sala*) = 1, 00,000.

Duration and No. of Members (*Tickets*) = 20.

Amount of subscription (*Installment Amount*) = 1, 00,000/20 = 5,000.

1st month total Contribution (*Chitty* Amount) = 20 X 5,000 = 1, 00,000.

Highest Bid: 20,000.

Then the Bidder gets Rupees 80,000 (1, 00,000 - 20,000).

Profit per Subscriber for the 1st month = 20,000/20 =1,000.

Amount of subscription for the 2nd month = 5,000-1,000 = 4,000.

2nd month's *Chitty* Amount = (20 X 4,000) + 20,000 (1st months bid amount) = 1,00,000.

2nd month's Highest Bid: 18,000.

Then the Bidder gets Rupees 82,000 (1, 00,000 - 18,000).

Profit per Subscriber for the 2nd month = 18,000/20 = 900

And it goes on till the 20th month.

Local variation in the operation of unregistered *Chit fund* (*Chitty / Kurri*).

Unregistered *Chit* funds operate in different ways and locally known as *Bar Chitty / Bar Kurri*. Here the *Chit* fund subscribers had to contribute the prefixed subscription amount regularly, without reducing the bid amount. The bid (*Bar*) amount will be carried forward to the next auction. Again the bid amount for the 2nd month is added with the bid amount of the 1st month and the cumulative amount is carried forward to the 3rd month. This process goes on till the bid amount becomes large enough to conduct an additional auction in a month. It means there will be two auctions in that month reducing the total periods (months) by one. This process continuous and results in the reduction of more moths from the total period. The end result will be that a *Chitty* which is to be ended after a specific period say 20 months, will end well in advance (before the 20th month) say after 16 or 17 months. But the total auctions will be equal to the proposed duration. It happens because there will be more than one auction (generally two) in a few months reducing the total duration.

Example:

Chitty Amount (*Sala*) = 1, 00,000;

Duration and No. of Members (*Tickets*) = 20.

Amount of subscription (*Installment Amount*) = 1,00,000/20 = 5,000.

1st month total Contribution (*Chitty* Amount) = 20 X 5,000 = 1,00,000.

Highest Bid: 28,000.

Then the Bidder gets Rupees 72,000. (1,00,000- 28,000)

Balance (Bid amount) = 28,000

Amount of subscription for the 2nd month = 5,000

2nd month's *Chitty* Amount = (20 X 5,000) = 1,00,000.

2nd month's Highest Bid: 25,000.

Then the Bidder gets Rupees 75,000 (1, 00,000- 25,000).

Cumulated Bid amount = 28,000 + 25,000 = 53000.

Suppose in the 3rd month the highest bid was rupees 23000; then the balance (cumulated) amount in the bid account will be 76000(53000+23000).

And in 4th month is possible to conduct 2 *Chitties* at a time. One with the regular subscription received and the other from the balance in the bid account. And this process goes on till twenty *Chitties*, in number, are over. (Twenty numbers will be over before the completion of twenty months). Profit to the subscribers is the early completion of the *Chitty*. They need to pay only a less number of installments than the prefixed numbers without a change in the *Chitty* amount (*Sala*).

Variations in working between registered and unregistered *Chit fund*.

1. Ownership : Owners of the registered *Chit funds* are generally individuals, firms or corporate bodies who had taken registration under respective *Chit fund* Acts and operate for profit. Owners of unregistered *Chit funds* are Not for Profit Organisations such as Clubs, Schools, Religious Organisations / Institution, Professional Associations, Group of Individuals having same interest and in a few cases individuals. In most cases motive is to raise fund for acquiring assets or for meeting working capital needs. But if the owner is an individual then the fund is operated for profit.

2. Security : Security is a compulsory requirement for a registered *Chit funds*. The highest bidder gets the money only on providing adequate security. In unregistered *Chit funds,* there is no need of security. The foreman provides the money to the bidder based on personal relationship and mutual trust.

3. Subscribers Characteristics : In the case of registered *Chitty Funds,* the subscriber can be any person who agrees to meet the contractual liabilities under the *Chit fund* Act which rules the *Chitty* scheme. In an unregistered *Chit fund,* the members are individuals who are personally known to the foreman. It means there will be clear personal / social relationship between the foreman and the subscribers.

4. Bid Limitations : The maximum reduction possible from the *Chitty* amount as bid amount is 25% as per the prevailing *Chitty* Act and if there is more than one subscriber interested in bidding at 25% reduction, the numbers of such bidders will be put to a draw. In the case of unregistered *Chit funds* there is no such restriction.

5. Foreman's Commission : The foreman is entitled to a certain percentage - not more than 5% - of the *Chitty* amount as his commission from each member in the case registered *Chit funds*. It unregistered *Chit funds*; commission is equal to the *Chitty Amount* (*Sala*). It means foreman's commission from each member is equal to one subscription.

Working of Unregistered *Kurries*

In some parts of the area studied, *Kurries* and *Chitties* are used interchangeably. But they are basically different. *Kurries,* which have colloquial names such as *Ambala*[9] *Kurri / Veetha*[10] *Kurri,* work in a different way. A *Kurri,* in general, will have duration of one year and the closing date will be fixed based on some important events like *Onam*[11] or local religious festivals.

Kurries, like *Chitties,* are generally operated by Not for Profit Organisations such as Clubs, Schools, Religious Organisations/ Institution and in few cases by individuals. The working of a typical *Kurri* is as follows.

Like a *Chit fund, Kurri Runners* also collect periodic subscription from the subscriber, which is known as *Share*. *Share* can be any amount starting from Rupees 5, and in multiple of 5, based on the capacity of the subscriber. Normally the subscription is collected in a time interval of 14 days (Two weeks). There are several local variations to this period such as 7 days, 30 days etc. The *Share,* thus collected will be distributed to the person / persons, preferably a subscriber to the scheme, who is in need of money. General principle is that only 70% of the total amount paid by a subscriber as *Share* can be given to him as loan. Further, loan from a *Kurri fund* can be given only to a person who is a subscriber of the *scheme.* But it is a universal practice to lend the maximum possible amount after analysing the need, payment history and ability to repay. It will be decided by the *Kurri Runner* (Foreman). Loan from a *Kurri fund* is also given to outsiders, who are not subscribers, but personally known and trusted by the *Kurri Runner,* if no subscriber is in need of money or if there is available balance. The rate of interest is high when compared to bank rate but low when compared to Money Lenders. Normal rate charged by Kurri Runners is 3% monthly (roughly 36% annually) on the amount outstanding. Important point is that, interest thus collected is not the income of the *Kurri Runner* but it is divided among the subscribers in proportion to their *Share*. The people who take the loan have to pay the interest monthly and can settle the loan amount at any time. If such person is a subscriber, then he can settle the outstanding on closing of the fund with the amount due to him. The revenue of the *Kurri Runner* (Foreman) is one *Share* amount from each subscriber. He is responsible to collect *Share* amount, interest on loan and due amounts. He is also responsible to keep proper account of the fund.

Working of the Local Money Lenders.

Local money lenders' working in the study area is same as in the other parts of the country. Following are the important facts observed through interview with regards to the working of the local Money Lenders.

1. Rate of Interest : The rate of interest charged by them is very high. The rate is in between 4% to 6% per month. The rate of interest will differ based on social acceptance of the borrower, quantum of money required, financial strength and repayment history. Money lenders charge different rates on different persons at the same period of time. It a universal practice among the lenders to collect the interest monthly.

2. Lending Period and Security : Lending is done generally for a period of one year or less. The security needed will be three times of the principal amount plus the total interest payable for the credit period. Security can be post dated cheques along with a written agreement in the case of salaried persons and in all other cases title-deed of the land or gold is need. Now it a common practice among Money Lenders to accept gold as a security than land.

Very short lending for a day or two is a practice in the urban area. Rate of interest vary in between Rupees 8 to 10 for each 100 Rupee per day. Only amount after reducing the interest amount in advance is given as loan. Illustrating this, if a person takes a loan for Rupee 100 at an interest rate of Rupee 8 per day, then he will get only Rupees 92 in the morning and in the evening he has to repay Rupees 100. Hawkers and peddlers engaged in the business of fish, vegetable or small tea shops are the main user of this credit. They are in need of additional fund due to variation in prices or as working capital. The peculiar feature of day lending is that it will have duration of 12 to 48 hours only. Lending is done on trust and no security is needed.

3. Existence of a Middle Man : Another feature noted in the presented study that differs from many previous studies is the existence of a middle man. The study revealed that the local Money Lender uses the help of a socially accepted person in the locality in lending money. He acts as a link between the person in need of money and the Money Lender. He also pretends the role of guarantor of the borrower for ensuring smooth repayment of interest and principal. It is also found that in most cases middle man gets commission from the Money Lender.

Summary of the Interview with Various Low Income Groups Who Uses Informal Credit Sources

The study was carried out to know the important financial needs, various credit requirements, credit sources and reason for low use of bank credit by the low income groups. Low income groups, for this study means; small income earning persons, small fixed shop traders and hawkers / peddlers (fish, vegetable & small tea shops) as detailed in table 6. The response collected through interview from the various categories of low income groups did not differ in their perception with regards to different objectives of the study. Thus the important findings are summarised and listed below as a single unit.

1. Important Financial Need : The most important financial need of low income groups is the availability of low rated, hassle-free credit. Sample size studied confirmed this with a 100% tally mark. This was the most important financial need than having a bank account or using other financial services such as taking DD, bill payment or getting insurance product. It was found that 53 out of 57 sample population studied had at least one bank account. It constitutes 93 % of the total sample.

2. Credit Needs : Meeting medical emergency is the most important credit need of low income groups. For this, the needy person may approach Money Lenders which is the least preferred informal source.

Second important credit need of low income groups is the business need of exploiting an opportunity such as, selling vegetables / flowers in the *onam* season or selling crackers in the *Vishu*[12] /*Deepavali*[13] or for meeting short term working capital requirements. The low income group mostly uses either *Chitty* or *Kurry* funds for this purpose since the need can be anticipated.

Third important credit requirement of the low income groups are the timely repayment of the installments of comparatively larger loans they have taken from banks or other formal credit sources. This credit may be either for purchasing or acquiring assets like house or for meeting social obligations having large financial cost like marriage. Here the *Chitty* or *Kurri* funds act as a potential channel for saving small amounts so that the timely repayment of large loan installment amounts can be ensured.

3. Source of Credit : Most important credit source of the low income groups are *Chitty funds* followed by *Kurries.* The least preferred source of credit is Money Lenders. Though the bank or institutional credit is preferred than Money Lenders, it is an unapproachable source due to many reasons.

4. Problems with the Bank credit : Bank credit is the less preferred source of credit to the low income groups than *Chitty funds* or *Kurries* due to following reasons.

Most significantly, the credit from a *Chitty fund* or *Kurri* is having an element of savings. This is a periodic savings of small amounts which makes the low income groups eligible for comparatively large amount of credit without any effortful process and time. This is not possible in the case of bank or institutional credit.

Getting bank credit will takes an effortful process and long time which will obstruct the purpose of taking credit. Due to the nature of credit needs, it is not possible for the low income group to wait for bank or institutional credit. Attitude of the bankers towards the low income groups who they treat as less credit worthy is negative.

In *Chitty funds* or *Kurries* there is a group element which acts as a pressure or catalyst for ensuring prompt transaction among the low income groups. This lacks in the case of bank or institutional credit. It may result in late repayment and thus assessing them as low credit worthy customers.

In *Chitty funds* or *Kurries* a humanitarian consideration is possible and such consideration is not an exceptional case. For example in a *Chitty* the bid amount can be a negligible due to abstention of other subscribers from bidding because of certain humanitarian consideration towards the bidder. It is because, in *Chitty funds* or *Kurries,* participants know each other so that an individual consideration is possible. None of this is possible in bank or institutional credit.

FINDINGS

Present study on the non-institutional credit sources, credit requirements and credit sources of selected low income groups - give out the following significant findings.

1. Having a bank account cannot solve the problem of financial inclusion. Most important financial problem faced by the low income groups is the problem of getting cheep and timely credit. This finding goes along with the findings of Salagrama, Venkatesh and Thaddeus, Koriya. (2008); RBI's report on Currency and Finance 2006-08 (2008) and NSSO (2005).
2. Among the various credit needs of the low income groups, the most important one is to meet the medical emergencies, followed by business needs and short term working capital requirements. Third important credit need is for timely repayment of the large loan's installment.
3. There are number of problems faced by the low income groups when they approach the banks for credit. Getting credit having favourable condition to satisfy the *most important credit needs* is almost an impossible task to low income groups. Bankers' attitude towards the low income groups, whom they treat less credit worthy, is very negative.
4. In the case of unregistered *Chitty funds* and *Kurries*, the benefit of high rates (*bid/bar* or high rate of interest as the case may be) goes to the members. It is a group effort that works on mutual trust and belief. The lion's share of the scheme's benefits goes to members. Moreover there is a humanitarian consideration while lending in exceptional cases.
5. Unlike bank or other institutional credit, the credit schemes in *Chitty funds* and *Kurries* is directly related to Savings element. A person in need of a credit has to

initiate an obligatory savings by way of *subscription* or *share*. This automatically ensures the repayment of the loan if any. It was found that the amount of bad debts is nil or negligible in unregistered *Chitty funds* and *Kurri* schemes.

6. Due to the high lending rate and inhuman behaviour, credit from the local Money Lenders is the least preferred source. Normally, the low income groups approach the Local Money Lenders when they have to meet some medical emergencies. Now it is a usual practice among the Money Lenders to lend through a socially accepted intermediary and in most cases they get commission.
7. Hawkers and peddlers, who are engaged in the business of fish, vegetable or small tea shops, are the main users of the 'Day Lending' done by the Money Lenders. This is the most exploited category among the low income groups due to high rate of interest. At the same time there is no other credit source from where these hawkers and peddlers could get a credit for 12 to 48 hours and without a security.
8. There is a towering need for new group based and savings related credit product that can offer common man an easy and cheep source of credit.

SUGGESTIONS

Based on the significant findings of the study, we put forward a few suggestions for further deliberations and dialogues by the academic community, policy makers, Governments, Regulators, and Bankers. These suggestions may improve the present state of financial inclusion and can guide future policy formulation.

1. The programme of financial inclusion should start from answering the vital question - 'What is the significant

financial need of a common man particularly of small income groups?' Only then such an inclusion programme can be successful. Here a planning from the bottom approach is needed.

2. Deliberations and discussions for the development of a new *Banking Product* having the important features of unregistered *Chitty funds* and *Kurries* are needed. Such a *Banking Product* should offer a credit facility linked to savings and should have a group element.

3. An improved system, from what is presently adopted by the micro finance institutions promoted by the Government, can be considered for providing adequate credit at low cost to the small income groups.

4. A product similar to that of Call Money Market ought to be introduced in the urban and rural areas in small scale. This can satisfy the very short term credit needs of the low income groups like hawkers and peddlers. This can improve the living standard of them. The objective behind the establishment of Regional Rural Banks was to create a supplementary channel for flow of credit from the central money markets to the rural areas through refinance for supporting productive activities in the rural areas (Estimates Committee: 13th Lok Sabha, 2003). Steps should be taken to materialise this objective.

5. Establishing new specialised Co-operative Societies for providing credit facilities having duration of 12 hours to 3 months can be considered by the Government. Alternatively the Government can consider providing such credit facilities through the existing specialised Co-operative Societies established for the sole benefit of a specific group such as fisher man or vegetable marketers.

6. A major research may be conducted to study the

different ways through which the common people satisfy their credit requirements. Present study revealed that the Money Lenders are not the impotent source of non-institutional credit. There are sources like unregistered *Chitty funds, Pana Payattu* and *Kurries.* A detailed study of such sources can aid in formulation of a better credit product for the rural and low income peoples.

CONCLUSION

A news report published by *The Hindu* on 17th August 2010, titled, '*Microfinance for small-time traders soon*' says that in Karnataka, a microfinance scheme will be introduced through co-operative banks that facilities small-time traders to get a loan ranging from rupees 1000 to 50000, at low interest rates of 10%, to free them from the clutches of private money lenders and finance companies. We see this as a positive measure by the Karnataka Government in satisfying the credit needs of the small income groups like small traders. A financial inclusion programme, like any other programme for common people should start from the targeted population; from their needs, wants and peculiar characteristics. It should not be something that is coming from upper levels but it should start from bottom level. Only then the objectives of such programmes can be achieved. A research on various credit sources used by the rural and low income people in India will help in formulating new credit products that can serve them in a better way.

REFERENCES

1. Agrawal, Amol. (2008), *The need for Financial Inclusion with an Indian perspective.* Mumbai: IDBI Gilts Limited.
2. All India Debt and Investment Survey. (January-December 2003), NSSO 59th Round Report. Government of India.
3. Committee on Financial Inclusion. (2008), *Report of the*

Committee on Financial Inclusion; Economic Advisory Council to the Prime Minister. New Delhi: Government of India.

4. Estimates Committee: 13th Lok Sabha (April, 2003), *Regional Rural Banks.* (16th Report, Ministry of Finance and Company Affairs -Department of Economic Affairs – Banking Division) New Delhi: Lok Sabha Secretariat.

5. Jeromi, P. D. (2007), *Regulation of Informal Financial Institutions: A Study of Money Lenders in Kerala.* (Reserve Bank of India Occasional Papers Vol. 28, No.1) Mumbai: RBI.

6. Kochhar, Sameer. (2009), *Speeding Financial Inclusion.* Mumbai: Skoch Development Foundation.

7. Leeladhar, V. (2005), *Taking Banking Services to the Common Man -Financial Inclusion.* (Lecture at Federal bank 1/12/2005). Mumbai: RBI.

8. NABARD. (2006), *Profile-2006,* Mumbai: NABARD.

9. NSSO. (May, 2005), *Situation Assessment Survey of Farmers - Indebtedness of Farmer households.* (NSS 59th Round -January - December 2003) New Delhi: Government of India.

10. Pitt and Khandkar. (1995), *Grama Bank, Bangladesh Rural Advancement Committee RD12.* Dhaka: Government of Bangladesh. p 45-49.

11. Rao, Preethi. (2007), *Chit Funds - A Boon to the Small Enterprises.* (Working Paper Series, Small Enterprise Finance Centre) Chennai: Institute for Financial Management and Research.

12. Rangarajan C. (2007), *Financial Inclusion: Some Key Issues.* (Lecture at Mangalore University on 10/08/ 2007) Mumbai: RBI.

13. Reserve Bank of India (2005), *Annual Policy Statement 2004-05.* Mumbai: RBI.

14. _____ (2005), *Mid Term Review of the Policy 2005-06.* Mumbai: RBI.

15. _____ (2006), *Annual Policy Statement 2005-06.* Mumbai: RBI.

16. _____ (2008), *Report on Currency and Finance 2006-08.* Mumbai: RBI.

17. _____ (2007), *Report on Trend and Progress of Banking in India*

2006-07. Mumbai: RBI

18. Salagrama, Venkatesh. Thaddeus, Koriya. (2008), *Assessing Opportunities for Livelihood Enhancement and Diversification in Coastal Fishing Communities of Southern India*. Chennai: United Nations Team for Tsunami Recovery Support, UN India.
19. Subbarao, Duvvuri. (2009), *Financial Inclusion: Challenges and Opportunities*. (Talk at Bankers' Club on 9/12/2009. Kolkata) Mumbai: RBI.
20. The Hindu. (August 17, 2010), *Microfinance for small-time traders soon*. Bangalore Edition.
21. Thorat, Usha. (2007), *Financial Inclusion -The Indian Experience*. (Speech on 19/6/2007 at the HMT-DFID Financial Inclusion Conference, London). Mumbai: RBI.
22. http://www.hindu.com/2010/08/17/stories/2010081750780300.htm

16

Growth of Micro Credit and SHGs in India: An Evaluation

K . V Vinesh Kumar

INTRODUCTION

Worldwide economic analysts identified that the policy adopted during the period 1961-1970 did not achieve the goal of the first United Nations decade of the development of poorer nations. During the period of this policy it was not successful in yielding benefits from the reformulation of development goals, which seemingly aimed to take greater account of poverty and establish strategies to meet humanity's basic needs. The experiences of the three decades to 1990 led to a dominant argument that the development investments had not achieved the goal of transforming the poverty situation in poorer countries, and in many cases, the investments made had actually exacerbated the conditions in these countries. Following this, there were moves to develop a system based on micro credit facilities. As a result, during the 1990s, micro credit programme emerged as one of the mainstream development interventions to address poverty alleviation and to help women's empowerment particularly in developing countries (Hashemi *et al.*, 1996; Johnson and Roglay, 1997; Mayoux, 1998; Amin *et al.*, 1998; Kabeer, 1998; Ditchter, 1999; Wright, 1999; Rahman, 1999). Micro Credit is defined as provision of thrift, credit and other financial services and products of very small amount to the poor in rural, semi-urban and urban areas for enabling them to raise their income levels and improve living standards. Micro Credit Institutions are those, which provide these facilities. (As per RBI Master Circular, 2008). Micro credit is an alternative and a financially viable alternative to the previously existing methods of addressing poverty especially in the perspective of gender through the provision of credit. The emergence of micro credit in recent years has questioned the fundamentals of the credit system in developing countries for channelling credit to the poor .A Self Help Group (SHG) has an average size of about 15 people from a homogeneous class. They come together for addressing their common problems. They are encouraged to make voluntary thrift on a regular basis. They use this pooled resource to make small interest bearing loans to their members. The process helps them imbibe the essentials of financial intermediation including prioritisation of needs, setting terms and conditions, and accounts keeping. This gradually builds financial discipline in all of them. They also learn to handle resources of a size that is much beyond individual capacities of any of them.

MICRO CREDIT SYSTEM IN INDIA

There are two major models under microfinance, *i.e.*, Self-Help Group (SHG)-Bank Linkages and Micro-Finance Institutions (MFI) - Bank Linkages being operated in the country. Despite having a wide linkage of rural bank branches in India which executed detailed poverty alleviation programmes that sought creation of self-employment opportunities through bank credit for almost two decades a very large number of the poorest of the poor continued to remain outside of the crinkle of formal banking system. In this situation NABARD of India launched its pilot phase of SHG bank linkage programme in February 1992. The NABARD led pilot project instigated with the support of Reserve Bank of India from 1992 onwards aimed at promoting and financing 500 SHGS the entire country.The Reserve Bank of India (RBI) is highly concerned with soaring inflation and the humiliating impact of the weight of rising prices of essential commodities on the common man. The initial pilot study gained acceptance from the banking system and the results were promising, the RBI encouraged this positive initiative by issuing instructions to banks in 1996 to cover SHG financing as a main watercourse activity under their priority sector lending assortment.

SHG BANK LINKAGE PROGRAMME

The SHG - Bank Linkage Programme can be regarded as the most potent initiative since Independence for delivering financial services to the poor in a sustainable manner.SHG are the real grass root level set up for micro credit growth. They disclose the poorest sectors in rural setting as well as vesting around India. The SHG-Bank linkage programme in which SHGs are linked to banks in a gradual way-initially through savings and later through loan products- is considered to be an effective strategy to ensure financial inclusion. In this backdrop, this study has been undertaken with the specific objective of analysing the impact of SHG-Bank linkage agenda on the financial inclusion. The poor were encouraged to come together to save small amounts regularly and extent micro loans among themselves. The focus of micro finance initiatives is largely on those rural poor who have no access to the formal banking system. The target group broadly comprises small and marginal farmers, landless agricultural and agricultural labourers, artisans and crafts man and other rural poor engaged in small business such as vending and hawking. As per the operational guidelines of NABARD, SHGs are sanctioned saving linked loans by banks.

As on 31 March 2010, a total of 69.53 lakh SHGs were having saving bank accounts with the banking sector with outstanding savings of 6198.71 crore as against 61.21 lakh SHGs with savings of 5545.62 crore as on 31 March 2009, thereby showing a growth rate of 13.6 per cent and 11.8 per cent, respectively. Thus, more than 97 million poor households were associated with banking agencies under SHG-Bank Linkage Programme. Bank loans disbursed to SHG in the year 2009-10 was 15.86 lakhs SHGs with 14453 crores loans disbursed as against 16.09 lakh SHG with 12253 crores bank loans in 2008-09. The bank loans outstanding with SHGs 42.24 lakh SHGs improved to 48.51 lakh SHGs. The programme continued to enlist massive support of the rural poor women into the self-managed and door-step based micro-finance movement (Table 1).

As on 31 March 2010, the Commercial Banks lead with savings accounts of 40.53 lakh SHGs (58.3%) with savings amount of 3673.89 crore (59.3 %) followed by RRBs having savings bank accounts of 18.21 lakh SHGs (26.2%) with savings amount of 1299.37 crore (21.0%) and Cooperative Banks having savings bank accounts of 10.79 lakh SHGs (15.5 %) with savings amount of 1225.44 crore (19.8%). There is a massive level increase in the co-operative banking sector because most of the banks are operating in the rural sector(Table 2).

During 2009-10, banks have financed 15.87 lakh SHGs, including repeat loan to the existing SHGs, with bank loans of 14,453.30 crore as against 16.10 SHGs with bank loans of 12,253.51 crore during 2008-09, registering a decline of 1.4

Table 1. Growth of self-help group and micro credit in India

Particulars	*2007-08*		*2008-09*		*%growth 08-09*		*2009-10*		*%growth -09-10*	
	No of SHGs (lakhs)	*Amount (crores)*	*No of SHGs (lakhs)*	*Amount (crores)*	*No of SHGs (lakhs)*	*Amount (crores)*	*No of SHGs (lakhs)*	*Amount (crores)*	*No of SHGs (lakhs)*	*Amount (crores)*
Savings of SHGs with Bank	50	3785.3	61.21	5545.6	22.2	46.5	69.53	6198.7	13.6	11.8
Bank loans disbursed to SHGs	12.2	8849.2	16.09	12253.5	31.1	38.5	15.86	14453.3	1.4	17.9
Bank loans outstanding with SHGs	36.2	16999.9	42.24	22679.8	16.5	33.4	48.51	28038.2	14.8	23.6

Source: NABARD

Table 2. Saving with SHG agency wise positions in India

Agency	*Position as on*	*Total SHGs savings with the banks as on 31st march 2009-10 (Rs in crores)*			
		No of SHGs(lakhs)	*%share*	*Amount*	*%share*
Commercial bank (public & private sectors)	31-3-2009	35.49	58.0	2772.99	50.0
	31-3-2010	40.53	58.3	3673.89	59.3
	%growth	14.2		32.5	
RRBs	31-3-2009	16.29	26.6	1989.75	35.9
	31-3-2010	18.21	26.2	1299.37	21.0
	%growth	14.5		34.7	
Cooperative banks	31-3-2009	9.44	15.4	782.88	14.1
	31-3-2010	10.8	15.5	1225.44	19.8
	%growth	14.5		56.5	

Source: NABARD

per cent of SHGs but a growth of 17.9 per cent in bank loans disbursed. Out of the total loans disbursed during 2009-10, SHGs financed under SGSY accounted for 2.67 lakh (16.9%) with bank loan of 2198.00 crore (15.2%) as against 2.65 lakh SHGs (16.4%) with bank loan of 2015.22 crore (16.4%) during 2008-09. Growth rate of SHGs and its bank loan disbursed is high in the cooperative banking sector. It was 16.6 percentage SHGs and 34.1 percentages in bank amounts (Table 3).

Table 3. Bank loans Disbursed to SHGs

Agency	*Position as on*	*Total SHGs savings with the banks as on 31st March 2009-10(Rs in crores)*			
		No of SHGs (lakhs)	*%share*	*Amount*	*%share*
Commercial bank (public & private sectors	31-3-2009	1004587	62.4	8060.53	65.8
	31-3-2010	977521	61.6	9780.18	67.6
	%growth	2.7		21.3	
RRBs	31-3-2009	405569	25.2	3193.49	26.1
	31-3-2010	376797	23.7	3333.20	23.1
	%growth	7.1		4.4	
Cooperative banks	31-3-2009	199430	12.4	999.49	8.2
	31-3-2010	232504	14.7	1339.42	9.3
	%growth	16.6		34.1	

Source: NABARD

Based on the MIS, banks have financed to 691 MFIs with bank loans of 8062.74 crore as against 581 MFIs with bank loans of 3,732.33 crore during 2008-09, representing growth rate of 116.5 per cent in bank loans disbursed (Table 4). As on 31 March 2010, the outstanding bank loans to 1513

MFIs was ' 10147.54 crore as against 5009.09 crore to 1915 MFIs as on, 31 March 2009, showing doubling of bank loan over the previous year. Further, during the year 2009-10, SIDBI had financed to 88 MFIs with financial assistance of 2665.75 crore and the loan outstanding against 146 MFIs as on 31 March 2010 was 3808.20 crore. As such the total exposure of banks and financial institutions to MFIs as on 31 March 2010 was to the tune of 13955.74 crore (Table 5).

PROGRAMME IMPACT

The major findings and recommendations of three studies on the impact of the SHG - Bank Linkage Programme are summarised as

- Reduced the incidence of poverty through increase in income, and also enabled the poor to build assets and thereby reduce their vulnerability.
- Enabled households that have access to it to spend more on education than nonclient households. Families participating in the programme have reported better school attendance and lower dropout rates.
- Empowered women by enhancing their contribution to household income, increasing the value of their assets and generally by giving them better control over decisions that affect their lives.
- Reduced child mortality, improved maternal health and the ability of the poor to combat disease through better nutrition, housing and health - especially among women and children.
- Contributed to a reduced dependency on informal money lenders and other non-institutional sources.
- Facilitated significant research into the provision of financial services for the poor and helped in building "capacity" at the SHG level.

Table 4. MFI Bank Linkage in India

Particulars	*2007-08*		*2008-09*		*Growth during 08-09(%)*		*2009-10*		*Growth during 09-10(%)*	
	No of MFIs	*Amt.*	*No of MFIs*	*Amt.*	*No of MFIs*	*Amt.*	*No of MFIs*	*Amt.*	*No of MFIs*	*Amt.*
Bank loans disbursed to MFIs	518	1970.1	581	3732.3	12.2	89.4	691	8062.7	18.9	116.0
Bank loans outstanding to MFIs	1109	2748.8	1915	5009	72.7	82.2	1513	10147.5	21	102.6

Source: NABARD

Table 5. Bank loan provided MFI in India (agency wise)

Agency	*Years*	*Amount of loan disbursed to NGOs/MFIs*		*Loan out standing against NGOs/MFIs*	
		No. of MFIs	*Amt.*	*No. of MFIs*	*Amt.*
CBs (public,	2008-09	522	3,718.93	1,762	4,977.89
private,	2009-10	645	8,03861	1407	10,095.32
foreign)	%growth	23.5	116.2	20.1	102.8
RRBs	2008-09	59	13.40	153	331.20
	2009-10	46	24.14	103	52.22
	%growth	22	80.1	32.7	67.4
Co-op. Banks	2008-09	0	0.00	0	0.00
	2009-10	0	0.00	3	0.007
	%growth	NA	NA	NA	NA
Total all banks	2008-09	581	3,732.33	1,915	5,009.09
	2009-10	691	8062.74	1,513	10,147.54
	%growth	18.9	116.5	21.0	102.6
SIDBI	2009-10	88	2665.75	146	3808.20
Total all banks &SIDBI	2009-10	779	10728.49	1659	13955.74

Source: NABARD

- Finally, it has offered space for different stakeholders to innovate, learn and replicate. As a result, some NGOs have added micro-insurance products to their portfolios, a couple of SHG federations have experimented with undertaking livelihood activities and grain banks have been successfully built into the SHG model in the Eastern Region. SHGs in some areas have employed local accountants for keeping their books, and IT applications are now being explored by almost all for better management information sytems

(MIS), accounting and internal controls.

The main challenges facing the SHG - Bank linkage model are:

- The pace of expansion of the programme.
- The role of NGOs is very low
- The per capita credit outlays are small and not commensurate with the costs involved in.
- Bringing the SHGs to the banking main stream.
- SHGs working with multiple agenda especially for government sponsored programmes.
- RBI and Government as part of their development role, NABARD, which is spearheading this programme, and banks who are the main promoters of the programe, may initiate the following effective steps to overcome these shortcomings:
- The long term sustainability of the SHG model may require a federal structure, without severing the linkages that the SHGs have with the local bank branches. The assumption that the federation structure should not be supplanted on the SHGs and can be addressed when the demand emerges needs reconsideration.
- Database of SHGs and MFI is the main problem. In India NABARD is the only authentic source to keep these statistics
- Role of Corporates in Micro Finance: Corporates in India, has shown keen interest in the SHG movement as it provides an alternative business opportunity for them besides being a means to actualize its corporate social responsibility objectives. Many corporates have realized that the people at the bottom of pyramid can be brought into their business model. The group also sees a critical role of the corporate sector in providing

market linkage to the products of the rural areas on a sustainable basis. The following are the examples

- ITC (through e-choupal model).
- Hindustan Lever Ltd (through Stree sakti project).
- Mahindra & Mahindra (through Mahindra Subh labh).
- Tata Group (through Tata kisan sansar).

A salient feature of MFIs has been that they have sprung up spontaneously to meet a market demand similar to the creation of micro businesses. These institutions which have been set-up at first as small village based voluntary associations to cater to each other's needs have gone through an evolutionary process to become sometimes national level MFIs. Despite varying sizes, MFIs handle other people's money and, therefore, the viability and solvency of these institutions have become a crucial issue in MFI policy frame works. Given the fact that they function as depositories for the most vulnerable groups at the bottom of the income pyramid, a failure of an MFI may entail greater social costs from a welfare point of view than that of a higher level lending institution

CONCLUSION

Micro credit progeamme has become an important tool for to eradicate poverty in India. It is gathering to become a major force in India. The self-help group model with bank lending to group of poor women without collateral has become an accepted part of rural finance. In India forming and nurturing small, homogenous and participatory self-help group of the poor has today emerged as a potent tool for human development.After the pioneering efforts of the last ten years, the Micro Finance Scene in India has reached a take-off point. With some efforts substantial progress can be made in taking MFIs to the next orbit of significance and sustainability. This needs innovative and forward-looking policies, based on the ground realities of successful MFIs. This, combined with a commercial approach from the MFIs in making Micro Finance Financially Sustainable, will make this Sector vibrant and help achieve its single-minded mission of providing Financial Services to the Rural Poor.

It is necessary to recognize that we, in India, have to focus on extending financial services in both rural and urban areas for ensuring financial inclusion of all segments of the population. At the same time, one should avoid the temptation of creating one set of banking and financial institutions to cater to the poor or the unorganized, and another for the rest. The medium to long-term objective should be to ensure inclusion of all segments in the mainstream institutions while taking advantage of the flexibility of multiplicity of models of delivering a wide range of financial services. In this light, a comprehensive framework to revive the cooperative credit system, revitalize the Regional Rural Banks and reorient commercial banking system needs to get a high priority while simultaneously encouraging and enabling the growth of micro-finance movement in India, which has been very successful. We need to build on its strengths and extend it to vast areas, which are inadequately covered by both banking and micro-credit entities.

No doubt, micro credit has come a long way. And still now it has a long way to go. Micro credit institutions have not been completely successful in its pursuits because of some inherent weaknesses and restraints. Speedy actions are needed to remove the obstacles to microcredit's development. Inadequate regulation is one element curbing this sector's healthy expansion. Considering the potential of the sector, a review of the Bill to rectify the above drawbacks is essential.

REFERENCES

1. Ansari Saghir Ahmad (2007), "Micro Finance in India", *Asian Economic Review*, August, Vol. 49(2), pp 327-336.
2. Basu, Priya, and Pradeep Srivastava. (2005) "Scaling up Micro finance for India's Credit and Microfi nance. Mumbai. Available at *www.rbi.org.in*.
3. Fisher, T., Sriram, M.S. (2002), Beyond micro-credit: Putting development back into micro-finance, New-Delhi: Vistaar Publications.
4. Ghate, Prabhu.(2007) Indian Microfi nance: The Challenges of Rapid Growth. New Delhi: Sage publications.
5. Goetz, A.M. R. Sen Gupta,(1996) "Who takes the Credit? Gender, Power, and Control Over
6. Loan Use in Rural Credit Programme in Bangladesh", *World Development*, Vol.24, No. 1:
7 Mahajan, Vijay and Bharti Gupta Ramola,(2004) "Microfinance in India - Banyan Tree and Bonsai," BASIX Quarterly Review
8. A Study ofMicro finance in India: Sectoral issues and challenges (2004) Y.S.P. Thorat, Managing Director NABARD.
9. Microfinance India conference and a look at the expanding market by Sukhwinder Singh Aurora,Financial sector team ,policy division ,DFID,United Nations Capital Development Fund (UNCDF) ,Issue 13 / June 2005
10. NABARD (2010), Status of Micro finance In India
11. Rangarajan, C (1996), "Rural India, the Role of Credit", *Reserve Bank of India Bulletin*, Reserve Bank of India, Mumbai.
12. Reserve Bank of India. (2005) Internal Group to Examine Issues Relating to Rural Poor." *World Bank Policy Research Working Paper 3646*.
13. Vijayachandran Pillai,B ", Harikumar,V., (2006) "Self- Help Groups in Kerala", *Kurukshetra*, Vol. 54,No. 9: 30-33.

17

Demand and Supply of Financial Capital towards Poverty Reduction in Tanzania: Perceptions of Customers of Financial Institutions in Mwanza City, Tanzania

Jairus B. Amayi
Clifford G. Machogu
Nicas Nibengo

INTRODUCTION

Since 1961, the Government of Tanzania has been adopting various measures for economic growth and poverty reduction through fiscal and monetary policies. In the 1990s, attention focused on economic growth as the means of achieving improvements in human welfare with the mind set of 'trickle down effect of economic growth'. However, Poverty and Human development Reports of the years 2007 and 2008 which assessed the trend of poverty in 2007 based on Household Budget Surveys (HBS) of 2006/07 and 2007/08 revealed that despite the high economic growth of 6.8% to 7.8%, respectively, 36% of Tanzanians were living below poverty line. In the year 2007/08, it was estimated that 19% of Tanzanians lived below the food poverty line (Poverty and Human Development Report, 2008). The report indicated that the percentage of households below poverty line, by region, 2007/08 for Mwanza was 48% (HBS: 2007/08).

Despite the financial system reforms initiated in 1990, the National Microfinance Policy of 2000 and Small and Medium Enterprises Development Policy of 2003 (URT: 2003), which enabled availability and access to financial capital (*Chijoriga: 2000*): credits, hire purchase, lease financing, agro-inputs loans, agro-input vouchers; saving schemes and insurance schemes, public perception on the contribution of financial capital on income poverty reduction was not known. Besides, income poverty remains high in Tanzania, a marvel that has not been known with the current financial capital paradigm?

The study therefore was an endeavour to determine the level of Public awareness on contribution of financial capital on income poverty reduction. The study analyzed the driving forces for demand and supply of financial capital and the magnitude of financial capital contributions on income poverty reduction.

LITERATURE REVIEW

The study was based on the concept that financial capital, if correctly perceived can play an important role in increasing efficiency and productivity. Although growth is not a sufficient condition for poverty alleviation, there is evidence that higher incomes in the community benefit the poor segments of the population proportionately (Ikara, 2003). Financial sector is a key element in generating growth, and thus, it is an important ingredient in poverty reduction. Dollar and Kraay (2000), indicated that on average the poor do benefit from growth, as an increase in the rate of GDP per capita leads to a one for one increase in the average income of the poorest. The Financial Sector provides the best alternative source of capital to poor population, especially through micro financing. According to Collins and Borthworth (1996), the use of factor productivity in growth diagnostics, assesses the relative contribution of the factors of production and Total Productivity (TFP). The production functions are mainly founded on econometric work of different levels of sophistication from standard two inputs case to multi-inputs case. Thus Q= f (k, l) in the two input case, where Q= output, k = **Capital,** l= labour input and f=function. This model provides an incremental reasoning on the contribution of capital in economic development. The role of financial and non financial institutions is to provide capital to deficit units which invest this capital in different economic activities.

Financial capital theory suggests that, as financial capital increases within networks of transacting partners, the average level of benefits increases and the disparity of benefits decreases. In part, this inverse relationship between disparity of income and average income results from terms of trade in financial capital-rich networks which favours transacting partners, from increased investment in real assets and ultimately provide opportunities independent of one's income.

FINANCIAL CAPITAL AND POVERTY

The connections between financial capital and poverty are two fold: Financial capital and poverty reduction are connected in that financial capital is an important resource that if properly managed can be used to reduce poverty. Utilization of financial capital directly reduces poverty through spill-over-effects of investment. Attitude toward investment will direct individuals' life cycle (Eakins, 1999). The lesson of the past several decades is that the productivity of physical, social, human and natural forms of capital depends on financial capital.

FINANCIAL CAPITAL PARADIGM

A paradigm, Robison at el; (2002), is a description of a subject that includes definitions, identification of and description of variables, and expected cause and effect relationships. As paradigm mature, the proposed view of the subject becomes generally accepted by experts in the field. A mature paradigm can facilitate cooperative action in a particular area, because it reduces conflict and cost of obtaining agreements. The financial capital paradigm describes the influence of relationships on financial goods, and economic transactions and contains concepts drawn from nearly all of the social sciences

The elements of financial capital paradigm, beside financial capital, include perceptions, financial systems, participants, financial institutions, financial markets, financial instruments, policies and regulations.

THE LINK BETWEEN FINANCIAL CAPITAL AND POVERTY REDUCTION IN TANZANIA

Financial Capital schemes through financial institutions and markets delivery in Tanzania were initiated early 2000 to meet different objectives. The most commonly mentioned objectives included: poverty alleviation and improved living standards, offering financing to the poor (Harper et al; 2009), women empowerment, and the development of business sector as a means of achieving high standards and reducing market failure (Chijoriga; 2000)

According to Blomström and Kokko, (2003) and Borenzstein, De Gregorio, and Lee (1998), the contributions of Financial capital to the development of a country are widely recognized as filling the gap between desired investment and domestically mobilized saving, increasing tax revenues, and improving management and technology, as well as labour skills. These could help the country to fight its way out of poverty.

RESEARCH METHODOLOGY

This was a survey study design. The study collected information from households, financial institutions, non-financial institutions, experts, opinion leaders, business community, and salaried workers from Nyamagana and Ilemela districts in Mwanza City Tanzania. The financial institutions' population was drawn from 8 commercial banks, 3 non bank financial institutions 3 foreign bureau and 54 savings and credit cooperatives. The total population of financial institutions was 68. The business population was drawn from 4,570 registered trade/industrial businesses, which included whole sellers and retailers. The government sample was drawn from 1 branch of Bank of Tanzania and 2 district councils. The population of financial market was drawn from Dar es salaam Stock Exchange Market since Mwanza has no its own registered stock exchange market. Total sample size studied was 175 of which 125 were households and 50 key informants. Households sample was extracted from individual lists, which was obtained from list of borrowers from financial institutions and markets. Primary data were obtained using interviews with key informants and individual households' members.

DATA ANALYSIS, DISCUSSION AND FINDINGS

Level of Awareness on Contribution of Financial Capital on Income Poverty Reduction

As shown in figures 1 and 2 responses from key informants, households and focus group discussion helped to assess the level of public awareness on uses and access of financial capital and its contribution to poverty reduction. When respondents were asked the question, "do you know what the financial capital is all about", 89.60% of house hold respondents said they did, while 10.40 % said they did not. On the other hand, 96% of key informants said they knew, while only 4.00% of them said they did not .On average 91.43% of respondents said they were aware of the meaning of financial capital, while 8.73% were not aware of the meaning of financial capital.

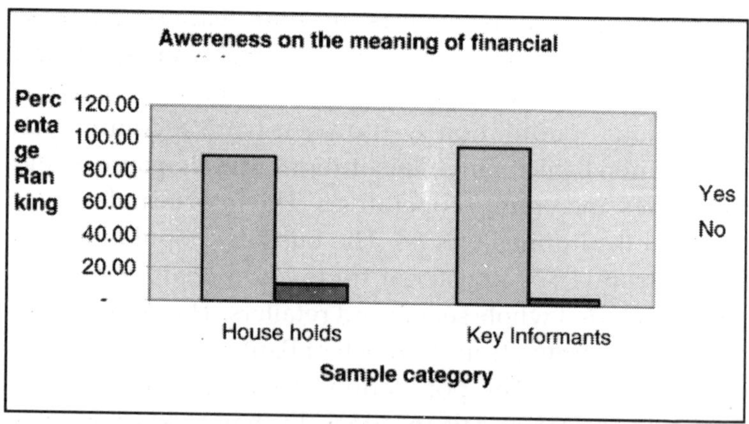

Fig. 1. Awareness on the meaning of financial capital

Source: **Field data, (2009)**

Given the findings as indicated in table1, financial capital contribution to the growth of industrial sector is ranked with the lowest perception at 81.71%, followed by agricultural sector with 65.14%, services and infrastructure with 57.71%, natural resources with 51.43%, health with

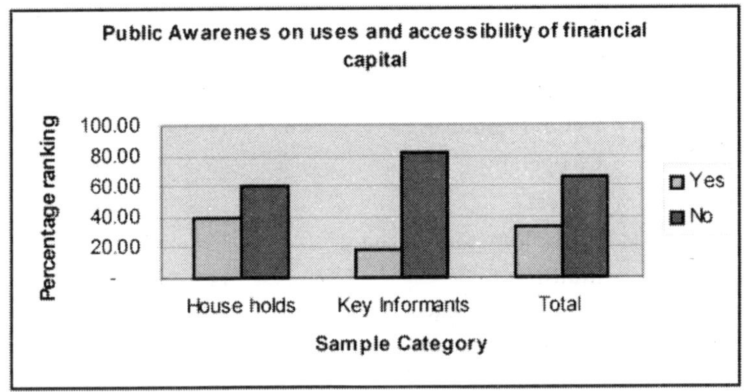

Fig. 2. Public awareness on uses and accessibility of financial capital

***Source*: Field data, (2010)**

50.86%, building and construction with 43.43% and cooperatives with 41.7%. The highest perception rating was as follows: Education sector was rated highest by 89.71%, trading and commerce 81.1%, vending 69.71 %, cooperatives 58.29 %, building and construction 56.57 %, health 49.14 percent, natural resources 48.57 %, services and infrastructures 42.29 %, agriculture 34.89 % and industrial sector 18.29 %.

Table 1. Perception on the performance of financial capital contribution to economic growth

Respondent ranking on contribution financial capital to Economic Growth	*Sectors*	*Very low*	*low*	*High*	*Very high*	*Total*
Households	Agriculture,forest,fishing	42	38	12	33	125
	Industry	54	45	16	10	125
	Trade and commerce	12	23	67	23	125
	Services &infrastructure	33	34	26	32	125
	Vending	6	52	67	0	125

	Education	0	23	98	4	125
	Health	23	34	43	25	125
	Building &constructions	12	44	56	13	125
	Natural resources	87	14	7	17	125
	Co operatives	3	56	54	12	125
Key	**Sectors**					
respondents	Agriculture,forest,fishing	8	16	23	3	50
	Industry	29	11	2	8	50
	Trade and commerce	7	6	67	0	50
	Services &infrastructure	8	17	23	2	50
	Vending	4	27	13	6	50
	Education	1	3	41	5	50
	Health	6	12	32	0	50
	Building &constructions	6	17	24	3	50
	Natural resources	18	7	19	6	50
	Co operatives	0	13	35	2	50
Combined	Sectors					
key infor-	Agriculture,forest,fishing	50	54	35	36	175
mants &	Industry	83	56	18	18	175
households	Trade and commerce	19	29	104	23	175
	Services &infrastructure	41	51	49	34	175
	Vending	10	79	80	6	175
	Education	1	26	139	9	175
	Health	29	46	75	25	175
	Building &constructions	18	61	80	16	175
	Natural resources	105	21	26	23	175
	Co operatives	3	69	89	14	175

Source: Field Data (2010)

Driving Forces for Demand of Financial Capital in Mwanza City

Both Household and Key informant respondents mentioned nine reasons that drive people to seek financial capital assistance; financing working capital 25.71 %, education development 17.14 %, medical expenses 9.14%,

Table 2. Driving forces for demand for Financial capital in Mwanza

Demand for financial capital	*Driving forces by percentage rating*									
	Working capital	*Education development*	*Medical expenses*	*Building and construction*	*Farming and live stock*	*Machinery tools and equipment*	*Long term investment*	*Home furniture*	*Car and motor vehicle*	*Total*
Household	25.60	17.60	8.80	9.60	12.00	4.00	0.80	12.80	8.80	100
Key informants	26.00	16.00	10.00	12.00	4.00	6.00	16.00	4.00	6.00	100
Average	25.71	17.14	9.14	10.29	9.71	4.57	5.14	10.29	8.00	100

Source: Field Data(2010)

building and construction 10.29 %, purchasing machinery, tools and equipments 4.57 %, long term investment 5.14 % and purchasing motor vehicles 8 %(Table 3)

Driving Forces for Supply of Financial Capital in Mwanza City

The forces that drive financial institutions to provide financial capital to the public include: Profit accounting 46%, provision of capital to the public 39%, pressure from political forces 29%, financial institutions sustainability and growth 21 % and 9 % respectively, economic growth stimulation 17% and public service provision 14 %.

Constraints for Demand of Financial Capital

Constraints for demand of financial capital as mentioned by respondents include: Public inadequate entrepreneurial and business management skills 18.29 %, High interest rates associated with financial capital 17.71%, non formalization of business activities 17,14%, unconducive business environment 13.14% , unfavourable terms and conditions associated to financial capital 12.57%, poor property regulation 12% and little awareness of credit information 9.14% (Table 4)

Constraints Facing Financial Institutions In Supply of Financial Capital to the Public

Constraints mentioned include; Public inadequate entrepreneurial and managerial skills 22.29%, poor regulatory environment 16.57%, limited availability of reliable credit information from the public 13.71%, high transaction costs for small volume 10.29%, high costs for financial intermediation 9.14% and high costs for establishing rural branches 7.43%.

Providers of Financial Capital in Mwanza City

Eleven actors that provide financial capital to the public

Table 3. Perceived driving forces for institution supply of financial capital

Supply for financial capital	*Driving forces for supply of financial capital*							
	Profit making	*Institution sustainability*	*Institution growth*	*Public service provision*	*Capital provision*	*Economic growth stimulation*	*Political forces*	*Total*
Household	23.20	10.40	-	11.20	26.40	11.20	17.60	100
Key informants	34.00	16.00	18.00	-	12.00	6.00	14.00	100
Average	26.29	12.00	5.14	8.00	22.29	9.71	16.57	100

Source: Field data, (2010)

Table 4. Constraints for Public Demand of Financial capital

Constraint for demand of financial capital	*Constraint for demand of financial capital*							
	Inadequate entrepre-neurial skill	*Little awareness of credit information*	*Non formalisation of business activity*	*Poor property rights*	*Unfavourable credit terms and conditions*	*Un Conducive business environment*	*High interest rates*	*Total*
Household	11.20	7.20	20.00	9.60	16.80	12.80	22.40	100
Key informants	36.00	14.00	10.00	18.00	2.00	14.00	6.00	100
Average	18.29	9.14	17.14	12.00	12.57	13.14	17.71	100

Source: Field data, (2010)

in Mwanza City include; NMB bank with 24.57%, CRDB bank 20%, NBC 8.57%, saving and Finance 5.71%, Postal Bank 1.14%, Azania Bank 8.57%, Stanbic Bank 2.29%, Bank of Africa 2.29%, SACCOS 12.5%, NGOs 4 % and TUNAKOPESHA 10.29%.

Perceived Magnitude on the Contribution of Financial Capital on Business Activities

Respondents mentioned financial capital to contribute to growth of business sales revenue 32.57%, profit increase 25.71% increase in business assets 15.43%, opening new branches 8 percent, provision of employment, 8.57% and increase in business linkages and networking 9.71% (Table 5).

Table 5. perceived magnitude on the contribution of financial capital on business activities

Contribution of financial capital on business	*Perceptions in the contribution of financial capital on business*						
	Sales revenue increased	*Profit increased*	*Business assets increased*	*Increase in business branches*	*Employ more staff*	*Business linkage and networks*	*Total*
Household	36.00	26.40	14.40	9.60	8.00	5.60	100
Key informants	24.00	24.00	18.00	4.00	10.00	20.00	100
Average	32.57	25.71	15.43	8.00	8.57	9.71	100

Source: Field data, (2010)

Perceived Magnitude on the Contribution of Financial Capital on Personal Well being

Perceived contribution were in terms of: increased personal commitment and accountability 9.71%, improvement in education 37.71%, improvement in shelter and housing 24% , acquisition of household items and furniture 7.43%, increased accessibility to food 12% and improvement in general health 9.14%.

Perceived Forms and Experiences of Financial Capital Services

The perceived forms and experiences in accessing and usage of financial capital as mentioned by respondents include: short term loans 85.14%, long term loans 28 percent, salaried workers loans 56%, overdraft facilities 28%, agricultural loans 31.43%, livestock loan 13.71 %. Leasing 2.29% and housing loans 29.14%.

Qualitative Contribution of Financial Capital on Growth of Economic and Social Indicators

Respondents qualitatively ranked the contribution of financial capital to ten economic and social indicators. The low perception rating was as follows: industrial sector rated lowest by 81.71%, agricultural sector 65.14%, services and infrastructure 57.71, natural resources 51.43 %, health 50.86%, building and construction 43.43 %, cooperatives 41.71 % and education 10.29 %. The highest perception rating was as follows: Education sector was rated highest with 89.71 %, trading and commerce 81.14%, vending 69.71%, cooperatives 58.29 %, building and construction 56.57%, health 49.14 %, natural resources 48.57%, services and infrastructure 42.29 percent, agriculture 34.89% and industrial sector 18.29 %.

Statistical Analysis and Description on the Findings

using the median as measure of central tendency the results indicate that, over half of the population believes contribution of financial capital to growth of economic activities and social well being is high. Conversely, less than half the population believe contribution of financial capital to economic growth and social well being is low.

CONCLUSION

Finance is an important component of development, including poor people. Indeed, evidence from this study has shown that more than half the population perceived financial capital to have reduced income poverty and lowered income inequality. In addition to facilitating overall economic growth, financial capital had helped individuals smooth their income, insure against risks, and broaden investment opportunities. Testimonies have been evidenced in promoting individuals education, facilitated trade and commerce and improved individual accessibility to food and good health.

Despite this positive contribution, productive sectors such as industrial and agriculture have been perceived to have low accessibility to financial capital, hence less contribution to GDP. Therefore the most important factor for a prosperous future of contribution of financial capital on income poverty reduction lies in honesty and mutual concern by financing industrial, agricultural, infrastructural and construction sectors.

RECOMMENDATION

Based on the findings above, the study makes the following recommendations to improve the contribution of financial capital on income poverty reduction.

The Financial System

The financial system should be at the service of man, systems, and governments, by allowing individuals and societies to come to their utmost fulfilment by assuming responsibility for their own development.

Supplier of Financial Capital

Supplier of financial capital i.e. financial institutions and Markets should improve accessibility of financial capital services by: (1) Lowering interest rates that help to facilitate the growth of client businesses. (2) Financing industries, agricultural and construction sectors. (3) Offering training and couching their clients on entrepreneurship and business management skills. (4) Promote their financial capital services to the public to make them aware of the facility. (5) Be flexible and offer favourable credit terms and conditions.

Users of Financial Capital

Users of financial capital i.e., the society should: (1) Formalize business activities to be able to attract financiers. (2) Formalize property rights and documentation. (3) Observe credit agreements, adhere to honesty and accountability. (4) Invest in most productive sectors, such as industry, agriculture and construction

The Government

The government should: (1) establish entrepreneurship incubation centres to enable the community to acquire entrepreneurship skills and be competent in investment and business undertaking. (2) improve monetary system, fiscal policy and regulatory environment to protect both lenders and borrowers..

International Community

International Community should have a political will to stop World financial institutions such as World Bank and IMF from wasting productive capacity on financing the manufacture of arms and then selling the same to poor countries. Instead, they should finance production that is geared towards the satisfaction of real human needs.

AREA FOR FURTHER RESEARCH

This study recommends further research in Innovation and Inclusions in financial system issues, strategies and options in Developing Countries.

REFERENCES

ADAM, R.H. 2004. *Economic Growth, Inequality and Poverty*: Estimating the Growth Elasticity of Poverty

ALBERT, Ernest. 2008. The Disinherited of the Earth, ORDISEF

Association, Kampala Uganda

MBELLE, Amon .2006. *Prospects for achieving broad-based and equitable growth in Tanzania:* A research report presented to eleventh REPOA Research Workshop White Sands Hotel, Dar es Salaam, Tanzania

ATKINSON, A.B .1991. *Comparing Poverty Rates Internationally: Lessons from Resent Studies in Developed Countries*: The World Bank Economic Review Vol. 5no.1.pp.3-21

BAGACHWA, M.S.D. 1994. *Poverty alleviation in Tanzania*: Dar es Salaam. Dar es Salaam University Press

BANDERA, O.M.S. 1997. *Micro and small enterprises Potentials for Development: General Considerations*: A paper presented to the workshop of Micro and Small Enterprises Research, November, Dar Es Salaam

CHIJORIGA, M.M. 2000. *The performance and Sustainability of Microfinance Institutions in Tanzania*: Working paper

COLLINS, S and B. Bosworth. 1996. *The Empirics of Growth*: Brookings Institution

DORWARD, A; J.Kydd, J. Morrison and I. Urey. 2004. *A Policy Agenda for Pro-poor Agricultural Growth;* World Development, Volume 33, Number 1, January, pp.73-90

EELE, G,J. Semboja, S.B; Likwelile and S.Ackroyd. 2000. *Meeting International Poverty Targets in Tanzania;* development Policy Review, Vol.18 pp.66-88

HARPER, V.L et all.1999. *Measuring Transformation assessing and improving the impact of Micro Credit*; Paper Presented at Micro Credit Summit meeting of councils in Abidjan Cote de'Ivore, June

KOTHARI, C.R. 1990. *Research Methodology: Methods and Techniques;* H.S Poplai 2nd Edition

KUZILWA, J.A .2002. *The role of Credit for Small Business Success;* A study of the National Entrepreneurship Development Fund in Tanzania, A paper presented at the 6th Annual International Conference on Entrepreneurship and Small Business Development (ICAESB), White Sand Hotel, Dar es Salaam

PACK, H.and C. Paxson.2001. "Is Africa Manufacturing Skill Constrained?"

SZIRIMAI, A and Ranis, G; F.Stewart and A.Ramirez. 2000. "Economic Growth and Human Development "World *Development*" Vol.28 No 2, pp 197-219

SEVERINE SA.Kessy and Fratern M.Urion. 2006. *The contribution of Microfinance Institutions to Poverty Reduction in Tanzania;* REPOA Research Report no 06.3 Mkuki na Nyota, Dar Es Salaam Tanzania

18

Micro Financing in India: Diverging from Objectives?

K. Rajesh
Salini K

"Microfinance is not a charity. It is a way to extend the same rights and services to low-income households that are available to everyone else. It is recognition that poor people are the solution, not the problem." — **Kofi Annan**

INTRODUCTION

The incredible growth and spread of Indian Microfinance in both rural and urban areas across the country has gained national and international attention. India's micro credit has swelled through increased number of self help groups and the amount of savings mobilized by these groups. Similarly, the number of microfinance lending institutions has also shown an upward trend during this decade. State and Central government agencies, Non-Governmental Organizations, commercial banks and external (both national and international) donors are playing a vital role in the extension of micro credit. Using this credit, the groups with entrepreneurial talent would make profit and leads to poverty reduction. Microfinance is thus considered as a strong apparatus and potent instrument to bring in social and economic upliftment. There has been a tremendous increase in the number of institutions providing microfinance services in India. The performances of these institutions were trust worthy until recently. However, recent reports from various part of the country, especially from Andhra Pradesh, raised apprehensions among the proponents of micro finance. The issue of sustainability made many Micro Finance Institutions (MFIs) to stand and work on for profit. This situation may lead to defeat the "very purpose" of its existence of this novel concept. The basic premise of this paper is to empirically analyze the operational framework of these institutions and provide a critical assessment of the major issues of microfinance in India. The paper is expected to provide certain suggestions to overcome these problems.

MICRO FINANCE: ORIGIN, DEFINITION AND SCOPE

The concept of micro credit was introduced (during 1970's) and revolutionised by the Bangladesh visionary Muhammed Yunus through his popular concept of Gramin Banks, which was rewarded by Nobel Prize for Economics in the year 2006. Muhammad Yunus's Grameen Bank has now been replicated on five continents (Beatriz and Morduch, 2005). Approaches started in Latin America have found their way to the streets of El Paso and New York City; experiments in Bolivia have given birth to institutions in Uganda and Azerbaijan; and policymakers in the world's two most populous countries, India and China, are now developing their own home grown micro finance versions. Recognizing the energy and activity, the United Nations designated 2005 as the International Year of Micro credit (*Ibid*). The most notable revolution happened during the first decade of the 21st century is the shift from "micro credit" – which refers speciûcally to small loans – to "micro-finance" (*Ibid*).

The term 'microfinance' was described as 'the provision of financial services dealing with very small deposits and loans'. It means, providing very poor families with very small amount of credit in the form of micro credit, essentially to help them to grow their tiny business and maintain their income (Rutherford, 2000). United Nations defined microfinance as loans, insurance, savings, transfer services, other financial products for low-income clients (UN, 2005). According to NABARD microfinance means the "provision of thrift, credit and other financial services and products of very small amounts to the poor in rural, semi urban or urban areas, for enabling them to raise their income levels and improve living standards" (NABARD, 1999). Before the year 2000, 'microfinance' is commonly referred to as small loans. But later, it has diversified to include additional financial services such as savings, insurance and remittances and is commonly called as Microfinance (Vonderlack-Navarro and Sherraden, 2007). Microfinance institutions (MFIs) are those, which provide thrift, credit and other financial services and products of very small amounts mainly to the poor in rural, semi-urban or urban areas for enabling them to raise their income level and improve living standards.

The microfinance programs basically aim at removing poverty by establishing micro enterprises and encouraging productive activities (Mohindra, 2003). Such activities are commonly undertaken by community groups and local authorities. Many microfinance programs target women as they are the most vulnerable and powerless. A special emphasis was given to women in such poverty alleviation activities in the first International Women's Conference in Mexico in 1975 (Mayoux, 1997). This was further strengthened by the Micro Credit Summit Campaign in 1997, which had 'reaching and empowering women' as the second important goal after 'poverty reduction' (Mayoux, 2006). Figure 1 clearly shows the scope of microfinance that is how it helpful to escape the poverty of the people by providing improved nutrition, better health care and better education. Microfinance is the provision of collateral free loans to the poor people, especially women in rural areas, at affordable rates and in different frequencies. Borrowers are organized into groups and repayment is guaranteed through peer pressure. Microfinance is thus considered as an effective strategy not only to reduce poverty, but also to improve health, sanitation, education and other living standards. Many micro credit programs normally intents women as their 'beloved beneficiaries' as they are the most vulnerable groups in the society. By providing employment and income generation opportunities, women have improved their autonomy, confidence, financial freedom, security and status within and out the household and thus it helps in the development of women empowerment.

OBJECTIVES AND OPERATIONS OF MICROFINANCE

As observed earlier, that the microfinance schemes are featured by relatively small amount of loans, short repayment period, absence of collaterals, involvement of women beneficiaries, and participation of Non-Governmental Organizations. Specifically, the objectives of microfinance can be listed as below: (Central Bank of Nigeria, 2005)

- To promote the habit of saving and thrift
- To encourage proper repayment habit among the rural poor
- To organize the women in different units and teach them to handle collective responsibility

- Educate the poor and illiterate to handle issues with banks, government offices and other agencies professionally
- To encourage lending and proper repayment among the poor
- To establish a financial discipline
- To impart training in the required field like paddy cultivation, poultry farm, self employment etc
- To mobilize and utilize optimally the available resources like capital, intellectual potential, space etc
- To teach the needy about resource sharing like machinery etc and share the return from the shared resources
- To ensure financial independency among the beneficiaries

It is also worthwhile to note that microfinance programs are based on group based lending upon joint liability and peer pressure. Generally, the group consists of ten-to-twenty people, within the same locality with more or less same financial background. These self selected groups, which are commonly knows as Self Help Group (SHGs), are homogeneous groups with varying degrees of participation in microfinance program. Peer pressure and joint liability principles, ensure effective utilization and prompt repayment. This joint liability will in turn results in joint ownership of assets and resources. This transforms mere 'beneficiaries' into real 'clients' of microfinance program. This enhances the financial empowerment of the poor by facilitating the financial freedom. The creation and management of SHGs are generally done by Non-Government Organizations (NGOs). Groups promoted by NGOs authorize poor people to access formal finance. There are other types of microfinance operations also. This group based approach has been widely recognized as an effective method to empower the marginalized in rural areas, especially women. The groups are formed by NGOs (in most cases) upon mutual trust and accountability. At the same time, these group approach suffers from serious limitations like the limited extend of empowerment in some cases, process of group formation, the selection criteria of members, efficiency of lending schemes, utilization of micro credit and exclusion of real poor from the group (Reinke, 1998). Microfinance institutions all around the world are keen to build suitable products and services to avoid barriers which kept women from formal financial institutions.

MICROFINANCE IN INDIA

India's first Microfinance Institution 'Shri Mahila SEWA Sahkari Bank was set up as an urban co-operative bank, by the Self Employed Women's Association (SEWA) soon after the group was formed in 1974. Microfinance for the rural poor began when NABARD initiated a pilot project in 1992 with about 500 women's SHGs across the country. This was called the SHG-bank linkage programme (SBLP). Under the 1992 guidelines, the SHG functions as a joint liability group, replacing other collateral for the loans. The Small Industries Development Bank of India launched its micro credit scheme in 1994 and formed the SIDBI Foundation for Micro Credit in 1998. Early results achieved by SHGs promoted by NGOs such as MYRADA, led NABARD to offer refinance to banks for collateral-free loans to groups (Tankha, 2002)

Microfinance in India is synonymous with micro credit; this is because savings, thrift, and micro insurance constitute a minuscule segment of the microfinance space. In India, most microfinance loans are in the range of Rs.5,000 to Rs.20,000(Mahapatra and Dutta, 2010). MFIs are the main players in the microfinance space in India; their primary product is micro credit. The list of top ten performers of micro

players in the microfinance space in India; their primary product is micro credit. The list of top ten performers of micro finance institutions in India are presented in Table 1.

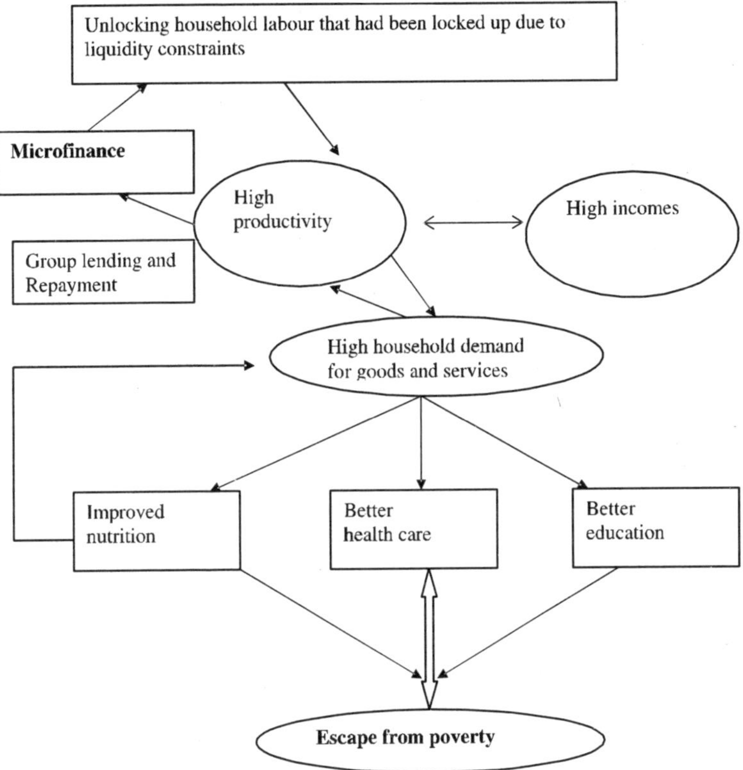

Fig. 1: Scope of micro finance

From table 1 it is clear that most of the microfinance insurance institutions are centred in the state of Andhra Pradesh. In addition to major MFIs, there are banks and insurance companies, agricultural and dairy co-operatives, corporate organisations and the postal network which actively involve and contribute in the field. Additionally, there are specialised lenders, called apex MFIs that provide both loans and capacity building support to MFIs.

The main models of microfinance that are in vogue

Table 1. Top 10 performers of micro finance institutions in India

Name of MFI	*Headquartered in*	*Legal Status*
SKS Microfinance Ltd (SKSMPL)	Secunderabad, Andhra Pradesh	Pvt. Ltd Company (NBFC)
Spandana Sphoorty Financial Ltd (SSFL)	Hyderabad Andhra Pradesh	Public Ltd.Company (NBFC)
Share Microfin Limited (SML)	Hyderabad Andhra Pradesh	Public Ltd.Company (NBFC)
Asmitha Microfin Ltd (AML)	Hyderabad Andhra Pradesh	Public Ltd.Company (NBFC)
Shri Kshetra Dharmasthala, Rural Development Project (SKDRDP)	Dharmasthala, Karnataka	Trust
Bhartiya Samruddhi	Hyderabad Andhra Pradesh	Public Ltd.Company (NBFC)
Bandhan	Kolkata, West Bengal	Society
Cashpor Micro Credit (CMC)	Varanasi,Uttar Pradesh	Section 25 Company
Grama Vidiyal Micro Finance Pvt Ltd (GVMFL)	Tiruchirappalli, Tamil Nadu	Pvt. Ltd. Company (NBFC)
Grameen Financial Services Pvt Ltd (GFSPL)	Bangalore,Karnataka	Pvt. Ltd. Company (NBFC)

Source: CRISIL, 2009

SHG-bank linkage programme still has the highest volumes in the country. SHGs are considered safer as lending is conditional to saving. Group saving is mostly used for productive purposes. In the case of MFIs it is only lending. MFI got into big lending in 2005-2006 (Mahapatra and Dutta, 2010). Figures NABARD released show that till 2009, the outstanding SHG loans amounted to about $23,000 crore, about twice the size of the MFI portfolio. Between 2006 and 2009 MFIs had 83 per cent annual compounded growth rate while that of SHGs during the same period was 41 percent (*Ibid*). In its annual publication on Status of Micro Finance in India for 2009-2010, NABARD has indicated that the total exposure of banks and financial institutions to MFIs as on March 31, 2010, was Rs. 13,956 crore, representing a growth of more than 100 per cent during the year (Business Line, 2011).

In the MFI-bank linkage model, covering ûnancing of MFIs by banks and other ûnancial institutions such as Small Industrial Development Bank of India (SIDBI) for on-lending to small borrowers, the penetration is predominantly in six States – Andhra Pradesh, Tamil Nadu, Karnataka, Orissa, Maharashtra and West Bengal – though they also exist in Gujarat, Delhi, Rajasthan and Uttar Pradesh. NABARD has reported that in 2009-10, the banks have disbursed Rs 8,062.77 crore to MFIs – more than the Rs 2,665.75-crore loans provided to them by SIDBI.

The total demand for micro-credit in the country has been predicted to Rs.50,000 (Mahapatra and Dutta, 2010). The Reserve Bank of India (RBI) estimated that in 256 of India's 626 districts the credit gap is at least 95 per cent or more. This huge demand justifies the promotion of news entrants into the micro finance industry in India.

MAJOR CONCERNS ABOUT INDIAN MICROFINANCE

Though, Indian microfinance gained a lot of attention from all over the globe, it suffers from some serious limitations. These pitfalls deserve a lot of concern from scholars, practioners and academicians. The apprehensions over micro insurance were at the peak due to the recent developments in Andhra Pradesh. India's micro-finance institutions claim they followed the fabled Grameen Bank model of Bangladesh. However, the pace of growth of these institutions disproves their claims. One example can be pointed from, SKS Microfinance, the biggest player in India.

The table2 explains the growth of this company over four years. Table 2 made clear that SKS has grown 90 per cent annually for the last four years from just two lakh members to 40 lakh members. The loan disbursement has gone up from just Rs 150 crore to over Rs 4,400 crore in four years, which further anticipate problems in future. Being the first listed company SKS Microfinance officially declared their change in their operations. Though they are unlisted Share Microfin and Spandana Sphoorty are also known for their exponential growth in business and exploiting the beneficiaries (Economic Times, 2011) particularly in Andhra Pradesh. According to the Government of Andhra Pradesh, more than Rs. 25,000 crore has been lent to over 80 lakh poor families. On an average each family owes Rs. 30,000. According to the information submitted by MFIs on October 29 to the state government, 50 per cent of rural poor households in the state have taken multiple loans (Mahapatra and Dutta, 2010). The interest rate ranges from 21.2 per cent to 60.5 per cent. Some MFIs seem to use strong-arm tactics in loan recovery, with a few reported suicides. The Andhra Pradesh Government reacted with an ordinance to regulate MFIs. The Andhra Pradesh ordinance has not introduced any ceiling, except for saying that the interest should not exceed the principal. It was also observed that the concept of self help group (SHG) was not followed in Andhra Pradesh and other states. M.S.Sriram (2010) traced the use and abuse of an ingenious shareholding vehicle called mutual benefit trusts (MBTs) that was central to this lopsided promoter poor women relationship. All these led to the suicide of more than 50 MFI beneficiaries in Andhra Pradesh during September to October 2010, which forced the state Government to temporarily ban on these lending institutions.

Another issue is that whether MFIs need to be brought under the regulatory ambit of an apex institution such as NABARD or RBI or be left to be self-regulated

Table 2. Operational Information of SKS micro finance (2006-2009)

Operational Information	*2006*	*2007*	*2008*	*2009*
Branches	80	275	771	1354
Districts	19	102	235	336
Staff	574	2389	6425	12814
Members (lakh)	2	6	18.7	39.5
Loan (Rs. Cr.)	152	445	1679	4399

Source: Business Line, dated 15.01.2011

(Kanagasabapathy, 2010). The consensus now seems to be in favour of a comprehensive regulatory framework. The Bill in this regard is already before Parliament, but awaits revisions to incorporate additional features emanating from the Andhra Pradesh episode and the recommendations expected from the RBI-appointed Malegam group. Flagging off concerns with major suggestions of Malegam group including the income status of the borrower, fixing loan limit upto Rs.25,000/- and restrict lending to non income purposes to 25% of the total lending etc were criticised for its superficial nature. After re-examining the breathing literature on Malegam committee report it could be concluded that which is primitive to make a restructuring in the whole procedure of micro finance industry in India to that of Bangladesh.

The other major drawbacks in the microfinance in India are similar to that of other countries which are listed below:

a) Persistence of poverty after microfinance programs: Not only in India, but also in countries like South Africa, where microfinance programs are very popular and operational, the level of poverty remains to be very high. It is to be noted that, a majority of the poor are the beneficiaries of microfinance in these countries (Imran, David and Rutherford, 1999).

b) Exclusion of the poorest of the poor: The microfinance programs is designed for the social and economic upliftment of the poor, it is highly censured for not including the deserved poor. The conventional programs exclude the most vulnerable and ultra poor from participation in many parts of the country.

c) Excuse for the responsibilities: This is particularly true in the Indian context where the microfinance programs have become an excuse for the government to abdicate their role in providing social security to the vulnerable and the poor. Other poverty eradication programs ceased to exist under the shadow of microfinance. The insistence of steering poverty eradication activities through self help groups may result in exclusion of the deserved in some cases.

d) Bankers' responsibility shifting of priority sector lending: Bankers have also found this as an excuse not providing small loans to poor and the needy. They deny providing small loans directly to the poor suggesting to approach in group form. This tendency is worsened with the frequent transfer of bank officials in the rural branches.

e) Slow graduation from micro credit to micro enterprises: Many researchers have found that, there is either no or slow graduation from micro credit to micro enterprises. The financial aid received as micro credit is not fully utilization for developing small but productive enterprises. It requires a serious attention. Such micro credit beneficiaries faced serous difficulties in repaying the loan and becoming more poor and indebted than before.

f) Lack of a long term sustainable solution to poverty: The programs though aimed at poor and very poor, it does not offer a long term sustainable solution to poverty. The credit delivered can enhance the standard of living of the poor, but the long term sustainability is still under doubt.

g) Lack of a multi-dimensional view: Most of the programs are viewing poverty from only one angle - on money terms. But there are other aspects like children's education, healthcare of the family, social security, equal opportunity and gender empowerment.

Policy analysts say that when a few MFIs transform from a not-for-profit enterprise to for-profit outfit, they must perforce feed the insatiable appetite of the investors, who are invariably looking out for dividend and capital appreciation. It urges invariably to meet two objectives, i.e., the need of the poor on the one hand and the interest of the stake holder on the other. Therefore, the suggestions or policy pertaining microfinance should be in such a manner to meet the objectives of these two groups.

SUGGESTIONS

Microfinance program is meant for the poor and by the poor and all the efforts taken by SHGs and NGOs are to be appreciated. Still certain suggestions have also come up from a primary analysis. These suggestions or recommendations can also be considered for the solving the issues and improving the performances.

a) Regulation, either from Centre or from state or from apex institutions like RBI, is essential for financial intermediation.

b) The survival and success of the micro enterprises depend upon the individual capability of the micro entrepreneur. Hence, along with micro credit, non-micro credit initiatives should also be imparted and encouraged.

c) A concept of synergy can be introduced among the participants and encourage them to act in union. Not only the beneficiaries, but the MFIs and SHGs in general also should be given proper training in this regard.

d) The strategy should be focusing on poor rural women and the SHG members to increase their income through the development of micro enterprises.

e) A small impetus towards entrepreneurship development and small amount of credit to start small income generating programs will create enough self employment opportunities which will greatly improve the quality of lives of people living in rural areas.

f) The success of any microfinance activity depends mostly upon the formation and operation of self help groups. The major purposes of SHGs include routing of micro credit and allied services. Group activities initiated and solving of issues at the group level will enhance the sense of belongingness. The main role of SHGs is based on the principle 'Help people to help themselves'

g) Encourage NGOs to promote SHGs as autonomous bodies which would help the women to work for poverty alleviation, gender equality, work discrimination, injustice and exploitation at home, village and wider levels. Establish SHG linkage between insurance companies, banks and other training institutions which assist them to identify income generating programs and ensure its sustainability.

Motivate and encourage women in SHGs to view micro credit as a way of empowerment, not an end in itself. This credit activity is only one element of credit in an integrated approach of empowerment. Empowerment is a holistic approach covering her personal life, domestic sphere, political, economical arenas. Rajesh and Salini (2011) observe that provision of micro insurance along with microfinance products, especially micro credit, will mutually benefit each other.

CONCLUSIONS

No room for doubt, that the poor is economically and psychologically helped with the introduction of microfinance activities. Microfinance enabled the beneficiaries to manage their financial needs better, especially considering the seasonal nature of agriculture. It is believed that the availability of micro credit reduced the over dependence on informal money lenders and sources. Although absolute poverty is not eradicated, the program could bring in considerable positive impact in reduction of poverty. Due to the immense scope for business potential many NBFCs are entering into the Indian micro finance market. In order sustain their business it is important to treat micro finance as a business rather than a charity. At the same time, one should draw a line between the social benefit and private profit, which emphasise the need for a controlling mechanism like RBI. Another problem that observed from the Indian micro finance market is the diverging of funds by the beneficiary. Neither the provider nor the beneficiaries are bothered about this divergence. Rather the providers consider only the repayment, which also lead to the imminent breakdown of this novel concept. This issue also should be taken care of the purview of the monitoring mechanism. Since, India is vast due to population and geography which became the need of the hour. Better results are expected if the academicians and authorities discuss and implement the indicative suggestions listed above. Acknowledging the shortcomings, the community or group based initiative holds tremendous potential for poverty eradication and empowerment of poor women, especially living in rural parts of the country.

REFERENCES

Beatriz, A.A., and M. Jonathan, (2005), *The Economics of Microfinance*, Cambridge, Massachusetts Institute of Technology.

Business Line, (2011), "Microfinance, India's sub-prime crisis", dtd: 15.01.2011.

Central bank of Nigeria, (2005), *Microfinance Policy, Regulatory and Supervisory Framework for Nigeria*, Available at: *http:// www.cgap.org/gm/document-1.1.5907/Microfinance%20Policy, %20 Regulatory%20And%20Supervisory%20(2005).pdf*

Economic Times, (2011), "ET Investigation: Two Faced Relationships, Women Share-holders Miss MFI Wealth Creation Pie", The Economic Times, dtd.31.01. 2011.

Kanagasabapathy K., (2010), "MFI Crisis in Perspective", Business Line dated, November. 26.

Mayoux L., (1997), *Participatory Learning for Women's Empowerment in Micro-finance Programmes: Negotiating Complexity, Conflict and Change*, http:// www2 .ids.ac.uk/impact/files/ institutionalisation/Mayoux_particiaptory_learning.pdf

Mayoux L., (2006), *'Women's Empowerment through Sustainable Microfinance: Rethinking 'Best Practice'*, Discussion Draft, Feb 2006, Available at: http://www. gen-finance.info/ Documents/Mayoux_Backgroundpaper.pdf

Mahapatra, R., and A.P.Dutta, (2010), "Profits from the Poor", Down to Earth, November.

Mohindra K S, (2003), "A Report on Women Self Help Groups In Kerala State, India: a Public Health Perspective", A Report prepared for FCRSS/IRSC, Montreal, Université de Montréal Départemement.

United Nations, (2005), UN Conference on Pangea Model at Lenoir Rhyne University, Hickory, North Carolina. Available at: http://hickory international council .com /modelun/the-general-assembly

Rajesh, K. and K. Salini, (2010), "Micro Insurance in South Asia: Road yet to be Developed for Rural Development". In *Growth with Equity Financial Inclusion*, D.Lazar, A.Aravanan and M.Deo (Eds), Chennai: Vijay Nicole Imprints Private Ltd., pp.280-289.

Reinke J. (1998), "Does Solidarity Pay? The Case of the Small Enterprise Foundation". *Development and Change*, Vol. 29, pp. 553-576.

Rutherford, Stuart (2000), *The Poor and Their Money*, UK: Practical Action Publishing.

Sriram , M.S., (2010), *Commercialisation of Microfinance in India: A Discussion on the Emperor's Apparel*, Indian Institute of Management, Ahmedabad

Tankha, Ajay (2002), "Self Help Groups as Financial Intermediaries in India: Cost of Promotion, Sustainability and Impact", *ICCO and Cordaid*, The Netherlands. Available at: *http://www.sa-dhan.net/Adls/Microfinance/Perspective Microfinance /Self-helpGroupsasFinancial.pdf*

Vonderlack-Navarro R., Sherraden M. (2007), "Microfinance, Women's savings and Financial Security in a Honduran Barrio, *Social Development Issues*, Vol. 29(1), pp.65-80.

19
Financial Inclusion without Financial Literacy Does More Harm Than Good

Dr Ushakumari L

1. THE BACKDROP

Financial Inclusion[a] - the mission to mainstream the marginalised- is the buzz word of the day (Canara bank 2008). In an era where all sorts of financial agencies and institutions- banking as well as nonbanking – strive towards widening and deepening the dimensions of Financial Inclusion (IIBF 2010), it will be worthwhile to have a look at how far the benefits of such efforts percolate to the society.

Debt financing is a common phenomenon in the rural economic scene (IIBF 2008). The pressure of debt burden is powerful enough to compress the life span of a debtor as evidenced by the increasing suicides reported by media (Deshpande 2002; Kusanna 2004; Sainath 2010;). The efforts of Primary Cooperative Agricultural and Rural Development Banks of Kerala [Hereafter referred to as the Primary Banks] towards deepening Financial Inclusion by way of granting of loans to the rural agriculturists were significant and praise worthy (sharma 2001). A survey into end results of the prevailing lending practices from the borrowers' angle is considered to be worthy and useful to get an idea about how far the Primary Banks could contribute towards inclusive growth.

A bank loan, if utilised for productive purpose, remains self-liquidating in nature (Chavan and Ramakumar 2002). The repayments can be made out of the income generated from investment of loan amount. Figure-1 illustrates the expectations about the operations of a credit cycle. [please, follow the order of sequence by the number given in brackets.]

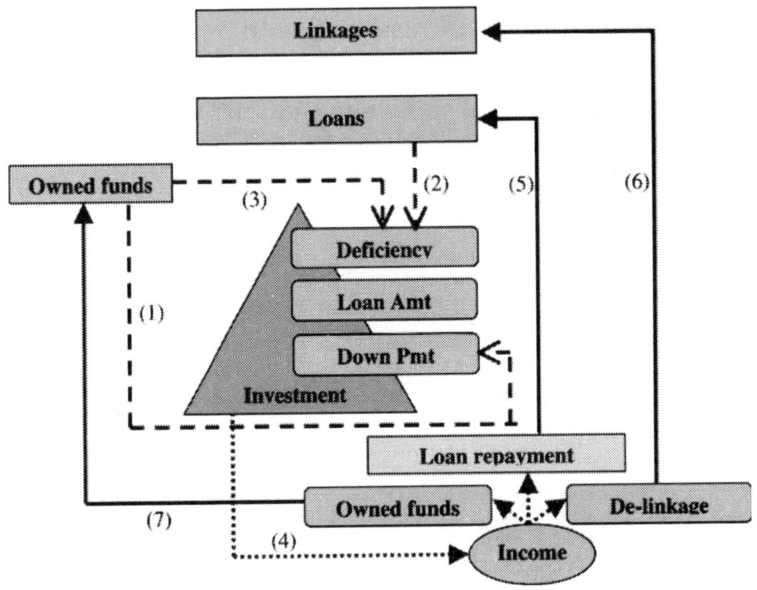

Fig. 1. Expected Credit Cycle

The loanee–

- Makes down payment from owned funds (**1**)
- Invests loan amount released from the bank for the purpose for which it is given (2).
- Has to adjust the deficiency from his owned funds, if the loan amount is not sufficient for completing the investment project (3).
- Shall obtain income generated from the investment project (4).
- Will be able to repay loan instalment dues together with interest from such income generated (5).
- will be able to delink his existing linkages to the to informal sources by making use of the excess cash in flow left after servicing the loan (6), and above all
- Is also expected to eke out a reasonable life and to improve his standard of living from the cash flows of a properly implemented loan project plan (7) (Kahlon and Singh 1992)

The theme of this paper hovers round the issues listed in the following section.

THE OBJECTIVE OF THIS STUDY

The issues addressed in this paper are:

- How far the Financial Inclusion efforts of the primary banks by way of granting of loans to rural public could succeed in terms of delinking the loanees from the informal sources?
- Do the loans remain self liquidating in nature by generating enough income to repay the loans? How do the loanees repay the loans?

METHODOLOGY

This study is based on the cross sectional data collected

in a sample survey among the loanees of Primary Cooperative Agricultural and Rural Development Banks of Kerala using interview schedules. A multi-stage stratified random sampling design was followed to select 300 sample loanees, 50 each, from the 6 sample banks operating in the three sample districts (Alappuzha, Palakkad and Kasargod) selected on a geographical basis. The samples of loanees were drawn from each bank, in such a manner that the Defaulters[b]and Prompt payers[c] would get an equal representation (i.e., 25 each) in it. The sample loanees were frank enough to disclose the details regarding the utilisation and diversion of the loan funds without much hesitation. By resorting to spot verification, observation and probing, almost all the required information could be collected.

Chi-square analysis is the tool used to test the association between selected variables and the status of repayment.

DISCUSSION AND FINDINGS

If the loan amount granted is used for non-productive purposes, it will not enhance the repaying capacity of loanees (Balishter et al.1998). On the contrary, it will produce adverse impact on the repaying capacity. Thereby the diverters are forced to seek additional borrowings (Chavan and Ramakumar 2002).

At the outset an investigation is made to find out answer to the question –"Is there any clogging in the credit pipeline?"

For this purpose, the actual Credit Cycle is traced. The pipelines, through which credits from the bank really flow, are depicted in Figure 2. The numbers in bracket indicate the sequence of operations of the cycle.

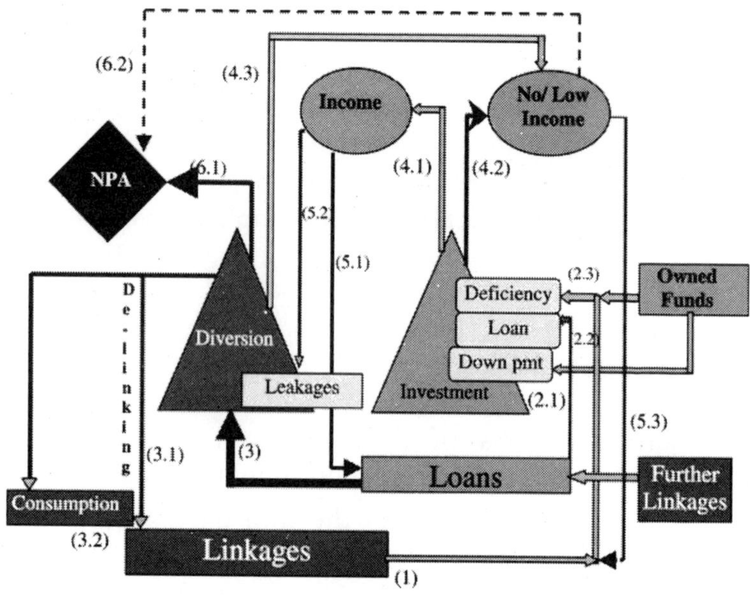

Fig. 2. Actual Credit Cycle

Like many other field studies, this study also reveals that the reality is far apart from expectation. The studies bring to light certain unethical practices of loan linkages to informal sources (Deshpande 2002; Purkayastha 2001; Rao 2001) and loan leakages (Ushakumari 2011) for undesirable purposes. The lay out of the credit pipelines shows the following facts:

- Many loanees who approach the bank are already indebted to informal sources (table.2) for one reason or the other (1).
- The source for contributing towards the down payment requirement of 'loan investment project' is not limited to owned funds. Private borrowing for meeting down payment requirement (col.2 of table.4) is a common phenomenon (2.1)
- The primary bank loans are granted for specific purpose investments(2.2)

- For a vast majority of loanees, the loan amount granted was not adequate for the requirements of loan investment projects. Therefore, many loanees depended on informal sources for covering the inadequacies of loan amounts (col.3 of table 4) sanctioned by banks (2.3).
- The heavy indebtedness towards informal sector, together with emergent requirements for consumption (table 3) tempted loanees to divert loan funds to the purposes for which they are not meant for (3; 3.1; 3.2).
- Only a limited number of loan projects could generate income to the expected level (4.1).
- Many loanees who utilised the amount in full for the set purpose were unable to generate reasonable income from their loan investment projects (4.2).
- The diverters could not generate income for obvious reasons (4.3).
- Only a few loanees repaid out of income generated from the loan investment projects (row.1 of table 6). (5.1)
- Even those who received reasonable income diverted the same either for delinking from informal sources or for meeting their consumption requirements (5.2).
- A good number of loanees who earned low/ no income and those who diverted income for their personal requirements were forced to depend on informal sources for making repayment of dues towards the primary banks (5.3). Some others sold their assets to raise money required for loan repayment. There were loanees who used income earned from other sources and by other members in the family to settle the dues to primary banks.
- Diversion of loan funds, diversion of subsequent income generated from loan projects(6.1), and the low

income generated from the loan projects (6.2) were the broad reasons for the dangerous virus "NonPerfoming Assets[d]".

The NonPerfoming Assets choke the credit pipeline of primary banks. The pipeline contains harmful components in its hold. It is soul searing to find that the primary banks meant for the amelioration of the rural people (Narayanasamy and Sunderam 1980) are now instrumental in pushing the loanees to the vicious circle of borrowing due to the unethical practices of leakages and linkages.

The following sections analyses the linkages of loanees and leakages of loans with a view to ascertain the association between them if any.

LINKAGES

It was established in many earlier studies that the financial requirements of rural poor would not be fully met by organized sector (Chandra 1993; Swamy 1997). It is worthwhile to verify the above statement through evidence from the field. The revelations at the time of field interview regarding the different sectors to which loanees were indebted were tabulated in the following section. The formal or institutional, and informal or non-institutional are the main sectors, that provide financial assistance to the loanees.

The distribution of loanees on the basis of their dependency on multiple sectors for credit can be captured visually from Table 1.

As the sample was drawn from the loanees of the primary banks, all the 300 loanees selected for the study were indebted to primary banks and hence indebted to institutional sources. Only 31 per cent of them could restrict their borrowing to Formal sector alone. Unfortunately a vast majority (69 per cent) of loanees being not satisfied with the sources in the formal sector approached informal agencies also, simultaneously.

Table 1. Sector-Wise Dependants of Credit

Sectors	*Loanees (No)*	*Loanees(%)*
Formal Sector only (FS)	94	31.3
Formal andInformal Sector (F&I)	206	68.7
Total	**300**	**100**

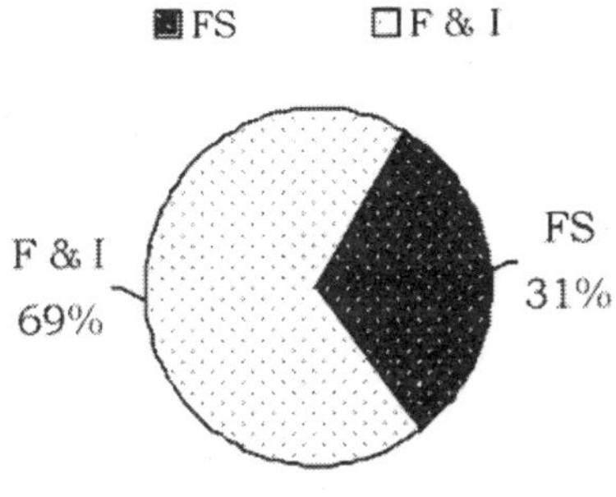

Fig. 3

Source: **Survey Data**

Thus the data collected from the field survey establish the dictum that rural people depend on more than one sector of credit to meet their financial requirements. Thus even among the financially included sections, presence of linkages is identified.

In order to get a full picture of linkages, it was imperative to mine more into the depth, by including more variables to the analyses. 'Time' and 'purpose' of borrowing from informal sector were the two variables selected for further examination.

Time of borrowing from informal sector

A survey was made among those sample loanees who had linkages with informal agencies. They were asked to reveal the time of borrowing from such informal sources in comparison with that from the Primary Banks. When the time of borrowing is subjected to observation, there arose four possible outcomes, which are exhibited in Table 2.

Table 2. Time of Borrowing from Informal Sources

Sample Loanees	*Borrowing Time*				*Total*
	Before(B)	*After(A)*	*Before & After (B-A)*	*Never(N)*	
Defaulters	19(51.4)	67(59.3)	29(51.8)	35(37.2)	150(50)
Prompt Payers	18(48.6)	46(40.7)	27(48.2)	59(62.8)	150(50)
Total	37 (100) (12)	113 (100) (38)	56 (100) (19)	94 (100) (31)	300 (100) (100)

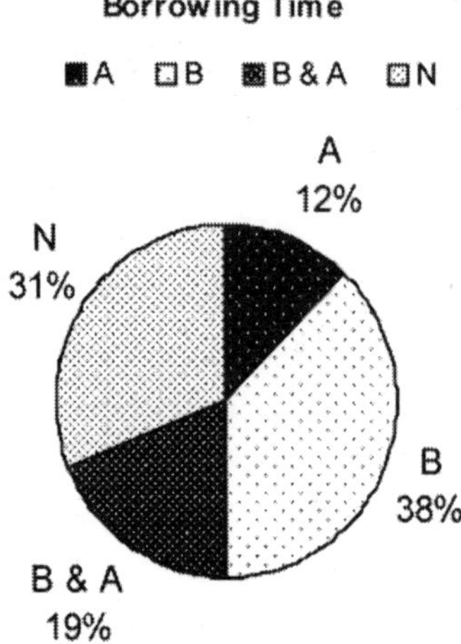

Fig. 4. Chi-square value: 10.129 D.F: 3 P-value: 0.018

***Note*: Figures in parentheses are percentages in totals**

***Source*: Survey Data**

This analysis was not relevant in the case of 31 per cent of sample loanees who were not indebted to the informal sources on the date of survey. More than 12 per cent of loanees borrowed from the informal sources quite before the incident of borrowing from the primary bank. In their case, it was not the incident of borrowing from primary banks that made them dependants of informal sources. But 38 per cent of loanees depended on informal sources only after the incidence of borrowing from the primary banks. In their case it may be this borrowing from primary banks that made them the dependants of informal sources. As much as 19 per cent of loanees used to borrow, before and after borrowing from primary banks. It is difficult to draw a specific conclusion about them. Their debt to informal sources may or may not be the effect of formal borrowing.

Regarding their nature of repayment the following observations are made. Majority of non dependants of informal sector repaid their dues in proper time. Majority of the loanees who become dependants of informal sector after availing loans from the primary banks happened to be defaulters. The remaining loanees did not show any particular trend in repayment. The chi-square test proved the presence of a relationship between the time of borrowing from informal sources and repayment to primary banks.

Thus an association between borrowing from primary banks and informal sources is identified. In order to identify the dire need which pushed the loanees to the informal sector it was necessary to dig deeper.

PURPOSES FOR WHICH THE LINKAGES ARE MADE

All the formal sources provide loans only for some predefined and enlisted purposes that are approved by the authorities. So, for purposes, which remain out side the purview of the approved list, there is no other go than to depend on informal sources (Komaraiah 2000). This throws light on the need to study the purposes for which loanees approach informal sources.

At the time of interview 206 out of 300 sample loanees were indebted to various informal agencies. The information regarding the purposes for which they approached the informal sources were collected and classified into 3 main divisions: consumption , investments , and bank loan-linked.

- All expenses incurred in a family on a day-to-day basis, and all the occasional requirements of medical, educational, employment and social nature, which arise only once in a while, were included in the division, "**consumption**".
- Asset purchases which consist of purchase of land, machinery, building, furniture, and home appliances, together with the investments made in business were classified as "**investments**".
- The financial requirements in relation to the loans already availed, either from the primary banks or from other banks were included in the class, "**bank loan-linked**".

It was learnt from the field that loanees depend on the informal sources for more than one purpose. In such cases the dominant purpose was taken into consideration. The repayment nature of the sample loanees was cross tabulated against the reasons for depending on informal sources as exhibited in Table 3.

Table 3. Reasons for Depending on Informal Sources

Sample Loanees	*Not Depended (ND)*	*Consumption (C)*	*Investment (I)*	*Bank loan linked (BLL)*	*Total*
Defaulter	35(37.2)	11(42.3)	9(64.3)	95(57.2)	150(50)
Prompt payer	59(62.8)	15(57.7)	5(35.7)	71(42.8)	150(50)
Total	94(100)	26(100)	14(100)	166(100)	300(100)
	(31)	(9)	(5)	(55)	(100)

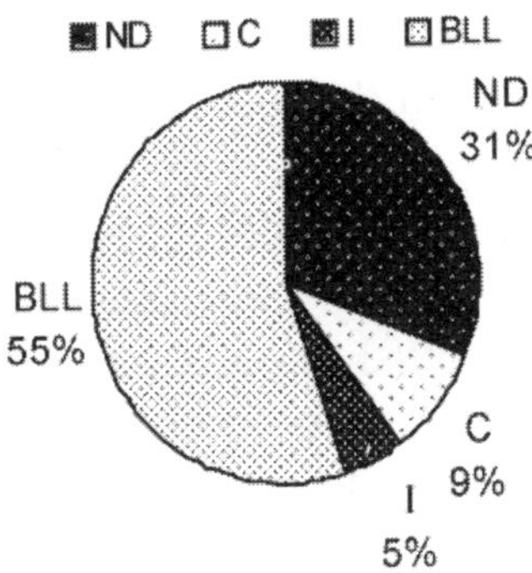

Fig. 36.5. Reasons for Depending on Informal Sources

Chi-square value: 11.356 D.F: 3 P-value: 0.010

Note: **Figures in parentheses are percentages in totals**

Source: **Survey Data**

Table 3 shows that more than 55 percent of loanees depended on the informal sources for meeting the requirements linked to the existing loans. Another important area, to which the formal sector failed to cater, was consumption which consisted of emergent and occasional requirements for funds.

A cursory glance at Table 3 reveals that, majority of non-dependents of informal sources and majority of the dependents for consumption purposes repay more promptly. Majority of the loanees who depended on the informal sources for investment, and for purposes linked to the bank loans could not repay in time. A strong relationship was found to exist between the nature of repayment and the purposes for depending on informal sources.

Having realized the influence of the loan-linked requirements in making a loanee a defaulter, a further analysis of these requirements was made with a view to identify the sub reason which had the highest influence on the repayment behaviour. Borrowing for down payment, for compensating the inadequacies in loans, for repayment of loans availed from the primary banks (Arunachalam and Palanisamy 1991), and that from other banks were the main requirements linked to the loans taken from the banking sources.

Table 4 cross-tabulates the repayment behaviour of the loanees who borrowed from informal sources for meeting various bank loan-linked requirements. Requirements for down payment, compensating inadequacies in loan amount, repayment of loans from primary banks and repayment of loans from other banks are the main items linked to bank loans.

Table 4. Different Bank Loan Linked Purposes for Depending on Informal Sources

Sample Loanees	*Not applicable* 1	*Down Payment* 2	*Balance Inadequacy* 3	*Repayment of Primary Bank Loan* 4	*Repayment of Other Loans* 5	*Total*
Defaulter	55(41)	21(52.5)	6(28.6)	56(64.4)	12(66.7)	150(50)
Prompt payer	79(59)	19(47.5)	15(71.4)	31(35.6)	6(33.3)	150(50)
Total	134(100) (45)	40(100) (13)	21(100) (7)	87(100) (29)	18(100) (6)	300(100) (100)

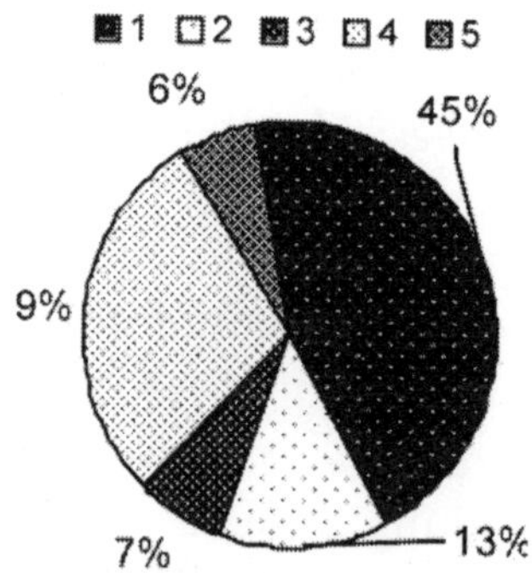

Fig. 36.6. Reasons for Bank Loan Linked Purposes

Chi-square value: 17.440 D.F: 4 P-value: 0.002

Note: **Figures in parentheses are percentages in totals**

Source: **Survey Data**

Out of the 55.3 percent of (i.e., 166) loanees, who depended on informal sources for meeting the bank loan-linked requirements, the purpose of 29 percent was to repay the loans taken from the primary banks. Another 6 percent of loanees borrowed to repay the dues to other banks. Thus 35 per cent (29 + 6) of loanees, borrowed from informal sector for the purpose of the repayment of already existing loans availed by them either from primary banks or other banks. Some loanees had no regular source of income for making repayment of loans. That was one of the reasons for depending on the informal sources. The second important purpose for depending on informal sector was to satisfy the requirement for down payment of the loans sanctioned to them from the primary banks. Yet another seven per cent of loanees depended on this sector in order to compensate the inadequacy of loan amount sanctioned by the primary banks

As is evident from Table 4, the vast majority of the loanees, who were indebted to the informal sources for the purpose of making repayment of loans availed from the primary banks (64.4 per cent) and from other banks (66.7 per cent), were defaulters. But the majority of non-dependants and dependants for compensating the inadequacies in loans from primary banks were found to be prompt payers. In the case of loanees who remain indebted to the informal sources for making the down payment, the percentage of defaulters slightly outweighed that of the prompt payers. On testing, the two variables – reasons for depending on informal sources for bank loan-linked purposes and the repayment nature of loanees – were found to be related significantly.

LEAKAGES

Quite often loanees divert the loaned money towards purposes for which these were not meant (Johl 2007). Generally such purposes may either be unproductive or productive. Unproductive diversion occurs when the diverted money does not generate any additional income from the use of it. Hence the loanee will have to repay from some other sources of income. Inadmissibility of any purpose for which a loanee has more pressing needs, like consumption, swapping of costly debts, etc. come under this category. This study agrees with the observations of Reserve Bank of India in the matter of leakages. In its Malegam Committee report (2011), RBI observed that only 25.4 per cent of every new loan was spent on income generation, while 20.4 per cent was used for repaying old loans.

Another type of leakage occurs when the credit money is used for productive purposes other than the one for which it is borrowed for. In an ambition to enhance their fixed assets some of the loanees divert their loans (from primary banks) to meet their fixed investment deficit for which it is difficult to borrow (Kahlon and Singh, 1984). Diversion turns productive when the diverted funds are used for the needs of education, employment or investment. Even if leakages are channelled through productive investment canals, due to the difference in the pattern of flow of returns, the repayment capacity of the loanee goes out of line and he becomes a defaulter. This section, therefore, attempts to map various reasons for diversion of loans, as it exists among the loanees of the primary banks.

For the purpose of analysis, leakages from loan amounts were broadly classified into three: debt swapping, consumption, and investment. "Debt swapping" in this study stands for delinking the loanees from their existing debts to informal agencies. This debt may or may not be linked to the sample loan. Consumption represents unproductive purposes. Most of the investment purposes are productive in the sense that it generates income. The distribution of loanees on the basis of the type of leakages incurred is exhibited in Table 5.

Table 5. Reasons for Loan Leakages

Reasons for Leakages	*Loanees (No)*	*Loanees(%)*
Debt swaps (D)	51	17
Consumption (C)	62	20.7
Investment (I)	48	16
Non leakages (N)	139	46.3
Total	**300**	**100**

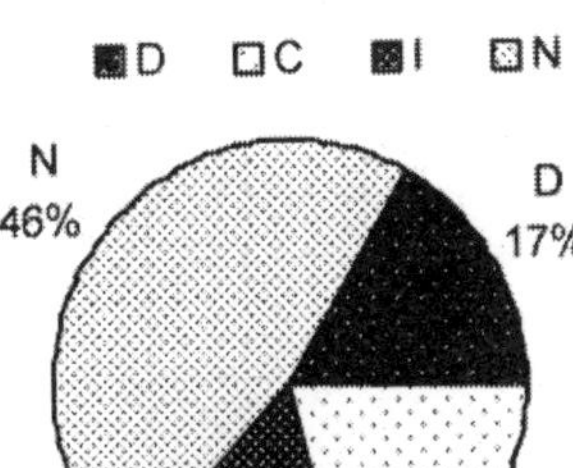

Fig. 36.7

Source: **Survey Data**

As per the figures, the consumption remained as the most common reason for leakages, followed by the debt swaps and the investment. As 17 percent of loanees diverted loan amounts for clearing their prevailing debts, it can be inferred that Linkages is the cause for leakages to a certain extent.

THE SOURCE OF REPAYMENT

Each loan project is expected to generate income for the repayment of instalment dues and even more. But, in this study, in the case of a vast majority of loanees, this expectation went wrong. While sorting out the financial mess at micro as well as macro level, it is not uncommon to solve a current problem of debt with additional borrowings / debt (Malegam 2011; Wade 2009). Likewise, the sample loanees depended on sources other than project income for the repayment of instalments due on the loans availed from the primary banks. Table 6 exhibits the tabulation of the data on the sources from which the loanees repay their loans.

Table 6. The distribution of loanees on the basis of Sources of Repayment

Sources of Repayment	*Loanees (No)*	*Loanees(%)*
Income from Project (IP)	13	4.3
Own funds (OF)	162	54.0
Banking sources(BS)	20	6.7
Money-lenders(ML)	72	24.0
Friends and Relatives(F&R)	33	11.0
Total	**300**	**100.0**

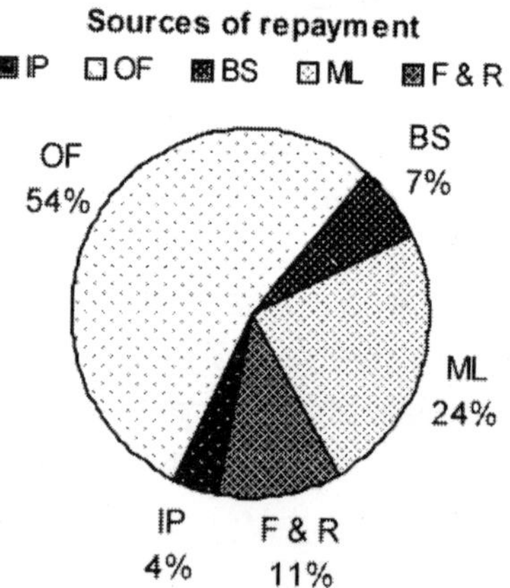

Fig. 36.8

***Source*: Survey Data**

Only 4.3 percent of loanees could repay from their projects. The vast majority of 95.7 per cent had to depend on sources other than income from the projects for repayment.

Borrowed funds constituted the main source for nearly 42 percent of loanees. Of this 35 percent had to depend on informal sector to clear the dues towards the primary bank. Thus borrowing from primary banks leads to linkages. The majority of loanees could repay out of their owned funds (54 percent). But this consisted of income received from other sources, income earned by other members in the family and/ or income from realisation of their assets. Thus, most of the loanees had to either forgo their income from other sources or sell their properties to settle their dues to the primary banks. In consequence, endeavours to strengthen the financial position end up in the erosion of the same.

CONCLUSION

Even after decades of efforts put in aiming at the inclusive growth, primary banks could not succeed in delinking loanees from the informal sources completely. This study supports the findings of the Expert Committee on Rural Credit under the chairmanship of Vyas (2000) in this respect. The bank financed projects are not self liquidating in nature as perceived by the policy makers.

The "bank loan-linked debts" in general and "the repayment of primary bank loans" in particular , were the dire needs of loanees which make them dependants of money lenders. This calls for urgent attention. The percentage of those who borrowed from the informal sources after the incident of borrowing from the primary banks was more than the percentage of those who borrowed before. It is soul searing to learn that the borrowings from primary banks make the loanees dependants on the informal sector to a considerable extent.

Today people are not bothered about the requirements of repayments of tomorrow. The panacea lies in enabling them to distinguish between needs and wants, and to spend within their means .

SUGGESTIONS

This points towards the relevance of Financial Literacy. Diversion of loans as well as diversion of income generated from loan projects, low income generating capacity resulting from poor project management, and stress at individual and family levels can be minimised through Financial Literacy, Financial Planning and Credit counselling, if not eliminated (Swanker 2007; Throat 2007). The recently devised Self Employment Training Institutes, Farmers Clubs, Knowledge centres for farmers etc can be considered as infrastructures for skill development and capacity building among the rural poor. Training has been recognised by many financing agencies as one of the pre requisites for giving financial assistance to the loanees (Swamy 1997).

Thus Financial Education is the basic infrastructure that supports the smooth flow of financial services. Efforts for promoting Financial Inclusion by way of providing credit to those who have little financial education steered them to the vicious circle of borrowing. Though the credit money neither served the very purpose nor benefitted the loanees in the anticipated manner, it required repayment. Like preparation of land is a prereqisite for good cultivation, promotion of financial literacy / education should precede introduction of measures for financial inclusion.

NOTES

a Financial inclusion denotes delivery of credit and other financial services at an affordable cost to the vast sections of the disadvantaged and low-income groups (Rangarajan Committee)

b Defaulters are loanees who have committed defaults to the primary banks in the repayment of one or more instalments and were defaulters as on 30-06-2004.

c Prompt payers, in this study, are loanees who have

never committed any default in the matter of repayment

d NonPerfoming Assets are the assets which which remains out of order for 180 days. Usually such assets do not generate income in the regular course.

WORK CITED

Arunachalam R., and A. Palanisamy(1991): "Utilisation and Payment of Cooperative Crop Loan." *Indian Cooperative Review* 29.2 : 180-186.

Balishter and Roshan singh and Mithilesh (1998): "Institutional Financing of Agriculture under Service Area Approach – A study in Agra District of Uttar Pradesh." *Land Bank Journal,* 37. 2 : 1-16.

Canara Bank (2008): "Financial Inclusion: towards Sustainable Economical Empowerment." In: *Ideas and Insights,* Corporate Business Plan Conference 2008-09: pp 88-92.

Chandra, Dinesh (1993): *Rural Credit- Role of Informal Sector.* New Delhi: Segment Books.

Chavan, Pallavi, and R. Ramakumar (2002): "Micro-Credit and Rural Poverty: An Analysis of Empirical Evidence." *Economic and Political Weekly* 37.10 : 955-965

Deshpande R S (2002): " Suicide by Farmers in Karnataka: Agrarian Distress and Possible Alleviatory Steps." *Economic and Political Weekly* 37.26 (2002): 2601-2610.

Indian Institute of Banking and finance (2008): "In Vidarbha, Farmers Prefer MFIs" Micro Finance, *IIBF Vision,* Vol. 1. Issue.1 August:5

– (2010): " Govt Banks to be Judged by Rural Drive" Top Stories, *IIBF Vision,* Vol. 2. Issue.11 June:1

Johl S. S., Reserve Bank of India (2007): Report Of The Working Group To Suggest Measures To Assist Distressed Farmers. *http://www.rbi.org.in*

Kahlon, A. S. and Karan Singh, (1984). *Managing Agricultural Finance-Theory and Practice.* New Delhi : Allied Publishers(P)Limited.

– (1992). *New Directions in Agricultural Credit System and Rural Financial Market.* New Delhi : Allied Publishers Ltd.

Komaraiah Bala J (2000): "Impact of Institutional Finance on Tribal Economy." *Land Bank Journal,* 39.2: 23-37.

Kusanna Dasanoor M (2004). "Indian Farmer's Suicides Have Become a Social Stroke: A view on Karnataka." *Land Bank Journal,* 43.1: 27-50.

Malegam Y.H, Reserve Bank of India (2011): Report of the Sub-Committee of the Central Board of Directors to Study Issues and Concerns in the MFI Sector 19 Jan, Available at *http://www.rbi.org.in*

Narayanasamy N., and K.K. Sunderam (1980): "Repayment of Loan- Farmers' Perception." *Indian Cooperative Review.18.2* : 51-62.

Purkayastha Gautham (2001): " Rural Indebtedness in Assam: Changing Scenario." *Economic and Political Weekly,* 36.25 : 2239-41.

Rao, Ramachandra K S., A K Tripathi (2001). "Indebtedness of Households: Changing Characteristics." *Economic and Political Weekly,* 36 .19 : 1617-25.

Sainath P (2010): "Farm Suicides a 12- year saga" *The Hindu Daily.* Kochi (Edn) Jan.25,: 8

Sharma B D (2001) " Role and Vision of Cooperatives in New Millennium", Background Papers of 14th Indian Cooperative Congress, NCUI, New Delhi, Sept 22-23: 1-24.

Sridhar Naga G and K. Ram Kumar(2011): " Without new loans, SHGs owe MFIs Rs 7,000 cr." Business Line, 9 April

Swain B.K. (2010): "Financial Access For All Still Miles To Go.", National Institute of Rural Development. Available at http://www.skoch.in/

Swamy, B.K. Narayana (1997). "Synthesising Development Potential with Rural Credit Plans at Grass root Level and Resource Planning for Development Lending by Nationalised Banks for Rural Development." Agricultural Banker : 33-38.

Swarnkar C.P., Reserve Bank of India (2007): Report of the Working

Group to Examine the Procedures and Processes of Agricultural Loans. Available at *http://www.rbi.org.in*

Thorat Usha, Reserve Bank of India (2007): Report of the High Level Committee to Review Lead Bank Scheme. Available at *http://www.rbi.org.in*

Ushakumari l (2011): "Misutilisation of Loans: a highway to Nonperforming Assets." In: Banking Sector in the Global Scenario, C Thilakam (Ed). Chennai: Maruthi Publishers, pp.385-387.

Wade Robert (2009): "Steering out of Crisis." *Economic and Political Weekly*, 44.13 : 39-46.

20

Financial Exclusion: A Theoretical Approach

B. Pradeep Kumar
P. J. Philip

INTRODUCTION

The problem of financial exclusion has gained wide currency in recent times owing to the aggressive persuasion of financial sector reforms in India, downsizing government share in nationalized banks, liberalizing the bank licensing policy and allowing the entry of foreign banks. The unfettered competition injected in to the financial sector with liberal agenda has in fact spawned a number of sea changes in the financial scenario. The vigorous pursuit of profit in place of the objective of "social and development banking" has paved the way for a shift from "mass banking" to "class banking" resulting in the exclusion of a segment of population from the mainstream financial framework, who are regarded as "credit unworthy" in financial parlance. The ICT enabled banking services have also kept some people away from the financial services, leading to the technical exclusion of these people. Financial exclusion is not a new phenomenon, although its dimensions have been changed in tune with the policy and technology related changes in recent times. This paper intends to focus on financial exclusion with a theoretical perspective.

This paper is structured as follows. The following second section is set aside to give an account of the definitions of financial exclusion. Third section sheds light on the prominent theories of financial exclusion. The fourth section elaborates on the strategies to address the problem of financial exclusion. Final section offers conclusion.

DEFINING FINANCIAL EXCLUSION

Defining financial exclusion is a very complex task as many academicians, practical researchers and financial analysts have attempted to define it in divergent ways. Notwithstanding the minute differences across various definitions, once could conveniently categorize these definitions under two broad heads: One, based on banking experts' perceptions of defining financial exclusion associated primarily with their commitment to fulfil the target of attaining cent percent financial inclusion as directed by the RBI, and the other based on how financial economists define it in a way as to connect the issue of financial exclusion with other broad fundamental issues like social and economic exclusion. Obviously, the former category of definitions conveys a very narrow but practically relevant meaning of financial exclusion whilst the latter defines it from the perspective of a theoretical background encompassing all dimensions of financial exclusion and its intertwining with other core areas like social and economic exclusion. Needless to say that of the two categories of definitions, the latter serves the purpose of a fundamental researcher in a better way. Nevertheless, a detailed account of the all definitions of financial exclusion is worthwhile as it helps one to comprehend the broad meaning of this phenomenon.

If one attempts to trace out the origin of the term financial exclusion, it can be seen that this term first came into the financial literature in 1993 to describe a situation of limited physical access to banking services on account of the bank closures. It means that in its original form financial exclusion meant not the lack of access to financial products like banking and insurance products and the like which ameliorate the vulnerability of the people but merely the lack of geographical access to banks. But it was in 1999 the term financial exclusion began to be used to designate the condition of not having access to mainstream financial services (Kempson and Whyley, 1999).

Unsurprisingly, financial exclusion appears to have been associated with social and economic exclusion. Some definitions of financial exclusion encompass this association in a meaningful manner. We now attempt to have a bird's eye view of such definitions. First of all financial inclusion (or, alternatively, financial exclusion) has been defined in the context of the larger issue of social inclusion (or exclusion). One of the oldest definitions by Leyshon and Thrift (1995) defines financial exclusion as referring to those processes that serve to prevent certain social groups and individuals from gaining access to the financial system. According to Sinclair (2001), financial exclusion means the inability to access necessary financial services in an appropriate form. In a speech in 2006, RBI deputy governor Rakesh Mohan said, "financial exclusion signifies the lack of access by certain segments of the society to appropriate, low cost, fair and safe financial products and services from mainstream providers". Usha Thorat (deputy governor, RBI) expressed similar views in a speech in 2007, as "by financial exclusion we mean the provision of affordable financial services, (viz., access to payments and remittance facilities, savings loans and insurance services) by the formal financial system to those who tend to be excluded".

THEORIES OF FINANCIAL EXCLUSION

It appears that financial exclusion is more associated with the broader form of exclusionary processes like economic and social exclusion. Hence, providing a theoretical framework to financial exclusion will have to take into account the fundamental and institutional variables, which have been at work in a country, manifesting itself into the concerns of economic and social exclusion. In countries plagued by fundamental economic and social disequilibria, the genesis of financial exclusion could be traced to factors causing such disequilibria viz. the prevalence of a multiple form of social stigma, religious fundamentalism, retrogressive social mind set up, existence of administrative bottlenecks, poor execution of state sponsored welfare schemes, terrain geographical setting and economic inequality brought about by the failures of pro-government initiatives like land reforms. These factors partially describe the reasons of financial exclusion as it evolves today whereas they may well explain why financial exclusion existed in days prior to the implementation of pro-liberal financial policies across the world particularly in India. Earlier literature on financial exclusion exhibits the fact that people at large were excluded from accessing basic mainstream financial products in India primarily on account of the lack of branch expansion in rural areas and private ownership of majority of banks. With banks having achieved considerable progress in branch expansion thanks to the nationalization of banks in 1969, geographical dimension to the problem of financial exclusion almost ceases to exist except in some uninhibited or marginally inhibited places, emphasis has now been shifted to other dimension of exclusion like, access especially conditional access, technological access etc. Competition among the banks unleashed by the aggressive financial sector liberalization policies since 1991 has forced banks particularly the nationalized banks to shift their priority from the "social and development banking" to "profit oriented banking". This has had undoubtedly wide-ranging ramifications in the realm of social and economic life of the country. The entire issue of financial exclusion needs to be looked into from this perception and practical change in the nature and functioning of the financial sector.

Here, we try to unearth the theoretical framework, which can illustrate the kind of financial exclusion that happens due to factors purely economic in nature. It must be born in mind that while today's financial exclusion is more attributed to factors associated with technology, financial crisis and market driven motives, the fundamental causes viz. lack of income, assets etc need to be stressed.

We have two theories to explain the process of financial exclusion.

1. Free Market Model.
2. The Theory of Asymmetric Information.

Free Market Model

We technically label this model as the "Share holder Wealth Maximization Model, hereafter abbreviated as SWMM or simply as the Free Market Model. Needless to say, that the true free market model has a long history and the usefulness of such a model to sort out many fundamental economic problems has been well documented and still debated. There are different variants of such model. But, the variant, which we rely on here for our analysis, is the one dealing with financial market.

A good chunk of economic theories starting from the time of Adam Smith has immensely contributed to the development of projecting "Market" as the sole panacea for all illness of an economy. In its sum and substance, these theories argue that a deregulated economy has an inherent tendency to move closer to "Pareto Optimum" where, technically speaking, all resources are well spread out and employed in a manner, which ensures maximum possible wealth creation. As encrypted in the concept "Pareto Optimum", such a condition does not envisage an economic agent's position being deteriorated following the enhancement of the gain of other persons. Starting from the time of Classical writers as Adam Smith and David Ricardo it has been claimed that competition unleashed by the policy of "laissez faire", will shower the benefits of rooting out all ills that an economy is likely to confront with. Intervention by the policies of government will take away the economies from the path of attaining growth accompanied by the removal of all type of imbalances. The free market model as we explain here has been built on this philosophical foundation.

Unlike in the past, now financial institutions indulge in stock market operations to collect fund for their fundamental functions. Most of the leading financial institutions encompassing banking institutions have embarked on placing their shares in the capital market with much advertisement. Besides the new generation private banks thronging on the capital market to collect fund, nationalized commercial banks in India have also followed the suit, thanks to the policy change of government in favour of disinvestment policies. As a testimony to this, one can notice the recent announcement by the Finance Ministry that it has decided to offload 49% of the government stake in the State Bank of India. Fallout of this sweeping change in the financial basis of these institutions has been a tendency to show that they are rated high by the internationally reputed rating agencies like Standard and Poores. Thus, the pressure of making the Financial Institution worth of stock market investing has in fact forced these institutions to abstain from risky lending.

At this juncture one could find a paradox that whilst deregulation, as the proponents of market driven strategies opine, appears to increase financial inclusion, the opposite, financial exclusion, seems to have surfaced as a growing problem. The argument that deregulation should have resulted in financial inclusion rather than financial exclusion rests on the principle that market driven strategies always lead to the spawning of suitable financial products in response to the market demand. But the problem is that as more financial products are brought into the market, the risk in lending also increases which forces the banks to focus more on certain groups, rather than on customers in general, leading to the financial exclusion of a majority of 'Non-Valuable Customer groups and more strategic inclusion of 'valuable' customer groups. Banks generally believe that inclusion of more 'valuable customer group' even at the cost of the exclusion of the underprivileged or the least 'valuable' will immensely enrich the "value-added' in SWM sense. Most of the new generation banks and private banks seem to have been adopting this strategy. For instance, certain new generation private banks in India do open savings accounts provided that there is minimum cash balance of Rs.5,000/-. This stipulation in fact testimonies the fact that 'valuable customers' are sought after compared to those who wish to open an account with a nil or frill balance. As Boyce (2000, p.649) rightly opines: 'Customer valuation is shown to have become a means to increase shareholder income and wealth, almost inevitable at the cost of further marginalizing the poor and disadvantaged'.

The deregulation of the financial sector in force in India since the onset of the neo-liberal policies has in fact exacerbated financial exclusion. Coupled with this deregulation, the financial crisis, which has become the order of the day, attenuates the financial exclusion process. It has been observed that whenever there is a financial crisis, there is an aftermath of some kind of 'flight to quality' and an emphasis on risk reduction by the financial industry. The result of this herd behaviour of becoming more conscious of financial operation is the 'abandonment and retreat to a more affluent client base'. This also applies to particular geographic localities. This is called the 'financial desertification' process. Leyshon and Thrift (1995, p.312) explains this economic process as 'increasingly exclusionary in response to a financial crisis founded in higher levels of competition and extreme levels of indebtedness'. Evidences show that in many financial systems, financial exclusion has its roots in the changing macroeconomic structural circumstances. Thus, it is evident that financial exclusion is the result of the enhanced competition triggered by globalization and deregulation. Leyshon and Thrift however have argued that not all banks have joined this folk in responding to the neo-liberal call of globalization and deregulation. This argument appears to be correct in Indian context as well especially in the case of those banks in which the government of India has the highest stake and say. Unarguably this shift that these banking institutions have made to 'valuable customers' in the pursuit of enhancing their 'value addition' can right be called as a "strategic shift" which has been underway in banking operations world over. This strategic shift has in fact led to a separation between lower income customers and higher income customers mainly in the case of financial products to which they have access. This separation has been intensified by a lot of other factors including technological advancement that the world in general and banks in particular have gained in recent times, whereas these 'advancements' appear to be not accessible to a large number of lower customers. Equipped with this technical advancement, the higher income customers have moved themselves to the level of 'global financial citizens' who possess instantaneous access to financial information, transactions and value transfers of their wealth. This emergent status of 'global financial citizenship' apparently has rendered these groups with a new kind of higher v/s the lower income customers. Consequently, as a source of 'value additivity' this former group has become a target of banks especially new generation private and foreign banks in the context of Indian financial system. The overemphasis being laid on this group on account of the above reasons has led either to the intensification of the already existing financial exclusion or to the emergence of the financial exclusion of the 'un-banked' or 'marginally banked' groups. They appear to have apparently less information about the products being launched by the banks, and they are not so heavily targeted for new products innovated by the banks. In short, the market dynamics of the banks appear to have exacerbated the polarization between the low-income customers and high-income customers. In short the above description provides us an understanding of how competition, deregulation and finally the financial crisis brought about by the globalization accelerate the process of financial exclusion. Now we turn to the other two drivers which prompt financial institutions to move after valuable customers and exclude low income and socially disadvantaged customers from accessing financial products. These two drivers viz. securitization and retail disintermediation, which require our immediate attention, are outlined below.

To put in simple parlance, Securitization means corporate relying on the capital market for fund rather than the financial institutions. In other words Securitization is the shifting of credit intermediation primarily by the corporate sector out of the banking system into capital markets. In this sense this is a disintermediation process which makes the financial intermediaries like banks irrelevant. Retail disintermediation on the other hand describes the shift of savings out of the banking system into money-market mutual funds and offshore vehicles. That means people do not save money with financial institutions like banks, rather they invest in capital markets seeking more returns. This process restricts the investment capacity of the banking system. On the other hand, securitization reduces the corresponding demand for commercial bank lending. Thus from both sides, the securitization and disintermediation together, the financial industry has been squeezed to an extent which drives it to resort to banking practices contrary to what they have been supposed to do. These trends have led to the development of investment banking in countries like USA. Thus, banks have responded to securitization and financial disintermediation by re-examining their core banking business. They have started seeking new ways to 'lock in' their customers and make more profit through a process - value addition in SWM language. The following are the main strategic shifts in response to this:

- Innovation of new varieties of deposit instruments.
- Improving risk management and risk mitigation techniques.
- ABS or Asset-Backed Securities techniques in lending.
- Moving into new areas of lending.

All these development viz. competition, deregulation, securitization and disintermediation have prompted banks to follow a kind of 'standardization' in their functioning. The development and the spread of ICT enabled technology revolution have also added fuel to this 'standardization process. Financial institutions like banks and even the corporate banks have started using software to assess credit risks, loan selection and the pricing of financial products. The application of computer based technology has naturally forced banks to reduce their staffing and the old brick mortar banking has become a thing of the past in many countries. All these are in the search for greater cost efficiency in the operation of the financial institutions. Having developed an array of different financial products, banks can now easily target standardized customers for cross selling its new products. Low-income profile customers may not be capable of purchasing multiple products that the banks are ready to offer. In US market, for instance, banks have been directed towards searching for profitable 'standardized' customers mainly because of the fact they appear to be less risky while being capable of buying multiple products simultaneously.

In the era of unfettered tough competition that the banks have become subject to, many small banks find it easy to be merged with big ones believing in the saying "too big to fail". Merging is often the fastest way to achieve the desired result and helps to explain the US bank merging tendencies. It can be rightly remarked that 'Mergers and acquisitions are central to the dynamic of the standardized customer'. (Dymski and Li (2002, p.5). The pre-regulation banking is characterized by relatively low fixed costs and high marginal cost of servicing customers. But on the other hand, the post-deregulation phase, the phase of new mega banking, is an era of high fixed cost (of establishing ATMs, Creating software, Debit and Credit Cards, product design, testing and marketing) and low marginal costs of servicing customers (because of staff cutting). High fixed costs when spread over a long period does not pose any threat to the bank whereas low marginal cost becomes beneficial. The net effect is a lower cost of customer servicing in the long period. Therefore, the target of banks is to pursue the more profitable customer groups, develop these customer relationships through time and to target them for a wider range of products. Many new generation banks today look like the front room of a five star hotel or a big house. A few cushion chairs replace uneasy and arrogant chairs of the old time. The message is that these banks do not expect many more worthless customers. They want only a few valuable customers. The economic impact of the above process is very visible. That is the mainstream commercial banks increasingly 'desert' the less profitable household groups. If these groups are concentrated in a particular locality, the resultant financial exclusion has an inevitable geographic spatial dimension as well as social and economic. This kind of 'financial desertification' may constrain continued economic and financial development activities.

To put it in a nutshell, the 'Free Market Model" postulates that unchecked deregulation of the financial activities driven by the motive of profit and market signals has a clear message that if uncontrolled it may exacerbate the problem of financial exclusion further, leading to a catastrophe in the financial space of an economy. Two things can happen if the financial sector continues to be deregulated as it is today: One is, at the very least a deregulated financial system can increase the polarization between the financially included and excluded in the societal groups. The other is, at the worst the free market model may also increase the number of groups excluded as risk-based pricing becomes more sophisticated. Therefore, some kind of 'intervention' cum 'partnership approach' to financial exclusion is the need of the hour. In this context, 'intervention' connotes those directions that the government would require banks to do. These actions include government as a mediator to 'self regulation' by the financial industry itself. 'Self regulation' here covers those banking sectors whose primary mission is to develop their regions, and help the poorer sections of the customer-base. Institutions pursing this way have also scripted successful stories of more profit and greater efficiency in their financial operations.

The Theory of Asymmetric information

Now we start with a word on the crucial distinction that theoretically exists between the transaction in the goods market and transaction in the credit market, which would be worthwhile to comprehend how information asymmetry engenders and exacerbates the problem of financial exclusion. In the goods market the task and objectives of transaction are simpler and comparatively less cumbersome. In such a market, the seller of a commodity "does not worry about who the buyer is and what happens to the commodity after the sale as long as he gets paid" (Gilberto.M.Llanto, 1989). On the other hand, transaction or exchange in the credit market is much more complicated and cumbersome primarily because of the fact that most of the transactions are future contracts in nature. Hence, the relationship built upon a transaction lasts for a long period. For instance, the case of fixed deposit, a home loan, or a personal loan. It is obvious, hence, that in the case of the transaction of these products a great deal of information on the personal characteristics of the borrower is required. In this background, it is quite natural that banks spend a good part of the time in locating a "good" borrower and a "good" project. Unlike the commodity seller who does not worry about the buyer of the financial product, the bank also worries about what the borrower will do with the loan and whether he will abide by the terms and conditions of the contract (Clemenz, 1986).

Generally, it is observed that the banks lend money without complete certainty of whether or not the loan will become a non-performing asset. Since the borrowers know themselves better than the bank, they can gain from understating personal as well as the project's weaknesses and exaggerating positive qualities. If the borrowers do so then we can safely say that the information transfer is hampered by "moral hazards and incentive problems". To address this issue, the banks employ screening techniques to insulate themselves from default risk. This drives banks to exclude somebody from having access to banks. In short, the asymmetric information denies the borrower effective access to financial resources.

STRATEGIES TO ADDRESS THE PROBLEM OF FINANCIAL EXCLUSION

Now it would be pertinent to look into various strategies that have been suggested to address the problem of exclusion in general and financial exclusion in particular. First, we shall have a peep into the three financial development theories, which establish the relation between the development of the financial system and the economic development.

The Theory of Active Financial Development or Supply Leading Financial Development

Placing significance on the setting up of financial institutions as a tool for spreading the habit of engaging in financial dealings among the people, this theory articulates that financial development precedes economic development. Equipping the people with all apparatus of financial instruments is the key to tackle the problem of financial exclusion. Once adequate financial needs of people are legitimately met by the financial system, then the people will start building upon that, necessary other economic entitlements and this economic empowerment of the people will in course reinforce financial development. The wide scale branch expansion of major commercial banks in India since 1969, that is after they were nationalized, was in line with the preposition of this theory. Most of the financial inclusion strategies being envisaged and implemented by the leading commercial banks in India under the direction of Reserve Bank of India are based on the spirit of this theory. Opening up of No-Frill Accounts is an attempt to offer financial products to the hither to unbanked people with a view to attract them to the world of finance. The figure 1 illustrates the theory of Active Financial Development.

The Theory of Passive Financial Development or Demand Following Financial Development

Contrary to the argument of the theory of active financial development, this theory states that economic development and economic empowerment of people paves the way for financial development. It is argued that when the people are actively involved in economic activities generating employment and income, the demand for various kinds of financial products tailor made to their needs arises. This generation of demand for financial products will act as stimuli for the establishment of financial institutions. This is because of this stress on demand that this approach has come to be alternatively known as the Demand Following Financial Development. It is generally held that this kind of financial inclusion brought about by this path of financial development will be sustainable in nature compared to the Supply Leading Financial Development. The mushroom growth of informal financial entities in the rural areas of our country can be cited as a best example of how the need forces the people to go in for credit at any price from whatever sources available to them. The entire argument contained in this approach can be illustrated with the help of the figure 2.

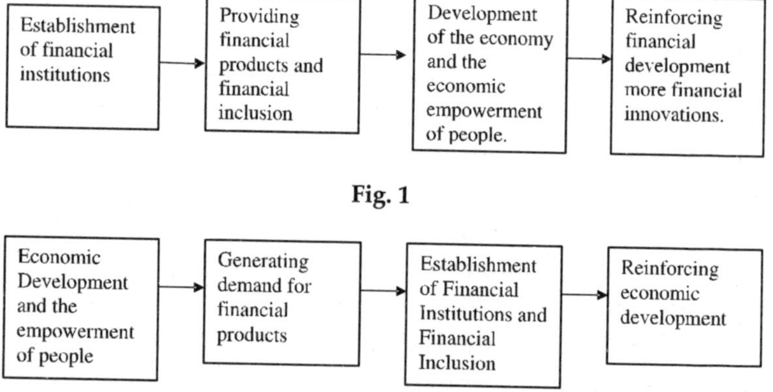

Fig. 1

Fig. 2

The Theory of Intertwining Financial Development

This theory different from other two theories narrated earlier argues that it is wrong to say that either financial development or economic development precedes each other. The theory articulates that sometimes financial development may lead to economic development and vice versa. Hence, it is difficult to point out where the process ends or starts. It can happen in both ways. The figure 3 captures the entire argument of this approach without any ambiguity.

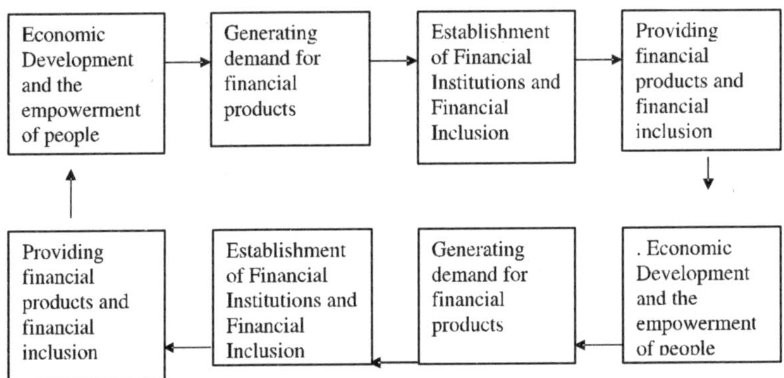

Fig. 3

Having gone through three main theories illustrating the relationship between financial development and economic development and thereby portraying the ways to address the problem of financial exclusion, now we turn towards other two theories, which are predominant in the realm of sociology in the analysis of the process of social exclusion. The increasing popularity of the concept of social exclusion among the sociologist especially since 1990s led to attempts to identify the multi-difficulties faced by the socially disadvantaged groups, and also to suggest measures to help the socially disadvantaged to overcome the multi-difficulties. Differences surfaced among the sociologists regarding the nature of solutions to be adopted to attain social inclusion. These differences entered around two views viz. whether to follow the pro-market policies or state led policies to tackle the problem of social exclusion. These divergent views led to two widely quoted discourse of social exclusion: The Social Integrationist Approach and the Redistributive Approach (Levitas, 1998). These approaches bear relevance to the problem of financial exclusion as well. Below, we attempt to relate these approaches to the problem of financial exclusion.

The Integrationist Approach to Financial Inclusion

The crux of this approach hovers around the whole dynamics of the Labour Market. This approach suggests that to wipe out the presence of financial exclusion we must provide the people with the opportunities to participate in the paid work in the labour market. Interestingly, this approach defines the concept of social exclusion in a different fashion that exclusion is nothing but exclusion from the paid work in the job market and hence it prescribes integration through paid work as the better panacea to solve the problem of exclusion. For instance, this approach endeavours to address the problem of the exclusion of the disabled from the labour market through the process of equipping them different with distinct skills, which are seemed suitable to enable them to enter into the labour market. To clean the education system, this approach argues that the system of education must be linked to the needs of the job market. In short, the social integrationists discourse supports a well-integrated society through paid work and relies heavily on the private market to find a lasting solution to the problem of financial exclusion. This approach in that sense appears to be friendlier with the notions of capitalism. It is known that workers do not produce all that they need. Instead, they exchange their labour power in the labour market for other products, which they could buy via the medium of money they are supposed to get from the labour market against the labour power they sell. Here money, in broader sense finance, plays a vital role in connecting the labour market with the product market, increasing the size of the product market and facilitating capital accumulation.

Integration with the labour market can be a best way to tackle the problem of financial exclusion as well. This is because once people are engaged in paid jobs in the labour market, the income generating from such paid works will definitely force them to demand various financial products and thereby leading to their effective financial inclusion. The Mahatma Gandhi National Rural Employment Guarantee Programme (MGNREGP), which has been successfully implemented in India, is a fitting example of how integration with the labour market can be a weapon for financial inclusion. Under this programme, every beneficiary that is the labourer will have to open an account with any nationalized bank for getting his or her wages regularly. The wage is disbursed through accounts. Here, so long as a person continues to work under the above said programme, he will have to be in constant touch with the banks, which will cultivate banking habit in that person.

Notwithstanding the bright side of this approach, critics argue that it has too many drawbacks viz. obscuring the inequality between the paid workers; overlooking the gender inequality in the labour market and ignoring the values of unpaid works such as taking care of the children in the family etc. (Levitas, 1998). Critics question the suitability of the labour market in generating employment for the people with learning difficulties.

The Redistributive Approach to Financial Inclusion

Quite different from the earlier approach, this one argues that the product and labour market are prone to creating inequality leading to the exclusion of those who cannot fall in line with the parameters of market. This approach is built on the premise that lack of an endowment to participate in the customary life of society is the cause that creates exclusion. The creation of a just society rerouting the movement of resources from the "abundant" hands to the "scarce" hands appears to be the solution to tackle exclusion, and hence active interventionist policies through the arms of tax reforms, expansion of benefit systems, reduction of earning differentials, financial recognition of unpaid works, introduction of minimum wages and minimum income for those who are unable to participate in the job market are called for to address the problem of exclusion. (Chau and Yu, 2002). This view associated with equitable society challenges the problems of inequality created by the product and labour market.

In addressing the problem of financial exclusion, the application of the elements of this approach could be found in many endeavours being adopted by the government. For instance, very often, having been misled by the fact that it is the price barrier, which prevents the disadvantaged in accessing credit from the formal credit market, nationalized banks in India adopt the practice of offering loans at subsidized rate of the interest to the low-income people, agriculturists and petty traders, SCs and STs. This subsidization of loan falls in line with the redistributionist discourse.

The difference between these two approaches lies in the division of responsibilities between the government and the market (labour market) in handling the problem of social exclusion. Both approaches recognize the difficulty that the disadvantaged group may face in the run up to be integrated into the mainstream of the society. The redistributionists argue that the market cannot create jobs for them as the market stands for those who are fit to work. Hence, they request the government to help them achieve a decent standard of living independent of the job market. The integrationists, on the other hand, question the government's ability to provide training to improve the employability of these people.

CONCLUSION

In short the problem of financial exclusion has to be tackled keeping in mind all the fundamental reasons that create and exacerbate the problem in various forms. The peripheral and eye washing strategies that have been implemented by the banks in India under the compulsion of government and RBI will not yield sustainable results unless and until fundamental problems are addressed.

REFERENCES

1. Boyce, G. (2000), 'Valuing customers and loyalty: the rhetoric of customer focus versus the realty of alienation and exclusion of (devalued) customers', *Critical Perspectives on Accounting,* 11.pp.649-689.
2. Clemenz.G, Credit Markets with Asymmetric Information, *Berlin: Springer Verlad,* 1986.
3. Frederic.S.Mishkin (1990), "Asymmetric Information and Financial Crisis: A Historical Perspective", Working Paper No.3400, *National Bureau of Economic Research, Massachusetts Avenue, Cambridge.*
4. Gilberto.M.Llanto (1989), Asymmetric Information in Rural Financial Markets and Interlinking of Transactions Through the Self-Help Groups" *Journal of Philippine Development,* 28, volume XVI No.1, 1989.
5. Leyshon.A. and N.Thrift (1994), 'Access to financial services and financial infrastructure withdrawal: problems and policies', *Area,* 26, pp.268-275.
6. Leyshon.A. and N.Thrift (1995),' Geographies of financial exclusion: financial abandonment in Britain and the US', *Transactions of the Institute of British Geographers, New Series,* 20.pp.312-341.

7. Sen, Amartya, (2000), "Social Exclusion: Concept, Application and Scrutiny", Working Paper, *Social Development Paper No.1, June, Bangkok"* ADB

8. Shaw.EW, (1973), "Financial Deepening in Economic Development", *New York: Oxford University Press,* 1973.

Section III : Financial Inclusion and Cooperatives

21

An Overview of Urban Cooperative Banks in India

Anupam Mitra

INTRODUCTION

In India, The cooperative societies act was introduced in 1904. The concept of cooperative banks was based on mutual co-operation i.e. each for all and all for each. This is the underlying spirit of the 100 years old co-operative movement in India. The first co-operative bank was set up in a small town in south India in 1904. The co-operatives were set up to cater the small needs of poor artisans, businessmen as an alternative to moneylenders. During the banking crisis in India in 1913-14, there was a trend of withdrawing deposits from non co-operatives and putting them in co-operative institutions.

Cooperative credit institutions may be of two types- (I) urban cooperative banks (UCB) and (ii) rural cooperative credit instititution (Chart 1). The urban areas are served by urban credit cooperatives. The credit cooperative has a three tier structure for the distribution of rural credit with Primary Agricultural Credit Cooperatives at the village level, District Central Cooperative Banks at the district level and State Cooperative Banks at the State level. As per the banking regulation act 1949, only urban cooperative banks, State Cooperative Banks and District Central Cooperative Banks are qualified to be called as banks in the cooperative sector.

Chart 1: Structure of Co-operative Credit Institutions (as on 31.03.2010)

Co-operative Credit Institutions					
Urban Co-operative Banks (1853)	Rural Co-operative Credit Institution (109924)				
	Short-Term Structure (109177)			Long -Term Structure(747)	
	State Co-Operative Banks (31) (SCB)	Central Co-operative Banks (371) (DCCB)	Primary Agricultural Credit Societies (94,942) (PACs)	SCARDB (20)	PCARDB (697)

The present study has been divided into nine sections. These are:

1. Introduction
2. Literature Review
3. Objective of the Study
4. Database and Methodology
5. Features of the Urban Co-operatives Banks
6. Progress of Urban Co-operatives in India
7. Findings
8. Conclusions
9. References

LITERATURE REVIEW

Urban cooperative banks also referred to as primary co-operative banks, play an important role in meeting the growing credit needs of urban and semi-urban areas of the country. They mobilize savings from the middle and lower income groups and purvey credit to small borrowers, including weaker sections of the society. These banks in India are financial cooperatives akin to credit unions found abroad, except that they can also accept deposits from non-members and form a part of the payments systems.

Market Share of UCBs

As on March 31, 2010 there were 1853 UCBs, 84 scheduled commercial banks, 133 Regional Rural Banks (RRBs) and 398 Rural Cooperative Banks (including 31 State Cooperative Banks and 367 District Cooperative Banks) in India. An analysis of market share of various bank groups indicates that the share of UCBs in total bank deposits is relatively low. Nevertheless, their market share grew steadily from 3.3% in 1990-91 to a high of 6.6% in 2004-05, but thereafter gradually declined to 4.8% (provisional) in 2009-10 (Table 1).

Table 1. Market share of deposits of all bank groups to total deposits (in percentage)

Year Ended 31st March	*Urban Cooperative Banks (UCB)*	*Rural Cooperative Banks (RCB)*	*Regional Rural Banks (RRB)*	*Commercial Banks*
2000	4.5	7.2	2.5	85.8
2001	4.9	7.6	2.6	84.9
2002	5.3	7.7	2.8	84.2
2003	5.6	7.8	2.8	83.8
2004	6.6	7.7	2.8	82.9
2005	6.3	7.2	2.9	83.6
2006	6.4	7.2	3.0	83.4
2007	6.3	7.0	3.0	83.7
2008	5.8	6.6	3.1	84.5
2009	5.3	6.3	3.1	85.3
2010	4.8	5.5	3.0	86.7

Source : RBI statistics

Growth of UCBs

In 1966 when the Banking Regulation Act was made applicable to UCBs, there were about 1100 UCBs with deposits and advances of Rs.167 crore and Rs.153 crore respectively. As at the end of 1996, the number of UCBs increased to 1501 and their deposits and advances rose significantly to Rs.24, 161 crore and Rs.17, 927 crore. The UCBs continued to grow at a fast pace till 2007, when their number increased to 1941 and their deposits and advances to Rs.1, 01,546 crore and Rs.64,880 crore respectively. Subsequently, the number of UCBs declined in 2010 to 1853 with total deposits of Rs.1, 12,237 crore and advances of Rs.70, 379 crore. An overview of their growth since the 2003 is given in Table 2.

Table 2. Growth of UCBs (amount in crores of rupees)

Year Ended March 31	*Number of UCBs*	*Deposits*	*% growth*	*Advances*	*% growth*
2003	1501	24161		17927	
2004	1502	40692	68.4	27807	55.1
2005	1618	80840	98.7	54389	95.6
2006	1854	93069	15.1	62060	14.1
2007	1941	101546	9.1	64880	4.5
2008	1926	110256	8.6	67930	4.7
2009	1872	105021	-4.7	66874	-1.6
2010	1853	112237	6.9	70379	5.2

Source : NAFCUB

The spectacular growth of UCBs in the late nineties and up to 2008, which had resulted in increasing their penetration, ironically, also led to certain weaknesses in the sector that adversely affected public perception and thereby, their competitiveness. A major reason for the decline in public confidence was the crisis faced in 2001 by a large multi-state bank in the state of Gujarat, when the bank witnessed a sudden 'run' on its branches, following rumours of its large exposure to a leading broker who had suffered huge losses in the share market. The large-scale withdrawal of deposits within short time had resulted in severe liquidity problems for the bank. The bank was also holding about Rs.800 crore of inter-bank deposits from a large number of UCBs in the state and from other states, which posed a systemic risk. In order to protect the interests of the general public and also that of the other cooperative banks, RBI had issued directions to the bank restricting certain operations (acceptance of fresh deposits, restricting payments to any single depositor to Rs.1000 and ban on fresh lending) and requisitioned the Central Registrar of Co-operative Societies, New Delhi to supersede the Board of Directors and appoint an Administrator. An order of moratorium was also enforced on the bank by the Central Government for a short period. The bank was subsequently placed under a scheme of reconstruction with the approval of Reserve Bank of India. The Gujarat episode was followed by another major crisis in the state of Andhra Pradesh in 2002, when one of the largest banks in the state faced a run, following a newspaper report regarding an inquiry instituted into the affairs of the bank by the State Registrar of Cooperative Societies. The bank was in a weak position, and ultimately, after attempts for its revival failed, its license was cancelled by the Reserve Bank in 2004. As on June 30, 2004, 732 out of 1919 UCBs were categorized in Grade III or IV signifying weakness and sickness.Recognising the systemic risks and keeping in view the needs of its clientele, Reserve Bank reviewed the entire gamut of legislative, regulatory and supervisory framework for these banks, and in March 2005, brought out a draft 'Vision Document for UCBs'. The vision document, which was drawn with the main objective of maintaining the viability and competitiveness of the UCBs, discussed the characteristics of the sector, analyzed the problems afflicting the banks and proposed strategies for dealing with problems affecting the sector.

OBJECTIVE OF THE STUDY

The information relating to Urban Co-operative Banks will be able

- To understand the need for credit for financing in urban areas.
- To identify the problem associated with urban co-operative banks.
- To evaluate the importance given by the Govt. of India as well as Govt. of West Bengal in respect of urban development by the UCBs for the overall development of the economy.
- Whether the UCBs are generating goodwill among the urban people.
- To assess the performance of UCBs.

DATABASE AND METHODOLOGY

This study is a modest attempt to examine the performance of urban co-operative banks in India. It is based on the secondary data which are available from various issues of reports of NAFCUB, RBI, and GOWB etc... In fact, the vast literature in this area has induced to undertake such a study because of the fact that there are very few studies concentrating on the performance of urban co-operative banks. Various statistical tools like correlation analysis, simple interpolation, regression analysis, etc to be used to analyze our data vis-à-vis to interpret the results.

FEATURES OF THE URBAN CO-OPERATIVES BANKS

The UCB sector is unique in that there is significant degree of heterogeneity among the banks in this sector in terms of size, geographical distribution, performance and financial strength. There is also diversity among the urban cooperative banks in the levels of professionalism, standards of corporate governance and access to advanced technology. Most importantly, the banks in this sector are under dual control, with a part of the powers vested in the State Government and a part with Reserve Bank.

Heterogeneity

While on the one hand, there are a number of small neighborhood banks functioning for mutual interest of their members, on the other, there are several large UCBs with a wide network of branches, large number of depositors and borrowers, many of whom are medium/large corporate. In the latter kind of UCBs, the cooperative structure remains only as an organizational arrangement and their business model and goals are more akin to commercial banks. The extent of heterogeneity can be gauged by size-wise, region-wise and grading-wise analysis of the UCBs. However, the density of network of urban cooperative institutions shows marked regional variations.

Size-wise distribution

The frequency distribution of UCBs in terms of deposits and advances their relative share is shown in Table 3. It is observed that at the lower end of the spectrum, 36.2% of the UCBs have a deposit base of less than Rs.10 crore and account for only 3.0% of deposits. At the same time, at the top end, only 14 banks had a share of 23% in the total deposits. More than 50% of the UCBs (962 banks) fell in the deposit base range of Rs.10 crore to Rs.100 crore and accounted for 29.5% of total deposits.

Region-wise distribution

The distribution of urban cooperative banks across the country is skewed, with significant concentration in southern and western regions. Table 4 gives the region-wise distribution of number of UCBs and share of deposits of each region.

Table 3. Size wise distribution of UCBs(as on 31.03.2010)

		No. of UCBs		*Deposits*	
	Amount (Rs in Crore)	*No.*	*Share in Total (per cent)*	*Amount (Rs in Crore)*	*Share in Total (per cent)*
1	>1000	14	0.8	25768	23
2	500 to <1000	16	0.9	11153	9.9
3	250 to <500	48	2.6	16947	15.1
4	100 to <250	142	7.7	21910	19.5
5	50 to <100	210	11.3	15164	13.5
6	25 to <50	302	16.3	10525	9.4
7	10 to <25	450	24.3	7374	6.6
8	5 to <10	333	18.0	2486	2.2
9	<5	338	18.1	910	0.8
	Total	**1853**	**100.0**	**112237**	**100.0**

Source : NAFCUB

Table 4. Region wise distribution of UCBs/their deposits (as on 31.3.2010) (amount in crores of rupees)

Region	*No. of banks*	*% Share in total*	*Deposits*	*% share in total*	*Advances*	*% share in total*
West	926	49.97	87063	77.57	54726	77.76
South	613	33.08	16003	14.26	10429	14.82
North	231	12.47	6389	5.69	3544	5.04
East	83	4.48	2781	2.48	1679	2.39
Total	1853	100.00	112237	100.00	70379	100.00

Source : NAFCUB

Grade-wise distribution

As part of its on-site inspection exercise, Reserve Bank has a system of categorizing banks into four grades based on objective parameters relating to capital adequacy, asset quality, earnings, compliance with CRR/SLR requirements and adherence to RBI guidelines and/ directives. Non-scheduled urban co-operative banks have been allowed to place deposits with strong scheduled urban co-operative banks; gold loans and small loans have been exempted from the 90-day norm for recognition of loan impairment; and the ceiling on certain categories of priority sector advances (loans to professionals, self-employed and the retail trade) has been raised. (Table 5)

Table 5. Grading-wise distribution of UCBs/their deposits (as on 31.3.2010) (amount in crores of rupees)

Grades	*No. of Banks*	*% share in Total*	*Deposits*	*% in Total*
I	716	39	64941	57.86
II	460	25	18580	16.54
I + II	1176	63	83521	74.40
III	407	22	13879	12.38
IV	270	15	14838	13.22
III + IV	677	37	28717	25.60
I + II +III + IV	1853	100.00	112237	100.00

Source : NAFCUB

The central bank also scrapped the "weak" and "sick" tags for classifying financially unsound urban co-operative banks. They are now classified into four grades – I, II, III, IV. While Grade I covers banks with no major supervisory concerns, the other three grades would indicate existence of supervisory concerns in increasing degree. Table 5 gives the grading-wise distribution of banks as on March 31, 2006 (as per provisional data). It is seen that 37% of UCBs in the country, accounting for 25.60% of total deposits, were in Grades-III and IV signifying weakness/and sickness, while the remaining major portion (63%) of UCBs, accounting for 74.40% of total deposits, were in Grades-I and II, indicating good/satisfactory performance/ financials.

PROGRESS OF URBAN CO-OPERATIVES IN INDIA

The distribution of UCBs across States showed that as at end-March 2010 one third of all UCBs, almost half of all branches of UCBs, around 60 per cent of total extension counters of UCBs and more than 85 per cent of ATMs of UCBs were located in Maharashtra state. Accordingly, more than 60 per cent of the total banking business of the UCB sector was concentrated in Maharashtra leaving very low volume of operations in rest of the States. The task of developing cooperative networking was initiated in the Second Five Year Plan on the recommendations of the All India Rural Credit Survey Report and was extended further in the Third Plan. In the post -liberalization period the urban cooperative banks, particularly those in larger towns are facing tougher competition from commercial banks. Even public sector banks have become very aggressive. One of the vital problems which vitiate cooperative networking is the interference of the politicians in the organization. Unless banking system more specifically urban co-operative banks are freed from political interference, the efforts to introduce transparency and accountability, a pre-requisite of good networking may not bring desired result.

FINDINGS

Priority sector lending targets introduced in 1983 were mainly aimed at directing a portion of total credit to some specific sectors of the economy which, inter alias, includes weaker sections, small enterprises, and housing. As at end-March 2010, about 65 per cent of total advances of UCBs went

Table 6. Financial Performance of Urban Cooperative Banks (As at end-March) (Amount in crore)

Item	*Scheduled*		*Non-Scheduled*		*All UCBs*	
	2008-09	*2009-10P*	*2008-09*	*2009-10P*	*2008-09*	*2009-10P*
A. Total Income (i+ii)	7,714	8,341	10,695	11,688	18,409	20,029
	(100.0)	(100.0)	(100.0)	(100.0)	(100.0)	(100.0)
I. Interest Income	6,803	7,593	9,828	10,865	16,631	18,458
	(88.2)	(91.0)	(91.9)	(93.0)	(90.3)	(92.2)
ii. Non-Interest Income	911	748	867	823	1,778	1,571
	(11.8)	(9.0)	(8.1)	(7.0)	(9.7)	(7.8)
B. Total Expenditure (i+ii)	6,133	7,156	8,814	9,756	14,947	16,912
	(100.0)	(100.0)	(100.0)	(100.0)	(100.0)	(100.0)
i. Interest Expenditure	4,444	5,226	6,241	7,013	10,685	12,239
	(72.5)	(73.0)	(70.8)	(71.9)	(71.5)	(72.4)
ii. Non-Interest Expenditure	1,689	1,930	2,573	2,743	4,262	4,673
	(27.5)	(27.0)	(29.2)	(28.1)	(28.5)	(27.6)
of which: Staff Expenses	815	1,192	1,548	1,670	2,363	2,862
C. Profit						
i. Amount of operating profit	1,581	1,185	1,881	1,931	3,461	3,116
ii. Provisions, contingencies, taxes	719	533	1,180	1,099	1,899	1,632
iii. Amount of net profit	862	652	701	832	1,562	1,484
Memo Item						
i. Return on Assets	1.1	0.7	0.6	0.7	0.8	0.7
ii. Return on Equity	9.2	5.7	5.1	4.9	6.8	5.2
iii. Net Interest Margin	2.9	2.5	3.3	3.1	3.1	2.8
iv. Non-Interest Margin	-1.0	-1.2	-1.6	-1.6	-1.3	-1.4

P : Provisional.

Note : 1) Figures in parentheses are percentages to total.

2) Ratios given as memo items are derived using average assets or equity as the denominator.

RBI statistics

to priority sectors of which more than 16 per cent of the total advances went to weaker sections. The composition of the priority sector lending of UCBs as at end-March 2010 showed that maximum loans under priority sectors went to small enterprises sector followed by housing and retail trade. Further, the composition of lending to weaker sections showed that almost one third of it went to the housing sector and another one fourth went to small enterprises.

Among initiatives taken so far, introduction of 'no-frills accounts' was one of the most important steps to expand the banking network. Notably, UCBs also opened a considerable number of 'no-frills accounts' so far. As the non-scheduled UCB sector handles more banking business than the scheduled UCB sector, the number of deposits accounts, 'no-frills' accounts as also loan accounts were higher in the non-scheduled sector as compared with the scheduled sector. However, the share of loan accounts of the non-scheduled sector vis-à-vis scheduled sector was particularly striking as the scheduled sector was having only eight per cent of the total loan accounts of the entire UCB sector (Table7).

In the banking sector, some major developments has taken place in the form of introduction of prudential banking norms (in respect of Income Recognition, Assets classification, Provisioning and Capital Adequacy Standard as prescribed by Bank for International Settlement i.e. (BIS) and intensification of competition. Unfortunately, the co-operatives remained largely impervious of such changes. The operational efficiency of urban co-operative banks is unsatisfactory and characterized by low profitability, ever growing non-performing assets (NPA) and relatively low capital base. Their situation gradually worsened due to heavy overdue and non-collection of loans advances by them. Probably the crucial challenge encountered by the banking sector, specially the UCBs, is the availability of quality assets. In case banks are unable to generate income due to NPAs, it will put the banks into liquidity crunch. The problems of increasing NPAs are adversely affecting the profitability, liquidity and solvency position of the UCBs. Major concern suffering this sector include high levels of loan delinquency, erosion of capital base, paucity of funds for fresh deployment, ineffective credit planning, lack of professionalism in conduct and management, deficiency in application of computerized system, poor management information system and inadequate internal controls governance structure. The large scale sickness in the UCBs has shaken the public confidence in co-operative banks.

Table 7. Details of Deposits and Loans Accounts of UCBs (As at end-March 2010)

Item	*Scheduled*	*Non-Scheduled*	*All UCBs*
Number of Deposit	2,19,15,317	3,98,45,850	6,17,61,167
Accounts	(35.5)	(64.5)	
Of which: No-frills	3,41,434	8,98,007	12,39,441
Accounts	(27.5)	(72.5)	
Number of Loan	12,51,546	1,43,03,228	1,55,54,774
Accounts	(8.0)	(92.0)	
Memo Item			
Credit-Deposit Ratio	61.0	59.8	60.3
Average Deposit per Account (in Rupees)	36,599	25,763	29,608
Average Loan per Account (in Rupees)	3,91,124	42,895	70,913

Note: 1) Figures in parentheses are percentages to respective totals.

2) The interpretation of average deposit per account as well as average loan per account may take into account the fact that there can be multiple deposit and loan accounts in the name of the same individual.

RBI statistics

There was an improvement in the asset quality of the entire UCB sector both in absolute and percentage terms as at end-March 2010 over the previous year. However, both gross as well as net non-performing loans of the UCB sector continued to be on the higher side. Along with a decline in the nonperforming loans, there was also an increase in the coverage ratio of UCBs at end-March 2010 over the previous year, indicating improvement in the financial soundness of the sector. As at end-March 2010, dominant portion of UCBs were complying with the minimum CRAR norm of 9 per cent. Nonetheless, about 13.7 per cent of total UCBs fell short of meeting the regulatory norm with regard to capital adequacy. Leverage was higher in the case of scheduled UCBs as compared with the nonscheduled category. Bank-wise data on CRAR of scheduled UCBs indicated that though majority of them were maintaining CRAR above the regulatory minimum of 9 per cent, some of the scheduled UCBs fell short of minimum level, and more alarmingly, nine UCBs within them reported negative CRAR as at end-March 2010.

CONCLUSION

Reserve Bank of India is taking certain revival strategies for the better functioning of urban cooperative banks. Only 1900 urban cooperative banks are trying their best to compete with the commercial as well as public sector banks. The urban co-operative banks are positioned to be responsive to the credit needs of the poor. But in recent time a series of scams starting with the crumbling of the Madhavpura Mercantile Co-operative Bank, followed by an Rs 70-crore bullion scam and a gilts scam which involved hundreds of crores of rupees have denied the trustworthy of co-operative sector.

Cooperative banks, though account for a small proportion of the total business undertaken by the banking system in India, have a prominent place in the Indian financial landscape owing to their potential role in furthering financial inclusion as also because of financial inter linkages that these institutions have with the rest of the financial system. As a result of the on-going consolidation initiatives in the UCB sector, the profile of UCBs witnessed a shift in favour of financially sound banks. The UCB sector reported overall net profits as at end-March 2010. However, the spillover effects of the global financial turmoil caused a decline in the profitability during the last two years. Some of the emerging issues which deserve attention in the UCB sector are negative non-interest margin, high level of nonperforming loans, presence of loss-making banks, banks with negative CRAR and skewed concentration of banking business.

Not surprisingly, the RBI has been tightening urban co-operative bank regulations to protect depositors' interests. But urban co-operative banks, which have a collective deposit base of close to Rs 100,000 crore and advances of around Rs 70,000 crore, are not ready to throw in the towel without a fight. Backed by politicians, these banks are ganging up as they feel that their democratic rights have been trampled upon.

The cooperative structure whether rural or urban are nowadays very weak in India. This sector is trying hard to revitalize its propositions. Therefore in urban co-operative banks there are needs of updated technologies, proper governance, branch network expansion etc. to co-opt co-operatives.

REFERENCES

1. Agarwal, K.P., Puhazhendhi V. and Satyasai KJS (1997): "Gearing Rural Credit for the Twenty first Century", Economic and Political Weekly (EPW),32(42), October 18-24.

2. Bhalla, GS (2006): *Condition of Indian Peasantry*, National Book Trust, India, Delhi
3. Center for Monitoring Indian Economy (CMIE) (1993): "Basic Statistics Relating to the Indian Economy, Vol. 1: All India, CMIE publications, Bombay.
4. .Das, MB, Palai, NK and Das K (2006) : *Problems and Prospects of the Cooperative Movement in India under the Globalization Regime*, XIV International Economic History Congress, Session 72, Helsinki
5. Dandekar, V.M. (1993): "Limits of Credit Not Credit Limits", Economic and Political Weekly (EPW), September 25.
6. Gadgil M.V. (1992)," Future of Institutional Agricultural credit of India: Likely Impact of Narasimham and Khusro Committee Reports", Indian Journal of Agricultural Economics (IJAE), Vol. 47, No.2, April-June.
7. *Government of India (GOI): Tenth Five-Year Plan, 2002-2007, Vol-1...*
8. *Hanumantha Rao, C.H. (1970): "Farm size and credit policy ", Economic and Political Weekly, Vol. V, No. 52, December 26.*
9. Joshi, Vijay and Little, L.M.D. (1997): "India's Economic Reforms 1991-2001", Oxford University Press, New Delhi
10. Karmakar. K. G. (1999): "Rural Credit and Self Help Groups", Sage Publication, New Delhi.
11. RBI (2010): Development in Cooperative Banking, *Report on Trend and Progress of Banking in India 2009-10*, Mumbai, pp. 108-135

22

X-efficiency in District Co-operative Banks in Kerala

P. S. Feroze

INTRODUCTION

Co-operatives in India have been undergoing a period of reforms aimed at enhancing their efficiency and effectiveness. Accordingly measurement and improvement of the performance of co-operatives is crucial. The quest for a co-operative that works better and costs less shall be the dictum of the policy makers and therefore a new system of performance assessment shall be initiated. Despite the importance of efficiency measurement in co-operatives it is only recently that econometric and mathematical programming techniques have been applied to co-operative institutions.

Co-operative banks differ from commercial banks as they are co-operatives in which the members supply capital and consume the financial services. That is the members are both the owners and the customers. Unlike commercial banks, the benefits of ownership in a co-operative bank neither lead to dividend nor capital gains on shares. Instead, the benefits of ownership materialise in the form of lower interest rates on loans, higher interest rates on deposits and better service quality for customers.

District co-operative banks are currently facing their greatest challenge from public sector banks and private banks especially from new generation private banks. The liberalization and globalization of the Indian economy is affecting the district co-operative banks (DCBs) and the entire co-operative sector itself. When customers are faced with a variety of innovative financial products, many of which are superior in quality, more convenient, and can compete on cost, DCBs need to re-examine their operational strategies and offer innovative banking products like mobile banking, ATM and insurance services. They need to focus on the efficiency with which they utilize their financial resources in offering financial services to their customers. It is in this background the present study makes an attempt to measure the X-efficiency of DCBs in Kerala using data envelopment analysis (DEA).

As a subsector within the banking sector co-operative banks are particularly suitable for an efficiency estimation using DEA. Their no-loss-no-profit character makes DEA the most appropriate technique for frontier estimation. Moreover, DEA does not require price data. Its flexible form is also specially suited for the financial service providers as it allows multiple input and output specifications.

The objective of this paper is to estimate the X-efficiency in district co-operative banks in Kerala, explore their sources of inefficiency and suggest potential improvements in the efficiency. While many similar studies have evaluated the efficiency of co-operative banks using ratio analysis, it is the first time (to the knowledge of researcher) that the efficiency of co-operative banks in Kerala is being evaluated using DEA. The rest of the paper is organized as follows. Section 2 provides a brief review of the literature on the efficiency of banks in India. Section 3 presents a conceptual framework for the measurement of efficiency of co-operative banks. Section 4 describes the methodology used in the study. The empirical results are discussed in Section 5 and the final section concludes the findings of the study with suggestions for future research.

REVIEW OF LITERATURE ON THE EFFICIENCY OF BANKS IN INDIA

Although literature on the efficiency of banks in developed countries is growing very fast, research on efficiency of banks especially co-operative banks is lagging far behind. This section discusses different strands of literature on the efficiency of banks in India.

Battacharya et al., (1997) examined the performance of various categories of banks in India. They employed DEA methodology to measure the efficiency of 70 banks for the period 1986-1991. Their study found public sector banks as the best performing banks in India.

Sathye (2003) evaluated the productive efficiency of banks in India. He employed DEA methodology to measure the efficiency of banks. Two models were developed to show how efficiency scores vary with change in inputs and outputs. The study found that mean efficiency score of Indian banks compares well with the world mean efficiency score whereas the efficiency of private sector commercial banks is lower than that of public sector banks and foreign banks in India.

Rammohan and Ray (2004) compared the revenue maximizing efficiency of public sector banks, Indian private and foreign banks during 1992-2000 using DEA approach. They used loans, investments and other incomes as outputs and deposits and operating costs as inputs in physical quantities. Their study revealed that the efficiency of public sector banks was higher than that of private sector banks. Furthermore, their study indicated that the difference in the efficiency of public sector banks and foreign banks was not significant.

Das et al., (2004) have estimated and analysed various efficiency scores of Indian banks during 1997-2003 using data envelopment analysis (DEA). The results of their study identified asset size, ownership structure, and the fact of being listed on the stock exchange as the factors which have positive impact on the average profit efficiency. They observed that the median efficiency scores of Indian banks in general and of bigger banks in particular have improved considerably during 1997-2003.

Sahoo et al., (2007) have examined the productivity trends of Indian commercial banks for the period 1997-98 – 2004-05. Their empirical findings are indicative in many ways: first, average annual trends in technical efficiency for all ownership groups have improved, indicating an affirmative gesture about the effect of the reform process on the performance of the Indian banking sector, second, foreign banks have a leading edge over nationalized banks and Indian private banks. And finally concerning the scale elasticity behaviour, the technology and market based results differ significantly supporting the empirical distinction between returns to scale and economies of scale.

Sunil Kumar and Rachita Gulati (2008) have measured technical, pure technical and scale efficiencies in Indian public sector banks using data envelopment analysis. They reported that public sector banks in India (PSBs) have an overall technical efficiency of 88.5 per cent in the year 2004-05. This would imply that PSBs can reduce inputs by 11.5 per cent without sacrificing output.

Khankhoje and Sathye (2008) investigated whether the

restructuring of regional rural banks in India, undertaken in 1993-94 has helped improve their production efficiency. They measured production efficiency using non-parametric technique of DEA. They measured efficiency most directly using interest income and non-interest income as outputs and interest expenses and non-interest expenses as inputs. Efficiency scores were calculated for the years 1990-2002. The study found that efficiency of rural banks has significantly improved after restructuring.

Pradeep Kaur and Gian Kumar (2010) have examined the cost efficiency of Indian commercial banks by using DEA technique over the period 1990-91 – 2007-08. The findings of their study revealed that average cost efficiency of public sector banks is 73.4 per cent and for private sector banks it is 76.3 per cent. The results of their study suggest that to some extent merger programme has been successful in Indian banking sector.

EFFICIENCY MEASUREMENT: A CONCEPTUAL FRAME WORK

Measuring Co-operative Bank Efficiency

Financial ratios are traditional tools, used by analysts for measuring financial performance and quality of management of a co-operative bank. These easy to use tools often express operating costs as a percentage of its assets or gross income. Data needed to construct these ratios are readily available from annual financial statements of co-operative banks. Although ratios are easy to construct and use they are capable of being manipulated through changing accounting practice. Myopic interpretation of cost ratios can be misleading. An increasing ratio need not signal inefficiency or a declining ratio does not necessarily result in increase in efficiency. The major drawback of ratio analysis is its inability to deal simultaneously with multiple input and output variables.

Co-operative banks use a combination of inputs to produce a combination of outputs. Their reported aggregate cost figures will depend just as much on the mix of inputs and outputs as on the rate at which they use those inputs to produce outputs (Mester, 1987). A co-operative bank is said to be operating efficiently, if it can reduce the use of inputs without a proportionate decrease in output or if it can produce more output without a proportionate increase in inputs.

Efficiency can be defined in terms of the extent to which a decision making unit (DMU), typically a business, can increase its outputs without increasing its inputs, or reduce its inputs without reducing its outputs (Liu & Tripe, 2002). Efficiency can be of scale, scope and X-efficiency. Traditional micro economic theory states that economies of scale exist where increased volumes of output are produced with less than proportionate increase in quantities of input (increasing returns to scale). After sometime economies of scale get exhausted, and diseconomies of scale prevail (decreasing returns to scale).

Scope efficiency measures a bank's ability to produce multiple outputs from the same combination of inputs at lower cost in terms of inputs, than if they specialise in producing only one type of output. In the context of financial service providers, there exists a situation where a firm produces loan and deposit services, using the same staff and branch networks, rather than specialising in just one of these functions. The economies of scale and scope assume a uniform production function that applies to all firms in the market: if two firms are producing the same combination of outputs at the same volume, their cost will be the same (Tripe, 2003). Berger et al., (1993) suggest that managerial ability to control costs or maximise revenues appear to be greater than the cost effects of the choice of scale and scope of production.

X-efficiency measures the effectiveness with which banks are transforming multiple inputs into multiple outputs. The presence of X-efficiency in a firm implies management's success in controlling costs and generating revenues. Existing studies reported that X-inefficiencies form 20% or more of costs while scale and scope inefficiencies account for less than 5% of costs in banking.

There is no consensus on the appropriate procedure for measuring X-efficiencies. Berger and Humphrey specify five different approaches to determine the efficiency frontier. The efficiency frontier encompasses the best practice co-operative banks (which then become the benchmark for efficiency).The existing methodologies for constructing an efficient frontier can be divided into parametric and non-parametric. The three parametric approaches to estimate efficiency frontier are the Stochastic Frontier Approach (SFA), the Distribution Free Approach (DFA) and the Thick Frontier Approach (TFA), while the two non-parametric approaches are Data Envelopment Analysis (DEA) and the Free Disposal Hull (FDH) method.

DEA and FDH are non-parametric methods for estimating the best practice frontier. The benefit of DEA is that it does not require the explicit specifications of a functional form and imposes very little structure on the shape of the efficient frontier and so captures the interplay between various inputs and outputs of different dimensions (Bauer et. al., 1998). The principal problem with the non-parametric approaches is that they cannot distinguish random error arising from measurement error or exceptional financial performance. Exceptional events not related to the fundamental economic performance of the DMU may lead to over statement of efficiency, thus making other DMUs look comparatively inefficient.

The DEA Model

The efficiency measure proposed by Farrell (1957) did not receive much attention until Charnes, Cooper and Rhodes formulated a mathematical programming approach to frontier estimation in 1978. They coined the term Data Envelopment Analysis for the first time. The DEA model developed by Charnes, Cooper and Rhodes had an input orientation and assumed constant returns to scale (CRS). The CRS model offers best solutions only when all firms are operating at optimal scale. Subsequent studies by Banker, Charnes and Cooper have considered alternative sets of assumption and introduced a variable returns to scale model (VRS). The VRS model measures technical efficiency devoid of scale efficiency effects.

DEA is a linear programming model initially formulated to evaluate the efficiency of public sector non-profit organisations. DEA is a special application of linear programming which measures the relative efficiency of individual decision making units (DMUs). A DMU could be any financial service provider, banks or co-operative banks which use multiple inputs to produce multiple outputs. DEA makes use of mathematical programming technique to identify best practice DMUs from the observed data on inputs and outputs. The constructed relative efficiency frontiers are non-statistical or non- parametric in the sense that they are constructed through envelopment of the DMUs, with the best practice DMUs forming frontier.

DEA measures the relative efficiency of a DMU in the particular sample. It compares the performance of each of the DMU with the best practice DMU in the observed input-output combinations. Measuring efficiency against best practices, an inefficient DMU can identify its less-efficient practices and improve its efficiency. An important advantage of DEA is that it identifies a reference set or possible peers for inefficient DMUs. A peer is an efficient DMU with a similar combination of weights as that of an inefficient DMU. Where there are two or more efficient units for an inefficient DMU, they form a peer group. These reference sets represent the DMUs most similar to the relatively inefficient DMU in their mix of inputs and outputs. Reference sets are very important in DEA as they can be used to identify the amount of resources that could be saved if an inefficient DMU became efficient. DEA captures best practice DMUs that can be considered as role models for improving efficiency.

DEA employs linear programming technique to obtain best possible solution for each DMU. It measures the distance necessary to move an inefficient DMU to the efficiency frontier and then translates that distance into the amount of resource (inputs) that may be reduced to make the DMU efficient relative to DMUs on the frontier. As an efficient frontier technique, DEA identifies the inefficiency in a particular DMU by comparing it to similar DMUs regarded as efficient, rather than trying to associate a DMU's performance with statistical averages that may not be applicable to that DMU (Sathye, 2003).

DEA is an alternative approach to regression analysis. Regression technique involves the computation of an average production for each co-operative bank being evaluated, using one or more independent variables and one dependent variable. Co-operative banks are then ranked in terms of their residual values. Co-operative banks with positive residuals are considered as best performers, co-operative with negative residuals, poor performers.

Regression analysis cannot generate a single overall measure of relative performance. It does not compare co-operative banks on the basis of optimum performance, but it is based on average performance. DEA evaluates each co-operative bank distinctively, producing individual efficiency scores relative to all the co-operative banks in the sample data. A great merit of DEA is that unlike regression analysis, it does not require a priori assumption about functional form of production function. Instead, it constructs the best practice production function on the basis of observed values making it difficult to misspecify the production technique.

DEA assigns mathematically optimal weights to all input and output variables rather than requiring a priori determination of weights by the management. DEA determines the weight to be assigned to the various input-output variables in the sample by assigning maximum weight to those variables for which an individual DMU compares most favourably and minimum weight to those variables for which an individual DMU compares least favourably.

DEA generates a simple, easily interpretable relative measure of efficiency (called DEA score) for each DMU included in the particular sample. The DEA score is a value ranging from 0 to 1.00. A DEA score of 0 means that a DMU is most inefficient compared to all other DMUs in that sample. A DEA score of 1.00 means that DMU is 100 per cent efficient.

METHODOLOGY

The present study is designed as descriptive one mainly based on secondary data. The study uses Data Envelopment Analysis (DEA) methodology to measure the X-efficiency in district co-operative banks in Kerala. Of the various methods to measure the services produced by banks, production and intermediation approaches are widely used in the previous studies. The study uses intermediation approach which considers bank as a financial intermediary, transforming deposits into loans and investments. Inputs are measured in both physical and financial terms. Input variables include number of employees, number of branches, and working capital, while the output variables include the value of loans and investments (Table 1)Inputs and outputs are specified considering the availability of data and approach chosen for measuring the efficiency. It may be noted that data on interest expense, non-interest expense, interest income and non- interest income are not available in the panel of data compiled by the National Federation of State Co-operatives Banks Limited (NAFSCOB).

Table 1. Input-Output variables used in DEA Models

District Co-operative Bank	*Inputs*			*Outputs*	
	No. of Emp.	*Working capital (Rs. in lakhs)*	*No. of Branches*	*Loans (Rs. in lakhs)*	*Investments (Rs. in lakhs)*
Alappuzha	388	94734	55	63662	26031
Ernakulam	457	18210	54	99458	83632
Idukki	295	84425	47	100371	12325
Kannur	445	167909	50	116643	62103
Kasargod	255	40098	29	31940	182
Kollam	515	112926	56	48220	47429
Kottayam	426	100476	55	55395	34730
Kozhikode	327	91032	43	59639	27073
Malappuram	302	75723	42	59121	24079
Palakkad	243	99122	38	56696	57706
Pathanamthitta	366	58226	55	38275	24158
Thiruvananthapuram	681	195255	68	71817	48291
Thrissur	465	153097	49	108690	49175
Wayanad	140	27130	26	30561	15926

CCR and BCC are two popular models of DEA which are run on the selected input and output data to obtain X-efficiency (Technical efficiency) scores. CCR model generates X-efficiency scores under the assumption of constant returns-to-scale (CRS). CCR X-efficiency score is a measure of technical efficiency (TE). On the other hand, BCC model provides X-efficiency score under the assumption of variable returns-to-scale (VRS). BCC X-efficiency score is a measure of pure technical efficiency (PTE) devoid of scale efficiency (SE). SE measures the divergence of DMUs from the most productive scale size (MPSS). MPSS indicates the size of operation where output is maximized per unit of input. SE is obtained by dividing CCR score by BCC score (SE=CRR/ BCC).

There are two directions for DEA models - either an input orientation or an output orientation. An input orientation aims at reducing input amounts as much as possible while keeping at least the present output levels, while an output orientation aims at maximizing output levels without increasing the use of inputs (Cooper et al., 2000). This study makes an attempt to estimate X-efficiency scores using both CCR and BCC models of DEA with an input orientation.

This study employs DEA-SOLVER Software developed by Kaoru Tone to estimate X-efficiency scores of all the 14 district co-operative banks (DCBs) in Kerala in India. The data on inputs and outputs have been collected from the annual reports of district co-operative banks compiled and published by National Federation of State Co-operative Banks Limited, Mumbai.

EMPIRICAL RESULTS AND DISCUSSION

This section discusses the X- efficiency (technical efficiency) scores obtained from the CCR and BCC models of DEA. Table 2 shows X- efficiency scores of all the 14 district co-operative banks (DCBs) in Kerala for the year 2008-09. The results unfold the magnitude of disparity in the X-efficiency scores of DCBs obtained from CCR model. The X-efficiency scores range between 0.419 and 1. The average X-efficiency score is 0.73.

This score is comparable with the mean efficiency score

of Indian banks reported in the previous studies that employed DEA and followed intermediation approach. Ernakulam, Idukki, Kannur and Palakkad DCBs are most efficient banks as they are the banks with X-efficiency score equal to 1. These 4 efficient banks form efficiency frontier and are called peers and are considered as banks with best practices. They also form reference set for inefficient banks.

The average technical inefficiency (TIE) score is 27 percent. This implies that inefficient DCBs can become efficient by emulating the practices of efficient DCBs and reducing their inputs on an average by 27 percent without sacrificing the present level of output. But the exact percentage reduction in inputs may vary from bank to bank (see Table 4 in Appendix). It is evident from Table 2 that Alapuzha, Kasargod, Kollam, Kottayam, Kozhikode, Malappuram, Pathanamthitta, Thiruvananthapuram, Thrissur and Wayanad DCBs are the banks with X-efficiency score less than 1 and hence they are considered as relatively inefficient. X-efficiency scores of the inefficient banks vary between 0.419 (Pathanamthitta) and 0.963 (Thrissur). These inefficient DCBs can improve their efficiency by reducing inputs and increasing outputs. Pathanamthitta and Thrissur DCBs may reduce their input levels, on an average, by 58.14 per cent and 3.70 per cent respectively while retaining their current output levels.

Of the inefficient banks Pathanamthitta and Thruvananthapuram DCBs are most inefficient as their scores are below the efficiency at first quartile. These two banks require special attention of the policy makers while restructuring district co-operative banks in Kerala. Thrissur district cooperative banks may be considered as marginally inefficient as it operates at high level of efficiency (i.e. 96.3 per cent) and is located close to the efficient frontier. This bank also deserves special consideration of the policy makers as it may attain 100 percent efficiency by making slight improvements in its resource utilisation.

Table 2. X-efficiency score for district co-operative banks in Kerala for 2008-09

District Co-operative Banks	*Efficiency Score*	*Inefficiency (%)*
Alapuzha	0.578	42.23
Enakulam	1.000	0.00
Idukki	1.000	0.00
Kannur	1.000	0.00
Kasargod	0.537	46.33
Kollam	0.547	45.31
Kottayam	0.516	48.36
Kozhikode	0.663	33.72
Malappuram	0.691	30.90
Palakkad	1.000	0.00
Pathanamthitta	0.419	58.14
Thiruvananthapuram	0.508	49.25
Thrissur	0.963	3.70
Wayanad	0.819	18.07
Average	0.731	27.00

SOURCES OF INEFFICIENCY IN DISTRICT COOPERATIVE BANKS

The decomposition of X-efficiency helps investigating sources of inefficiency in DCBs. The inefficiency in the bank may be due to inefficient operations of the bank or due to inappropriate bank size. In this section the study examines the sources of inefficiency comparing input-oriented CCR and BCC scores. X-efficiency score obtained from CCR model under constant returns-to-scale is known as technical efficiency (TE). On the other hand, X-efficiency score obtained from BCC model under the variable returns-to-scale is known as pure technical efficiency (PTE). In DEA literature the banks with TE score equal to 1 are called as 'globally efficient' banks and banks with PTE score equal to 1 are called as 'locally efficient' banks and banks with 100 percent efficiency in both CCR and BCC scores are known as the most productive scale size (MPSS) banks.

Table 3 presents technical efficiency (TE), pure technical efficiency (PTE), and scale efficiency (CCR / BCC) scores of all the 14 banks. It is observed from the Table 3 that 5 banks - Ernakulam, Idukki, Kannur, Palakkad and Wayanad acquired the status of 'locally efficient' banks by accomplishing 100 per cent pure technical efficiency. Of these

Table 3. Decomposition of X-efficiency score for district co-operative banks

DCBs	*TE*	*TIE (%)*	*PTE*	*PTIE (%)*	*SE*	*SIE (%)*
Alapuzha	0.578	42.23	0.655	34.48	0.882	11.82
Ernakulam	1.000	0.00	1.000	0.00	1.000	0.00
Idukki	1.000	0.00	1.000	0.00	1.000	0.00
Kannur	1.000	0.00	1.000	0.00	1.000	0.00
Kasargod	0.537	46.33	0.910	9.02	0.590	41.01
Kollam	0.547	45.31	0.637	36.27	0.858	14.20
Kottayam	0.516	48.36	0.620	37.97	0.833	16.75
Kozhikode	0.663	33.72	0.795	20.53	0.834	16.60
Malappuram	0.691	30.90	0.818	18.21	0.845	15.51
Palakkad	1.000	0.00	1.000	0.00	1.000	0.00
Pathanamthitta	0.419	58.14	0.530	47.00	0.790	21.02
Thiruvanantha-puram	0.508	49.25	0.577	42.29	0.879	12.05
Thrissur	0.963	3.70	0.978	2.20	0.985	1.53
Wayanad	0.819	18.07	1.000	0.00	0.819	18.07

Notes: DCBs: District co-operative banks, TE: Technical efficiency, TIE (%):Technical inefficiency=(1-TE)×100, PTE: Pure technical efficiency, PTIE(%): Pure technical inefficiency=(1-PTE)×100, SE: Scale Efficiency, SIE: Scale inefficiency=(1-SE)×100

5 'locally efficient' banks 4 banks have emerged as 'globally efficient' banks by scoring 100 per cent technical efficiency. These 4 banks are 100 percent efficient in both the CCR (TE) and BCC (PTE) scores, and operating at most productive scale size (MPSS).

An analysis of PTE and SE scores for the district co-operative banks indicates that the technical inefficiency is caused by the inefficient utilisation of the inputs and the failure to operate at MPSS (SIE). The average pure technical efficiency score for district cooperative banks is 0.82. This suggests that about 0.17 points inefficiency in 0.27 points technical inefficiency stems from their divergence from best management practices and following incorrect input-output mix. The rest of the technical inefficiencies (pure technical inefficiencies) is attributed to their inappropriate scale of operations. Wayanad district cooperative bank is a 100 percent BCC efficient with 81.93 percent scale efficiency score. This would mean that the technical inefficiency of the Wayanad district co-operative bank is due to unfavourable regional conditions prevailing in Wayanad district.

EFFICIENCY IMPROVEMENT

One advantage of DEA is that it identifies areas of inefficiency which help an inefficient bank to improve upon to move onto efficient frontier. It provides information on the direction and magnitude of improvements in inputs and outputs required by inefficient bank to attain the status of globally efficient one.

On proportional reduction in inputs and addition in outputs an inefficient bank may attain 100 per cent X-efficiency. Table 4 provides information on potential reduction in inputs and potential addition in outputs for inefficient district co-operative banks.

It is observed from the table that Pathanamthitta DCB, the most inefficient bank, should reduce employees by 58.14

per cent and use 58.14 per cent less working capital and reduce branches by 62.59 per cent to attain 100 per cent X-efficiency. Similarly Kasargod DCB, another inefficient bank, should get employee reduced by 57.91 per cent, working capital and branches by 46.33 per cent and deploy additional funds in investments by 999.90 per cent to move onto the efficient frontier.

Table 4. Potential improvements for inefficient district cooperative banks

District Co-operative Bank	*Score*	*Input reduction (%)*			*Output addition (%)*	
		No. of Employees	*Working capital*	*No. of Branches*	*Loans*	*Investments*
Alappuzha	0.578	42.23	42.23	42.23	-	-
Ernakulam	1.000	-	-	-	-	-
Idukki	1.000	-	-	-	-	-
Kannur	1.000	-	-	-	-	-
Kasargod	0.537	57.91	46.33	46.33	-	999.90
Kollam	0.547	49.68	90.85	45.31	16.97	-
Kottayam	0.516	48.36	48.36	48.36	-	-
Kozhikode	0.663	33.72	33.72	33.72	-	-
Malappuram	0.691	30.90	30.90	30.90	-	-
Palakkad	1.000	-	-	-	-	-
Pathanamthitta	0.419	58.14	58.14	62.59	-	-
Thiruvananthapuram	0.508	56.03	68.03	49.25	-	-
Thrissur	0.963	13.67	03.70	03.70	-	05.12
Wayanad	0.819	18.07	18.07	38.23	-	-

CONCLUSION

Co-operative banks play a vital role in the financial system of Kerala economy in terms of their reach, volume of operation and purpose they serve. Co-operative banks aim at fulfilling the banking requirements of rural populace. They have been established with the prime objective of meeting the credit needs of the rural sector. Therefore greater degrees of efficiency among co-operative banks would result in greater accessibility of finance, higher profitability and increased financial services for rural people. Efficiency of co-operative banks often lies in the efficiency of each co-operative bank which contributes to the total efficiency of the co-operative banking system.

This paper makes an attempt to estimate the X-efficiency in district co-operative banks operating in Kerala for the year 2008-09, using data envelopment analysis. The empirical results of the study reveal that the level of X-efficiency in DCBs is 73 per cent and the magnitude of inefficiency is 27 per cent. 4 DCBs obtains X-efficiency score equal to 1 and formed the efficiency frontier. On comparing CCR and BCC scores, it is found that 4 DCBs emerged as 'globally efficient' banks among 14 DCBs in Kerala. The sources of inefficiency in DCBs stem from both managerial inefficiency and inappropriate size. The study suggests potential improvements in the efficiency of inefficient DCBs in terms of potential reduction in inputs and potential addition in outputs.

This study points to the scope for future research in four directions. First, future research could compare X-efficiency of DCBs and commercial banks, second, use Malmquist index to examine the changes in X-efficiency of DCBs over time, third, estimate the cost and profit efficiency of DCBs, and four, investigate the relationship between efficiency and profit in DCBs.

REFERENCES

1. Banker, R. D., Charnes, A., Cooper, W. W. (1984): "Some Models for Estimating Technical and Scale Inefficiencies in Data Envelopment Analysis", *Management Science* 30: 1078-1092.

2. Bauer, P.W., Berger, A.N., Ferrier, G.D. and Humphrey, D.B. (1998): "Consistency Conditions for Regulatory Analysis of Financial Institutions: A Comparison of Frontier Efficiency Methods", *Journal of Economics and Business*, 50: 85-114.

3. Berger, A.N, and D.B. Humphrey. (1997): "Efficiency of Financial Institutions: International Survey and Directions of Future Research", *European Journal of Operation Research*, 98: 175-212.

4. Bhattacharya, A., Lovell, C.A.K., and Sahay, P. (1997): "The impact of liberalization on the productive efficiency of Indian commercial banks", *European Journal of Operational Research*, 98: 332-345.

5. Charnes, A., Cooper, W. W., Rhodes, E. (1978): "Measuring efficiency of Decision Making Units", *European Journal of Operation Research*, 2: 429-444.

6. Cooper, W.W., Seiford, L.M., and Tone, K. (2000): *Data Envelopment Analysis, A Comprehensive Text with Models, Applications, References, and DEA-Solver Software*, Boston, Kluwer Academic Publishers.

7. Das, Abhiman., Nag, Ashok., and Ray Subash C. (2004): "Liberalisation, Ownership, and Efficiency in Indian Banking: A Nonparametric Approach", *Economic Working Papers*. Paper 200429: 2-26. http://digitalcommons.uconn.edu/econ_wpapers/200429.

8. Farrell, M. (1957): "The Measurement of Productive Efficiency", Journal *of the Royal Statistical Society*, 120: 253-281.

9. Khankhoje, D., and Sathye, M. (2008): "Efficiency of Rural Banks: The Case of India", *International Business Research*, 2: 140-149.

10. Liu, B & Tripe D.W.L. (2002): "New Zealand bank mergers and efficiency gains", *Journal of Asia-Pacific Business*, 4, 4: 61-81.

11. Mester, L.J. (1987): "Efficient production of financial services: scale and scope economies", *Federal Reserve Bank of Philadelphia Business Review*,15-25.

12. Misra, Biswa Swarup (2003): "Allocative Efficiency of Indian

Banking System in the Post Reform Period: A State Level Analysis". *RBI Occasional Papers,* 24, 3: 161-177.

13. Pradeep Kaur and Gian Kaur. (2010): "Impact of Mergers on the Cost Efficiency of Indian Commercial Banks". *Eurasian Journal of Business and Economics,* 3, 5: 27-50.

14. Ram Mohan, T.T. and Ray, S.C. (2004): "Comparing Performance of Public and Private Sector Banks: A revenue maximization approach". *Economic and Political Weekly,* 39: 1271 - 1276.

15. Sahoo, B.K., Sengupta, J.K., and Mandal, A. (2007): "Productive Performance of Evaluation of the Banking Sector in India using Data Envelopment Analysis". *International Journal of Operational Research,* 4, 2: 63-79.

16. Sathye, M. (2001): "X-efficiency in Australian Banking: An Empirical Investigation." *Journal of Banking and Finance,* 25: 613-630.

17. Sathye, M. (2003): "Efficiency of banks in a developing economy: The case of India". *European Journal of Operational Research,* 148: 662 -671.

18. Sunilkumar and Rachita Gulati. (2008): "An Examination of Technical, Pure Technical, and Scale Efficiencies in Indian Public Sector Banks using Data Envelopment Analysis", *Eurasian Journal of Business and Economics,* 1, 2: 33-69.

Section IV : Banks Fraud and Instability

23

Frauds and Security Threats Associated With the Use of ATM

A. S Dileep
T.Rajesh

INTRODUCTION

Electronic Banking

In the post consolidation era the ability of commercial banks to satisfy and retain customers depend largely on the development of information technology infrastructure. To meet the challenges posed by the customers and to improve the quality of their service delivery every bank have invested much on technology and have widely adopted electronic and telecommunication network for delivering a wide range of value added products and services. Automated Teller Machine (ATM) is one of the most prominent product of electronic banking and in now a days the use of ATM is increasing at alarming rate.

Automated Teller Machine (ATM)

Automated Teller Machine is a computerized telecommunications device that provides the customers of a financial institution with access to financial transactions in a public space without the need for a human clerk or bank teller. On most modern ATMs, the customer is identified by inserting a plastic ATM card with a magnetic stripe or a plastic smartcard with a chip that contains a unique card number and some security information, such as an expiration date. Security is provided by the customer entering a personal identification number (PIN).

Although ATMs were originally developed as just cash dispensers, they have evolved to include many other bank-related functions. In some countries, especially those which benefit from a fully integrated cross-bank ATM network, ATMs include many functions which are not directly related to the management of one's own bank account, such as: Paying routine bills, fees, and taxes (utilities, phone bills, social security, legal fees, taxes, etc.), Printing bank statements, Updating pass books, Loading monetary value into stored value cards, Purchasing and so on.

THE BENEFITS OF ATMS

According to Brain (2000), the benefits that can be derived from ATM usage are so numerous, some are outlined below:

- Flexible account access allows clients to access their accounts at their convenience
- MFI personnel are not required to be present for transactions and have more time to serve clients.
- Increased hours of operation fit client schedules.
- More clients can be reached beyond the branch network, such as in smaller population centers.
- More low-cost funds are available because ATMs make

it easier for clients to deposit savings, etc.

The other side of the coin

The use of ATM is not only safe but is also convenient. This safety and convenience, unfortunately, has an evil side. This evil side is reflected in the form of "ATM frauds" that is a global problem. The use of plastic money is increasing day by day for payment of shopping bills, electricity bills, school fees, phone bills, insurance premium, traveling bills and even petrol bills. The convenience and safety that credit cards carry with its use has been instrumental in increasing both credit card volumes and usage. The world at large is struggling to increase the convenience and safety on the one hand and to reduce its misuse on the other.

OBJECTIVES OF THE STUDY

The objectives of the study are as follows.

- To identify various fraud and security threats associated with the use of ATM
- To evaluate the users opinion on ATM fraud and how offender robs the victim of his/her ATM card, gets the PIN and then uses the card.

Methodology

In pursuance of the above mentioned objectives the following methodology was adopted for the study. The study is analytical one. Both primary and secondary data were collected and used for the study.

Secondary data

The secondary data for the present study have been collected from the discussions with the officials of the commercial banks and from various publications of numerous institutions

Primary data

The primary data required for the study have been collected from selected customers from selected commercial banks of Thiruvanathapuram District.

Sample Customers

Sample customers are selected from three commercial banks in Thiruvanathapuram District. The population of the study comprise of the customers of three banks in Thiruvanathapuram district, each with fifty ATM users were selected for the study. This gives a total of 150 ATM users.

Various frauds and Security Threads

Various ATM frauds can be discussed in two heads, one is related Automated Teller Machines and is another associated with Personal Identification Number.

Automated Teller Machines Frauds

Card Theft

In an effort to obtain actual cards, criminals have used a variety of card trapping devices comprised of slim mechanical devices, often encased in a plastic transparent film, inserted into the card reader throat. Hooks are attached to the probes preventing the card from being returned to the consumer at the end of the transaction. When the ATM terminal user shows concern due to the captured card, the criminal, usually in close proximity of the ATM, will offer support, suggesting the user enter the PIN again, so that he or she is able to view the entry and remember the PIN. After the consumer leaves the area, believing their card to have been captured by the ATM, the criminal will then use a probe (fishing device) to extract the card. Having viewed the customers PIN and now having the card in hand, the criminal can easily withdraw money from the unsuspecting user's account.

Skimming Devices

Another method of accessing a consumer's account information is skim the information off of the card. Skimming is the most frequently used method of illegally obtaining card track data. "Skimmers" are devices used by criminals to capture the data stored in the magnetic strip of the card. Reading and deciphering the information on the magnetic stripes of the card can be accomplished through the application of small card readers in close proximity to, or on top of, the actual card reader input slot, so it is able to read and record the information stored on the magnetic track of the card. The device is then removed, allowing the downloading of the recorded data.

PIN Fraud

This can take the following forms:

Shoulder Surfing : Shoulder Surfing is the act of direct observation, watching what number that person taps on to the keypad. The criminal usually positions himself in close but not direct proximity to the ATM to covertly watch as the ATM user enters their PIN. Sometimes miniature video cameras that are easily obtained might be installed discretely on the fascia or somewhere close to the PIN Pad, to record the PIN entry information.

Utilizing a Fake PIN Pad Overlay : A fake PIN pad is placed over the original keypad. This overlay captures the PIN data and stores the information into its memory. The fake PIN pad is then removed, and recorded PINs are downloaded. Fake PIN pads can be almost identical in appearance and size as the original. An additional type of overlay that is more difficult to detect is a 'thin' overlay that is transparent to the consumer. This method used in conjunction with card data theft provides the criminal with the information needed to access an unsuspecting consumer's account.

PIN Interception: After the PIN is entered, the information is captured in electronic format through an electronic data recorder. Capturing the PIN can be done either inside the terminal, or as the PIN is transmitted to the host computer for the online PIN check. In order to capture the PIN internally, the criminal would require access to the communication cable of the PIN pad inside the terminal, which can more easily be done, at off-premise locations.

AUTOMATED TELLER MACHINE SECURITY

Research on Bank ATM Security Advice states that ATM bank cash machines have been incorporated in our way of life. They offer a real convenience to those on the run, but at the same time offer an element of risk. Using a bank ATM machine safely requires awareness and a little planning. Just because a bank ATM machine is open and available 24-hours a day doesn't mean it is always safe to use it. Further some research identifies that Bank ATM robbers are usually males less than 25 years of age and most work alone. ATM robbers usually position themselves nearby (50 feet) waiting for a victim to approach and withdraw cash. Half of the ATM robberies occur after the cash withdrawal. Many ATM robbery victims are women and were alone when robbed. Most claim that they never saw the robber coming. Most ATM robbers used a gun or claimed to have a concealed weapon when confronting the victim and demanding their cash. in order to ensure security of Automated Telling Machine, most of the ATMs are equipped with personal security.

Analytical Results

The analytical results of the study are presented in the following sections.

Table 1 clearly shows that location of ATM is a high determinant to fraud or crime carried out at ATM point. From this table it is clear that nearly 75% of the respondents affirm that the location of ATM in secluded place contributes to the fraud perpetuated at ATM point. ATM within the banking premises is more secure than ATMs outside the bank premises. The Table 1 also states that the major form of ATM fraud is PIN theft which is carried out by various means; skimming, shoulder surfing, camera, key pad recorder etc. This study elucidates that the common type of fraud perpetuated is PIN theft which is mostly as a result of congestion at ATM points. Other forms of fraud that were enumerated by respondents were; force withdrawal, card theft, and skimming and congestion method fraud at ATM Table 2 discloses that majority of the ATM users are aware about the incidents of the ATM frauds and they are not majority of the respondents are not victim of ATM frauds. The table also shows that majority of the respondents are unaware about security guide and they feel that level of security is not sufficient.

Table 1. Causes of ATM frauds

Sl. No	*Question*	*Strongly disagree*	*Dis-agree*	*Neu-tral*	*Agree*	*Strongly agree*
1	Location of ATM at secluded and high risk areas contribute to fraud and crime perpetuated at ATM	7 (4.7%)	28 (18.7%)	34 (22.7%)	62 (41.3%)	19 (12.7%)
2	PIN theft and shoulder surfing are common ATM fraud perpetuated by fraudsters	10 (6.7%)	26 (17.3%)	45 (30%)	41 (27.3%)	28 (18.7%)
3	ATMs outside banks are more prone to fraud	21 (14%)	19 (12.7%)	37 (24.7%)	41 (27.3%)	32 (21.3%)

Source: Survey Data

Table 2. Incidences of ATM fraud and its Security

Sl. No	*Question*	*Yes*	*No*
1	Have you ever been a victim of ATM	65(43.3%)	85(56.7%)
2	Are you aware of incidence of ATM fraud	96(64%)	54(36%)
3	Do you think the level of security is sufficient	55(36.7%)	95(53.3%)
4	Are you aware of any security guide for the use	63(42.3%)	87(57%)
5	Is there any means provided by the bank that you can quickly report ATM Fraud incident to the bank	54(36%)	96(64%)
6	ATM fraud is carried out most during the Day	77(51.3%)	73(48.7%)

Source: Survey Data

FINDINGS

- The major findings of the study are as follows
- Location of ATM play a crucial role in committing frauds
- Pin theft is the most common method of ATM fraud.
- ATM outside bank premises is subject to more frauds.
- Majority of the customers are very aware about ATM frauds.
- The level of security system prevailing in ATM counter is not sufficient.

CONCLUSION

The adoption of ATM in Thiruvanathapuram banks for financial transaction keeps growing and people have realizes the convenience in using ATM. The research shows that customers are much comfortable with the electronic banking system, which ATM is just a segment out of various services of e-banking. As the usage of ATM is increasing so it openness to security threat is ascending. As the ATM technology is advancing, fraudsters are on drawing board to see how they come up with different fraud skills to beat the security. Various forms of fraud are perpetuated, ranging from; ATM card theft, Skimming, Pin theft, Card reader techniques, PIN pad techniques, force withdrawal and lot more. Despite this threat, the banks are putting up little effort which is not proportional to rate the fraudsters are working to defraud customers. The technology of ATM keep developing, the fraudsters keep improving ways of crime but the banks are not putting sufficient measures of control to avoid fraud at ATM. The security measures adopted by some banks are obsolete making the measures less significant and allowing fraud at ATM.

REFERENCES

1. Brunner, A., Decressin, J. and Kudela, B. (2004): Germany's Three-Pillar Banking System – Cross Country Perspectives in Europe, Occasional Paper, International Monetary Fund, Washington DC.
2. Chris E. M. (2006). Bank ATM Security Advice: Effective Method of Security Measures.Virtual Banking. Journal of Internet Banking and Commerce, 11(1)
3. Christolav E. A., Marianne A.H. and Jeanne M. H. (2003). US Consumer's and electronic banking 1995- 2003.Board Division of Consumers and Community Affairs. Los Angeles

24

Global Financial Crisis and Indian Banks

K. Venugopalan

INTRODUCTION

At present, the global economy is passing through a major recession. There is a breakdown of United States mortgage market and the reversal of the housing boom in various highly developed countries. It appeared more deep and persistent than expected in 2007 and beginning of 2008. The intensity of the crisis is so severe that some of the world's largest and oldest financial institutions have collapsed. It is extensively noticeable in September 2008. Several large United State based financial firms failed in that period. Bear Stearns collapsed in March, 2008. The competitors purchased others at lower prices. Bank of America Corporation purchased Merrill Lynch in September, 2008. It resulted in creation of disorder in the world financial markets. The governments of the richest nations have to undertake extensive post security and salvage packages in order to save some of their important banks and financial institutions. Many financial crisis associated with banking panics occurred in 19th and 20th century. Numerous recessions coincided with these panics. Likewise financial crisis is also associated with stock market crashes, currency crisis and sovereign defaults. The current financial crisis originated in United States of America. It is the worst of its kind since the great depression in 1930's. The global financial meltdown spread disaster particularly in United States and European economy and in the world economy in general.

Financial crisis refers to a loss of confidence in a country's currency or other financial assets causing international investors to withdraw their funds from the country. Some financial institutions or assets suddenly lose a large part of their value.

SUBPRIME MORTGAGE CRISIS

The international financial crisis originated in the subprime mortgage crisis which originated nearly three years ago (in 2007) in the United States. The term subprime refers to the credit states of the borrower which is less than ideal. Subprime lending is a general term that refers to the practice of making loans to borrowers who do not qualify for the best market rates of interest because of their deficit credit history. Subprime lending comprises of a variety of credit instruments such as prime credit cards, subprime car loans, subprime mortgages etc. Such prime lending is also called B-paper or second chance lending. The mortgage bankers offer subprime loan at a rate higher than A-paper loans due to the increased risk.

METHODOLOGY

The present study focuses on

1. The origin and causes of financial crisis
2. Its effect on world market.
3. The impact of crisis on the Indian banks

The study is entirely based on the secondary data.

1. The origin and causes of financial crisis

The current financial crisis originated in United States due the indiscriminate lending of housing loans in subprime mortgage market. Large inflow of foreign funds with low rate of interest during the boom years helped the banks to create easy credit conditions for many years. Banks lent money on the assumption that the house prices will rise continuously. In the scenario of low interest rates, excess liquidity, intense competition in the prime market, rising home prices and craze for home loans, a new class of lenders named mortgage bankers started lending. During the boom years the mortgage brokers encouraged buyers with poor credit to accept housing mortgages with little or no down payment. The brokers got high commission in this respect. Banks provided loans without checking credits worthiness of the buyers. Most of the borrowers could not regularly pay installments due to their poor income flow.

The growth of the secondary mortgage market allowed the mortgage lenders to export much of the risks to other investors who showed keen interest in acquiring mortgage backed securities carrying higher rate of interest as compared to the less risky investments. The lenders securitized these debts with high risk debts and they sold these securities to worldwide investors.

A number of banking authorities indicated that the United States housing market is the root cause of the financial crisis. Surplus stock of houses and increasing rate of interest led to the decline of housing prices in 2006-07. The reversal of the housing boom caused the derailment of the United States sub-prime mortgage market. The crisis has spread quickly and imposed extensive damage on markets and institutions of the financial system. Mass foreclosures due to loan defaults happened at one end of the economic spectrum. This created a credit pinch in the financial system. The loan defaults disrupted the ability of the financial institutions to provide credit or raise cash or liquidity in short term. This is the main reason of the financial crisis and subsequently the collapse of several large United States based financial firms.

The distribution of collateralized debt instruments worldwide effected many financial institutions all over the world due to financial crisis occurred in United States. That resulted in number of European bank failures and decline in various stock indexes.

Causes of Financial Crisis

The United States is currently experiencing the biggest financial crisis after the Great Depression. Just like the past worldwide economic downturn, marked with massive bank failures and the stock market crash in 1929, today we witness the unforeseen bankruptcy of big, trusted banks and extreme market volatility. This article will try to explain the original causes of the current US financial crisis, its effect on the world market and its impact on Indian banks.

1. The real estate bubble : Subprime borrowing is the major cause of the enhancement of ownership rates of houses. It increased the demand for houses. This demand helped to increase the price of houses and enhanced consumer spending. Most people started directly with the real estate market. It is the place where the crisis actually began. They focused on the subprime mortgages and the unprincipled lenders which really caused the unsustainable real estate bubble which began to collapse in 2006. Increase in house purchases during the boom period eventually led to the surplus inventory of houses which caused to decline of house prices. Easy credit along with the assumption that the house prices would continue to increase, has encouraged many prime subprime borrowers to obtain adjustable rates mortgages which they could not afford after the initial incentive period. One of the main factors which lead to the current financial crisis is this real estate bubble.

2. Speculation : The whole real estate bubble originated mainly as a response to the huge demand of financial assets. Not many places can actually provide such assets, naturally in such situations speculative bubbles come on the stage and become part of the supply response of financial assets to the demand of such assets. During 2006, 22 percent of the houses purchased for investment purposes and 14 percent houses purchased as vacation houses. That means nearly 40 percent of houses purchased are not for residential purposes. The speculators left the market in 2006, which caused a fall in house prices.

3. The Problem with Securitization of Mortgages : The excess capital globally pushed a massive amount of money into the United States mortgage market. Almost 80% of the United States mortgage market is securitized. Basically, securitization is a wonderful financial medium. Mortgages are pooled together as securities and sold to investors. The investors can resell it. Securitization creates diversification and liquidity. Securitization of housing loans for poor people with poor credit rating is another reason for this financial crisis. Subprime mortgages were also put in big pools of assets from which the so called "Mortgage Backed Securities" were created. The problem with securitization shoots from the fact that it does not provide protection against systematic risk. Unluckily, such a systematic risk was also not priced into the subprime mortgage pools.

4. Non consideration of systematic risk : Credit rating agencies has not considered the possible systematic risk and blessed the low risk securities with AAA rating. Pension funds, mutual funds, some money market funds, banks and investors from all over the world purchased such securities thinking that they are safe. Thus, the markets absorbed enormous amounts of these securities. Additionally, the investors leveraged these low risk securities. In other words they invest more than what they actually have. These instruments were widely spread among investors of all types and this caused as one of the factors of this financial crisis.

5. Inaccurate credit rating : It is another reason for the financial crisis. Risk rating agencies are unable to give proper rating to complex instruments. Credit rating agencies gave high ratings. This encouraged the flow of funds in mortgage backed securities which helped to finance the housing boom.

6. Poor regulation : In United States financial markets are poorly regulated. The fall of the financial institutions is a reflection of ineffective regulations. Some parts of the financial system are either loosely regulated or are not regulated at all. This regulatory failure helped to move funds towards unregulated segments.

7. Inability to remit mortgage payments : The subprime lending increased the homeownership rate in the United States significantly.

Nearly 5 million people went from tenants to homeowners. As a result, rents decreased and house prices went up till they reached unsustainable heights relative to rents. However, in contrast to the stock market, in the real estate market when the asset prices rise more assets are created through construction. Between 2001 and 2007 the construction of new housing units exceeded significantly. But this housing bubble could not grow up infinitely.

Thus, when the rise in housing prices stopped in 2006, inevitably many subprime borrowers had difficulty in making their mortgage payments. The housing bubble became more evident when many subprime mortgage lenders began declaring bankruptcy around March 2007. This problem started to gain crisis proportions and yet, the financial authorities and the Federal Reserve believed that it was an isolated phenomenon.

Effect in World Market

The financial crisis occurred in United States of America effected the world wide countries also. In mid-2007, the losses in the subprime mortgage markets generated astonishing disorder throughout the international financial system. The crisis spread with an amazing speed to other markets and even to financial institutions that had no direct revelation to the subprime mortgage market.

1. Loss of confidence : The stock market witnessed systemic weakness across financial sectors. The share prices for large, small, and investment banks extensively crashed and lost about a third of their value in between July 2007 and March 2008. Banks stopped trusting other banks. This interrupted interbank lending. Bear Stearns ended in the month of March and Indy Mac Bank went into receivership in July. But the deepest fall of all is the bankruptcy of Lehman Brothers in September, 2008. The financial system went in a standstill. After the events in September, 2008, the panic shot up and the crisis spread beyond the financial markets. Now it affected directly the mainstream also.

2. Decline in stock indexes and reduction in the market value of equities : The current financial crisis became prominent since September 2008 after the failure of few big financial American firms due to subprime mortgage crisis in the United States. The United States financial crunch hit other international markets. It is a negative impact of Globalization. It quickly developed a global credit crisis and deflation. That resulted in a number of European bank failures and decline in various stock indexes. This led to reduction in the market value of equities and commodities worldwide.

3. Tight market credit conditions : The crisis has given rise to extremely tight credit market conditions across the world. In the United states the disparity between the yields on safe, three-month government securities and the rate that banks charge each other for loans of the same duration has widened to more than 4.0 percentage points. More than $8 trillion of market value wiped out in stock markets worldwide.

4. Reduction of interest rates : The world's major central banks lowered their benchmark interest rates. The Federal Reserve, the European Central Bank, the Bank of England and the central banks of Canada and Sweden all reduced primary lending rates by a half percentage point. Switzerland also cut its benchmark rate, while the Bank of Japan endorsed the moves without changing its rates. The Chinese central bank reduced its key interest rates and reserve requirements. The Reserve Bank of India reduced its Cash Reserve Ratio (CRR) by 250 bps in releasing Rs 1,000 billion in cumulative terms. The International Monetary Fund (IMF) has marked down its growth projections for 2008 to 3.9% from 4.1% earlier and for 2009 to 3.0% from 3.9% earlier. The global economy had grown at 5 % in 2007.

Asian countries including India have not had a sub-prime mortgage crisis like many nations in the west. But their increasing incorporation with the west through trade and investment created incidental effects on their economies. Many Asian countries have seen a sharp downward movement in stock markets and currencies. Federal banks have tried all possible options. Most Reserve Banks have cut down the interest rates. On January 8, 2009 the Bank of England cut down base rate to 1.5%, the lowest in the Central Bank's history since its inception in 1694. The economy also affected by cuts in capital spending.

The impact of crisis on the Indian banks

Today Indian economy is a part of global economy. So we cannot be isolated from the present situation.US financial crisis affected European union, U.K and Asia along with American economy. The growth rate of these economies slowed down. India's growth rate in 2007-08 is 9 percent. But it is reduced to 6.7 percent in 2008-09. The Indian economy has registered a growth of 7.4 per cent in 2009-10, but it is not reached the level achieved in 2007-08. The economy began to slow down from the middle of 2007-08. A 9 per cent growth apparently could not be sustained, being clearly beyond India's potential rate of growth to be around 8.5 per cent.

However, global financial crisis shocked the Indian financial sector in several important ways.

1. Sharp depreciation of the rupee : Before the crisis, portfolio flows (mainly equity) financed largely India's current Account deficit. During the crisis the flow was reversed. Reversal of these flows led to a sharp depreciation of the rupee. Liquidity was sucked out of the markets, and also that risk capital more or less disappeared.

2. Severe liquidity crisis in the rupee market : After the bankruptcy of the US investment bank, Lehman, global credit markets dried up and the Indian corporate sector and banks are unable to roll over their short-term dollar liabilities. This created a severe liquidity crisis in the rupee market.

3. Deflation of a domestic asset market bubble : The global reduction in liquidity and risk appetite triggered the deflation of a domestic asset market bubble (in equities and real estate) and this placed strains on the domestic financial system.

4. The collapse of global demand effected export oriented sectors of the economy very badly. This resulted economic slowdown.

5. The sharp appreciation of the Swiss franc and Japanese yen against the US dollar as well as the steep depreciation of rupee created severe stress for miss-hedged corporate borrowers and their bankers.

The first round of adverse affects on banks

As per information with the RBI, Indian banks do not have any direct exposure or first round of adverse affects because our banks are not exceptionally exposed to subprime lending to sub-prime mortgages. The banking sector, through its overseas branches, has some exposure to distressed financial instruments and troubled financial institutions. But this exposure is part of their usual business and is quite small comparative to the size of their overall business. Only one of the larger private sector banks, the ICICI, is partly exposed to the financial crisis. But it is able to manage the crisis through a strong balance sheet and timely government action. The banking sector as whole maintained a healthy balance sheet and, over the third quarter of 2008. Actually that year is a nightmare for many big financial institutions around the world. India's banks reported encouraging results and witnessed an impressive jump in their profitability. According to reports, the RBI had estimated that as a result of exposure to collateralized debt obligations and credit default swaps, the combined mark-to-market losses of Indian banks at the end of July is around $450 million.

Second-round– impact of the crisis

However, the indirect –or second-round– impact of the crisis has affected India quite badly. The liquidity squeeze in the global market following Lehman Brothers' collapse has serious implications for India.

1. It led a massive outflow of Foreign Institutional Investment (FII) and compelled Indian banks and companies to shift their credit demand from external sources to the domestic banking sector. The period marked with massive FII outflow from India following redemption pressure of funds in their home countries. As a broad measure, overall foreign Investment in India as a percentage of GDP declined from 5% in

financial year 2008 to 1.7% in financial year 2009. It put forth pressure on domestic market liquidity, thus giving rise to a credit crunch (Table 1).

Table 1. Foreign Investment as a percentage of Gross Domestic Products

2005-06	2.6
2006-07	3.1
2007-08	5
2008-09	1.7
2009-10	4.9

Source : Complied data from RBI Bulletins

2. The collapse of the inter-bank market after the failure of Lehman left the Indian banking system in the position of having to repay large dollar liabilities that could no longer be rolled over. The Reserve Bank of India nipped this crisis in the bud by lending dollars to Indian banks out of its ample foreign exchange reserves. The central bank allowed banks to raise interest rates on NRI deposits so that more money would flow to India.

3. After Lehman, liquidity evaporated and the inter-bank rate averaged 11.6 per cent in the second half of September and 11.7 per cent in the first half of October. On the 10th of October, the rate hit 18.5 per cent. Even at these interest rates, there is no liquidity available.

Capital adequacy of Banks

Capital Adequacy measures the strength of the bank. Bank capital plays a very important role in the safety and soundness of individual banks and the banking system. Basel Committee for Bank Supervision (BCBS) has prescribed a set of norms for the capital requirement for the banks in 1988 known as Basel Accord I. These norms ensure that capital should be adequate to absorb unexpected losses or risks involved. If there is higher risk, then it needs to be backed up with Capital and vice versa. All the countries establish their own guidelines for risk based on capital framework known as Capital Adequacy Norms. Capital Adequacy Ratio is also known as Capital Risk Weighted Assets Ratio. Basel Committee has revised the guidelines in the year June 2001 known as Basel II Norms.

Under Basel II norms, 8% is the prescribed Capital Adequacy Norm. In case of Scheduled Commercial Banks Capital Adequacy Rate is 9%. For New Private Sector Banks Capital Adequacy Rate is 10%.

The minimum capital to Risk-Weighted Asset Ratio (CRAR) in India is placed at 9 per cent, one percentage point above the Basel II requirement. All the banks have their Capital to Risk Weighted Assets Ratio (CRAR) above the stipulated requirement of Basel guidelines (8 per cent) and RBI guidelines (9 per cent).

At the end of March 2008, there were 2 Scheduled Commercial Banks (1 Private Sector Bank and1 Foreign bank) having 0-9% of Capital Adequacy Ratio. 55 Scheduled Commercial Banks (28 Public Sector Banks, 17 Private Sector Banks & 10 Foreign Banks) were having Capital Adequacy Rate between 10%-15% and 22 Scheduled Commercial Banks (19 Foreign Banks and 3 Private Sector Banks) having Capital Adequacy Ratio of 15% and above according to RBI Publications.

The CRAR of Indian banks under Basel I framework, is on a steady increase since 2007. A marginal increase is shown during the crisis year. That is from 13.0 per cent at end-March 2008 to 13.2 per cent at end-March 2009. At end-March 2010, there is a further increase in the CRAR to 13.6 per cent. Under Basel II, CRAR of Indian banks as at end-March 2009 stood at 14.0 per cent, far above the stipulated minimum ratio by the Reserve Bank of 9 per cent. This indicated that Indian banks have successfully managed to meet the increased capital requirement under the changed framework.

CRAR of Indian banks in terms of Basel II norms is at 14.5 per cent as at end March, 2010 which is much higher than the regulatory direction. In 2008-09, the Indian banking system is able to survive the pressures of the global financial crisis. One of the factors that helped the regular functioning of the banking system even in the face of the largest global financial crisis is its vigorous capital adequacy (Table 2).

Table 2. Capital to Risk Weighted Assets Ratio – Bank group-wise(As at end-March)

(Per cent)

Bank group				*Basel I*		*Basel II*	
	2006	*2007*	*2008*	*2009*	*2010*	*2009*	*2010*
Public Sector banks	12.2	12.4	12.5	12.3	12.1	13.5	13.3
Nationalized banks	12.3	12.4	12.1	12.1	12.1	13.2	13.2
SBI Group	11.9	12.3	13.2	12.7	12.1	14.0	14.5
Old Private Sector banks	11.7	12.1	14.1	14.3	13.8	14.8	14.9
New Private Sector Banks	12.6	12	14.4	15.1	17.3	15.3	18.0
Foreign Banks	13	12.4	13.1	15.0	18.1	14.3	17.3
Scheduled Commercial banks	12.3	12.3	13	13.2	13.6	14.0	14.5

Source: Compiled from Reports on Trends and Progress of Banking in India, Reserve Bank of India

Present position of Indian banks

The Indian banking system is multilayered, comprising 82 scheduled commercial banks (SCBs), 92 regional rural banks (RRBs), 4 local area banks (LABs), 1,813 urban co-operative banks (UCBs) and 107,497 rural co-operative credit institutions and 34 foreign banks operating through branch route. 45 foreign banks are also operating in India through representative offices. Deposit of SCBs as of March 26, 2010 was Rs.4492825 crore while Bank Credit stood at Rs.3244788 crore. The Indian banking system has had no direct exposure to the sub-prime mortgage assets or to the failed institutions. It has very limited off-balance sheet activities or securitized assets. Indian banking industry is quite healthy. It remains safe.

Deposits

Following the financial crisis, new deposits have moved towards public sector banks. According to RBI's 'Quarterly Statistics on Deposits and Credit of Scheduled Commercial Banks: September 2009', nationalized banks, as a group, accounted for 50.5 per cent of the aggregate deposits, while State Bank of India (SBI) and its associates accounted for 23.8 per cent. The share of other scheduled commercial banks, foreign banks and regional rural banks in aggregate deposits are 17.8 per cent, 5.6 per cent and 3.0 per cent, respectively. Table 2 reveals that even in years of financial crisis the deposits of public sector banks in India are increasing.

Bank credit

With respect to gross bank credit, nationalized banks hold the highest share of 50.5 per cent in the total bank credit, with SBI and its associates at 24.7 per cent and other scheduled commercial banks at 10.2 per cent. Foreign banks and regional rural banks had a share of 3.5 per cent and 14.6 per cent respectively in the total bank credit(Table 3).

Bad times for the economy spell lower credit growth. In 2007-08, commercial credit growth slowed to 22%. It slowed further to 18% in 2008-09. But banks maintained their return on assets in 2008-09 at the same level as in the preceding boom years of 2004-08. This is truly astonishing. It suggests that no matter what the ups and downs of the economy, the Indian banking sector can deliver a return of 1% on assets, a benchmark of good performance in banking. India today seems to have a crisis-proof banking sector(Table 4).

Table 3. Annual Growth rate of Deposits (as at end March) (Percent)

Bank group	*2006*	*2007*	*2008*	*2009*
Nationalized banks	16.2	24.1	24.4	24.5
SBI Group	15.5	17.9	25.9	30.5
Regional Rural Banks	15.0	16.2	18.6	21.9
Foreign Banks	44.9	30.5	24.4	12.7
Other Scheduled Commercial banks	28.1	31.5	22.9	8.9

Source: Data compiled from quarterly statistics on deposits and credit of scheduled commercial Banks published by Reserve Bank of India

Table 4. Annual Growth rate of Bank Credits (As at end March) (Percent)

Bank group	*2006*	*2007*	*2008*	*2009*
Nationalized banks	30.6	28.3	25.0	24.7
SBI Group	31.1	28.9	20.7	21.0
Regional Rural Banks	21.2	22.1	21.6	14.6
Foreign Banks	28.2	29.2	27.8	3.5
Other Scheduled Commercial banks	32.3	29.0	18.8	10.2

Source: Data compiled from quarterly statistics on deposits and credit of scheduled commercial Banks published by Reserve Bank of India

Revival of confidence

The confidence of non-resident Indians (NRIs) in the Indian economy is reviving again. NRI fund inflows increased since April 2009 and touched US$ 47.8 billion on March 2010, as per the RBI's June 2010 bulletin. Most of this has come through Foreign Currency Non-resident (FCNR) accounts and Non-resident External Rupee Accounts.'

Reserves

To re-establish orderly conditions in the money, equity and forex markets and to improve the overall liquidity in the system, the RBI has cut the CRR to 6.5% from the earlier 9.0%. To help mutual funds, as a temporary measure, the RBI has allowed banks to avail of additional liquidity support of up to 0.5% of their net demand and time deposits. This is in addition to the ad hoc reduction in the statutory liquidity ratio to 24%. Foreign exchange reserves were up by US$ 1.69 billion to US$ 272.783 billion, for the week ending June 11, on account of revaluation gains. June 21, 2010.

Return on assets

Banks managed a return on assets of 1% in both 2007-08 and 2008-09, slightly higher than the 0.9% return of 2006-07. This should place the Indian banking sector amongst the most profitable in the world today. Banks elsewhere saw their capital eroded and required infusions of capital from governments. In India, capital adequacy actually improved in 2008-09.

Other income

Banks have woken up to the potential for fee income. Apart from conventional products that generate fees such as letters of credit, guarantees and mortgage products, banks now generate fee income from sale of mutual fund and insurance products.

CONCLUSION

Our country also adopted the policy of liberalization and globalization. The government followed disinvestment policy in all fields. But even now the financial market is dominated by public sector banks. They have not invested much in collateralized debt instruments and mainly depend upon the domestic market for deposits. That is why banking sector of India is able to sustain with full confidence at the time of financial crisis and present. Deposits of our banks are increased compared to deposits of foreign banks in 2007-08. The government is also able to take correct measures through Reserve bank of India. 34% of banks deposits are in government securities and cash with the RBI. Our banking industry is also subject to stricter prudential regulations with respect to capital and liquidity. Indian banking sector is better placed to cope with the adverse consequences of the ongoing financial turmoil in the west. Vigorous capital adequacy of the banks helped the banks for the smooth functioning even in the face of largest global financial crisis. Banks, of course, need to do more. We need more sophisticated products. There is the challenge of financial inclusion. We can overcome the challenge of financial inclusion only with the help of nationalized banks. So the government should not privatize banking sector fully and the present role of public sector banks should continue in the financial markets.

REFERENCES

1. Economic survey (2009-10): Ministry of finance, Government of India, New Delhi
2. Ghosal, S.N (2008): *'Sub prime crisis: what caused it'*, The Indian banker, Aug 6.
3. Ghosal,S.N(2009):. *'Global financial crisis-cause and impact'*, ICFAI Reader, March
4. Ghosh, D.K. (2009): *'The US Subprime crisis, Bursting Bubbles on whirlpool of speculation'*, The Indian Banker, Vol 4 Feb

5. Jayanth R Varma (2009): '*Indian Financial Sector and the Global Financial Crisis*' Vikalpa 'Vol.34: Nov 3.

6. Jayati Ghosh, C. P. and Chandrasekhar(2008): '*India and the global financial crisis*', Business Line October 21.

7. Mallya, M. D(2009): Chairman & Managing Director, Bank of Baroda, India '*Global Financial Crisis & Indian Banking Sector*', Talk on Global Financial Crisis & Indian Banking Sector Dubai Chapter of The Institute of Chartered Accountants of India: http://www.cgidubai.com

8. Rangrajan, C. (2009)'*The international financial crisis and its impact on India*'. Bureau of Parliament Studies and training, LokSabha, Parliament House. New Delhi.

9. RBI's 'Quarterly Statistics on Deposits and Credit of Scheduled Commercial Banks: September (2009)

10. Singh Dhananjay(200): '*Global Financial crisis- Positive for India*', ICFAI Reader, January.

11. Srinivasa Rao,.K.(2008): '*Global Crisis, Emerging Challenges for Indian Banks*', The Indian Banker, Vol 3 No:11, November.

12. Tapaskumar panda (2010), '*Economic recovery, signals end of crisis for India*' The Indian Banker, Vol: 5, Janaury.

13. The RBI Bulletin of August 2009 published by the Reserve Bank of India

Newspapers

Business line

Economic Times

The Hindu

Website

EconomyWatch.com

http://planningcommission.gov.in/reports

www.investopedia .org

www.banknetindia.com/banking

*Businessweek.com/***Indian-banking**

SECTION V : BANKING INNOVATION AND FINANCIAL INCLUSION

25

Investment in Gold Exchange Traded Funds (Gold ETF): A Safe and Novel Approach to Investment in Gold

Joshy Andrews

INTRODUCTION

Gold is always considered as one of the best investment alternatives available with a common Indian investor. Indians have considered investment in gold as a traditional method of investment. As world's top consumer of gold, India accounts for 20% of world gold demand. If we consider the price growth of gold since 2001, it has risen by as much as 450%. As the importance of gold investment increased due to extreme volatility in the financial markets, economic uncertainty and fears that national currencies will lose their value etc. forced the investment in gold. It is gold is always considered as the best means to hedge against market volatility. As its importance increased in the investment arena, gold is nowadays measured equivalent to investment opportunities in the mainstream financial markets.

THE DEMAND SCENARIO

According to the World Gold Council(WGC), India's gold import, which had already exceeded 2009 levels, is likely to cross the 750-tonne mark this year due to increasing consumer demand for jewellery despite soaring prices. As per their estimates, the gold imports would cross the 750-tonne mark this year, a level earlier achieved in 2007. In 2009, the total import of gold stood at 559 tonnes. In Q3 2010, India, the world's largest consumer of the yellow metal, has bought 214 tonnes of gold compared to 176 tonnes in the same quarter in 2009. It is a very good sign that the demand side is shooting up and give a confident signal to investors that the trend in gold prices is not a bubble. India's position in the world pool is shown in Table 1.

Table 1. India in World Gold Industry

Rounded Figures	*India (In Tons)*	*World (In Tons)*	*% Share*
Total Stocks	13000	145000	9
Central Bank holding	400	28000	1.4
Annual Production	2	2600	0.08
Annual Recycling	100-300	1100-1200	13
Annual Demand	800	3700	22
Annual Imports	600		
Annual Exports	60		

Source: *http://finance.indiamart.com/markets/commodity/gold.html*

PRICE TRENDS

As an investment opportunity, gold need to be considered as a long term investment option. It is because the increase in prices of gold always happens on a long term basis. It is imperative that gold prices will increase over long period of time. Analyzing the history of fluctuation in gold prices, it has shown fall in prices many times but the fall had only a temporary effect of short period of time ranging from 1 month to 2 years. In the long run, the price of gold always showed increasing trend as well as stability in value. It is because of the supply and demand mismatch in gold. The world supply of gold is almost stable but the demand of gold has increased all over the world. Considering as the biggest gold consumer in the world, the income level of an average Indian has increased overtime. At the same time, the saving population as well as purchasing power of investors of our country has also increased during the period. These reasons keep the value of gold soaring.

There are many reasons for the present skyrocketing of prices of gold. One of the reason is as mentioned earlier, the reason of supply and demand mismatch. Another reason is the Quantitative Easing2(QE2). Federal Reserve of US has been providing US dollar liquidity or availability since the start of financial crisis from 2008 onwards. The liquidity or availability provided here is called Quantitative Easing (QE). Federal Reserve of US is providing new US dollar liquidity or availability from Nov-2010 onwards. The fresh round of US dollar liquidity or availability from November 2010 is being called as phase 2 of Quantitative Easing (QE2). This move will cause further increase in supply of dollars which leads more spending or consumption by individuals and in turn will increase prices of goods thereby causing inflation. The rise in inflation will cause fall in the value of US dollar. The fall in US dollar will cause increase in price of gold, as gold price globally is quoted in US dollar. So in medium term also the probability of rise in price of gold is very high. If we analyze the price of gold with dollar value, we can see that there is an inverse relationship between the two. It is evident from Figure 1.

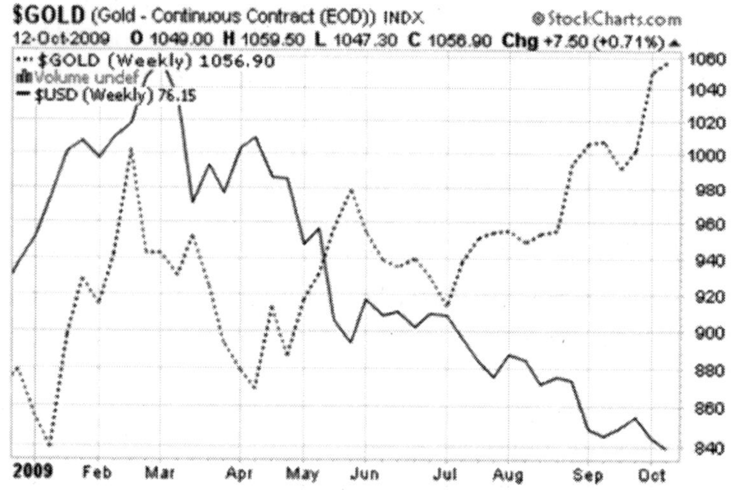

Fig. 1. Inverse relationship between price of Gold & Dollar

Source: **http://seekingalpha.com**

If the traditional way of gold investment was in ornaments, new investors opt for gold coins and biscuits. Banks and other financial institutions were offered gold coins of specific weights and purity. The Indian postal services recently introduced the same and attracted the gold thirst of common people.

GOLD EXCHANGE TRADED FUNDS(GOLD ETFs)

Exchange Traded funds are instruments which are traded like shares which are backed by physical holding of the commodity. These are open-ended mutual fund schemes which invest the pooled money in standard gold of 0.995 purity. The first ETF launched in India towards the end of

2001 by Benchmark Asset Management Company through its Nifty Benchmark Exchange-Traded Scheme(Nifty BeES). Since they are open-ended and listed on the stock-exchanges, it is possible to buy and sell them through out the days. They traded in exchanges in a small range around the value of NAV held by them. It can be considered as a hybrid of open-ended mutual funds and listed individual stocks. The working of Gold ETF is depicted in figure2.

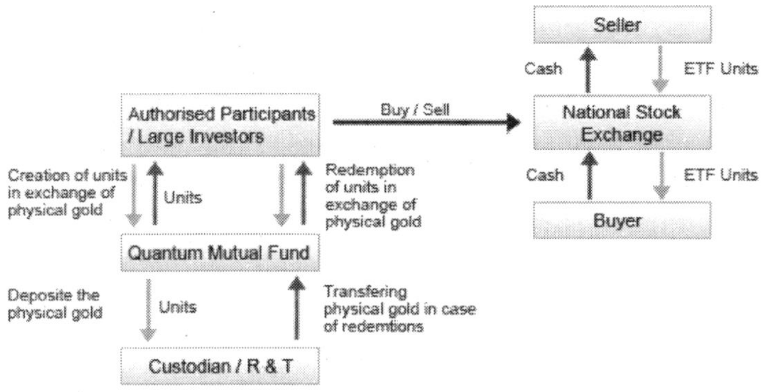

Fig. 2. Working of Gold ETFs

Source : ***http://www.quantumamc.com/SchemesNAV/gold_fund.aspx***

It is a new phenomenon concerned with India but getting popularity as investors become aware of investing in gold in a non material form. Comparing with physical gold, there are many advantages in investing gold ETFs. Gold ETFs allow an investor to invest in paper gold instead of physical gold. The units are issued in demat form and avoids the risk of holding physical gold. It can be easily bought and sold like any stock on the exchange through terminals spread across the country. It invests the investors' money in physical gold in the same way as equity mutual funds invest in equities. The investment made by investor is in units and one unit is equivalent to 1 gram of physical gold or as the asset management company fixes. There is no separate form filling for buying or selling units. It can be done by just a phone call to the broker or a click on the net. One can buy or sell the units during the market hours at prices that are close to the NAV of the scheme. A comparison table in this connection is given below

COMPARISON OF GOLD ETFs WITH OTHER FORMS

A comparison table is given below which compares the different parameters of investment with other forms of investment in gold. The following is a comparison of investment in gold in the most preferable routes by a common investor such as jewelry and bullion as well as coins offered by banks and other financial institutions with investment in Gold Exchange Traded funds. The standard investment here taken as 10 gm rate (Table 2).Considering the above comparison table, it is clear that investment in gold in the form of jewelry and bank offered coins costs higher compared to Gold ETFs of the same value and quantity. It is 11.70% more cost to buy 10gm Jewelry compared to 10 units of Gold ETF NAV of Benchmark BeES(which is almost exactly invested in 10gm of gold) and 10.66% more cost to buy 10 gm gold coin from SBI. Ie, in both the cases, the extra cost incurred than the actual market value of gold(margin of jeweler as well as banker) is a loss to the investor if they sell back gold in times of need and at the same time he may sometimes negotiate the price with the jeweler. In case of Gold ETF, an investor can avoid this margin and at the same time he can sell his Gold ETF at a price closer to the market price of Gold (Table 3).

GOLD ETF SCHEMES AVAILABLE

If we consider the Indian Gold Exchange Traded Fund (Gold ETF) market in India, Total 9 schemes are available at present. Among these, the funds launched by ICICI Prudential Mutual Fund House, Religare Gold ETF and HDFC Mutual Fund House are of recent origin. The various details regarding the nature of each scheme are mentioned

Table 2. Comparison of Gold ETF with physical Gold

Sl. no.	*Parameter*	*Jeweler*	*Bank*	*Gold ETF*
1	How Gold is Held	Physical (jewelry)	Physical (bar/coins)	Dematerialized form
2	Pricing	Differs from one to another neither transparent nor standard	Differs from bank to bank not standard	Linked to international gold prices and very transparent
3	Buying premium above gold price	Likely to be more	Likely to be more	Likely to be less
4	Making Charges	Charges incurred	Charges incurred	No charge incurred
5	Impurity risk	High	Nil	Nil
6	Storage requirement	Locker/safe	Locker/ safe	Demat account
7	Security of asset	Investor is responsible	Investor is responsible	Fund house take the responsibility
8	Resale	Conditional and uneconomical	Banks do not buy back	At secondary market prices
9	Convenience in buying and selling	Less convenient as gold needs to be moved physically	Less convenient as gold needs to be moved physically	More convenient as held in electronic form under demat account
10	Quantity to buy / sell	Available in standard denomination	Available in standard denomin-ation	Minimum is ½ or 1 gram according to the fund

Sl. no.	*Parameter*	*Jeweler*	*Bank*	*Gold ETF*
11	Bid / Ask	Very high Spread	Can't sell back	Very low
12	Risk of Theft	Yes, possible	Yes, Possible	No, Not Possible
13	Wealth tax	Yes	Yes	No
14	Long term capital gain tax	Only after 3 years	Only after 3 years	After 1 year

Source: HDFC MF Scheme info Document

Table 3. Comparison of Investment 10 grams of gold through different sources (value as on 12.01.2011)

Source	*Investment required (Rs.)*
Jewelry*	22,462
Bank offered coins **	22,200
Gold ETF***	19,833

* gold rate of 24 ct. @ 1gm = 2042 and minimum making charge of 10% also added. The applicable taxes are excluded.

** SBI gold coin rate (excluding VAT and other local taxes as applicable)

*** Gold ETF rate as per the NAV of Benchmark BeES (10 units)

below; (Table 4). The Average Asset Under Management(AAUM) and the Net Asset Value(NAV) of each fund available in India is given below. From the comparison is clear that the Benchmark Gold BeES occupy comparatively higher AAUM compared to other funds. If the NAV is taken into to consideration, it is almost same for different funds except Religare Gold ETF and ICICI Prudential Gold ETF. It is because almost all the funds are keeping near to 100 % of their AUM in physical gold (Table5). As in the case of NAV, when considering periodic evaluations of return of various schemes, it is more or less same and there is no significant difference in their return (Table 6). The taxation of Gold ETF is almost same as that of debt mutual funds. The most impressive tax implication in investing Gold ETFs is that it is not liable for wealth tax compared with investment in physical form. In relation to short term capital gain (STCG) tax, taxation is applicable incase of before one year and long term capital gain (LTCG)tax will be applicable after one year. Incase of Jewellery and coins, the STCG tax is applicable before 3 years and LTCG tax is applicable after three years (Table 7).

Table 4. Details of Gold ETFs Available in India

Fund	*Expense Ratio*	*Entry/ Exit Load*	*Launch date*	*Pricing Per unit*	*Proportion of Investment Gold : Current Assets*
Benchmark Gold BeES	1%	Nil	19 March 2007	Appr. 1 gm of gold	99: 09
Kotak Gold	1%	Nil	27 July 2007	Appr. 1 gm of gold	99.61:0.31
Quantum Gold	1.25%	Nil	22 Feb. 2008	Appr. ½ gm of gold	99.91:0.09
Reliance Gold ETF	2.50%	Nil	1 Nov. 2007	Appr. 1 gm of gold	90:10
Religare Gold ETF	-	Nil	23 Feb. 2010	Appr. 1 gm of gold	90:10
SBI Gold ETF	2.50%	Nil	30 March 2009	Appr. 1 gm of gold	90:10
UTI Gold ETF	1%	Nil	10 April 2007	Appr. 1 gm of gold	90:10
ICICI Prudential Gold ETF	2.50%	Nil	15 July 2010	Appr. 1 gm of gold	90:10
HDFC Gold ETF	1%	Nil	25 June 2010	Appr. 1 gm of gold	90:10

Table 5. Comparison of AAUM & NAV

Schemes	*Average Asset Under Management (AAUM) for the quarter October December 2010*	*NAV (Rs. / unit)As on 14/01/2010*
Benchmark Gold BeES	1,50,629.11	1971.89
Kotak Gold	24,331.66	1970.52
Quantum Gold	2,563.01	980.34
Reliance Gold ETF	34,060.53	1916.74
Religare Gold ETF	3,821.82	2026.16
SBI Gold ETF	15,548.25	2008.05
UTI Gold ETF	44,940.17	1971.15
ICICI Prudential Gold ETF	8562.31	2033.06
HDFC Gold ETF	31,529.50	2015.34

Source: *Company websites*

Table 6. Comparison of periodic return

Schemes	*6 Months*	*1 year*	*2 year*	*3 year*	*Since inception*
Benchmark Gold BeES	10.9	12	27.1	25.3	22.73
UTI Gold Share	11	12.1	26.9	25.3	23.27
Kotak Gold ETF	11	12	26.8	25.2	28.22
Reliance Gold ETF	10.9	12	26.7	24.3	24
SBI Gold ETF	11.2	11.9	N.A.	N.A.	25.03

Table 7. Tax Implications

Taxation	*Gold ETF*	*Jewellers*	*Banks*
Wealth Tax	No	Yes	Yes
Short- term capital gain tax	Applicable before one year	Applicable before 3 years	Applicable before 3 years
Long –term capital gain tax	Applicable after one year	Applicable after 3 years	Applicable after 3 years

CONCLUSION

Gold ETFs have a good future in India. Nowadays the portfolio managers advice investors to keep gold as a part of their portfolio. It is because gold always acts as a hedging tool against inflation. Keeping such a tool in the form of Gold ETF is more preferable as it will be cost effective than in physical form. In addition to that there are many advantages in investing in paper form of gold than in physical form of gold. Considering Indian investors, it is a new model of investment and needs to create awareness among the investors.

REFERENCE

1. *http://finance.indiamart.com/markets/commodity/gold.html*
2. *http://seekingalpha.com*
3. *http://www.quantumamc.com/SchemesNAV/gold_fund.aspx*
4. *http://www.gold.org*
5. *http://www.benchmarkfunds.com*
6. *http://www.kotakmutual.com*
7. *http://www.quantumamc.com*
8. *http://www.reliancemutual.com*
9. *http://www.religaremf.com*
10. *http://www.sbimf.com*
11. *http://www.utimf.com*
12. *http://www.hdfcfunds.com*
13. *http://www.pruicici.com*

26

An Islamic Microfinance Model - The Missing Dimension

E. Sulaiman

INTRODUCTION

Islamic microfinance represents the convergence of two rapidly growing industries: microfinance and Islamic finance. It has the potential to not only respond to unmet demand but also to combine the Islamic social principle of caring for the less fortunate with microfinance's power to provide financial access to the poor. Islamic microfinance is still in its infancy, and business models are just emerging. In 2007, global survey on Islamic microfinance conducted by the CGAP revealed that Islamic microfinance has a total estimated global outreach of only 380,000 customers and accounts for only an estimated one-half of one percent of total microfinance outreach. The supply of Islamic microfinance is very concentrated in a few countries, with the top three countries (Indonesia, Bangladesh, and Afghanistan) accounting for 80 percent of global outreach.

Islamic convictions on the responsibility go well beyond mere profitability goals and coincide with the renewed perception on business recently at stake within the most advanced sectors of western business and civil societies. Far from the limits imposed by neo-classical thought, this new wave implies new sorts of responsibilities on behalf of the company falling under the rubric of corporate social responsibility (Ferro, 2005). As its ultimate goal is the maximization of social benefits as opposed to profit maximization, through the creation of healthier financial institutions that can provide effective financial services for grass roots levels; and argue that Islamic finance, if inserted in a new paradigm, could be a viable alternative to the socio-economic crisis lived by the Western paradigm (Al Harran, 1996).

A relatively few studies and a few experiences are available on Islamic microfinance. Dhumale and Sapcanin (1999) drafted a technical note in which they tried to analyze how to combine Islamic banking with microfinance. They took into consideration the three main instruments of Islamic finance (*mudaraba, musharaka and murabaha*) trying to use them as tools to design a successful microfinance program. Concern over credit provision and finance accessibility for the poor via microfinance is also relevant to Islamic banks that should place greater social welfare responsibilities and religious commitments to achieve the Islamic economic objectives, including social justice, equitable distribution of income and wealth and promoting economic development. Many writers such as El-Gamal (2006), Al-Harran (1990, 1996, 1999), Akhtar (1996, 1998), Dhumale and Sapcanin (1998), Ahmed (2001), and others, believe in the great potential of Islamic banking to be involved in microfinance programmes to cater for the needs of the poor who usually fall outside the formal banking sector.

Islamic banking is concerned with much more than

just refraining from charging interest. It is a system that aims at making a positive contribution to the fulfilment of the socioeconomic objectives of the society. Islamic banks are expected to be guided by an Islamic economic objective to ensure that wealth is fairly circulated among as many hands as possible without causing any harm to those who acquired it lawfully. Hence the issue of financing the poor via microfinance initiative is not alien to Islamic banking.

OBJECTIVES AND METHODOLOGY

The present study discusses the conceptual framework of Islamic micro-finance and its relevance for fulfilling the financial requirements of marginalised sections of the society. It enunciates its basic principles, approaches, practices and applications in the area of financial products and services offered to the clients of micro-finance. The data used for the study were collected from the secondary sources such as journals, research reports, websites and books related with the subject.

RESULTS AND DISCUSSIONS

Islamic banks may emulate the existing model of microfinance practice; the activities must be carried out in ways, which do not conflict with the principles of Islamic finance. Islamic microfinance initiatives should be free from any involvement of activities prohibited by Islam and from elements like usury *(riba)*, gambling *(maisir)*, harmful substance (*darar*) and excessive ambiguity (*gharar*). Islamic banks can always learn from various approaches used by microfinance institutions to ensure effectiveness in providing finance to the marginalized society. In addition to the innovative approaches used by many microfinance institutions, Islamic banking can apply diverse financial instruments together with other available mechanisms such as *zakah,* charity and *waqf,* which can be integrated into microfinance programmes to promote entrepreneurship amongst the poor and subsequently alleviate poverty. The following sections delineate the various instruments in Islamic finance for mobilization of funds and financing the poor.

MOBILIZATION OF FUNDS

The conventional MFIs depend on interest-based deposits, government subsidies, donations and loans for the mobilisation of funds. On the other hand, Islamic MFIs can mobilise funds by way of using different financial instruments. The fund mobilisation of Islamic MFI's can be broadly divided into: (1) internal resources and (2) external resources.

Internal Resources : The internal financial resources can be mobilized internally to ensure self-sustainability and self-sufficiency. It can be further divided into two main categories, namely deposits and equity. The following describes the salient characteristics of Islamic deposits and equity that can be mobilised for microfinance purposes:-

(a) Deposits : Islamic microfinance can mobilise various forms of deposits such as *wadiah* (safekeeping), *qard al-hassan* (benevolence loan), and *mudarabah* (profit sharing). Under *wadiah* mechanism, the deposits are held as trust and utilised by the bank at its own risk. The depositors are not entitled to any return since the profit or loss resulting from the investment of these funds is entirely belonged to the bank. In the case of *qard al-hassan* mechanism, whereby the funds deposited in the bank is treated as a loan by the depositor. Here, the bank shall have to guarantee the principal amount but is not allowed to offer any return to depositors. *Mudarabah* deposits are based on profit sharing between the bank acting as the entrepreneur and depositors as the owner. The amount deposited is not supposed to be guaranteed and depositors are entitled to any return derived from the invested funds.

(b) Equity : Islamic microfinance initiative may also mobilise funds through participatory models such as *musharakah* and *mudarabah*. In *musharakah* model of fund-raising, public can buy shares and become owners of the whole microfinance programme initiated by Islamic banks or choose specific financing project of their choice. Any profits realised from the project are distributed annually to the shareholders. While losses incurred shall be shared proportionate to the amount of capital contributed by each participant.

External Resources : It is the common practice of microfinance institutions worldwide which rely on external parties to provide financial resources like government grants, subsidies and donations. In addition to this, an Islamic MFIs can use funds such as *zakah*, donations, gift and *waqf* to resolve the issue of financing the poorest of the poor or hardcore poor.

DEMAND-ORIENTED FINANCING

The instruments used by the Islamic MFIs to address various needs and demands of the clients especially among the poor entrepreneur can be broadly divided into: (1) participatory profit-loss-sharing modes like *mudarabah* and *musharakah*; (2) exchange modes like *murabahah* (cost plus sale), *bay' bithaman 'ajil* (deferred payment sale), *bay' al-Salam* (forward sale) and *bay' al-Istisna'* (commission to manufacture sale), *Ijarah* (leasing); (3) voluntary charitable contract, such as, pawning contract and benevolence loan (*qard al-hassan*) and (4) hybrid-modes like diminishing partnership *(musharakah mutanaqisah)*, hire purchase etc.

FINANCING THROUGH SPV

A major concern for banks to be involved in microfinance is how to manage their risk inherent in financing activities involving the poor and small entrepreneurs. One of the possible alternatives for banks to get involved in microfinance is through a SPV. An SPV is a legal entity created by a firm (known as the sponsor or originator) to undertake some specific purpose or restricted activity spelt out by the sponsoring firm. An essential feature of an SPV, which makes it promising as a vehicle to offer microfinance is its bankruptcy-remote in nature. The key elements of SPV financing (Figure 1) are as follows:

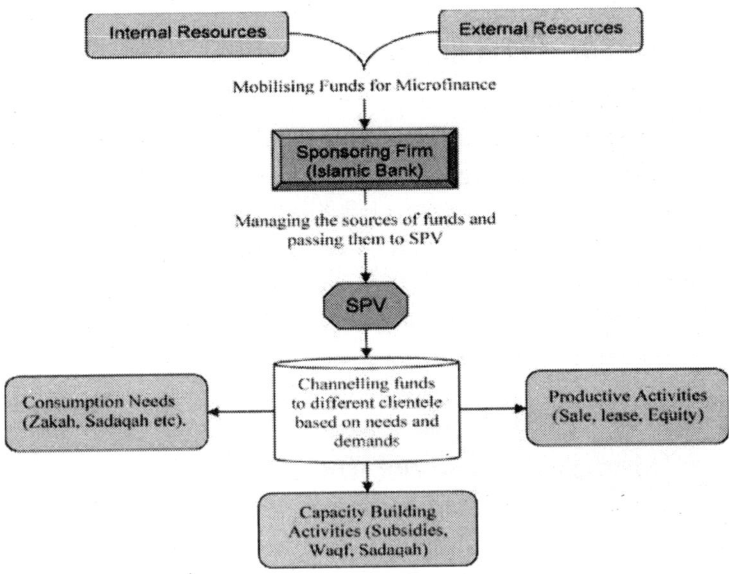

Fig. 1. Financing via SPV

- The bank mobilises various sources of funds with specific microfinance objectives.
- The bank creates a bankruptcy-remote SPV.
- The bank allocates certain amount of funds and passes it to the SPV.
- The funds are channelled to various clients depending on needs and demands.

PRACTICES OF ISLAMIC MICROFINANCE INSTITUTIONS

Islamic Micro-finance institutions focused on providing regular banking services needed by the community with an eye on community redevelopment using the principle of interest-free models. A number of financing products and structures which are commonly used in the mainstream Islamic finance industry could also be used in the Islamic microfinance products and services.

MARKET-BASED OR PROFIT MODEL

Islamic approach to poverty alleviation is a composite of a mission based and market-based interventions. Islam permits profit making and creation of wealth. The poor need a range of microfinance services, such as micro-savings, micro-credit, micro-equity, micro-insurance, and micro-remittance. In the context of mainstream Islamic finance, there are various markets based modes existing through which such services may be provided to the poor.

MICRO-SAVINGS

Micro-savings is a critical financial service for poor and excluded households. Micro-savers are motivated by a host of factors, such as, safety, convenience, returns, personalized service (door-to-door collection) etc. Various contractual options for designing Islamic savings products are: *wadia, qard hasan* and *mudaraba*. Under this mechanism, the deposits are held as a trust and utilized by the microfinance institution at its own risk. The depositor does not share in the risk or return in any form. Any profit or loss resulting from the investment of these funds accrues entirely to the microfinance institution. Another feature of such deposits is the absence of any condition with regard to deposits and withdrawals. These are also known as "sight deposits" or current accounts. Another view is to treat these deposits as *qard hasan* or benevolent loan by the depositor. Here, the microfinance institution is free to utilize these funds at its own risk. The depositor in its role as the lender is not entitled to any return as the latter would constitute *riba*.

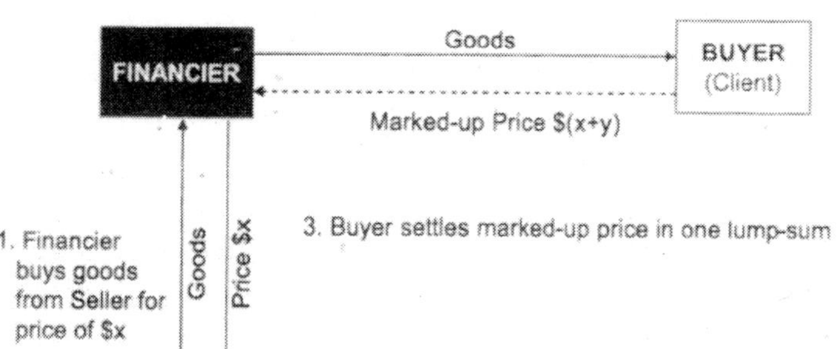

Fig. 2. Simple Murabaha

An alternative model is based on the mechanism of *mudaraba*. The microfinance institution now requires the depositors to authorize it for the purpose of investing the funds. Profits on investments are shared between depositor and microfinance institution as per a pre-agreed ratio. Losses are absorbed by depositor; effectively bringing down the value of the asset created with its investments and the value of the deposit. Under this mechanism, depositors have the right of withdrawal. Profits are calculated on the basis of the minimum balance maintained for a time period. The minimum balance maintained is deemed as the investment for that time period. A minimum balance is required to be maintained in order to qualify for a share in profits. *Mudaraba*-based savings products involve considerable downside risk. Therefore, these are rarely offered by Islamic microfinance institutions. It should be noted here that when the savings products are remunerated on the basis of revenue-sharing rather than profit-sharing, under which the depositor appoints the microfinance institution to manage its funds and considerable flexibility remains in the matter of prescribing the method and quantum of reward for the microfinance institution.

MICRO-CREDIT

The Islamic alternative to interest-based conventional loan is trade based or lease-based credit that permits the ownership and/or use of commodities or physical assets needed for productive enterprise while deferring the payments to future time periods. There are several such products developed by mainstream Islamic financial institutions involving *murabaha, ijara, bai-salam, bai-istisna, bai-istijrar* etc.

Murabaha (cost-plus mark-up) : *Murabaha* involves a finance party purchasing tangible assets from a seller and selling them to a buyer at a predetermined profit margin. In the context of trade finance, the buyer will settle the marked-up purchase price by way of immediate lump sum payment (Figure 2). In the context of consumer finance, the buyer will settle the marked-up purchase price by way of deferred installments. An asset is a highly liquid, the buyer will settle the marked-up purchase price by way of deferred installments but will also appoint the finance party as its agent to on-sell the assets on a spot basis and remit to the buyer the proceeds of any such sale (Figure 3). *Murabaha* is the most popular and flexible structure and is used in microfinance initiatives across Afghanistan, Bangladesh, Indonesia, Sudan, Syria and Yemen. Unlike profit-sharing mechanisms, *Murabaha* does not require the client to maintain written records that are often unavailable at the micro enterprise level or if available, the client may be unwilling to share them. There is also no opportunity for abuse on the part of the client through inaccurate or false record-keeping.

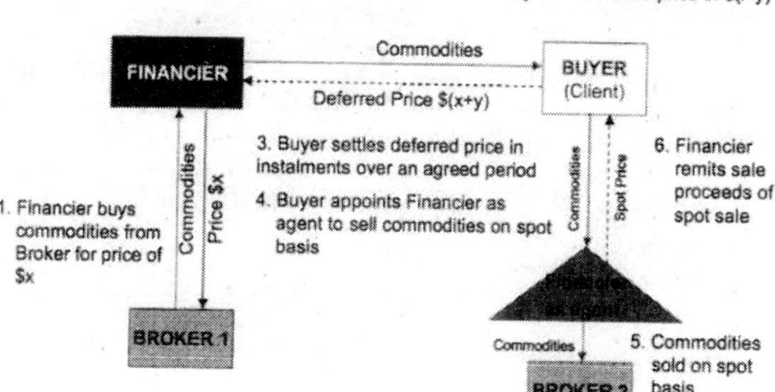

Fig. 3. Commodity Murabahad

Micro-Leasing (*Ijara*) : *Ijara* in simple terms implies leasing or hiring of a physical asset. It is a popular debt-based product in which the Islamic MFI assumes the role of a *lessor* and allows its client to use a particular asset that it owns. The client or (lessee) is in need of the asset. Through the *ijara,* it receives the benefits associated with ownership of the asset against payment of predetermined rentals. *Ijara* is for a known time period. In *ijara,* the MFI continues to be the owner throughout the *ijara* period while the client receives the benefits of using the asset. As such, risks associated with ownership of the asset remain with the MFI and the asset is supposed to revert back to the MFI at the end of the *ijara* period. The cash flows are structured in a way that cover the cost of the asset and provide for a fair return on the same to the MFI. The MFI after recovering its cost and fair return may simply donate the asset or sell the asset at a nominal price to its client (Figure 4). Micro-leasing or micro-*ijara* serves as a mode of microfinance. All kinds of income-generating equipment or physical asset, such as, tools and machines to manufacture commodities, rickshaws and boats to transport people, carts as also shops to sell merchandize, low-cost houses may be financed through this mode for the poor.

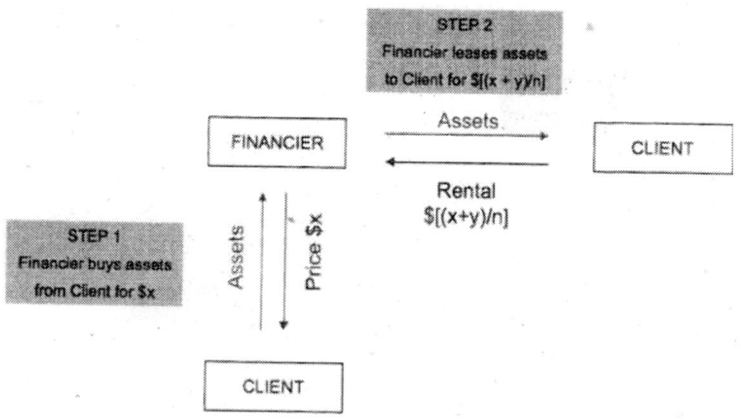

Fig. 4. Micro-Leasing (*Ijara*)

Bai-Salam : *Bai-salam* is a deferred delivery contract. It is essentially a forward agreement where delivery occurs at a future date in exchange for spot payment of price. It was originally designed as a financing mechanism for small farmers and traders. Under a *salam* agreement, a farmer or a trader in need of short-term funds, sells its output or merchandize to the MFI on a deferred delivery basis. It receives full price of the merchandize on the spot that serves its financing need at present. At a pre-agreed future date, it delivers the merchandize to the MFI. The MFI sells the merchandize in the market at the prevailing price. Since the spot price that the MFI pays is pegged lower than the expected future price, the transaction should result in a profit for the MFI. In practice, the MFI could be an association of the farmers or artisans or traders or an agency to undertake collective marketing of the members' produce.

Bai-Istisna : *Bai-Istisna* is a contract of manufacture. A seller under an *istisna* agreement undertakes to develop or manufacture a commodity with clear specifications for an agreed price and deliver after an agreed period of time. The unique feature of *istisna* is that nothing is exchanged on spot or at the time of contracting. The buyer makes payment of price in instalments over the agreed time period or in full at the end of the time period (Figure 5). In an *istisna*, the seller and the manufacturer may be different entities. This allows MFI to engage in *istisna* by assigning the job of development, manufacture or construction to a third party under a parallel *istisna* arrangement.

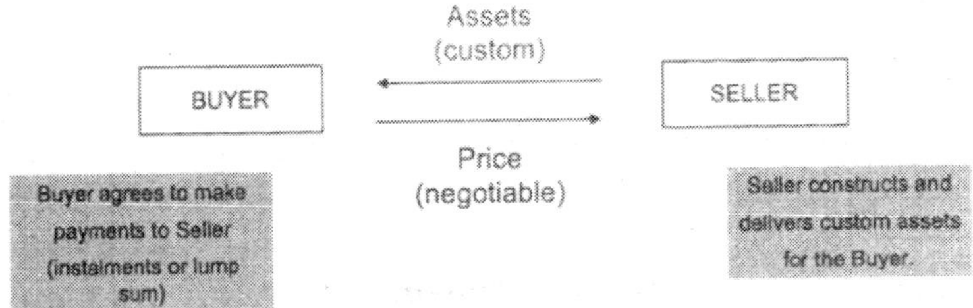

Fig. 5. ***Bai-Istisna***

Bai-Istijrar : *Bai-Istijrar* takes place when the buyer purchases different quantities of a given commodity from a single seller over a period of time. In other words, the seller delivers the total quantity of commodity purchased in instalments. This mode is ideal for microfinance where micro-entrepreneurs often buy their raw materials and inputs in small quantities from the same vendor over extended periods.

MICRO-EQUITY

An Islamic MFI may consider various partnership based modes or equity based modes for microfinance. Two classical modes commonly discussed in this context are *musharaka* and *mudaraba.* These equity-based products are unique to Islamic microfinance and in some sense, account for its superiority over conventional microfinance on grounds of ethics and efficiency.

Musharaka Model : A *musharaka* or a joint venture involves a partnership in which both the MFI and its micro-entrepreneur contribute to entrepreneurship and capital. It is an agreement whereby the micro-entrepreneur and the MFI agree to combine financial resources to undertake any type of business venture, and agree to manage the same according to the terms of the agreement. Profits are shared between the MFI and the micro-entrepreneur in the pre-agreed ratio. Losses are shared strictly in proportion to their respective capital contributions. A variant of the above called diminishing *musharaka* has great potential for the MFI as a microfinance product. While a classical *musharaka* aims to involve the MFI as a permanent partner in the venture, in a declining *musharaka,* the MFI's share in the equity is diminished each year through repayments of capital in instalments. The MFI receives periodic profits based on its reduced equity share that remains invested during the period. The share of the client in the capital steadily increases over time, ultimately resulting in complete ownership of the venture(Figure 6).

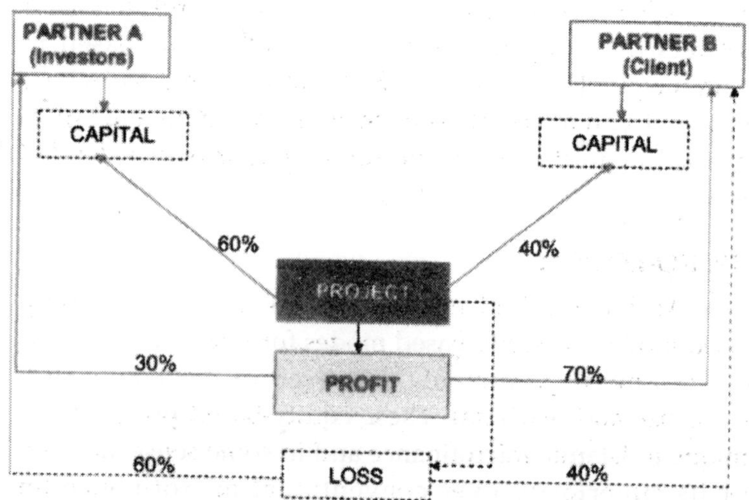

Fig. 6. *Musharaka* Model

Mudaraba Model : A *mudaraba* also known as trustee-partnership is a mode of microfinance through which the MFI provides capital finance for a specific venture indicated by the micro-entrepreneur. The micro-entrepreneur is responsible for the management of the business and provides professional, managerial and technical expertise for initiating and operating the business enterprise or project. Profit is shared according to a pre-agreed ratio. The MFI share any losses according to their respective funding contributions (Figure 7). *Mudaraba* may be of two types such as restricted or unrestricted. In a restricted *mudaraba* the MFI may specify a particular business in which investments may be undertaken. *Mudaraba* may also be an unrestricted, here the entrepreneur may invest the capital provided in any business he deems fit.

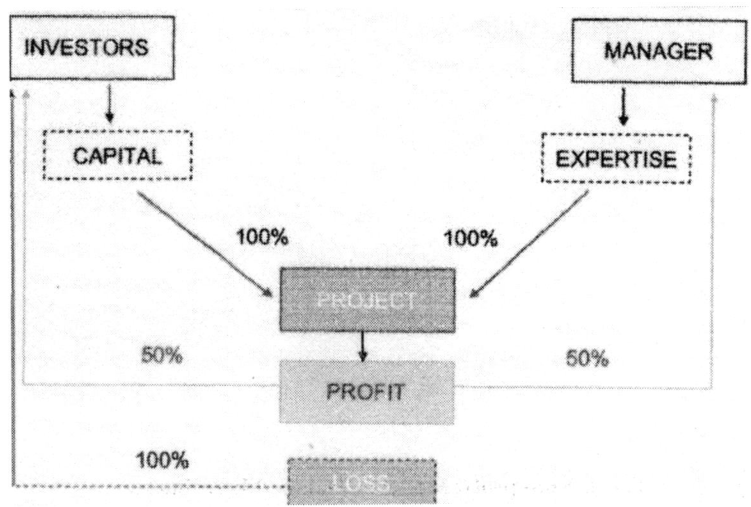

Fig. 7. *Mudaraba* Model

OTHER SERVICES

The poor also need many other services besides savings and financing, such as, remittance. These services may be easily provided by an Islamic MFI in a fee (*ujrat*) based framework. These services are to be provided in a *riba*-free manner, scholars insist that the quantum of fee is delinked from the quantum of funds involved and is based on the costs incurred in the process of offering the services.

NON-PROFIT MODEL OF MICROFINANCE

This is a model that uses non-profit modes only, but may be easily modified to incorporate for-profit modes as well. The Non-profit model of microfinance is presented in Figure 8.

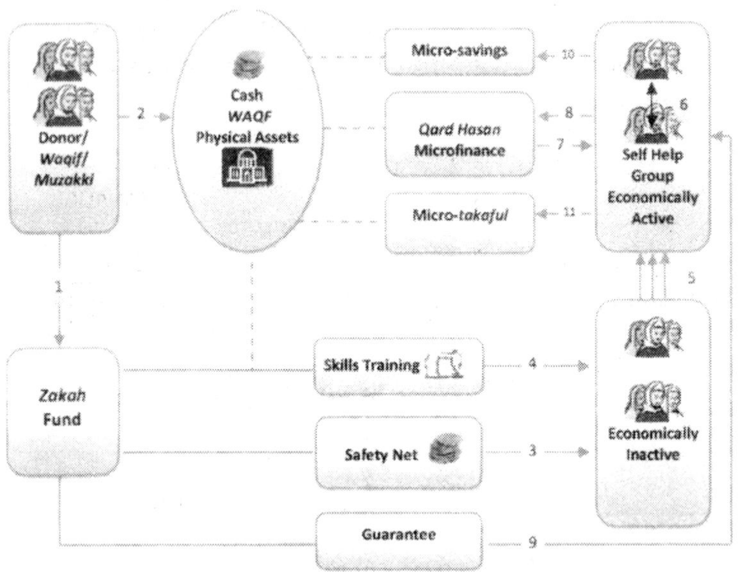

Fig. 8. Non- profit Model of Islamic Microfinance

The Non-profit model of Islamic microfinance may be described in terms of activities 1-11 as follows:

1. Islamic Microfinance Institution or Program creates a *Zakah* Fund with contribution from donor/*muzakki;*
2. Program facilitates *Waqf* of physical assets as well as monetary assets. The physical assets are used to facilitate education and skills training. The monetary assets may be in the form of a cash *waqf,* or simply as ordinary *sadaqa;*

3. Program carefully identifies the poorest of the poor and the destitute who are economically inactive and directs a part of *Zakah* Fund towards meeting their basic necessities as grant, seeks to provide a safety net;
4. Program provides skills training to economically inactive, utilizing community-held physical assets under *waqf*;
5. Beneficiaries graduate with improved skills and managerial acumen;
6. Beneficiaries are formed into groups with mutual guarantee under the concept of *kafala*;
7. Financing is provided on the basis of *qard-hasan* to the group; also to individuals backed by guarantee under the concept of *kafala*;
8. Group members pay back and in turn, are provided higher levels of financing;
9. Additional guarantee against default by the group is provided by the *Zakah* Fund and actual defaulting accounts are paid off with *zakah* funds; this is indeed the distinct feature of this model;
10. Group members are encouraged to save under appropriate micro-savings schemes;
11. Group's members are encouraged to form a *Takaful* Fund to provide micro-insurance against unforeseen risks and uncertainties resulting in loss of livelihood, sickness and so on. The distinguishing feature of this model is the use of *kafala* as a guarantee mechanism at the group or individual level. *Kafala* also forms the basis of designing a mutual guarantee (*takaful*) scheme against specific risks and uncertainties.

COMPOSITE MODEL OF ISLAMIC MICROFINANCE

When non-profit model of Islamic microfinance combines with profit model, it is can be named as composite model of Islamic microfinance. The composite model of Islamic microfinance is presented in Figure 9.

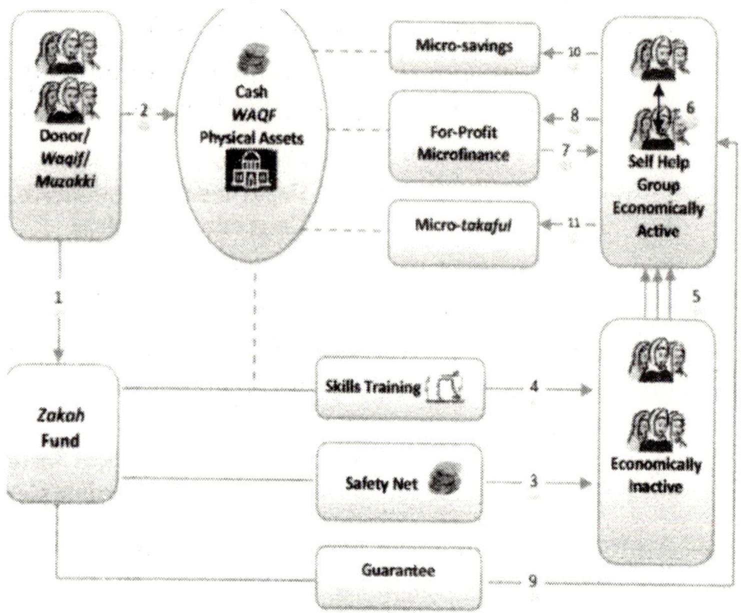

Fig. 9. Composite Model of Islamic Microfinance

The composite model of Islamic microfinance may be described in terms of activities 1-11 as follows:

- Islamic Microfinance Institution or Program creates a *Zakah* Fund with contribution from *muzakki;*
- Program facilitates *Waqf* of physical assets as well as monetary assets. The physical assets are used to facilitate education and skills training. The monetary assets may be in the form of a cash *waqf,* or simply as ordinary *sadaqa;*
- Program carefully identifies the poorest of the poor and the destitute who are economically inactive and directs a part of *zakah* funds towards meeting their basic necessities as grant, seeks to provide a safety net;

- Program provides skills training to economically inactive, utilizing community-held physical assets under *waqf*;
- Beneficiaries graduate with improved skills and managerial acumen;
- Beneficiaries are formed into groups with mutual guarantee under the concept of *kafala*;
- Financing is provided using a combination of profit based modes, such as, *bai-muajjal, ijara, salam, istisna* , *mudaraba* or *musharaka* or declining *musharaka*;
- Group members pay back their debt; and/or perform and meet the expectations of equity providers and, in turn, are provided higher levels of financing;
- Guarantee against default by the group is provided by the *Zakah* Fund and actual defaulting accounts are paid off with *zakah* funds;
- Group members are encouraged to save under appropriate micro savings schemes;
- Group's members are encouraged to form a *Takaful* Fund to provide micro-insurance against unforeseen risks and uncertainties resulting in loss of livelihood, sickness and so on.

CONCLUSION

The Islamic banking system has an in-built dimension that promotes financing activities to the poor. It is more concerned about poverty eradication, social justice and equal distribution of wealth at the same time of prohibiting involvement in illegal activities, which are detrimental to social and environmental well-being. The success of various approaches used in microfinance programme worldwide should be emulated by Islamic banks. An Islamic MFI may benefit from spectrum of sources of funds and offer a wide array of financing instruments catering different needs and demands of their clients. The Islamic MFI can be operated with profit motives as well as non-profit motives by combining corporate goals with social responsibilities and obligations of business. Further, the use of a bankruptcy-remote entity like SPV can protect Islamic banks from any adverse effect of microfinance activities. An Islamic bank can practice microfinance without compromising with institutional viability, competitiveness and sustainability.

REFERENCES

1. Ahmed, H. (2001): *Financing Microenterprises: An Analytical Study of Islamic Microfinance Institutions.* Paper presented at the 9th Intensive Orientation Seminar Islamic Foundation, Leicester.
2. Akhtar, M.R. (1996): "Practice and Prospects of Musharaka Financing for Small Enterprises in Pakistan", *Journal of Islamic Banking and Finance,* 13, 3: 7-27.
3. Allen; and Overy LLP. (2009): *Islamic Microfinance Report.* International Development Law Organization.
4. Al-Harran, S.A.S. (1990*): Islamic Finance: The Experience of the Sudanese Islamic Bank in Partnership (Musharakah) Financing as a Tool for Rural Development among Small Farmers in Sudan,* unpublished PhD thesis, Durham University, Durham.
5. Al-Harran, S. (1996): "Islamic Finance Needs - a New Paradigm", *New Horizon,* 48, 2:7-9.
6. Al-Harran, S. (1999): "Islamic Partnership Financing", *Arab Law Quarterly,* 14, 3:193-202.
7. Asyraf Wajdi Dusuki. (2008): "Banking for the Poor: The Role of Islamic Banking in Microfinance Initiatives", *Humanomics,* 24, 1: 49-66.
8. Al-ZamZami, A. and Grace, L. (2000): *Islamic Banking Principles Applied to Microfinance: Case Study of Honeidah Microfinance Programmes, in Yemen,* United Nations Capital Development Fund (UNCDF), New York,
9. Chiara Segrado. (2005): *Islamic Microfinance and Socially Responsible Investments,* Case Study, University of Torino.

10. Dhumale, R. and Sapcanin, A. (1998): *An Application of Islamic Banking Principles to Microfinance, United Nations Development Program,* Regional Bureau for Arab States, New York.

11. El-Gamal, M.A. (2006): *Islamic Finance: Law, Economics and Practice,* Cambridge University Press, Cambridge.

12. Habib Ahmed (2004): *Islamic Alternatives to Finance Poverty Focused Group-Based Micro-financing,* Presented at 26th Annual Meeting of IDB with NDFIS Tehran, September 13, 2004, Islamic Research and Training Institute, Islamic Development Bank, Jeddah.

13. Mohammed Obaidullah. (2008), "Introduction to Islamic Microfinance", International Institute of Islamic Business and Finance Net (P) Ltd, India, ISBN: 978-81-905822-2-3.

14. Obaidullah, Mohammed, Khan Tariqullah. (2008): *Islamic Microfinance Development: Challenges and Initiatives,* ITRI, Islamic Development Bank, Jeddah, ISBN: 978-9960-32-180-6.

27

Technology Innovations in Banking – Do They Reach Out the Common Man?

Dhanya K. A.
V. K. Janardhanan

Technology upgradation in banking is a new step towards expansion of banking services, providing efficient customer service and contribution to economic development at national level. Banking industry is one of the booming sectors in India and hence plays a significant role in developing the nation. *"Bankers own the earth. Take it away from them, but leave them the power to create money and control credit, and with a flick of a pen they will create enough to buy it back"* -- Sir Josiah Stamp, Former President, Bank of England. This shows the power of banking system. Technology and innovation enhancement in banking has actually begun in 1990s. Since then the banking sector in India has undergone huge transformation. The rate of transformation was high after 2000, when a number of innovations changed the way the banking was perceived. Now a days the banking services has been redefined with hi - tech services. Banks began to use new and improved technologies to provide quality services at greater speed. New innovations like ATMs, Electronic fund transfer, e-payment of utility service, online railway booking, mobile banking and what not. Internet and mobile banking made it more convenient for the customers to do banking at geographically diversified places. Gone are those days where people have to stand in long queues in bank branches and where they have to walk behind the bank officials to get things done. Conventional concept of banking has been changed with the advancement of technologies and now banks are so close to us that we can avail banking services from anywhere at anytime . But this is only the glittering part of the scene. On the other side there is a vast majority of public who is unaware of these innovations. There is a vast section that has no knowledge, no access and no availability of the so called hi - tech services. There is still another group who has the knowledge and access but still not using these innovative banking services due to one reason or other. Here comes the question: Can we claim the pride of technological advancement / innovations in banking when majority of the Indian people are not using these services. At this juncture the present study is of high relevance as it deals with both innovation and inclusion.

HISTORY OF BANKING

The Bank of Hindustan, set up in 1770, by the British rulers in India was the earliest bank in the country. Over the years, the British set up several other banks, notable among which were the three Presidency Banks in the Presidencies of Bengal (in 1809), Bombay(in1840)and Madras(in1843). These three banks were very powerful in their respective Presidencies and functioned as quasi-central banks, having even the power to issue currency notes. History of Banking in India can be traced back to 1865, establishment of The Allahabad, one of the oldest joint stock bank. Then came HSBC in 1869 and Punjab National bank in 1895. The period between 1906 and 1911, saw the establishment of a number of banks which have been survived to the present such as *Bank of India, Corporation Bank, Indian Bank, Bank of Baroda* etc. In the early 1990s, the policy of liberalization came and a small number of private banks were started. These came to be known as *New Generation tech-savvy banks,* and included Global Trust Bank (the first of such new generation banks to be set up), which later amalgamated with Oriental Bank of Commerce, *Axis Bank*(earlier as *UTI Bank*), *ICICI Bank* and *HDFC Bank.* This move, along with the rapid growth in the *economy of India,* revitalized the banking sector in India, which has seen rapid growth with strong contribution from all the three sectors of banks, namely, government banks, private banks and foreign banks. (Source: http.wikipedia.org) Around the turn of the 20th Century, the Indian economy was passing through a relative period of stability.

Significance of the study

Traditionally, banking meant 'borrowing and lending', but in the latter part of the 20th century, the word took on a different meaning. Banks no longer restricted themselves to traditional banking activities, but explored newer avenues to increase business and capture new markets. Banking activities also transcended their traditional scope and new concepts like personal banking, retailing and banc assurance were introduced. Banks began to use technology to provide better quality of services at greater speed. Now banking industry has developed to such a stage all transactions can be done with ease and quick as newer technologies like ATM, EFT, smart cards, internet banking, mobile banking etc are being introduced. Although the Indian banking sector has made rapid progress particularly in the number of innovations introduced, some analysts are skeptical about the efficacy and practical use of many of these services...Its true that though one side highlight the newer innovations, technological advancement, sophisticated features, technical know how etc there is a darker side were majority of the people are unaware of these developments or are not having access to these features. India being a country with vast majority of rural population, it's necessary to examine whether the innovations reach out the common man or not. At this juncture, the present study is of high relevance since it peeps into the extend of usage of technologies in banking industry by common people. The study seems to be unique as it includes three different sections of the society high income group, middle income group and a third group of Keralites working in metros outside Kerala. (named as metro customers trough out the study) . The study will be an eye opener for bankers, policy makes and regulators

Objectives of the study

- To identify the extent of usage of banking technology among different sections of society
- To asses the reasons for non usage of banking technologies.
- Specifically examine the satisfaction level of frequent users of new trends in banking services.

Scope of the study

The study covers northern and central part of Kerala. Two districts Malappuram and Thrissur are being selected for sample survey. The scope of the study is also confined to selected groups of categories of bank customers.

Methodology

Both the primary and secondary source is being used to collect data. A questionnaire was developed to collect primary data. Hypothesis were developed and tested to arrive at meaningful conclusions. Different statistical tools are used for data analysis

Data Collection

Primary data was collected using the structured questionnaire. Interviews with bank officials were also done wherever necessary. Secondary data was collected from websites, journals, magazines, periodicals etc.

Sampling and Sample Size

The study covers three groups of society like top class (educated/high status jobs), middle class (less educated / average workers) and the third group - people who are employed in metros outside Kerala. The low income group is not taken as a sample group as the unstructured interview with them itself reveals that those group are fully unaware and nonusers of technological advancement. 60 respondents from each group were selected and hence the total sample size for the study is 180. Out of the sixty 30 respondents are from Malappuram and 30 from Thrissur. Convenience sampling is used while selecting the districts. But purposive sampling is used in the selection of respondents. Special care has been taken to cover all categories of people except the lower income group which is not the part of study.

Tools for Analysis

Different statistical tools like percentages, mean, standard deviation etc are being used in the analysis. ANOVA is being used to test the hypothesis developed. The opinion of respondents regarding the different issues related to banking technologies were analyzed using Multi-Dimensional Scaling.

Hypothesis

H_0 : There is no significant difference in the awareness

level of banking technology among the selected groups

H_0: There is no significant difference in the frequency of usage of banking technology among the selected groups

H_0: There is no significant difference in the satisfaction level of banking technology among the selected groups

Limitations of the study

1. The study does not cover whole of Kerala
2. The sample size selected is less in proportion to the total population
3. Limitations of convenience sampling may adversely affect the results of the study

ANALYSIS AND INTERPRETATION

The study is based on the opinion collected from three different categories of bank customers. Respondents are divided into three sections, first group being high income customers like doctors, engineers, businessmen, lecturers, advocates etc.., second group being middle income group like school teachers, office staffs, clerks etc... and the third group being Keralites working in metros outside Kerala professionals, businessmen etc...

Demographic profile of customers

The above table 1 exhibits the classification of age group and education among the respondents selected. It can be noticed that care has been taken to have comparatively equal number of respondents in all classes of age group and education level. The study also shows that out of 180 respondents 35 are SBI customers, 20 are Federal bank customers, 18 are ICICI bank customers, 12 are Dhanalakshmi bank customers, 10 are having accounts in cooperative banks and balance 85 customers are having accounts in more than one of the above banks.

Table 1. Age wise and Education wise classification

Age group	*Frequencies*	*Education*	*Frequencies*
30 years and below	29	SSLC	13
31 to 45 years	82	Pre-degree	31
46 to 60 years	49	Degree	36
61 and above	20	Post graduation	48
		Technical	14
		Professional	38
Total	180		180

Source: Primary data

Awareness level of customers

One of the prime motives of the study is to understand the awareness level of customers with regard to the new trends and technological advancement in the banking sector. Hence five different variables like ATM, Net banking, Mobile banking, Electronic fund transfer, Credit card facilities and utility payment services are identified and the customers' awareness with regard to these aspects are ascertained.

Interpretation

Table 2 shows that maximum awareness level is for ATM (4.03) followed by credit card facilities and utility services. The least awareness is for mobile banking with an average of 2.24. The deviation in the opinion is maximum for mobile banking and utility payment services with a standard deviation of 1.37 and 1.15 respectively. It can be noticed that maximum awareness is for the ATM technology which is one of the initial developments in banking technology. Least awareness is for mobile banking which is a very recent technology enhancement in banking. Thus it can be said that the extent of awareness has got significant relation with the time period for which the particular technology has been using. Recent trends are having less awareness.

Table 2. Awareness level of Bank customers

Awareness	*Mean*	*Standard Deviation*
ATM	4.03	.90
Net Banking	3.1	1.04
Mobile Banking	2.24	1.37
Electronic fund transfer	2.37	.82
Credit card facilities	3.14	.95
Utility payment services	3.2	1.15

Source: Compiled from primary data

H_0 : There is no significant difference in the awareness level of banking customers among the selected groups

Among the three different groups of respondents, it was ascertained that the third group ie Keralites working in outside metros are having more awareness than the other two groups. The overall awareness level of three groups are High income group - 3.26 which means they lies between aware and fairly aware in a five point awareness scale. In the case of second group (middle income customers) the overall awareness is only 2.12 which show that middle income customers are less aware of new banking technologies. The third category Keralites working in metros are having the highest level of awareness of 3.65. The hypothesis developed is being tested using ANOVA (Table3).

Since the p value is .000 the null hypothesis is rejected even at 1% level. Hence it can be concluded that there is significant difference in the awareness level of customers between the three groups. ANOVA doesn't specify whether any two groups fall under same category. Thus a post hoc test of Tukey HSD has been done.The posthoc test shows that the awareness level of no two groups is same. All the three groups fall in three different subset. Thus we can conclude the awareness level of high income group is different from middle income group which is again different from third group. The high level of third group may be because of the exposure they get since they are the people who have to cope up the busy life schedules in metros like Mumbai, Bangalore, Chennai etc.

Table 3. Awareness level (Result of ANOVA and Tukey HSD)

	ANOVA			*TUKEY HSD*				
	Mean square	*F*	*Sig*	*category*	*N*	*Subset for alpha = .05*		
						1	2	3
Between Groups	38.601	270.211	.000					
Within Groups	.143			2.00	60	2.1223		
				1.00	60		3.2553	
				3.00	60			3.6723
				Sig.		1.000	1.000	1.000

Source: SPSS analysis

Frequency of usage

Even though the customers may have awareness in many cases they will be reluctant to frequently use the technologies due to several other reasons. Hence it is necessary to find out the frequency of usage of banking technologies by different customers. Frequency of usage of ATM has been checked on the basis of usage for cash withdrawal, password change and checking balances. The study shows that ATM is most widely used for cash withdrawal the usage rate being 3.27 which means the status of usage lies between occasionally and frequently in a five point scale of frequency. This is followed by checking balances where the average is 2.53 and the least usage of ATM is for password change in which case the mean is 2 which stands for rarely. In case of Net banking eight different variables like online shopping, online ticket booking, view account statement, order cheque books, to transfer funds, Utility bills, learn about banking products and to clear queries with bank are identified. The study shows that customers are using internet banking facility mostly for booking railway tickets online. The average usage level being 2.4. Next stands the usage of net banking for paying utility bills with a mean of 2.08 followed by learning banking products having an average of 2. Net banking is less used for ordering cheque books with an average of 1.43.

Table 4. Over all Frequency of usage of banking technology

Frequency of usage	*Mean*	*Standard Deviation*
ATM	2.62	1.27
Net banking	1.85	1.02
Mobile banking	1.22	.41
Mobile alerts	2.4	1.04
Credit cards	2.22	1.36

Source: compiled from primary source

Interpretation

Table 4 shows that ATM is the most frequently used technology with a mean of 2.62 followed by mobile alerts (2.4) and credit card usage(2.22) which means the usage level lies between rarely and occasionally . But the usage rate of net banking and mobile banking on an average is very poor say 1.85 and 1.22 respectively which means their usage status is between never and rarely. The standard deviation is more for ATM with 1.27.Thus it can be concluded that if we take the different sections of the society as a whole it can be noticed that the usage rate of technology advancement is very poor. But this may be due to the over influence of the behavior of a particular section. Hence it is necessary to study the behavior of three groups separately. If we take the high income customers, the average usage level of banking technology by this group is 3.11 which mean that they occasionally use the above said banking facilities. In case of middle income group the usage rate is only 1.45 which means that they never use the technologies on an average. In case third group the usage rate is 3.3 which means they use the banking technologies occasionally. But in all the three cases it can be noticed that no group has reached an average of 4 or 5 which shows that on an average the usage level is also poor. Though the average use of ATM by high income group for cash withdrawal seems to be 4 which mean frequently other usage of ATM like password change and checking account balance is rarely used by them. Hence the average will come down. But the usage rate of ATM for cash withdrawal by middle income group is only 1.7. Incase of internet banking facilities online reservation is the most widely used facility. Among the three categories it is the third group metro customers who use the online reservation facility more frequently with an average of 4.08. Category wise frequency usage is exhibited as Table 5.

Table 5. Frequency of Usage of ATM (Result of ANOVA and Tukey HSD)

	ANOVA			*TUKEY HSD*			
	Mean square	*F*	*Sig*	*category*	*N*	*Subset for alpha = .05*	
Between Groups	64.291	163.146	.000			1	2
Within Groups	.394			2.00	60	1.4327	
				1.00	60		3.1113
				3.00	60		3.3213
				Sig.		1.000	.162

Source: SPSS analysis

H_0: There is no significant difference in the frequency of usage of banking technology among the selected groups

This hypothesis has been tested using ANOVA and Tukey HSD. The test has been made separately for four different banking technologies like ATM, internet usage, mobile banking and credit cards usage. Results are exhibited below

ATM Usage

Interpretation

From the test ANOVA it is clear that p value is .00 which means that the null hypothesis is rejected even at 1% significance level. Hence it can be concluded that there is significant differences between the usage level of ATM by three groups. The post hoc analysis shows that category one and three falls in same subset which means there is no significant difference between the usage level of high income group and metro customers. But the middle income group falls in different subset which indicates that their usage level is different from that of the other two groups. Since the average of middle income group is 1.43 and other two groups are 3.11 and 3.32 it can be said that middle income customers are less users of ATM than others.

Internet Banking

Interpretation

Since the p value is .00 it can be said that there is significant difference in the usage level of internet banking among three different groups (Table 6). The tukey HSD test also shows that all the three categories fall in different subsets which means that the mean value of each group is different from each other. It can also be noted that the metro customers are more frequent users of internet banking than other two groups.

Table 6. Frequency of Usage of Internet banking (Result of ANOVA and Tukey HSD)

	ANOVA			*TUKEY HSD*				
	Mean square	*F*	*Sig*	*category*	*N*	*Subset for alpha = .05*		
Between Groups	57.631	451.988	.000			1	2	3
Within Groups	.128			2.00	60	1.1340		
				1.00	60		1.4557	
				3.00	60			2.9693
				Sig.		1.000	1.000	1.000

Source: SPSS analysis

Table 7. Frequency of Usage of Mobile banking (Result of ANOVA and Tukey HSD)

	ANOVA			*TUKEY HSD*			
	Mean square	*F*	*Sig*	*category*	*N*	*Subset for alpha = .05*	
Between Groups	1.489	9.367	.000			1	2
Within Groups	.159			2.00	60	1.1000	
				1.00	60	1.1667	
				3.00	60		1.4000
				Sig.		.631	1.000

Source: SPSS analysis

Interpretation

Since the p value is .00 it can be said that there is significant difference in the usage level of mobile banking among three different groups. The tukey HSD test shows that two groups first and second group i.e. .middle income customers and high income customers fall under the same subset while the third group metro customers fall in another subset. Though there is slight difference in the average usage level of three categories (1.10, 1.16, 1.4) the third group ie metro customers finds to be different from other two groups in the usage level.

Credit Card Usage

Interpretation

Since the p value is .00 it can be said that there is significant difference in the usage level of credit card usage among three different groups. The tukey HSD test also shows that all the three categories fall in different subsets which means that the mean value of each group is different from each other (Table 8). It can also be noted that the metro customers are more frequent users of internet banking than other two groups. Thus it can be concluded that the mean value of 1.26, 1.83 and 3.56 are significantly different from each other.

Table 8. Frequency of Usage of credit card (Result of ANOVA and Tukey HSD)

	ANOVA			*TUKEY HSD*				
	Mean square	*F*	*Sig*	*category*	*N*	*Subset for alpha = .05*		
Between Groups	86.156	93.670	.000			1	2	3
Within Groups	.920			2.00	60	1.2667		
				1.00	60		1.8333	
				3.00	60			3.5667
				Sig.		1.000	1.000	1.000

Source: SPSS analysis

From the above analysis it can be concluded that the usage level of three categories ie high income group, middle income group and metro customers are significantly different in case of internet usage and credit card usage. In both cases metro customers are highest users followed by high income and middle income group customers. But in case of ATM usage and Mobile banking there is a difference. With regard to ATM usage it can be noticed that both metro customers and high income group fall under same category while the ATM usage level of middle income group is significantly different. From the mean value it is clear that middle income group customers are less users of ATM than other groups. With regard to Mobile banking it can be noticed that both high income group and middle income group falls under the same category while metro customers fall under different category. It shows that metro customers are using mobile banking more frequently than that of middle and high income group.

Reasons for non usage of banking technology and MDS Analysis

From the above analysis it is clear that majority of the customers particularly the middle level and high level customers are rarely using the banking technologies. Hence it is necessary to analyze the reasons behind the non usage of banking technology. Eight reasons are being identified and customers are asked to rank them according to their relative importance. Multi dimensional analysis is being used to identify the relative distance between the ranks given by customers. The Euclidean distance model is given as (Table 9). The result is as follows :

Interpretation

The MDS analysis shows that incase of high income group lack of knowledge, lack of awareness are the components which lies near to origin and security problems

Table 9. Configuration drawn in two dimensions

Stimulus name	*Dimension 1*		
	High income customers	*Middle income customers*	*Metro customers*
Lack of Awareness	.659	1.40	1.7
Lack of knowledge	-.44	1.45	-.36
Security problems	-2.19	.66	-1.84
Transaction cost	1.29	-1.5	.33
Accessibility	1.27	1.02	.85
Problems while processing	-1.73	-1.67	-1.82
Poor quality of technology	1.88	-2.16	-.97
Not necessary	-.744	.812	1.1

Source: Compiled from MDS analysis

are the extreme one. Hence proper care should be given to these variables. Incase of middle income groups Poor quality, problems in processing, lack of knowledge and lack of awareness are all having stimulus coordinates more than 1 and all of them lies in extremes away from origin. For metro customers security problems and problems while processing are some of the practical issues related to the usage of banking technologies.

Satisfaction level of technology users

Before proceeding further and drawing a conclusion it is also necessary to assess the satisfaction level of frequent users of banking technology. For this purpose only two variables are selected one is ATM and the other one is internet banking facilities.

H_0: There is no significant difference in the satisfaction level of banking technology among the selected groups

ATM

Interpretation

Since the p value is .00 it can be said that there is significant difference in the satisfaction level on usage of ATM among three different groups (Table 10). The tukey HSD test also shows that all the three categories fall in different subsets which means that the mean value of each group is different from each other. It can also be noted that the metro customers are more satisfied of than other two groups as the average satisfaction score of third group is 4.

Table 10. Satisfaction level of ATM users (Result of ANOVA and Tukey HSD)

	ANOVA			*TUKEY HSD*				
	Mean square	*F*	*Sig*	*category*	*N*	*Subset for alpha = .05*		
Between Groups	22.363	126.724	.000			1	2	3
Within Groups	.176			2.00	33	2.5758		
				1.00	60		3.2667	
				3.00	59			4.0000
				Sig.		1.000	1.000	1.000

Source: SPSS analysis

Internet banking

Interpretation

Since the p value is .163 it can be said that there is no significant difference in the satisfaction level on usage of internet baking among three different groups. The null hypothesis is accepted. The Tukey HSD test also shows that all the three categories fall in same subset which means that the mean value of each group is not different from each other. It can also be noted that the metro customers are more satisfied of than other two groups as the average satisfaction score of third group is 3.5. Thus it can be concluded that all the three sections are having a 3.5 scale on an average which means they are between neutral and satisfied. Since it is around 3.5 it can be concluded that all are somewhat satisfied with the internet usage though not highly satisfied (Table 11).

Table 11. Satisfaction level of Internet banking (Result of ANOVA and Tukey HSD)

	ANOVA			*TUKEY HSD*		
	Mean square	*F*	*Sig*	*category*	*N*	*Subset for alpha = .05*
						1
Between Groups	.264	1.853	.163			
Within Groups	.142			2.00	16	3.3125
				3.00	59	3.4703
				1.00	14	3.5714
				Sig.		.083

Source: SPSS analysis

This section specifically examined the extent of usage of banking technologies by different class of people. It also examines the satisfaction level of frequent users of banking technologies. It can be noticed that the both the awareness level and frequency of usage is more for the third group ie metro customer. Further more the MDS analysis shows that for metro customers, the least important reason for non usage is 'not a necessary' which shows that the use of new technologies is a necessary for them since they have a very hectic schedule and they have more exposure with different people. This may be one reason why use of banking technologies is not advancing in Kerala.

FINDINGS OF THE STUDY

1. Metro customers and High income group have more awareness of 3.6 and 3.2 while for middle group it is only 2.12.
2. Among the different banking facilities ATM (4.03) is the most widely used one followed by utility payment services (3.2)and credit cards(3.1)
3. ATM is most widely used for cash withdrawal with a usage rate of 3.27.
4. Since the average usage level of middle income group is 1.43 and other two groups are 3.11 and 3.32 it can be said that middle income customers are less users of ATM than others.
5. The result of ANOVA shows that there is significant difference in the awareness level of banking technologies among the three categories of respondents.
6. The study shows that among internet banking facilities the most widely used facility is online reservation that also with a poor usage rate of 2.4. Least usage rate is for ordering cheque book or DD using internet banking facility.
7. Tukey HSD test shows that ATM usage rate is not significantly different high income(3.1) and metro customers (3.2) but significantly different for middle group. (1.4)
8. In case of mobile banking the usage rate is not significantly different for high income customers (1.1) and middle income customers (1.16) but different for Metro customers (1.4).
9. But both the credit card usage and internet baking usage rate is significantly different for all the three groups.

10. MDS analysis shows that security problems are the major concerns of high income and metro customers while the middle income group of customers are worried about the problems while processing, lack of technical knowledge etc...
11. It was found that other is significant difference in the satisfaction level of customers regarding ATM usage; Metro customers are satisfied mean value being 4, High income customers are neutral(3.2) while middle income customers are less satisfies (2.5)
12. In case of Internet Banking, it was found that there is no significant difference in the satisfaction level between the three categories of respondents. The mean value lies around 3.5 which means all the three categories lies between neutral and satisfied with regard to internet banking facilities.

CONCLUSION

Over the years, the banking sector has gone through several changes. The face of the industry is changing day by day. New innovations, technological advancements and new products are creeping in. Hence this is an area which opens wide scope for researchers and academicians to discuss on various topics. Appreciate the role of technology in increasing the convenience of customers and improving the efficiency of banking operations. But it is need of the hour to see whether the new inventions properly reach out the common man or not. The study throws light into the awareness, usage rate and satisfaction level of customers towards various banking technology services. It can be concluded from the study that on an average though customers have awareness about new technologies majority are reluctant to use these technologies mainly because of the security concerns and lack of technical knowledge. It can also be noticed that it's the metro customers who are having more awareness and usage rate than the other two groups which definitely highlights the point that necessity is a major factor which drives us towards the usage of new technological advancements.

REFERENCES

1. Ajai S Gaur et. al (2006): *Statistical methods for practice and research*, New Delhi, Sage publications.
2. Douglas and Bernardo (2002): *Information technology and commercial banking- A review and appraisal from historical perspective*, Econ WPA, Economic History.
3. Frances X Frei et.al (1998): *Innovation in retail baking*, Working paper, The Wharton School, University of Pensilvania
4. Jeevi Tha (2009): *Impact of Technology in Banking, News and society*: Economics.
5. Dr. Mithani D.M and Gordon.E (2006): *Banking and Financial systems*, Himalya pulications.
6. Nandagopal et.al. (2007), Research Methods in Business, NewDelhi Excel Books.
7. Tahir Masood et.al (2008), *CustomerAacceptance of Online Banking*, Journal of Internet Banking and Commerce, Vol 13 No1.
8. Vadlamani Ravi (2008): *Advances in Banking technology and management*, Research book news, Feb 2008 *http://www.wikipedia.org/*
9. IT in banking 2003 (special) *http://www.banknetindia.com/special/itbanking.htm*
10. Information technology innovations and commercial banking (Nov 2001) *http://jobfunctions.bnet.com/abstract.aspx?docid=129843*

ANNEXURE

Annexure 1. Category wise frequency usage

Category	*High income*	*Middle income*	*Metro customers*
ATM-withdrawal	3.9	1.71	4.14
Passwordchange	2.4	1.2	2.5
Check Account	3	1.35	3.21
Online shopping	1.7	1.22	1.96
Onliline resrvation	1.7	1.38	4.08
Account statement	1.63	1.25	2.9
Order cheque book	1.23	1	2.04
Transfer funds	1.46	1	2.14
Pay utility bills	1.23	1.16	3.81
Learn about banking products	1.4	1	3.55
Clear querries with bank	1.26	1	2.96
Mobile Banking	1.16	1.10	1.39
Mobile Alerts	2.1	1.62	3.44
Credit card	1.83	1.27	3.52

Source: Primary data

Annexture 2

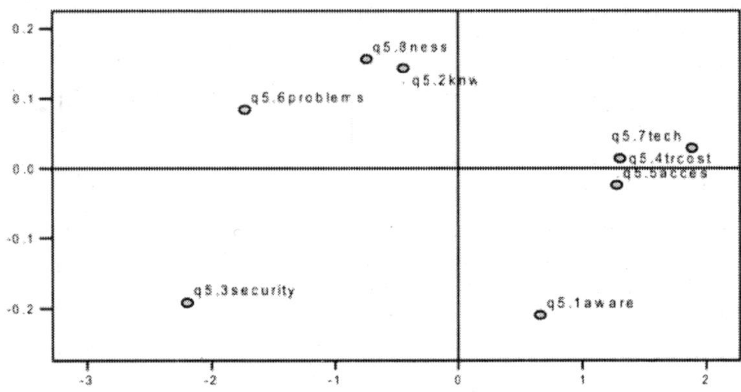

Graph 1: MDS analysis (High income level customers)

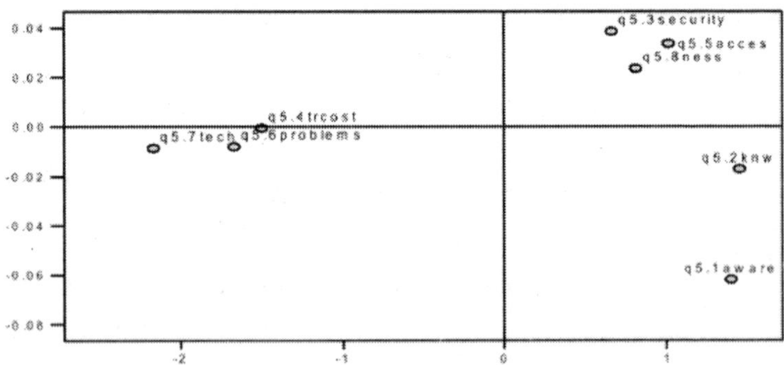

Graph 2 : MDS Analysis (Middle income level customers)

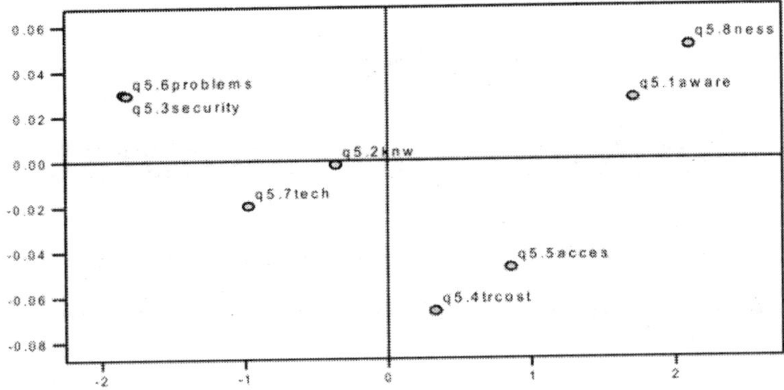

Graph 3: MDS Analysis – Metro customers

28
Banking and Corporate Social Responsibility

Jiya K. Shahani

INTRODUCTION

We live in a world of abundance and belief is that a bigger car, the latest appliances, the more trendy stuff will bring happiness. Corporations seeking profit by stimulating and feeding our unending appetite for stuff have trampled on the livelihood of a common man. Households are carrying credit card debt with interest rates that often make payoff nearly impossible and hence, people around the world are losing access to their own natural resources and economic sovereignty. In the mad rush of filling the bottomless pots, we forget that, happiness is not something we trust corporations to provide for a price, but rather something to be created by ourselves through social commitment and community development. Since, we no longer have the time, skills, extended families, and access to land that were commonplace just decades ago; we have become completely dependent on money. That dependency leaves us at the mercy of those who control the economy and money supply.

And those who accumulate money have inordinate influence over our government, which is, the departure from the way humans have lived for most of history. As a result, poverty continues to be a major concern in spite of registering a steady growth by India in recent years. While some level of growth is obviously a necessary condition for sustained poverty reduction, there is an increasingly unanimous view that growth by itself is not a sufficient condition for eradicating poverty (Ali and Son, 2007). Growth can marginalise the poor sections and increase inequality. High and rising levels of inequality can hinder poverty reduction, which in turn, can slowdown the growth process. One important indication of inadequate inclusion in India is that poverty reduction has been muted in the last decade even with rising growth. The poverty rate has declined by less than 1 per cent per annum over the past decade, markedly below trends in neighboring countries such as Nepal and Bangladesh, where both average income levels and growth are lower (World Bank, 2007). While the need for inclusive growth is stressed, it is to be seen, whether it is the inadequate growth of certain sectors like agriculture or the inability of certain groups like SC/STs to form part of the growth process or the lack of both physical and financial infrastructure that pull back the particular sections from enjoying the economic growth. It is possible that a combination of all these factors is keeping these sections out of the growth process and therefore, it is necessary to know the major determinants that pull down inclusive growth. The inter linkages between different development indicators and growth in the context of various regions and sections needs to be analysed to understand the nuances of India's growth process, because we can no longer allow such economy to grow like a cancer on our society until it takes over all facets of life. The economy needs to serve people, communities and the health of natural systems, not the other way round. Hence, instead of relying on footloose unaccountable global corporations, we must turn to strengthen local and regional production to serve our needs and provide sustainable employment, including small and medium-sized businesses, co-operatives, and farmer's markets etc. There is a huge underserved market in India for rural banking services. It is not the case of skill scarcity or lack in potential, however it needs a little bit of hand holding from banking and financial corporate network to come out of the clutches of poverty. Adopting sustainable inclusive growth, presupposes inclusive governance through empowerment, participation at the grass roots level and increased public accountability. Inclusiveness - a concept that encompasses equity, equality of opportunity, and protection in market and employment transitions - is an essential ingredient of any successful growth strategy (Commission on Growth and Development, World Bank, 2008). The Commission of Growth and Development (2008) considers systematic inequality of opportunity as "toxic" as it will derail the growth process through political channels or conflict. Hence, there is a need to act both decisively and quickly to build an enabling, rather than a limiting, banking sector in India.

The paper launches the central idea in the Introduction, followed by Objectives of the study and Methodology used. After this, the paper is divided into five sections; section I identifies the importance of economic democracy and role of micro-producers for the sustainable health of economy, section II emphasizes the intensive implementation of Corporate Social Responsibility practices and procedures through Banks and Financial Institutions, section III demonstrates the current outreach scenario of banking and financial services in terms of region-wise, state-wise credit-deposit ratio and also the distribution of credit and deposits of scheduled commercial banks in various population groups. It also explains the reasons for their low penetration.

Section IV recognises the role of technology in implementing financial inclusion agenda and highlights the need for financial support needed by green technology implementations, section V proposes a workable model for total penetration to rural sector, provides additional recommendations and concluding remarks on dynamic rural Indian economy.

OBJECTIVES

- Make banking products and services available to the entire population without discrimination
- To highlight the need for a greater investment in intangibles to enhance corporate value
- To analyse the contribution of Indian Banking sector in implementing the financial inclusion agenda
- Redirect Policy support for economically uplifting the resource poor

RESEARCH METHODOLOGY

Secondary research was conducted to study the multiple levels of financial inclusion and exclusion to assess the current scenario of financial inclusion in India. Data has been taken from Reserve Bank of India website, Economic Survey of India 2009-10, Indian Institute of Banking and Finance and Updated Master Office Files of Office of Registrar General and Census Commissioner, Government of India.

Insights into the existing needs of unbanked for banking products and services were acquired through socio-economic study conducted at few socially disadvantaged village populations near Gandhinagar, Gujarat. Informal interactions with representative of the two NGOs, namely 'SEWA' and 'DISHA" and the SHGs attached to these NGOs brought to light, the major challenges and hurdles in way of full financial inclusion. These social organisations are actively liaising between the underprivileged people in urban, semi-urban and rural areas and the financial organisations operating therein.

SEEKING ECONOMIC DEMOCRACY IN AN UNEQUAL WORLD

Economics is the foundation of any society and must exist above a mere subsistence level in order to support people in totality, where some are specialists not involved in basic survival modes of production. Money lending in one form or the other has evolved along with the history of the mankind. Even in the ancient times there are references to the moneylenders. Shakespeare referred to 'Shylocks' who made unreasonable demands in case the loans were not repaid in time along with interest. Indian history is also replete with the instances referring to indigenous money lenders, Sahukars and Zamindars involved in the business of money lending by mortgaging the landed property of the borrowers. But the paradox of the recent times is, in spite of the availability of extremes in the modern economy, many people have to do without even basic necessities. This occurs when there is a deception inside the group and a minority uses the surplus as a basis to enrich them and build a power base. When humanity thus splits within itself, the phenomenon of class division emerges, where we see that the real wealth is not equally available to each and every individual on an equal, per need and shared basis. A small group of people control vast amounts of this real wealth manipulated by the abstracted value of money, while most have barely enough to subsist and some are even too poor to survive. In some regions, far too many cannot obtain enough to live no matter how hard they work or hunt, while in other regions warehouses are brimming with everything conceivable that is of use to people. However, if there is "no market", resources are dumped instead of feeding starving people, all because of undemocratic economic manipulations in the hands of the few, the wealthy and therefore powerful. In a world of extremes in economy, mere political democracy fades into insignificance if not accompanied by economic democracy.

MICRO PRODUCERS - THE TRUE STRENGTH OF ECONOMY

Although globalisation has greatly influenced the Indian economy and made it a huge consumer market, it could not bring down unemployment and poverty to tolerable levels. Moreover, the recent deep decline in the world economy has left many countries in a severe state of depression. In such a global scenario, India and similar such countries, have withstood this shock of instability to a considerable extent. One of the important factors contributing to this strength is that our economy, to a large extent depends on small producers like small and marginal farmers with small land holdings, minor producers in the non-farm sector and small traders. Most of our establishments are based on micro or small activities, which contribute substantially to the stability of our economy. It is the small traders/farmers who are able to show strength and resilience in the face of droughts, floods and other natural calamities and are able to maintain some production even in the adverse circumstances. It is the micro-producer who lends stability to agricultural and industrial production, irrespective of political and other changes. Therefore, we must build on this basic strength and stability, which is imparted to our economy by the micro-entrepreneurs and never try to replace micro producers by big producers in our economic planning. But Table 1 reveals that the share of direct accounts with a credit limit of less than ' 25000 in total direct accounts declined from 93.4 percent in 1980 to 35.8

percent in 2008. The decline in share is observed across all the sectors, which is certainly threatening for the economic stability of the nation. Therefore, it is imperative to redirect and focus the policy formulations towards reversing this trend, because any attempt to replace the small and tiny sector by large sector will not only create large scale unemployment, but will also subject the economy, already fluctuating, to flashes as the big producers are subject to direct shocks of market sensitivity of the world economy. Micro-entrepreneurs are not only the producers of self-employment, but also contribute to the growth in a big way. There is already enough space for big businesses; the need is to develop an atmosphere conducive to small producers. For this, it is not only desirable, but indeed essential that commercial banks should be involved in providing financial support to micro-entrepreneurs. They have the necessary

Table 1. Percentage of Small Borrower Account to Total No. of Accounts

Occupation	*1980*	*1990*	*2000*	*2008*
Agriculture	96.7	97.3	85.4	51.4
Industry	56.9	83.4	69.4	34.4
Transport Operators	68.6	81.4	48.2	14.6
Professional & other services	96.5	91.6	76.5	22
Personal loans	-	-	59.6	22.7
Trade	86.3	96	77.1	44
Finance	94.4	91.6	60	29.7
All others	97.7	99.5	50.3	40
Total	93.4	95	72.2	35.8

Note: For 1980, the small borrowal account is defined as Rs. 10,000 and less.

Source: Basic Statistical Returns, Reserve Bank of India (various issues)

management expertise, systems and physical infrastructure in place. They are also able to accept deposits and have access to other sources of funds such as equity capital (Rhyne & Christen 1999). The success stories of few privately owned commercial banks show that with a high level of commitment and appropriate policies in place, it is possible to build mutually beneficial relationships with NGOs and MFIs for maximising their outreach to poor and the poorest.

CORPORATE SOCIAL RESPONSIBILITY (CSR) - A COMMERCIAL IMPERATIVE

While world is passing through a critical phase of rapid economic growth and deteriorating sustainable resources, every organization is looking for newer horizons to maintain the cutting edge. Due to the increased consciousness about the Energy, Environment and Economic sustainability, businesses are constantly growing concerned about their presence in the societal and environmental spaces, because society and environment are not among the stakeholders, but the very basis and purpose of their existence. It is widely demanded that organisations must take responsibility for the impact of their activities on environment and communities. Efforts to reduce their footprint on the environment and increase the same on society are visible throughout the globe by their recent attempts. There are many methods and approaches of performing these responsible acts. The crucial one, yet commonly ignored so far is Corporate Social Responsibility (CSR). CSR refers to operating a business in a manner that accounts for the social and environmental impact created by the business. It means a commitment to developing policies that integrate responsible practices into daily business operations, and to reporting on progress made towards implementing these practices. Companies can apply CSR in a wide range of areas: employment policy, customer relations, procurement and quality policy, risk management, environmental management, product design, distribution mechanisms etc., keeping in view the chief concern of inclusive and sustainable growth of policy planners. While discussing inclusive growth, a major factor to be examined is the socio-economic inclusiveness of the people. Inclusive growth being a long term process necessarily emanates from the inclusive nature of socio-economic development across regions and people. High growth is essential to generate resources for social spending. However, the benefits of growth should be shared equitably among all sections of society. This is the main logic behind emphasising the concept of inclusive growth as has been pursued in the Eleventh Five Year Plan. Easing the credit to people of small means thereby enabling them to acquire income generating assets can prove to be a remarkable step towards inclusive growth in the Banking and Financial sector. Therefore, governments have recognised credit as an important tool for alleviation of poverty, especially in developing nations. Banks in India have been disbursing a massive volume of credit to rural areas since past and traversed from the security oriented individual banking to subsidy oriented individual banking. However, the large amount of mandatory lending has piled up unmanageable non-performing assets and has affected the viability of the banks. Therefore, the search for a viable and sustainable means of purveying credit to the poor continues. Contrary to the experience of the past in the field of subsidised credit under government sponsored programs, the new experiments in microfinance are able to demonstrate that poor are bankable and microfinance is sustainable. Corporate houses too, are getting more focused on their efforts to mainstream CSR. Although, some view it as charity and philanthropy work, but for others, it is a vital investment in the future, essential to the top-line and bottom-line business success. In fact, CSR is now less a choice and more of a necessity. It has become a commercial imperative not only for banks but for all businesses to flourish.

Common CSR policy should include

- Adoption of internal controls reform
- Commitment to diversity in hiring employees and barring discrimination
- Management teams to view employees as assets rather than costs
- High performance workplaces that integrate the views of line employees into decision making processes
- Adoption of operating policies that exceed compliance with social and environmental laws
- Advanced resource productivity, focused on the use of natural resources in a more productive, efficient and profitable fashion (such as recycled content and product recycling)
- Taking responsibility for conditions under which goods and services are produced directly or by contract employees domestically or abroad.

INTENSIFYING CSR IMPLEMENTATION THROUGH BANKS AND FINANCIAL INSTITUTIONS

Banks are generally large companies that have powerful impacts on the economic fabric of the country. Therefore, bringing unbanked into the mainstream should be an important social goal of responsible banking. Their profession also leads them to play a key role in managing the social and environmental impacts of the activities of the companies that benefit from their financing. For the past two decades, this unique responsibility has been gradually integrated into the banks' practices, particularly due to the pressure from civil society. The aim for promoting CSR in banks is not only to help them strengthen their own CSR policy, but also to raise awareness amongst their clientele of the need to adopt best practices. For banks, there is a need to integrate CSR into both, in-house operations and the projects that are financed. For this, banks are required to create a sustainable development Charter/checklist for clients. Further, they must adopt both an in-house and a professional ethical charter, setting out commitment to CSR and develop such Strategic Orientation Plans that make CSR a cornerstone of the policy.

The strategy adopted or the commitment should scale up CSR in three areas:

- In-house CSR
  - Improving in-house working conditions
  - Rèducing the ecological footprint by financing appropriate projects
- Operational CSR
  - Developing a range of responsible products and services: green loans, Socially Responsible Investments (SRI), solidarity savings, credit plus services, pro-poor insurance schemes etc.
  - Defining an environmental and social risk management process for investments and other operations financed
- Transparency in external relations
  - In sponsorships and benefit schemes provision
  - In partnerships with NGOs, clients, microfinance institutions, self-help groups etc.

CURRENT OUTREACH SCENARIO

Across the developing world, millions of people survive by operating micro-enterprises. These working poor are typically locked out of mainstream financing by selective lending policies. For meeting their working capital needs, many turn to conventional financing sources. They have to pay back exorbitant interest rates at unsavory credit terms which reinforces the cycle of poverty. Although, the economic landscape of India has undergone a tremendous change with visible signs of growth momentum in all sectors, the benefits have not equitably percolated to different segments of our society. Even after establishment of cooperative banks, nationalisation of major commercial banks and creation of Regional Rural Banks, only 59 per cent of adult population in the country has bank accounts. Only 39 per cent of rural adults have access to accounts, while in the urban areas the percentage rises to 60. Mere 14 out of 100 adults have loan accounts on an all-India basis, while in rural areas it is just 9.5 percent. India is having one of the largest networks of bank branches in the world, but the hundreds of millions of poor in the country are largely out of it. The top six metros (Mumbai, Chennai, New Delhi, Kolkata, Bangalore and Hyderabad) alone contribute 45 percent to total deposit and 56 percent to credit, indicating lower penetration of banking services in the remaining parts of the country. All this indicates the extent of financial exclusion and reflects the lack of access to appropriate low cost, fair and safe financial and insurance products and services from mainstream providers. Banks in India were nationalised four decades ago with the hope and promise that their products and services would reach the poor. But the goal still remains a distant dream. Access to bank finances can be gauged from the credit-deposit (CD) ratio which has been provided in **Table 2**.

It can be observed from the Table that there is a wide disparity in CD ratio across the regions and states. The ratio remains above 80 percent in the Southern and Western Regions during 2009, which has increased from above 75 percent in 1985. On the other hand, the situation is not encouraging in the Northern Region where the CD ratio has become 68.5 percent in 2009, gone down from 76.1 percent

Table 2. Region-wise, State-wise Credit-Deposit Ratio

Region/State	*1980- (JUNE)*	*1985- (JUNE)*	*1990*	*1995*	*2000*	*2005*	*2009*
Northern Region	76.1	63.7	54.8	48.6	51.1	59.5	68.5
Haryana	66.1	67.6	**61.2**	45.5	42.4	51.4	**61.5**
Himachal Pradesh	28.6	44	38.6	26	23.8	36.3	38.5
Jammu & Kashmir	31.5	42.8	31.8	28.6	33.5	46.7	46.3
Punjab	38.6	44.6	45.5	41.4	39.4	50.1	65.5
Rajasthan	65.9	70.5	62.2	47.7	46.7	68.7	80.2
North-Eastern Region	**35.6**	**48.9**	**51.7**	**35.6**	**28.1**	**35**	**35.8**
Arunachal Pradesh	6.2	21.5	20.1	12.4	15.7	22	24.8
Assam	40.6	53.3	55.5	38.7	32	35.3	38.3
Manipur	25.1	70.5	69.9	58.2	37.4	42.4	38.7
Meghalaya	14.1	26.5	24.6	17	16.3	43.6	27.6
Mizoram	6	22.8	34.2	16.5	23.3	47.8	58.7
Nagaland	23.7	39.6	42.6	37.8	15.3	22.9	30.7
Tripura	51.3	72.9	72.2	47.5	25.7	28.6	29.8
Eastern Region	56.1	52	52.6	47.1	37	45.5	48.9
Bihar	41.8	41.7	40	32.5	22.5	27.7	27.3
Jharkhand	-	-	-	-	-	29.6	32
Orissa	61.1	92.8	81.3	54.5	41.5	61.8	50.8
West Bengal	60.9	51.9	54.9	53.9	45.5	52.3	60.8
Central Region	45.7	52.7	52.8	39	33.9	40.8	44.8
Chhattisgarh	-	-	-	-	-	43.6	53.3
Madhya Pradesh	52	62.6	68.6	49.6	49.1	43.6	57.4
Uttar Pradesh	43.5	49.2	47	35.1	28.2	37.9	42.1
Uttarakhand	-	-	-	-	-	24.3	25.6
Western Region	70.5	79.9	74	63.2	75.4	83.5	85.2
Gujrat	51.8	54.7	61.3	46.6	49	46.5	63.2
Maharashtra	79.2	90.8	79.7	69.5	86.4	94.9	90.8
Southern Region	77.6	84.4	87.4	69.4	66.2	78.1	88.4
Andhra Pradesh	71.5	78.3	87.1	73	64.2	74.8	97.6
Karnataka	77.8	86.7	91	65.8	63.3	73.8	76.6
Kerala	67.5	68.5	64	44.8	41.5	54.6	60.4
Tamil Nadu	88	98.6	99.4	86.7	88.6	101.2	108.9

Source : Statistical Tables Relating to Banks in India, Reserve Bank of India (various issues)

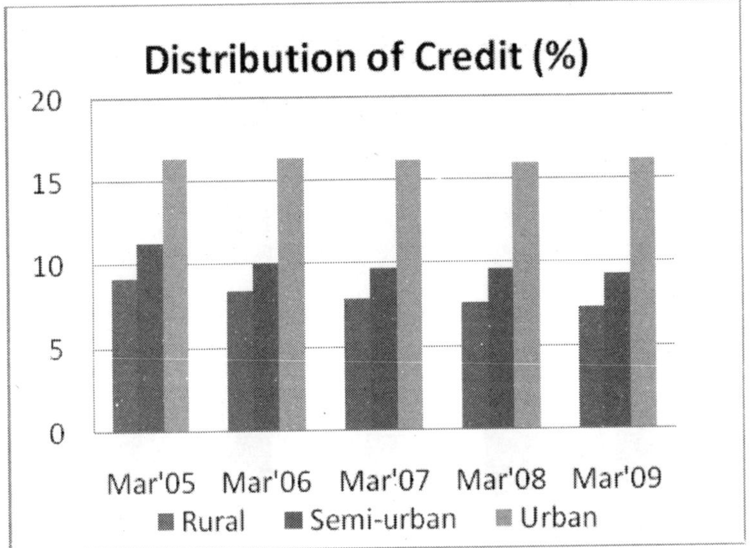

Chart 1

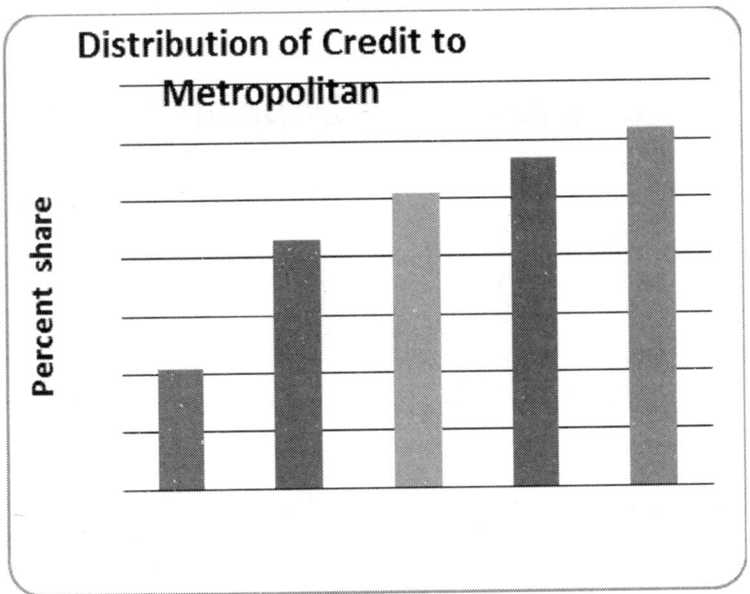

Chart 2

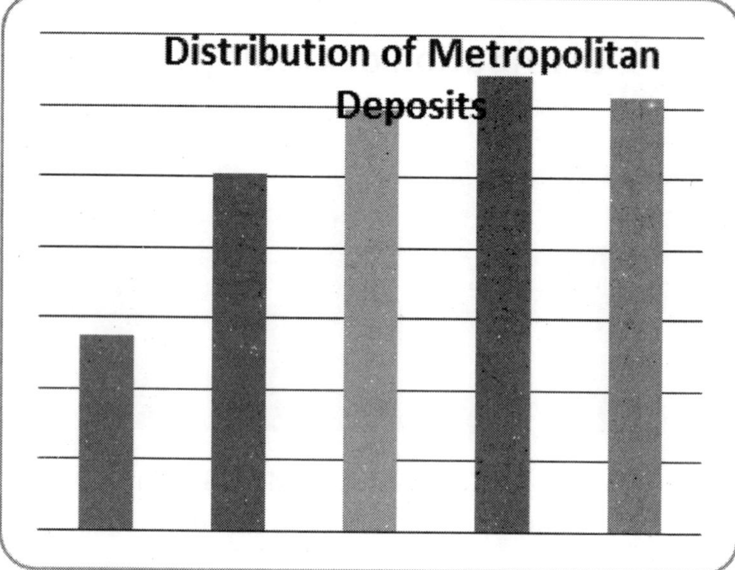

Chart 3

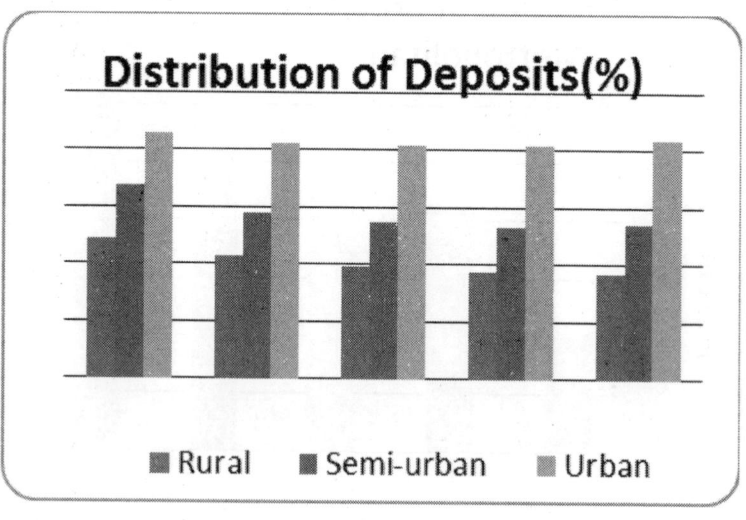

Chart 4

Source: **http://www.rbi.org.in/scripts/BS_PressReleaseDisplay.aspx?prid=23670**

in 1980. The condition is much worse in the Eastern, North-Eastern and Central Regions. While the CD ratio in the N-E Region and Central Region remained constant at 36 percent and 45 percent, respectively; it has gone down significantly from 56.1 percent in 1980 to 48.9 percent in 2009 in the Eastern Region during the three decade period. But, from the perspective of financial inclusion, an analysis of state-wise, region-wise performance of banks is not enough, as there is a wide disparity across state and regional performance. To probe further into the details, it is essential to study the population group-wise distribution of Deposits and Credits of scheduled Commercial Banks as provided by the charts 1 through 4.

It is clearly visible that banks have been hesitant in providing financial services to the rural and semi-urban populations. Following could be the reasons for their low penetration and distribution in such markets:

- Continuous pressure to maintain growth in their top lines as well as bottom lines leads them to concentrate more on the urban and metropolitan markets
- Little demand for financial products due to low levels of awareness and financial literacy
- Low investor base and lower concentration of commercial activities
- Lower scales of investment with rural households. According to a survey conducted by NCAER and MAX New York Life in 2005, the average income levels of urban households in India are 85% higher than that of the rural household.
- Preference of rural customers for ultra-local(doorstep) services
- Operational hurdles due to lack of infrastructural facilities
- Difficulty in promoting financial products due to

cultural and linguistic issues

In spite of these constraints, banks and the financial institutions are in search of solutions to cater to the important need of the society i.e. mopping up small savings at reasonable rates with range of alternatives, so that the common men have the option to park their savings under a few alternatives, including the small savings schemes introduced by the government from time to time. Banks today are free to determine their interest rates within the given limits prescribed by the RBI. It is now easier for the banks to open new branches, but the banking sector reforms are still not complete. A lot more is required to be done to revamp the public sector banks. Most of the credit-related schemes of the government to uplift the poorer and the under-privileged sections have been implemented through the banking sector. Thus, role of the banks has been important, and is going to be even more important in the future.

REACHING UNBANKED, THE FINANCIAL INCLUSION AGENDA

Financial Inclusion can be defined as the process of ensuring access or delivery of banking and financial products and services at an affordable cost to the vulnerable groups such as vast sections of disadvantaged/underprivileged and low-income groups in a fair and transparent manner by mainstream Institutional players. In the case of credit, the proper definition of the financially excluded would include households who are denied credit in spite of their demand. A well-developed financial system broadens access to funds; conversely, in an underdeveloped financial system, access to funds is limited and people are constrained by the availability of their funds and have to resort to high cost informal sources such as money lenders. Lower the availability of funds and higher their cost, fewer would be the economic activities that can be financed and hence lower the resulting economic growth (Rakesh Mohan, 2006). Apart from the credit, which is the major component, financial inclusion covers various other services such as savings, insurance, payments and remittance facilities by the formal financial system to those who tend to be excluded. Although, micro-finance has been successful in bringing the poor to a level of sustainability, its target group is not constituted by the poorest of the poor, who need food and health security, but the ones who do not have access to commercial banks' loans. There are two important ways in which banks can maximise their outreach:

a) By financing Green technology solutions

The green technologies are eco-friendly technologies developed by using natural resources and when adopted will not create any nuisance to the environment. In India there are number of R & D scientific organisations like Council of Scientific and Industrial Research (CSIR), Indian Council of Agricultural Research (ICAR), Indian Council of Medical Research (ICMR), Indian Institute of Technology (IIT), Conventional Universities, Agricultural Universities, Baba Atomic Research Centre (BARC) and number of private industrial research agencies that are contributing in evolving such eco-friendly technologies that can be called as green technologies. Today, there are number of green technologies available, namely renewable energy from wind, water, tidal energy, solar energy, development of bio-fuels from natural resources, bio-gas plants, bio-fertilisers, bio-manures, bio-pesticides, bio-waste recycling, bio-conservation, cattle farming and aquaculture, dairy and dairy products, pollution control and water purification, water conservation, rejuvenation for plantation and development of forest etc. Depending on the necessity and challenges that are required for the overall development of the rural sector, there is a need to bring in and implement at least some of the green technologies in such locations. For this purpose, a major pre-requisite is capital investment, which is possible only when finance is available. Access to finance and awareness on the availability of finance can play a major role in promoting the applications of green technologies. Integration of micro finance and technological applications will definitely generate employment, stimulate growth and lead to the overall development of the rural sector.

After witnessing a dip in 2009, on account of global financial crisis, the green sector in India is once again attracting the attention of investors and banks. Three favorable reasons for investing in rural sector include, high returns on equity, increasing investor comfort regarding renewable generation risk, and strong commitment from the central government to ensure renewable feasibility. The growth of the green sector can be catalysed by lending financial support through banks for implementing green technology projects. For example, Yes Bank has offered Rs 700crores for a project involving management of municipal solid waste and its disposal in an environmentally friendly manner. Moreover, State Bank of India has tied up with Managing Emission, a Mumbai-based company involved in business of setting up projects for renewable energy and energy efficiency with carbon embedded assets, to provide 20,000 energy efficient plants to rural India through micro finance loans. The project involves building bio-gas plants at farmers' houses. The project aims at reducing greenhouse emission by saving conventional fuel such as fire wood, LPG and kerosene. Under the project, farmers contribute 50 percent of the cost and the balance 50 percent is financed through low interest micro finance loans from the bank. The repayment of the micro finance loan is then structured in a manner by which the income received from carbon credits is used for repayment. Thus, micro-finance programs can be a success, if the banks realise it as a major business opportunity and not merely a social obligation. Such realisation will bring in more commitment which in turn will result into the much desired sustainability in these programs.

b) Through a technology ride

Reaching segments that are most difficult to penetrate requires technology support. The prime reason for the lack of penetration is the high risk and lower return on investment in rural sector. Lower unit transaction sizes are an added disincentive. However, an effective leverage of technology can reduce the cost of transaction, increase return on investment and make a risk worth taking. Banking services have evolved along with technology and the delivery of various banking products are carried out through the medium or high technology at a fraction of the cost to the customer. The concept of core banking has made 'Anywhere-Anytime' banking a reality. At the field level, technology is expected to address customer information processing and client related transactions. It should literally transform the field operator into a mobile banking. Many banks and financial institutions have already started using techno products, as they can connect millions and allow the consumer to receive disbursements, make loan payments and also conduct other transactions electronically. The main computing platform that forms the core of central workout should have the ability to handle huge data from varieties of customers and also process it. The field level technology can comprise card based solutions that could be used with mobile devices, handheld computers and mobile phones. Products like Point-of-Sale terminals, smart cards and biometrics are finding increasing significance in tapping the remote unbanked markets. Hardware commoditisation, coupled with new software paradigms and advancements in mobile telephony, will surely make PoS terminals economically viable and convenient. Smart cards are useful in supplanting cash, as they provide a relatively secure mode of transaction due to low risk of loss and fraud. Where large population in our country is still illiterate, widespread use of biometric characteristics, such as fingerprints can serve as a useful means for identification and authentication of customers. In this way, technology is playing a promising role in extending outreach and networking of micro-entrepreneurs. Although it has transformed banking services in urbanised area, there is a need to carry technology to the rural front and to the courtyard of the villages, which are yet to see the electricity, adequate drinking water and road connectivity. Thus continual innovation is actually required to keep-up with the growing demands of the market and serve the unbanked cost effectively, where technology can act as an enabler.

LINKING BANKS TO THE GRASS-ROOTS - THE PROPOSED MODEL

If we combine the means of capitalism with ends of communism, a new free enterprise can be built, from which the world benefits and equity is achieved, i.e., a new ideal, which states that not only each according to his ability, but each according to need can also be met. To bring millions of unbanked into the orbit of formal banking mechanism, RBI and Ministry of Finance should work together to develop an allocation policy based on area approach for allotting districts to each bank for total financial inclusion. Although the Lead Bank Scheme (LBS) was launched in 1969-70 with the same approach, but due to the inappropriate allocation mechanism, it could not achieve its objectives. Hence, there is a need to revamp and revitalize allocation mechanism. In the present model, district-wise allocation can be worked out as below:

Total number of districts in the country = 626

Total number of Scheduled Commercial Banks in the country = 171

Average number of districts per SCB = 626/171 = 3.67

As part of the mandatory CSR policy, each bank should be allotted 2–4 districts, depending upon the size, number of branches and current network (existing coverage). After distributing the allocation schedule, banks should be given 18-24 months' time to develop necessary infrastructure for meeting the target. Within first three months, banks must formulate and submit the phased plan for 100 percent coverage. Once the plan is approved, development work should be strictly monitored by the competent authority at regular intervals and no extension in any case should be granted, to avoid the chain reaction. Banks should be given freedom to design and develop customised products and services and explore new distribution channels as per the regional requirements. Penetration in dedicated districts will not restrict the banks from expanding in any other locations. In fact, the banks can synergise the efforts of each other by developing innovative inter-banking solutions. If required, they can opt for **Account number Portability** for simplifying the procedures.

As the target of achieving total outreach in two to four districts for any bank is not really a tough one, model should be accepted without any conflict. However, genuine suggestions for further enriching the model at any level can be fruitfully incorporated. Also, if need arises, responsibility of SCBs can be diluted by including non-scheduled banks into the cover.

ADDITIONAL RECOMMENDATIONS

- Development of a mandatory Environmental and Social support unit, which can help improve the environmental and social quality of financed operations by:

- defining the environmental and social due diligence to be conducted in projects
- advising project teams and all partners in its implementation (training, creating tools, etc.)
- contributing to intellectual production on the issue
- providing Financial education, Credit Counseling, Information sharing and problem solving on technical issues
- synergising and liaising with other organisations for value added services and development activities
- steering and guiding those under financial distress and educating others to avoid financial mess
- building partnerships with national and international working groups and participating in their proceedings

As per the UNDP report (2000) "the hard-core poor, having few assets, are reluctant to take on the risks of credit, and when they do, it is usually for emergencies and consumption, not for production." Therefore, instead of focusing only on micro credit, it should be used in combination with effective policies of land reforms and public employment programs for poverty alleviation, as the combination will be more effective than a single policy, because each of these will focus on different aspects of poverty.

CONCLUSION

Indian economy can be put on a firm footing only if benefits of economic growth percolate down to rural India. As we begin to relearn the skills and rebuild the relationships we lost in the pursuit of exponential economic growth, we will begin to find happiness that we are in charge of; one that is not dependent on the fluctuations of the stock market or the amount of stuff we own. Difficult as it may in the short run, but we can emerge from such crisis healthier and wealthier, with sort of wealth that really matters, i.e. strong community relationships and bonding, healthy ecosystems etc. There is a bold call from poor to the affluent world – 'Either be brave enough to share our pain equally, or generous enough to share your riches and privileges equally." This should be a wake-up call for all the banks and financial institutions to pursue 'inclusive growth' as a strategy of economic development. While income distribution schemes can allow people, to benefit from economic growth in the short run, inclusive growth allows people to "contribute to and benefit from economic growth in the long run". The fact that money attracts money demonstrates that, if you have got a little, it's easy to get more. The inability for unbanked is to acquire that little, and here banks have to extend their outreach to enable them to acquire that little through 'Financial Inclusion'. The benefits of Financial Inclusion are manifold for the banks, intermediaries and for the beneficiaries. Financial Inclusion drive for the underprivileged is the beginning of a strong empowerment drive and is a key player which will certainly transform India into a global economic power house. The success of CSR can be claimed only when every poor family is able to keep a child in school, send sick member of a family to hospital and build up secure savings. Visibility of CSR lies in seeing happy faces in the rural yards of the country, as the dynamism of the Indian rural market has the potential of not only bringing back the lost riches and prosperity to every Indian but also providing once again, the country, a lost status of Golden Sparrow.

REFERENCES

1. Agrawal Reena (2007) "Financial Inclusion: A Challenging Task Ahead", The Conference on Global Competition & Competitiveness of Indian Corporate, IIM K: *http://*

dspace.iimk.ac.in/bitstream/2259/485/1/271-286+.pdf

2. Blowfield Michael, Murray Allen (2009): *Corporate Responsibility, a critical introduction,* New York, Oxford University Press.
3. Campion Anita and Owens John (2005) "MABS: A sustainable Approach to Rural Microfinance." In: *Microfinance, Challenges and Opportunities,* S. Rajagopalan (Ed.). Hyderabad: ICFAI, pp. 179-187.
4. Clark Heather (2005) "Commercial Microfinance: The right Choice for Everyone." In: *Microfinance, Challenges and Opportunities,* S. Rajagopalan (Ed.). Hyderabad: ICFAI, pp. 10-22.
5. Dash R.N., "Financial Inclusion - An Assessment of New Modalities and Alternative Models": *http://cab.org.in/Lists/Knowledge%20Bank/DispForm.aspx?ID=12*
6. Dr. Vighneswara Swamy and Dr. Vijayalakshmi, "Role of Financial Inclusion for Inclusive Growth in India - Issues & Challenges": *http://skoch.in/fir/Role%20of%20Financial%20Inclusion%20for%20Inclusive%20Growth%20in%20India.pdf*
7. Draft Report of the High Level Committee to Review the Lead Bank Scheme (2009): file:///C:/Documents%20and%20Settings/Admin/My%20Documents/Rbi-bankg.htm
8. Elliott Larry (2010) "Budget will offer NI tax break for new firms in deprived areas": *http://www.guardian.co.uk/business/2010/jun/20/budget-tax-break-new-uk-firms-deprived-region*
9. Gelder Sarah van & Doug Pibel (2008) "Consciousness - Economics As If The People And The Planet Mattered": http://www.lifepositive.com/Mind/Money/Economics_As_If_The_People_And_The_Planet_Mattered32008.asp
10. Goss Salah (2010) "Broadening the Financial Inclusion Cast of Characters": http://technology.cgap.org/2010/12/16/broadening-the-financial-inclusion-cast-of-characters/
11. Kuttner Robert (2001) "The Power of Money": http://www.commondreams.org/views01/0218-09.htm
12. **M.S.SundaraRajan,**"ReachingtheUnbanked":*http://*

www.inclusion.in/index.php?option=com_ content&view= article&id=179

13. **MayuriRajbonshi(2010)** "Reaching the Unbanked": http://bismumbai.blogspot.com/2010/08/bis-1951-reaching-unbanked_1542.html
14. **Mosley Paul (2000)** "The Microfinance Experience of Developing Countries: Lessons for Banks in India." In: *Microfinance, Emerging Challenges*, Kishanjit Basu, Krishan Jindal (Eds.). New Delhi: Tata McGraw Hill, pp. 15-46.
15. **Nanda Y. C. (2000)** "Critical Issues in Microfinance." In: *Microfinance, Emerging Challenges*, Kishanjit Basu, Krishan Jindal (Eds.). New Delhi: Tata McGraw Hill, pp. 348-354.
16 **Rai Anurag & amrita Saha (2010)** "Financial Inclusion in Karnataka: A Study of Operationalisation of No Frills Accounts": *http://mpra.ub.uni-muenchen.de/26564/1/MPRA_paper_26564.pdf*
17. **Rangarajan C, (2008)** 'Report of the Committee on Financial Inclusion', Ministry of Finance, GOI
18. RBI, Report on Trend and Progress of Banking in India (1998-2007)
19. **Roland Christian (2005)** "Banking Sector Liberalization in India": *http://unpan1.un.org/intradoc/groups/public/documents/APCITY/UNPAN024227.pdf*
20. **Sen, Amartya, (2000)**: *'Development as Freedom'*, Anchor Books, New York, 2000.
21. **Sharma Anamika, (May 2009)**, "Challenges: For Building Financial Inclusive India, ICFAI Reader, pp 14-20
22. **Sheokand S. M. (2000)** "Reorienting Banking with the Poor: The SHG-Bank Linkage Way." In: *Microfinance, Emerging Challenges*, Kishanjit Basu, Krishan Jindal (Eds.). New Delhi: Tata McGraw Hill, pp. 291-318.
23. **Somnath V. S. (2009):** *Microfinance, redefining the future*, New Delhi, Excel Books.
24. **Thakore Abhishek (2003)** "Money – Abundance Unlimited": http://www.lifepositive.com/Mind/money/robert-kiyosaki.asp

25. **Varughese Suma (2009)** "Consciousness - The New Economy": http://www.lifepositive.com/Mind/Money/The_New_Economy32009.asp

26. **World Bank (2006)**, World Development Indicators, World Bank, Washington

27. **World Bank (2008)**: "Finance for All - Policies and Pitfalls in Expanding Access", World Bank, Washington

29

Payment & Settlement Systems – A Study of RTGS

D. Shiva Kumar

INTRODUCTION

Payment Systems encompass a set of instruments and means generally acceptable in making payments and includes the institutional and organizational framework governing such payments and the operating procedures and communications network.

A payment system, therefore, comprises – (a) a means by which the payer gives authority to his bank for funds to be transferred (b) a means of transmitting and exchanging the payment instruction and (c) a means of settlement between the banks involved.

SIGNIFICANCE OF PAYMENT SYSTEMS

Payment systems and financial stability : Any major payment system failure could result in failure to meet payment obligations leading to erosion of confidence of the markets and financial structure.

Payment systems and monetary policy implementation : In the course of maintaining monetary stability, central banks generally operate in the money market by influencing the short term interest rate and through it other rates. The choice of varying reserve requirements to achieve monetary policy objectives is also made use of. Both methods represent a market-oriented approach to monetary policy implementation. A reliable large-value payment system with same-day settlement is very much a requirement for meeting both of these conditions.

Payment systems and economic efficiency : If a payment system is inefficient and unreliable, payment instruction takes time to move from the payer's bank to the payee's bank and for the final recipient's account to be credited. Such inefficiencies inconvenience users and will give an adverse image about working of the economy.

The development of national payment system involves initiatives to:

- broaden the range of payment instruments and services;
- improve cost efficiency, particularly in terms of operating costs and access to, and usage of, liquidity;
- create more suitable oversight and regulatory regimes for the national payment system; and
- enhance the efficiency and stability of payment service markets.

In recent years, the development of electronic money payment systems have been gaining currency. The electronic money has the potential to take over from cash for big or small-value payments. Such transactions are becoming easier and cheaper for both consumers and merchants.

RESERVE BANK'S INITIATIVES

RBI has taken several initiatives to develop and promote electronic payments infrastructure. RBI introduced the following:

1. Electronic Clearing Service (ECS).
2. Real Time Gross Settlement (RTGS) system.
3. National Electronic Funds Transfer (NEFT).
4. Cheque Truncation System (CTS).

We will understand these in brief here.

ELECTRONIC CLEARING SERVICE (ECS)

To upgrade payment system to international standards, RBI took the initiative and set up Electronic Clearing Service in India in mid 1990s. Electronic Clearing Service is the counterpart of the automated clearing house (ACH) system of US. ECS has two variants. **ECS - Credit Clearing and ECS - Debit Clearing**

The Credit Clearing operates on the principle of 'single debit-multiple credits' and is used for making payment of salary, pension, dividend and interest, etc. The Debit Clearing functions on the principle of 'single credit-multiple debits' and is used for collecting payments by utility service providers like electricity, telephone bills as well by banks for receiving principal / interest repayments for housing and personal loans from the borrowers.

At present, about 18 million transactions flow through the ECS system every month. This facility is currently available at 74 centers in the country.

The National ECS is a product developed by the RBI to enable centralised processing of all ECS transactions, in contrast to the existing ECS system that has decentralised operations at 74 locations, spread all over the country. Under the National ECS, the processing of all the ECS transactions would be centralised at the National Clearing Cell at Nariman Point, Mumbai. The new centralized ACH solution will consolidate the current multiple ECS systems in due course of time. ACH system would provide technology platform to enable participants to implement end to end straight through processing mechanism. and sponsor banks would need to only upload the relative files to a web server, with online data validation facility.

REAL TIME GROSS SETTLEMENT SYSTEM

The payment systems in the country largely follows the deferred net settlement regime, under which the net amount is settled between banks on a deferred basis. Such a dispensation entails an element of settlement risk. Hence, as a step towards risk mitigation in the large value payment systems, the RTGS was operationalised by the RBI in March 2004, which enables settlement of transactions in real time, on a gross basis between banks. Almost all the inter-bank transactions in the country and many time-critical customer transactions are now settled through this system.

RTGS is fully secured electronic funds transfer system where banks and customers can receive payments on real time basis. The outreach of RTGS transactions has also grown geographically. Out of about 75,000 bank branches in the country, more than 66,178 bank branches now accept requests for remittance through RTGS system for customer transactions as well as inter-bank transactions.

A minimum threshold of rupees two lakh (increased from one to two lakh recently) has been prescribed for customer transactions to ensure that RTGS system is used only for large value transactions and retail transactions take an alternate channel of electronic funds transfer. The daily average of number transactions is over 1.7 lac and value of transactions over Rs.2.5 lakh crore per day.

NATIONAL ELECTRONIC FUND TRANSFER

The NEFT was launched by the RBI in November 2005 as a more secure, nation-wide retail electronic payment system to facilitate funds transfer by the bank customers especially for transactions below the cutoff limit of RTGS between the networked bank branches in the country.

The RBI provides, free of charge, intra-day liquidity to the banks for the RTGS transactions. The service charges to be levied by banks from their customers for RTGS & NEFT have, however, been deregulated and left to discretion of the individual bank. While some of the banks have rationalized their service charges and a few have made it even cost-free to the customers.

CHEQUE TRUNCATION SYSTEM (CTS)

The latest electronic payment product introduced by the RBI is the Cheque Truncation System (CTS), which was launched, on a pilot basis, in the National Capital Region of New Delhi on February 1, 2008, with the participation of 10 banks. At present all the banks are participating in the system through 53 direct member banks.

The main advantage of cheque truncation is that it eliminates the physical presentation of the cheque to the clearing house; The CTS would enable the realisation of cheques on the same day, and provide a more cost-effective mode of settlement than manual and MICR clearing.

Necessary amendments have been made to the Negotiable Instruments Act, 1881, which provides legal recognition to the electronic image of the truncated cheque. These amendments provide a legal basis for the cheque truncation system. .

CLASSIFICATION OF BANK PAYMENT SYSTEMS

Payment systems can be classified as

Value of funds transfer : (a) Large-value funds transfer – where individual payments are of high value and therefore time sensitive and (b) Retail funds transfer – where the value of transactions are of relatively low individual value but the volume of transactions put through it large.

Modality : (a) Net settlement where payments are set off against receipts over a large number of transactions taken up for settlement and (b) Gross Settlement – where each transaction is settled independent of other transactions.

Timing of settlement : (a) Real-time systems – where the transaction is settled as soon as it enters the system and (b) Deferred settlement systems – where the transactions are settled at pre-designated time intervals or at the end of the day.

RBI in 2005 set up the Board for Payment and Settlement Systems, released a vision document incorporating a proposal to set up an umbrella institution for all the RETAIL PAYMENT SYSTEMS in the country.

National Payments Corporation of India (NPCI) was incorporated in December 2008 as a Section 25 company and the Certificate of Commencement of Business was issued in April 2009.

NPCI has the vision of achieving any where, any time, payment services which is simple and easy to use, safe and secure, fast and cost effective. The objective of the NPCI is to consolidate and integrate all retail payment systems such that they are inclusive, customer friendly, varied yet simple, universally accessible, available round the clock, affordable to all, fully automated and world class.

STUDY OF RTGS - METHODOLOGY

This research confines to retail and is based on views, opinion, feed back and the suggestions from business segment, interviews of bank managers and secondary data from published sources in RBI site and other sources.

Questionnaires are used to collect data from business segment. 60 units responded though 250 units were approached. Scheduled Interview method is adopted for information from branches of banks.

The sample size consists of 60 business/industrial units in Bangalore selected randomly from the Population. And the other set of sample consists of 10 branches of different banks in Bangalore.

STATEMENT OF THE PROBLEM

To trace the emergence of payment and settlement system in India and to assess the extent of awareness and usage in practice of the efficient, fast and latest instrument of remittance viz., RTGS by user.

The important objectives of the study are:

- To study the emergence, process and procedures of latest products in payment systems in brief,
- To study the general public awareness and opinion about RTGS, and the extent of its usage; and
- To find out ground level deficiencies if any, for use of these instruments from customers angle and to recommend steps that may be needed to make the scheme widely acceptable.

Limitation : Sample study was confined to Bangalore city, and to the business units owned/run by Rotarians of Rotary Dist 3190 in Bangalore. Time was another constraint. Respondents providing information not actually referring to data might have resulted inaccuracies. Nevertheless since the respondents were actually dealing with these issues, the responses can be taken as reliable.

ANALYSIS : Primary Data collected has been tabulated in 3 master tables. There were 18 questions in the questionnaire and the sequence of analysis goes according to the questionnaire design and analysis of data reveals following information.

Out of 60 responses received, 20 were from Manufacturing units, 16 from Trading and 24 from Service Industries.

NATURE OF BUSINESS

Out of 60 responses received, 33% of responses came from manufacturing industrial units, 27% from trading units and 40% from service units. The response pattern, however, does not reflect the contribution of the respective sectors to the GDP or the ratio in which the remittance facilities are used by the universe (Table 1 & Graph 1).

Table 1

Type	*Industries*	
	No of Units	*Per Cent*
Manufacturing	20	33
Trading	16	27
Service	24	40

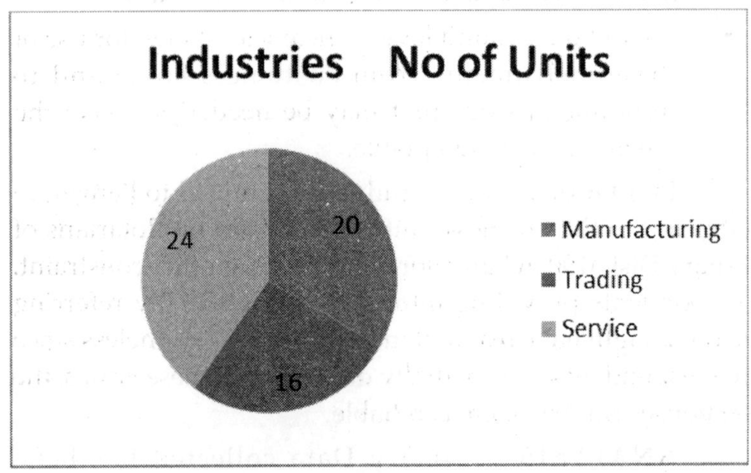

Graph 1

The responses regarding turnover is classified in to 5 groups. The first category is below Rs.25 lakhs and the last category is regarding turnover of above Rs.5 crores. Out of 60 units, 6 units (10%) had a turnover of less than Rs.25 lakhs. 14 units (23%) had turnover between Rs.25 lacs to Rs.50 lacs, 16 units (27%) had turnover between Rs.50 lacs and Rs.1 crore, 14 units (23%) between Rs.1 crore and Rs.5 crore and 10 units (17%) had a turn over of above Rs.5 crores (Table 2 & Graph 2).

Table 2. Turnover Of Business Units

	TypeTurnover in lacs				
	< 25	*25-50*	*50-100*	*100-500*	*>500*
Manufacturing			2	9	9
Trading	2	3	7	3	1
Service	4	11	7	2	0

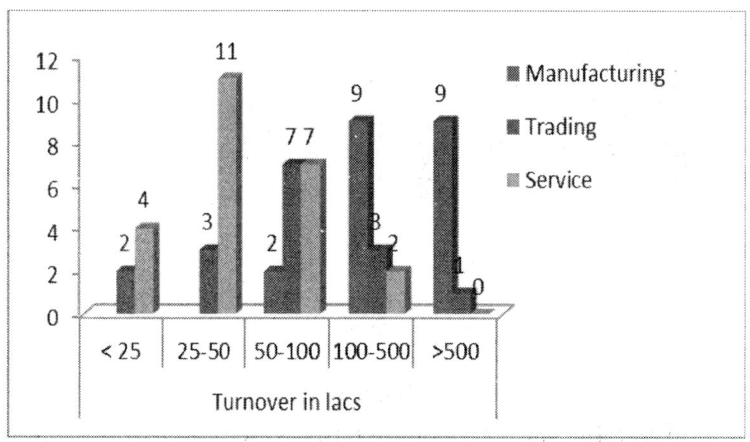

Graph 2

The manufacturing units had substantially higher turnover. 18 of 20 units had turnover of over Rs.1 crore, 9 out of them reported turnover of over Rs.5 crores. In trade category, maximum number units i.e., 7 reported a turnover of Rs.50 lacs to Rs.1 crore. Only 1 unit had turnover of above

Rs.5 crore. No service unit reported a turn over above Rs.5 crore. 11 units were placed in the category 2 with turnover of Rs.25 lacs to Rs.50 lacs.

The inference is that manufacturing units which responded were bigger in size , while trading units were moderate in size and the service units, comparatively smaller in size viewed from turnover angle (Table3).

Table 3. Bankers to the Business Units

	TypeBankers to the Business units							
	SBI Group	*Can Bk*	*Sy Bk*	*Vij Bk*	*Corprn*	*ICICI*	*Axis*	*Ors*
Manufacturing	2	2	1	1	1	5	4	4
Trading	6	2	1	2	2		1	2
Service	5	4	3	2	3	3	3	1

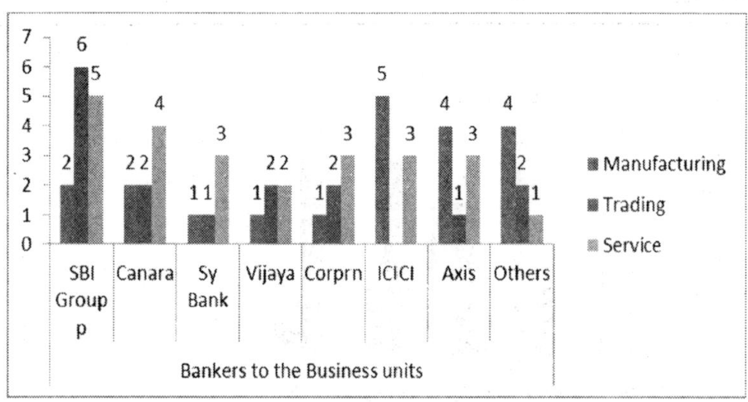

Graph 3

The table shows the main bankers to the business units responding to our questionnaire. As per the information, SBI group was the main bankers for 13 units (22%). There was a good dispersal of business among banks. However, surprisingly, 23 units (38% of units) had dealings with the new generation private banks. Among nationalized banks, Canara Bank had 8 units, Syndicate Bank and Vijaya Bank had 5 units each. Corporation Bank had 6 units dealing with them (Graph 3).

HOW BUSINESS UNITS RECEIVE MONEY?

All the 60 units responded informed that they receive payment in all the 3 modes i.e, by cash, by cheques and DDs and also through electronic mode (Table 4, Graph 4 & Graph 5).

Table 4.

Type	*Mode of Receipt of Money by Units*		
	Cash	*Cheque/DD*	*Electronic*
Manufacturing	20	20	20
Trading	16	16	16
Service	24	14	24

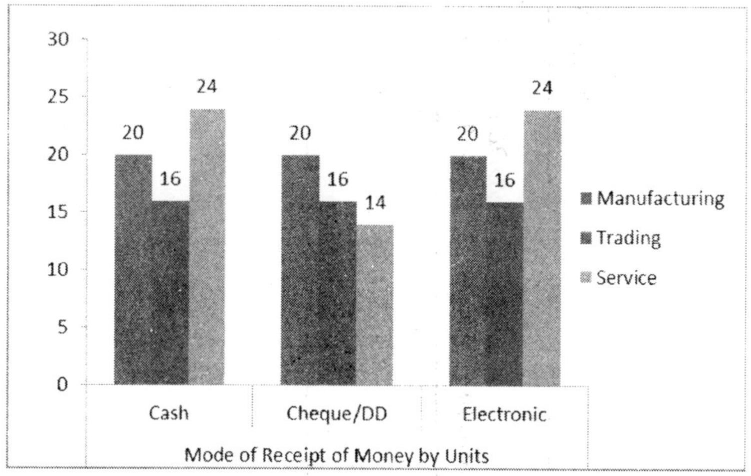

Graph 4

All units in manufacturing, trading and service sector receive payments in cash. But the per cent receipt is nominal. All business units receive only 5 to 10% of their total receipts in cash (Table 5).

Table 5

						TypeReceipts pattern in %					
	Cash			*Cheque/DDElectronic*					*Mode*		
	5 to 10	*5 to 10*	*10 to 25*	*25 to 50*	*50 to 75*	*75 to 100*	*5 to 10*	*10 to 25*	*25 to 50*	*50 to 75*	*75 to 100*
Mfg	20	3	11	6					6	11	3
Trading	16	1	5	4	6			6	4	5	1
Service	24	2	3	7	7	5	5	7	7	2	3

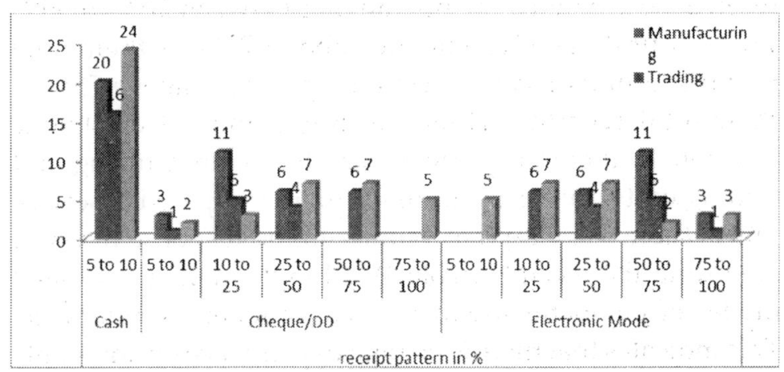

Graph 5

Manufacturing Units : Manufacturing units receive payments through cheques. But the proportion is not more than 50%. 6 units (30%) receive cheques ranging upto 50% of their total receipts. 11 units (55%) receive cheques between 10 to 25%. And 3 units receive cheque payments of 5 to 10%. The total receipts, however, is higher through electronic mode. The receipts through electronic mode is above 75% in case of 3 units, 50 to 75% in case of 11 units and above 25% in case of 6 units. This indicates that while cash transactions continue at a small level, the receipts through electronic mode is on the rise vis a vis cheque/DD receipts.

Trading Units : Trading units receive cheque payments ranging from 5% to 75%. One unit receives cheques/DDs ranging upto 1% while 6 units receive upto 75%. No unit receives cheque/DD payment above 75% of their total receipts. Payments through electronic mode is showing improving trends. 6 units receive payments upto 25%, 9 units between 25 to 75% and 1 unit receives payments above 75% of their total receipts. Again indicating the growing importance of electronic mode of receipts.

Service Units : The figures indicate that trend with regard to cheque/DD receipts and electronic receipts continue to be almost same. While 14 units receive cheques ranging between 25 to 75% of their total receipts, 14 units receive electronic payments ranging between 10% to 50%. While 5 units receive cheques above 75% of their total receipts, 3 units receive electronic payment above 75% of their total receipts. Thus the importance of electronic payment is increasing. However, the manufacturing and trading units use electronic mode more compared to service units (Table 6 & Graph 6). Similar to the response received regarding the receipts (table 4), all units make use of all 3 modes of payments to pay to their suppliers/vendors etc. This indicates that there is no total dependence on any single mode of payment, though the level of dependence on different modes is not equal but varies.

Table 6. Payments Mode by Cash etc.

Type	*Payment Pattern %*		
	Cash	*Cheque/DD*	*Electronic*
Manufacturing	20	20	20
Trading	16	16	16
Service	24	14	24

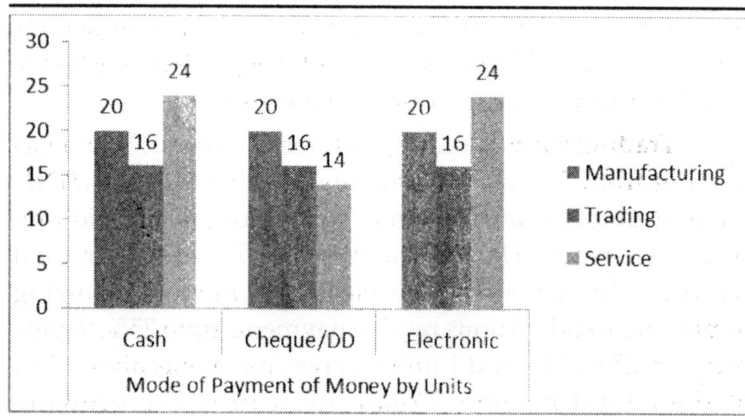

Graph 6

PAYMENTS PATTERN

All units in manufacturing, trading and service sector make payments in cash. But the proportion of cash payment

Table 7

	TypePayments pattern in %										
	Cash	*Cheque/DD*					*Electronic Mode*				
	5 to 10	*5 to 10*	*10 to 25*	*25 to 50*	*50 to 75*	*75 to 100*	*5 to 10*	*10 to 25*	*25 to 50*	*50 to 75*	*75 to 100*
Mfg	20	3	11	6					6	11	3
Trading	16	1	5	4	6			6	4	5	1
Service	24	2	3	7	7	5	5	7	7	2	3

is nominal. All business units make payments in cash only to the extent of 5 to 10% of their total payments (Table 7).

Manufacturing Units : Manufacturing units make payments through cheques. But payments by cheques is not more than 50% of their total payments. 6 units (30%) make cheque payments ranging upto 50% of their total payments. 11 units (55%) pay by cheques from 10 to 25% of their total payments. And 3 units pay by cheque up to 10% of their total payments. The payments, however, through electronic mode is higher compared to other modes of payments. The payments through electronic mode is above 75% in case of 3 units, 50 to 75% in case of 11 units and above 25% in case of 6 units. This indicates that while cash transactions continue at a small level, the payments through electronic mode is on the rise vis a vis cheque/DD payments or cash.

Trading Units : Trading units make payments by cheques ranging from 5% to 75%. One unit pays cheques/ DDs ranging upto 1% while 6 units pay upto 75%. No unit pays cheque/DD payment above 75% of their total payments. Payments through electronic mode is showing improving trends. 6 units pay payments upto 25%, 9 units

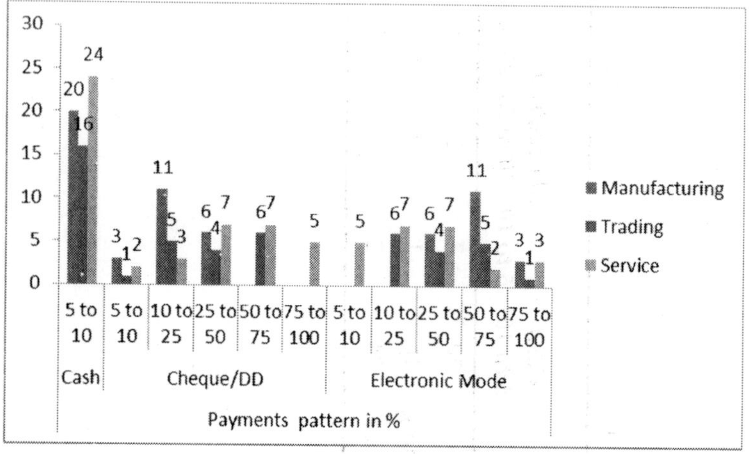

Graph 7

between 25 to 75% and 1 unit pays payments above 75% of their total payments. Again indicating the growing importance of electronic mode of payments (Graph 7).

Service Units : The figures indicate that trend with regard to cheque/DD payments and electronic payments continue to be almost same. While 14 units pay cheques ranging between 25 to 75% of their total payments, 14 units pay electronic payments ranging between 10% to 50%. While 5 units pay cheques above 75% of their total payments, 3 units pay electronic payment above 75% of their total payments. Thus the importance of electronic payment is increasing. However, the manufacturing and trading units use electronic mode more compared to service units.

AWARENESS ABOUT NEFT/RTGS

All the respondents have informed that they are aware of the schemes of electronic remittances, NEFT and RTGS. The depth of their awareness was not sought to be found out. But it can be reasonably assumed that all are very much aware of the RTGS and NEFT (Table 8 & Graph 8) since every business unit which responded has remitted or received money using RTGS or NEFT. The smaller units, however, have made use of this mode less frequently than the medium and bigger units.

Table 8

Type	*Awareness about RTGS/NEFT*	
	Nos	*Per Cent*
Manufacturing	20	100
Trading	16	100
Service	24	100

HOW DID THEY COME TO KNOW ABOUT RTGS/NEFT

In the previous table, we have seen that all the business units were aware about the RTGS and NEFT. The responses

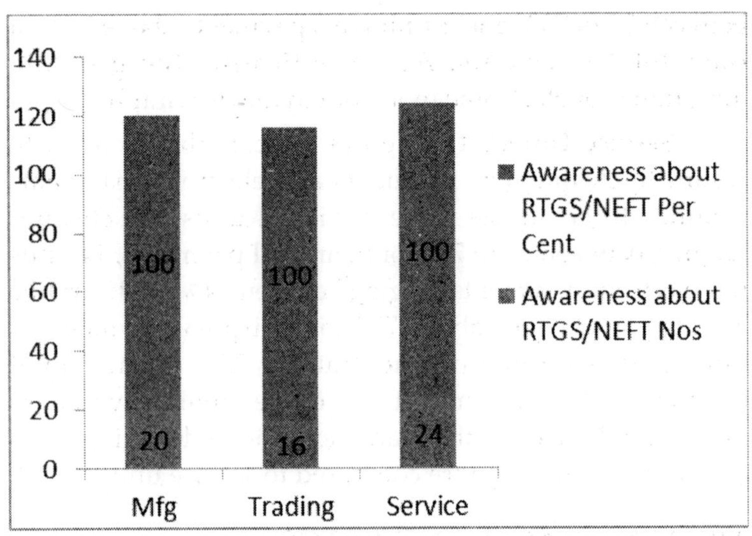

Graph 8

to Q.No. 13 indicates that all of them came to know about this mode of remittance through their banker and business colleagues and clients. Thus sufficient awareness has been created about these modes of remittances by the banks and other agencies involved (Table 9).

Table 9

Type	*How did you learn about RTGS/NEFT*	
	From Bankers	*from Friends/Clients*
Mfg	20	20
Trading	16	16
Service	24	24

Whether Recommended To Others To Adopt Rtgs/Neft?

We have seen earlier that all those who responded are aware of the schemes. They have come to know about RTGS through their bankers, friends and clients. Q.No.14 was aimed at knowing whether the respondents are also spreading awareness about this mode of remittances to their friends. The responses indicate thatrecommending to others to make use of RTGS was more pronounced in manufacturing sector. This response, coupled with what we had seen Table 5 and Table 7 indicate that the business units in manufacturing sector desire faster and efficient movement of funds keeping in view their requirements for funding the various operations. Compared to this, the trading sector used electronic mode less frequently and encouraged less number of times to others to use RTGS mode. The trend is further dominant in service sector. In this sector, less usage of electronic mode is seen and also the units do not recommend others to use RTGS/NEFT mode. More dominant form of payment and settlement in this sector is through cheques (Table 10 and Graph 9).

Table 10

Type	*Recommended to Others*	
	Yes	*No*
Mfg	16	4
Trading	4	12
Service	2	22

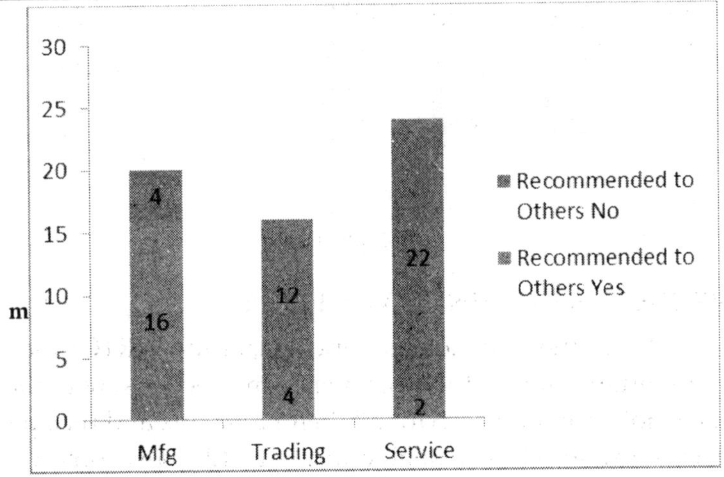

Graph 9

DO YOU PREFER RTGS MODE FOR ALL REMITTANCES?

The chart and the table indicate that all respondents have expressed the view that they want to make use of the RTGS mode of remittance for all their payments and settlements (Table 11 & Graph 10).

Table 11

Type	*Do you prefer RTGS for all your receipts/payments* *YES*	*Per Cent*
Mfg	20	100
Trading	16	100
Service	24	100

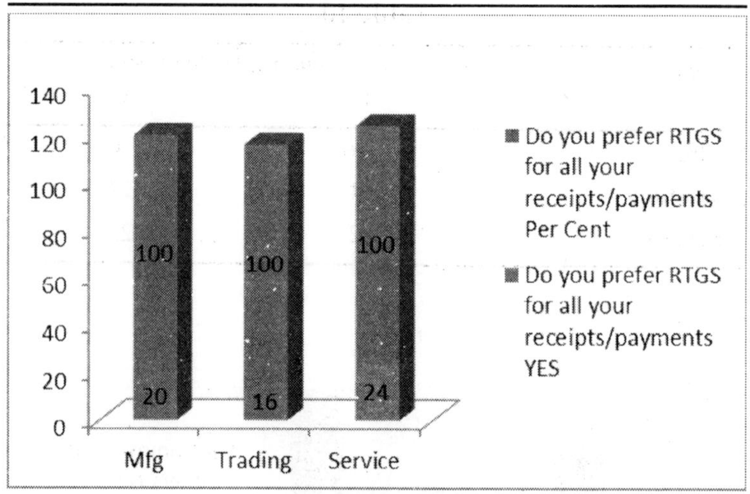

Graph 10

PROBLEMS IN USING RTGS FULLY

While the respondents want to make use of RTGS mode of remittance for all their payments and receipts, why they have not adopted RTGS for all their payments and receipts? The information as available in table 12 gives some clue about it.17 respondents in case NEFT and 46 respondents in

Table 12

Type	*PROBLEMS if any in using RTGS/NEFT 100% for all receipts/payments*						
	Visiting branch for NEFT	*Visiting branch for RTGS*	*Branch not RTGS Compliant*	*Difficult to get IFSC Code*	*Delay in receiving credits*	*No of times there was delay*	*No of days it took to resolve*
Mfg	8	12		13			
Trading	6	13		16			
Service	13	21		23			

case of RTGS inform that one problem they face is visiting the branch for effecting remittances (Graph 11). Banks have provided online facility to internet banking customers. However, some banks require customers to visit branches to remit funds, more so in case of RTGS. This is mainly for security considerations. This is mentioned as a problem in adopting RTGS for 100% payments and receipts. Non availability of IFSC code or difficulty in finding IFSC code is mentioned as a reason by 87% of the respondents. This aspect needs to be looked into for making RTGS widely adopted

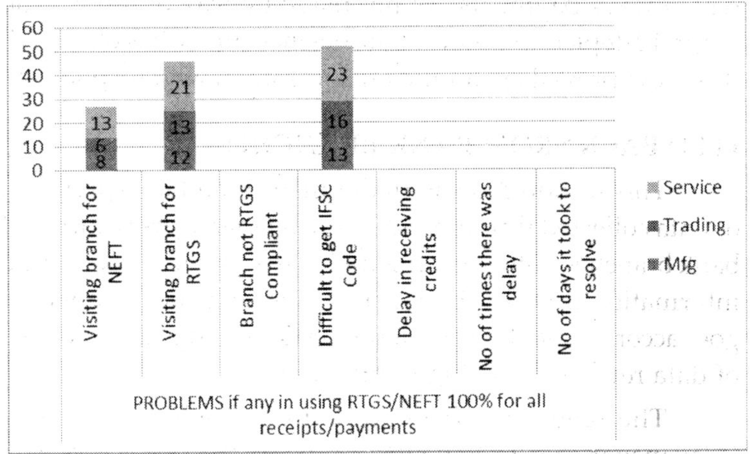

Graph 11

for payment and settlement. It is important that there was no branch which was not RTGS compliant. It indicates that all branches had core banking solutions and RTGS enabled. It is also to be noted that no respondent has experienced any delay in credit of RTGS amount to the account of the beneficiary at the destination. Hence, in the absence of any such problem, there was no waiting for getting the problems resolved.

If the RTGS mode is so fast and efficient and less costly, is there any other issue in adopting it fully for remittances. The table13 , however, gives an interesting input from the users point of view. None of the respondents felt that not being aware of how RTGS works is not coming in the way of using RTGS for payments/receipts. Procedure of RTGS is not cumbersome, indicate the responses. What is significant is the response regarding ready cash requirement for RTGS. Payment by cheque is giving some time for arranging for funds since there is a transit time for clearance, and a few days in case of outstation clearance. All the respondents have felt that receipt or payment by cheque will give them some breathing time to arrange for funds. This is one of the reasons why always payments are not made by way of RTGS. The graph 12 depicts this view of the business units. It is observed, this view prevails in all the business units who responded.

FEED BACK FROM BANK BRANCHES:

This section deals with the analysis and interpretation of data collected through interviewing managers/officers of bank branches. Interview method was adopted for collecting information from bank branches. The sequence of analysis goes according to the interview questions design and analysis of data reveals following information.

The feed back from 10 bank branches located in Vijayanagar area of Bangalore indicate that the RTGS is a) fast, efficient and low cost remittance scheme, b) Customers

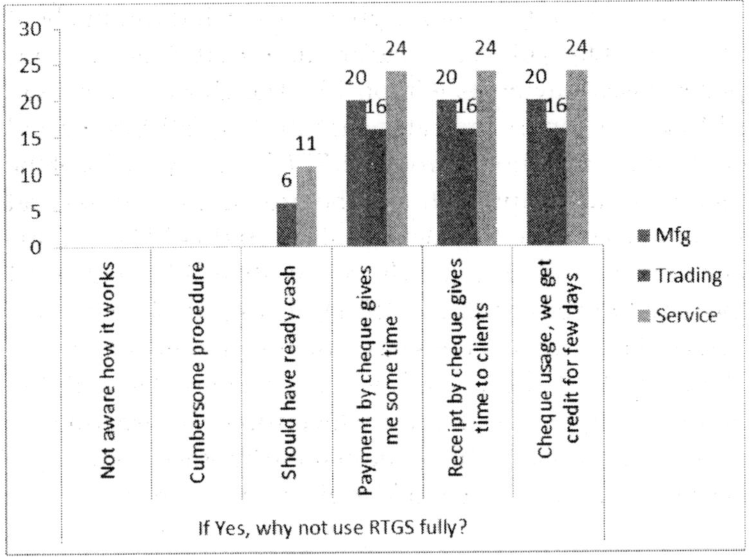

Graph 12

find it very useful and fast mode of remittance facility and charges are very low, c) The branch offices were not aware of any problems experienced by the customers, d) Customers are making use of RTGS on a larger scale now than earlier, e) Branches are not aware of the volume of RTGS transactions since large number of transactions take place on line, but the branches provide all assistance to customers who come to branch to make use of this facility including finding out the IFSC code of beneficiary branch, f) Branch Officers inform that there is a definite shift from DD remittance to RTGS usage.

ANALYSIS AT MACRO LEVEL

This section deals with the analysis and interpretation of data collected through secondary sources with regard to retail payment systems. The sources for secondary data are published material of RBI and other banks in print or in electronic media, internet and unpublished material from the bank branches.

The secondary source gives a clear indication about the increasing volume of electronic remittances vis a vis paper based payments (Graph 13). The above graph from RBI annual report indicates that in Aug 2010, the retail electronic transactions through NEFT/RTGS was 67% of the total volume. Graph 14 traces the growth in volumes and value in electronic transactions since 2003-04. The volume of electronic transactions which was about 12% in 2003-04 increased to about 40% in 2010-11till Aug 10. Similarly, the values of these transactions has shown a quantum jump from about 30% to about 90% during the same period (Graph 15). Share of Paper based versus Electronic Transactions is available in Similarly, the value of these transactions in paper based versus electronic mode is given in Graph 16 .

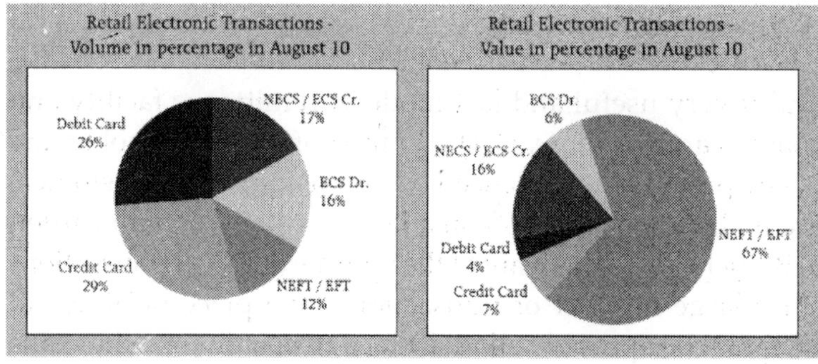

Graph 13

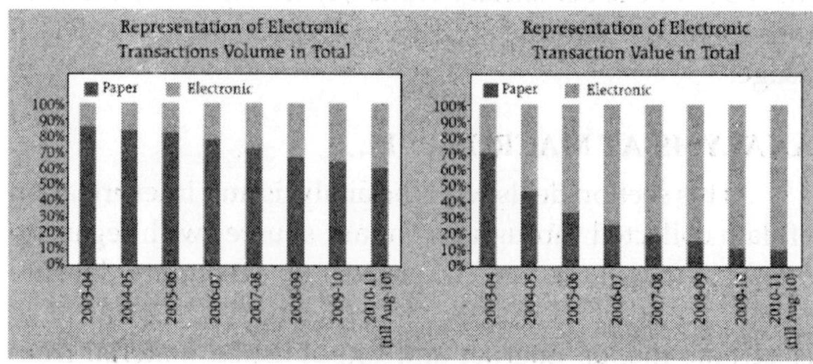

Graph 14

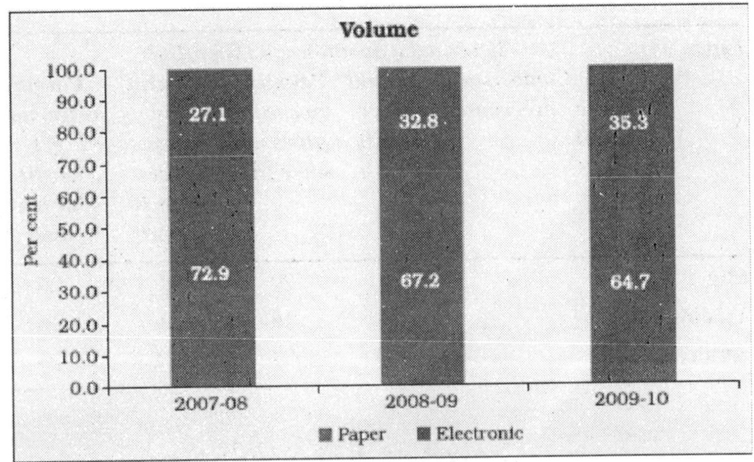

Graph 15

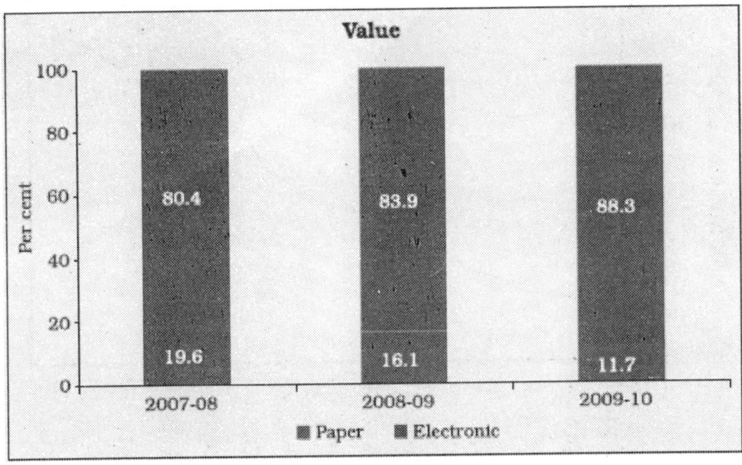

Graph 16

RTGS

Looking to the RTGS specific information, the below graphs and the tables taken from RBI report clearly indicate in increasing volumes and also values of RTGS transactions (Graph 17). A glance at the graph18 shows the increase in

Table 13

Type	*If Yes, why do not use RTGS fully?*					
	Not aware how it works	*Cumbersome procedure*	*should have ready cash*	*Payment by cheque gives me some time*	*Receipt by cheque gives time to clients*	*Cheque usage, we get credit for few days*
Mfg				20	20	20
Trading			6	16	16	16
Service			11	24	24	24

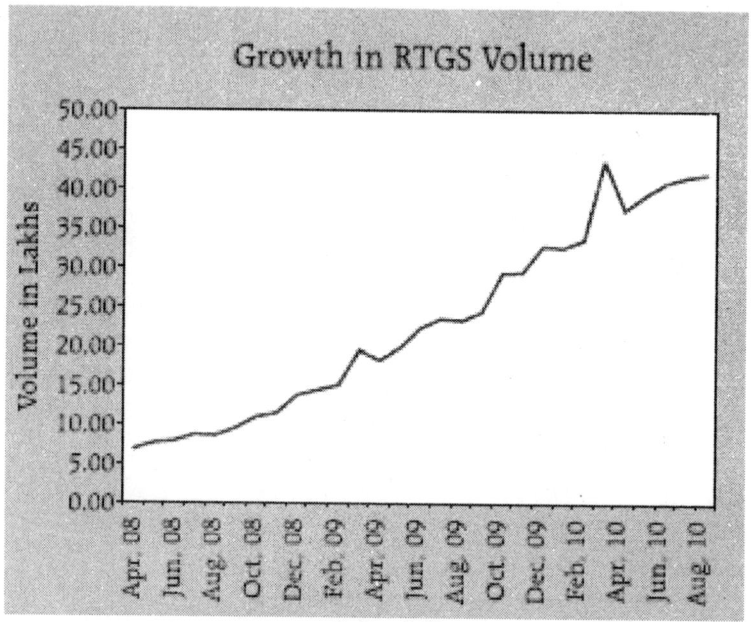

Graph 17

value of these transactions over a period from 2008 till Aug 2010. Coming to RTGS specific volumes, since its launch, there is a quantum jump which is indicated in the following table. The table gives year wise growth since launch. It significant to note that the customer transactions have grown by geometrical proportions both in volume and in value indicating the wider acceptability of the RTGS.

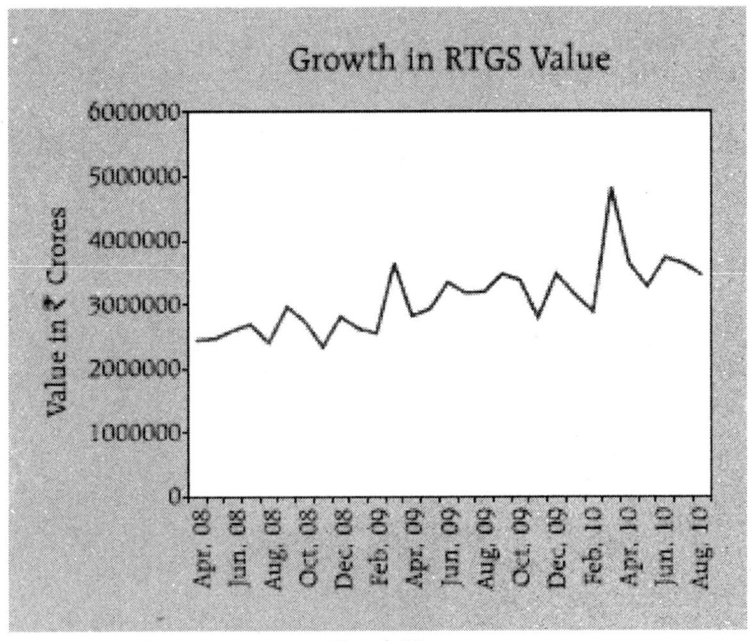

Graph 18

The growth of RTGS since inception in depicted in this table 14. The graph19 summarizes the performance of RTGS increase in values and volumes with interbank and customer break ups. Graph 20 shows that the number of transactions of customers has increased from about a million to nearly 33 million since 2005-06. The values have increased substantially for customers while there is a reduction in interbank values.

CONCLUSION

RTGS is regarded as the centre piece of an integrated payments system. It enables real time and on-line fund management for the financial system. Migration to an RTGS environment is the main objective of payments system reforms.

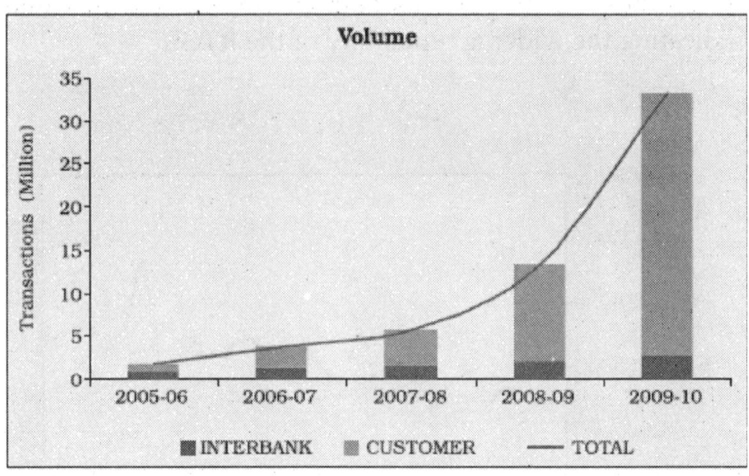

Graph 19

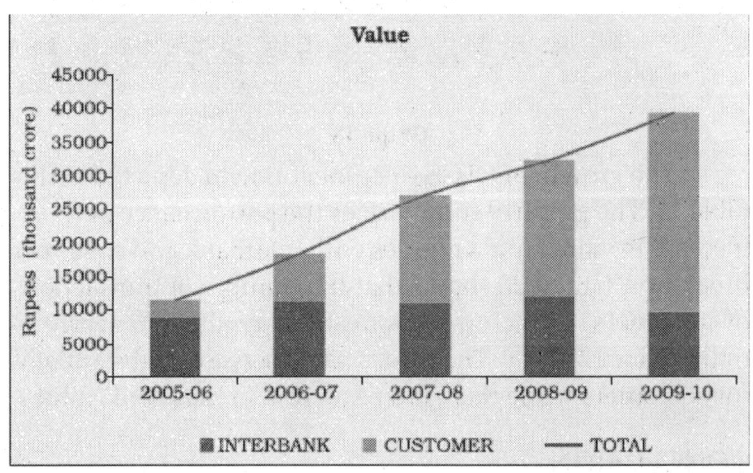

Graph 20

This paper had the objective of an overview of payment system, and also study the awareness level and problems, if any, in retail remittances.

Table 14

	Number	*Amount*
2003-04	1	1.965.49
2004-05	460	40,66,154.00
2005-06	1767	1,15,40,836.25
2006-07	38.8	2.46.19.179 99
2007-05	58.54	4,82,94,558.97
2008-09	133.84	6,11,39,912.44
2009-10	332.53	10,11,69,930.98
2009-10		
April	18.15	74,83,009.75
May	1951	93.67.545.14
June	22.32	1,00,45,166.89
July	23.45	99.66,068.81
August	23.24	92.45,113.39
September	24.34	92,58,141.64
October	29 26	84,49,696.31
November	2940	77,80,524.10
December	32.76	76,68,126.33
January	32.56	73.34,90073
February	33.57	69.00,93155
March	43.65	76,67,703.33
Total (upto Mar, 10)	**332.53**	**10,11,69,930.98**
2010-11		
April	37.35	70.71.951.51
May	39.31	56.77.573.95
June	40.87	68,40,564.36
July	41.55	67.16,06559
August	41.95	50.39.022.01
Total (upto Aug, 10)	**201.02**	**3,13,45,507.72**

All the units which responded made use of all the 3 modes, cash, cheque and electronic mode for receiving or making payments. Cash transactions were less than 10% of the total receipts or payments. Electronic mode has become a major method of effecting payments, both for institutional as well as retail payments. Electronic mode was used more by manufacturing units, comparatively lesser extent by trading and service units. All preferred electronic mode but for some ground level issues and awareness was very good.

The secondary data clearly establishes the growing importance of electronic payments.

The 3 issues at the ground level are a) **requirement of visit to branch**, a wider usage of net banking takes care of this problem. b**) IFSC code not known,** user friendly net banking sites will solve this. And c) **pre funding requirement for RTGS remittance.** Better working capital funds management by business units and genuine needbased working capital sanctions by banks should take care of this issue.

The electronic modes of payment and settlement systems and RTGS has taken deep roots, widely used for interbank payments and also for customer remittances. This along with ECS/NECS, NEFT and mobile banking is going to replace the paper based payment systems to a maximum extent. However the customers will continue to use cash and cheque modes, albeit, to a small extent. The interest free period for arranging funds is an advantage available for cash starved business units. This is one strong reason why paper based payment and settlement system is not going to vanish completely.

SUGGESTIONS

All banks may permit their customers to make use of internet banking for RTGS remittances.

The bank sites may be made more customer friendly making it easy to search and locate IFSC codes of the beneficiary branches.

The bank personnel handling the RTGS/NEFT desk should have a thorough understanding of the functioning of the system and encourage and educate users about the superiority of RTGS as regards speed, efficiency and cost.

Banks/branches may consider sanction/enhancement of cash credit limits to meet customers' genuine requirements. Improved working capital funds would have a bearing on further usage of NEFT/RTGS.

All large value and time critical payments shall be processed only through RTGS.

All bank branches have to be enabled with IFSC codes. The reach of RTGS and NEFT should be extended to all banks including Regional Rural Banks.

Improved RTGS, migration to its new version of 24x7 and one to one fund transfer system on the lines of Faster Payments Service in UK by modifying the NEFT system for 24x7 have to be the next developments.

The concept of a domestic payment card is in the offing and may come in to existence in 2011. The mobile payment network is expected to revolutionize the payment system in the country. There are 600+ million mobile connections in the country, may be more than bank accounts and this has tremendous potential for having a cost and hassle free payment system for small retail payments

REFERENCES

1. RBI-*Risks Associated with Payment Systems and Risk Mitigation Measures, 2008*
2. *Article on Indian Banking Sector: "The challenges that the banking sector in India faces" Knowledge Base website 'mbaknol' and other articles*

3. *RBI website, the speech of Sri V.Leeladhar Dy Governor, in Sept 2008, on P&S Systems,*
4. *RBI website-speech of Sri Vasudevan, Executive Director, RBI, Sept 2008 in the conference at IDRBT,*
5. *RBI annual report, June 2010*
6. *RBI – Payment System Vision 09-12*
7. *RBI Web sites and internet banking sites of various banks,*
8. *NPCI website, latest data available in the site as on Oct10 and information of mobile banking*
9. *IBA site home page on P&S Systems*

30

Innovations in Modern Banking – A Tool for Inclusive Growth

C. A. Visalakshi

INTRODUCTION

Banks are the financial epicentres of economic growth and progress of the country and its citizens. They are the catalysts and changing agents responsible for bringing economic prosperity and improvements in the lives of millions. Their responsibilities lie in bringing the gap of economic inequality by providing equal opportunities to all rural and urban, poor and rich, across states, regions and communities. "A good bank is not only the financial heart of the community, but one with an obligation of helping in every manner possible to improve the economic conditions of the poor."

Even after passing of four decades of bank nationalization and increasing number of banks and their coverage across India, the extent and degree of financial exclusion is large. It is in this context that expanding banking access assumes far more significant today. Banks have to play a very crucial role in fulfilling this dream of covering every household and citizen in the formal banking net and making India realize its true potential as a vibrant economy with prosperity all-round.

Driving financial inclusion through enhancing banking access is in the national forefront of national policy agenda and is viewed as a right step towards achieving the inclusive growth objectives

The objective of this paper is to examine the opportunities and challenges posed by technological innovations in banking in achieving inclusive growth.

WHAT IS FINANCIAL INCLUSION

The committee on financial inclusion headed by Dr. Rangarajan, 2008, defines "financial inclusion is the process of ensuring access to financial services and timely and adequate credit where needed by vulnerable groups such as weaker sections and low income groups at an affordable cost."

Financial inclusion means the provision of affordable financial services, viz, access to payments and remittance facilities, savings, loans and insurance services by the formal financial system to those who tend to be excluded (Thorat, 2006)

Thus financial inclusion is about providing cost effective financial services to those who have been hitherto excluded through expanding banking access and providing all financial services like small value payments and remittances, savings, loans and insurance services.

NEED FOR FINANCIAL INCLUSION IN INDIA

A society beset with instances of neglect and exploitation requires development from a holistic approach. Every individual should be incorporated in the development process. Development from the angle of welfare programs by the government cannot ensure proper growth unless the financial system becomes a part of it. This was the logic of bank nationalization and other rural programmes like integrated rural development programme (IRDP), National Rural Employment Programme (NREP), 20point program, and national rural employment guarantee scheme. To include beneficiaries into the financial ambit, banks opened accounts and provided financial assistance to people. There is an urgent need to extend banking and financial services to every part of the country for achieving the objective of inclusive growth. The eleventh plan document tries to restructure policies in order to make growth faster, broad based and inclusive by reducing fragmentation of the society. Broadly the policies aim at increasing the income and employment opportunities on the one hand and on the other they try to finance programmes which are capable of making growth more inclusive. According to K.C.Chakrabarty ,Deputy Governor, RBI, "though the Indian economy achieved a high growth momentum from 2003-04 to 2007-08,it could not bring down unemployment and poverty to tolerable levels .Further a vast majority of the population remained outside the ambit of basic health and education facilities during this high growth phase. This made inclusive growth the focal point for the economic development exercise.

VARIOUS PHASES OF FINANCIAL INCLUSION IN INDIA

1950-70 : Consolidation of the banking sector &facilitation of industry & trade.

1970-90 : Focus on channeling of credit to neglected sectors and weaker sections.

1990-05 : Focus on strengthening the financial institutions as part of financial sector reforms

2005 onwards financial inclusion was explicitly made as a policy objective.

FINANCIAL INCLUSION -SOME INDICATORS

Number of No-frill Accounts : 4.15crore (as on June 30,2009)

Number of Rural Bank Branches : 31,727 constituting 39.7%of total bank branches.(As on June 30,2009)

Number of Atms : 47,953(as on July 31 2009) (chart 1)

Number of Pos : 5,22,148 (as on July 31,2009)

Number of Kisan Credit Cards : 76 million (source: CMIE publication 2007-08)

Number of GCC Issued By PSBS : 52,824 (as on march 31,2009)

Number of Mobile Phones : 403 million (as on April 30,2009),out of which 187 million (46%) do not have a bank account.

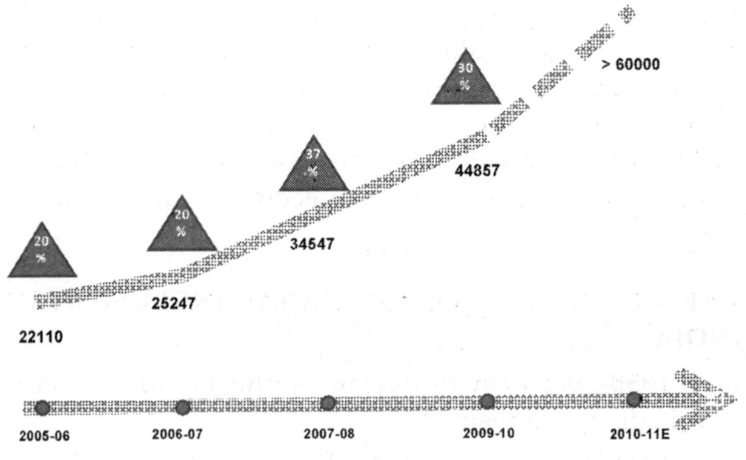

Chart 1. Growth of ATMs in India

***Source*: Cyber media research DQ Estimates**

FINANCIAL EXCLUSION - SOME INDICATORS

Estimates based on various studies and Market Surveys:

- Only 17 credit accounts per 100 persons with all the institutions.
- Only 54 savings accounts per 100persons with all the institutions
- Only 13% are availing loans from the income bracket of less than Rs.50,000
- 53% are taking loans from the institutional and non institutional sources only for emergency purposes.
- Critical exclusion in terms of credit is manifest in 256 Districts across 17 States and Union Territories (Dadra & Nagarhavely).
- Even rich people are excluded and have to depend on non institutional sources for loan purposes (chart 2).

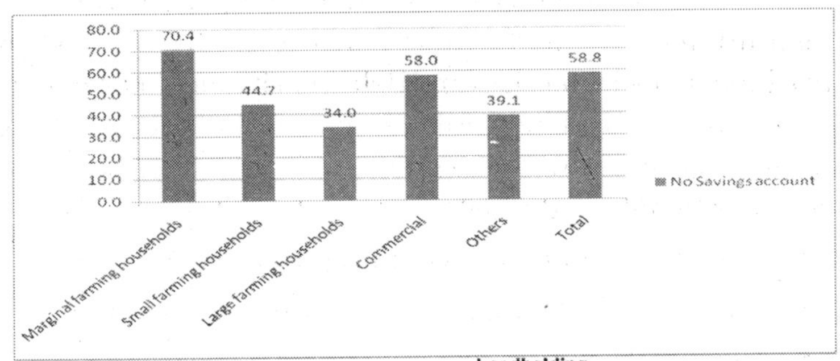

Landholding
Marginal farming households < 1 acre
Small farming households = 1 to 4 acres
Large farming households > 4 acres

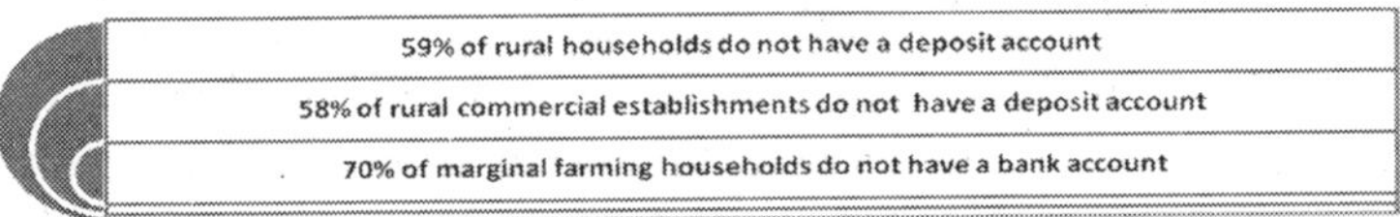

Chart 2. Percentage of Unbanked Rural Households

TECHNOLOGY FOR INCLUSIVE GROWTH

Technology has revolutionised every industry in the world by rendering faster and cost effective delivery of products and services to customers, who in the normal course could not have afforded the same, and at the same time the producers of goods and services would remain viable and profitable. Technology is surest and most appropriate way of bringing inclusion in respect of any product or service.

As regards the banking sector, technology has completely changed the nature and pace of delivery of banking services the world over. It has not only improved the speed but also the quality of the services delivered and has ensured tremendous reduction in transaction costs for the banks as well as the customers and made it possible to provide customer service through various delivery channels.

Technology would be required for providing banking access and other relevant information to customers, as also to enhance the product range. By leveraging IT, financial institutions can extend their reach to create flexible far reaching financial services and delivery channels more suited to rural areas. The following are the areas where technological innovation could provide greater access to credit or financial services.

- Savings, credit and insurance products.
- client access to market and product information
- institutional management information systems
- credit scoring
- financial education

In a developing country like India, technological advancement enabled a broader and inclusive banking sector and in the process, is a key driver for the sustained and inclusive growth of the economy. RBI, having realised the close association between technology, inclusion and economic growth, with the help of institutions, such as IDRBT on the one hand and banking sector on the other, have actively involved in utilizing technology for the development of Indian banking sector.

The changing face of banking sector aided by technological innovations can be seen from various developments in the recent past. Important among them is usage of ATM technology. The success of ATMs had made the banking sector develop more innovative delivery channels to build on cost and service efficiencies. As a consequence, banks have begun to introduce Tele-banking, Call centres, Internet banking and Mobile banking.

Tele banking is the good medium for customers to make routine queries and also an efficient tool for banks to cut down their manpower resources. The call centre is another channel that captured the imagination of banks as well as customers. At these centres enormous amount of information is at the fingertips of trained customer service representatives. Mobile banking can be regarded as 'the delivery channel of the future. This is because it offers portability and convenience to the user. It is just like having a 'bank account in the pocket.'

Without an appropriate banking solution, it would not have been possible for banks to give the full benefits of telebanking, mobile banking, internet banking ,card banking (multiple delivery channels) to all its customers .Centralised Core Banking System(CBS) has been one such development which has revolutionalised the banking sector. CBS can be defined as a solution that enables banks to offer a multitude of customer centric services from a single location, supporting retail as well as corporate banking activities, as well as all possible delivery channels, existing and proposed. Using CBS, customers can access their accounts from any branch, anywhere, irrespective of where they have physically opened their accounts.

CHALLENGES

Financial exclusion : It has been found that financial services are used only by a section of population. There is demand for these services, but it has not been provided. The excluded ones are rural, poor regions, and also those living in harsh climatic conditions where it is difficult to provide these financial services. The excluded population then has to depend on informal sector for availing finance.

High cost : Banks and their customers have to incur relatively high costs to access financial services in rural areas because of large costs of covering the huge numbers (cost of enrollment) and relative high maintenance costs for such accounts. It has been seen that the poor living in urban areas don't use the financial services as they find financial services costly and thus are unaffordable. Hence, even if financial services are available, the high costs deter the poor from accessing them

Non price barriers : Access to financial services also requires documents of proof regarding a person's identity, income etc. The poor people do not have these documents and thus are excluded from these services. They may also subscribe to the services initially but may not use them as actively as others because of long distance between the bank and the residence, poor infrastructure etc.

Behavioral aspects : Research in behavioral economics has shown that many people are not comfortable in using formal financial services. The reasons are difficulty in understanding language, various documents and conditions that come with financial services etc.

- In rural areas people are reluctant to go to bank - 91% of villagers do not have a branch within 2km and almost one in four does not have a branch within 10km radius.
- Rural sector continues to depend predominantly on

cash transactions. While servicing rural customers, banks might have to find out low cost ATMs with innovative features, keeping the demand profile of the rural customer in mind. There is a need to extend the shared network of ATMs for the use of hitherto excluded people.

- In India, banking penetration itself is very low and most of the rural people are hostile to the modern technology banking concept. Most of them even today believe in traditional banking methods of accounts keeping and would like to interact with a human over the counter rather than punching a few keys to transact their hard earned money.
- Technologies like Internet banking, Mobile banking, Phone banking etc, has helped banking service evolve into customer oriented and customer driven process. All the processes and systems exist to make the consumers' interaction better, simple and easy to his convenience and satisfaction. Many people do not use internet banking as they are content with the way they source their banking services. Some customers associate risks especially security risks with using internet and mobile technology.
- Consumers perceive lack of control over technology and feel overwhelmed by it. The reason is lack of communication as to what will happen after the command is executed and the request is placed on-line. Banks should ensure that the communication is clear and loud to the customer that the basic process of banking is the same as the human interaction model involved in the branch banking.
- Illiteracy and unfamiliarity with the technology - A good number of rural centres are lacking the basic infrastructure facilities like uninterrupted power

supply, communication media, technical back-up services and requisite skills and knowledge. Technical illiteracy makes the rural masses stay away from availing the modern banking services.

Small ticket size for each transaction, need for communication modes suited to the illiterate and in local language, affordability of the product or service, need for local acceptance and involvement of locally acceptable personnel are the other challenges of financial inclusion.

STEPS TAKEN BY RBI

Banks have been asked to open no frill accounts with minimum or zero balances. Banks are required to make available all printed material used by retail customers in the concerned regional language(chart3).

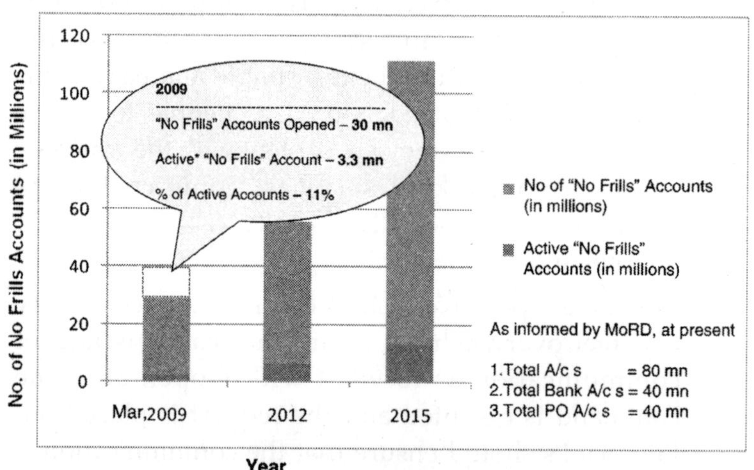

Active Accounts are those with more than two transactions per year

Chart 3. No Frills" Bank Accounts

***Source*: Speeding Financial Inclusion - Skoch Development Foundation(20th Skoch Summit, 16-17 July 09, Mumbai - Inclusive Growth 2.0) National Seminar on Launching a National Initiative for Financial Inclusion (NABARD) - September, 09**

Simplification of KYC norms

Credit counseling centres and financial education centres to be opened at the district level by banks. A multilingual website in 13 Indian languages on all matters concerning banking and the common person has been launched by the Reserve bank on 18 June 2007.

Introduction of IT enabled financial inclusion using smart cards for opening bank accounts through biometric identification.

Banks have been asked to consider introduction of a general purpose credit card (GCC) facility up to Rs. 25000/- at their rural and semi urban branches. The credit facility is in the nature of revolving credit entitling the holder to withdraw upto the limit sanctioned. Based on assessment of household cash flows, the limits are sanctioned without insistence on security or purpose. Interest rate on the facility is completely deregulated.

Banks have been advised to utilize the services of self help groups and Non Government Organisations to provide microfinance facilities through the use of business facilitators (BF) and business correspondents (BC).

State governments are encouraged to route social security payments under various programmes including NREGS through such smart cards.

A working group constituted to examine the experience of date of the BC model and suggest measures to, enlarge the category of persons that can act as BCs keeping in view the regulatory and supervisory framework and consumer protection issues.

Allowing RRBs/Co-Operative banks to sell insurance and financial products.

100 % financial inclusion - so far 431 districts have been identified by SLBCs for 100% financial inclusion - as on March 31st 2009, 204 districts in 18 states and 5 union

territories have reported having achieved the target.

OPPORTUNITIES

Lack of infrastructure can be addressed in a variety of ways by leveraging technology. The new technologies and information based systems can be used for expanding the coverage of Indian banking and financial systems to underserved markets. The use of smart card technology, mobile ATMs, coverage of post offices under electronic payment networks in remote areas could play a significant role in providing financial services to unbanked and under banked people. Smart cards can be used to provide other financial services like low cost remittances and insurance. Link to mobile or hand held connectivity devices ensure that the transactions are recorded in the bank's books on real time basis.

One key driver which can bring a sea change in the financial inclusion process is the application of information and communication technology (ICT). ICT, due to its scalability can change the cost structure and increase the banking services' accessibility in a major way.

Banks must be encouraged to adopt IT solutions that are secure, amenable to audit and ensure inter-operability among different systems. The use of IT also enables banks to handle the enormous increase in the volume of transactions for millions of households for processing, credit scoring, credit record and follow up.

RBI should initiate steps to reach out to remote villages with a focus on financial education to educate low income groups to demand financial services and to encourage banks to supply the financial services needed by the poor.

Banks have to realign their systems to enable BC models simultaneously preventing chances of frauds and misappropriations.

In today's world of cut-throat competition in the banking sector, retaining customers along with growing customer base has become very important. In order to enhance the effectiveness of the various channels such as branch banking, mobile banking and internet banking, banks may consider the use of a comprehensive customer relationship management (CRM) solution which would enable them to access the entire customer details and provide a 360 degree view across channels and products and enhance service quality. CRM can be defined as the process that has the potential to make the right offer to the right client at the right time via the right channel. CRM is thus recognized as an avenue for banks to go beyond other banks in terms of customer retention and increase in business volumes.

Since 2002, mobile subscribers have grown faster than bank account holders. There is a need to leverage mobile technology & penetration to provide basic financial services to the unbanked (chart 4 & 5)

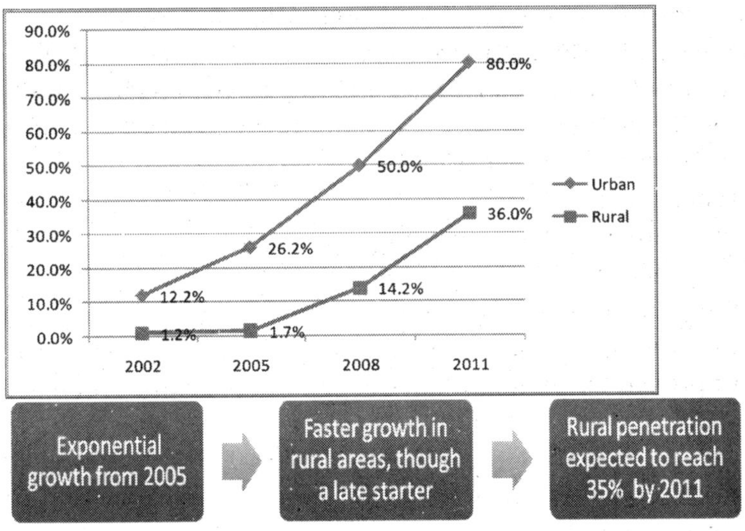

Chart 4. Mobile Growth Story

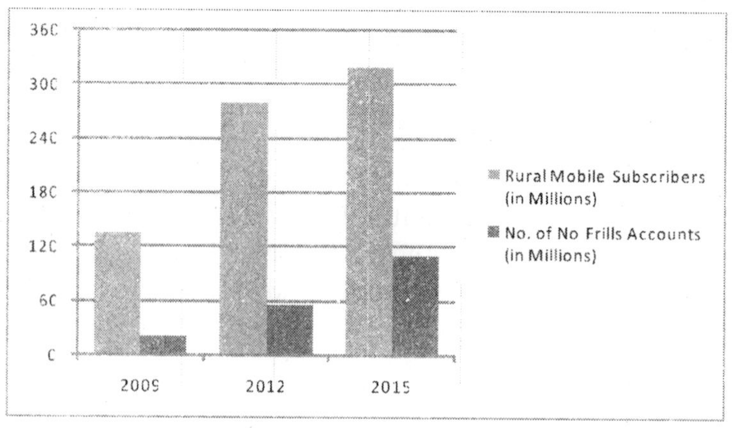

Chart 5. Mobile Subscribers Vs. Bank A/c Holders (Rural)

CONCLUSION

Inclusive growth has appeared to be an essential part of economic planning and financial inclusion has been accorded importance for making inclusive growth a successful venture. A large section of the community remains financially excluded where institutional sources of finance have not been able to reach and bring them into the ambit of the developmental and financial process. With the help of technology and increased usage of e - banking, banks can reach larger masses of people at low costs and with innovative products, allowing customers to access them from anywhere and at anytime. In short, technology has to enable the branch to go where the customer is present instead of the other way around .By adopting vibrant, innovative and improved technological modes of banking, banks can reach out to the poor and low income clients and provide them with affordable financial services tailored to their needs and there by lifting them up, to be at par with the privileged class.

REFERENCES

1. Rangarajan Committee Report on Financial Inclusion, 2008
2. Usha Thorat- - Financial Inclusion - The Indian experience
3. Website of Reserve Bank of India
4. Website of IDBI
5. Indian Banker-Nov &, Dec 2008, Oct, NOV-2010.
6. Economic Research-March 2008

31
Electronic Banking In India- Issues And Challengs

M. Ramanjaneyulu

INTRODUCTION

Electronic banking has been around for some time in the form of internet banking, automatic teller machines, telephone and mobile banking transactions. E- Banking is the banking of new era banking. Making banking products and services available to wholesale and retail customers, through an electronic distribution channel is called E-Banking. E-Banking is the outcome of technological innovation and competition. In fact, banks have been using electronic and telecommunication network for delivering a wide range of value added products and services.

The evolving concept of E- banking is the process of delivering banking services and products through electronic channels. E- Banking has the capacity to improve efficiency, convenience and speed of delivery and transactions. Telecommunications, information technology, plastic money, bar code, hologram, magnetic strip and apical memory card and ATM (Table 1) More recently, it has been transformed by the Internet, a new delivery channel for banking services that benefits both customers and banks. Access is fast, convenient, and available around the clock, whatever the customer's location. In addition, banks can provide services more efficiently and at substantially lower costs. For example, a typical customer transaction costing about $1 in a traditional "brick and mortar" bank branch or $0.60 through a phone call costs only about $0.02 online (Figure 1).

Table 1. Telephones and Internet and Mobiles in India 2008

Telephone Penetration	
1. Mobile and fixed line phone subscriptions per 100 people	14%
2. Population covered Mobile Phones network	61%
3. % 'Growth Population based on 2000-2008	979
Interenet	
4. Internet users per 100 people	45%
5. Broad Band Subscriptions per 100 people	0.50%
6. Personal Computer per 100 people 2006-08	3.20%
7. % 'Growth Population based on 2000-2008	850%
Mobiles	
8. Mobile phone connections charge Accessibility and Cost	2.30%
9.Fixed Line Phone "Connections charges 2006-08	6.90%
10. Price per 3 minutes local fixed line phone call	2

Source: Real Wealth of Nations Pathway to Human Development HRD-2010 UNDP.

Note: 5,000 'Telephone Towers every year in the next five years is needed.

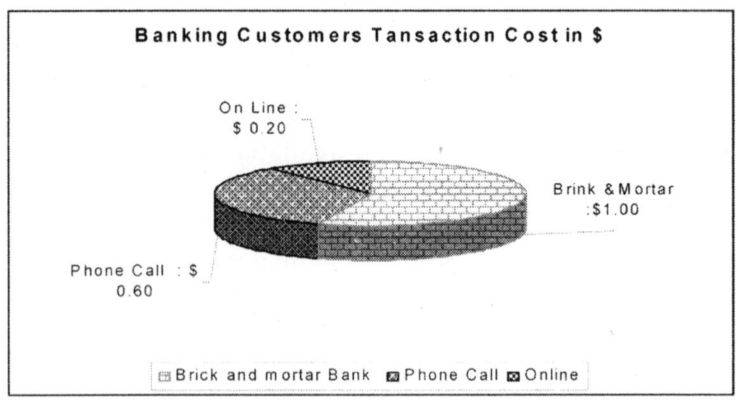

Fig. 1

TRENDS IN ELOCTRONIC BANKING

Trends in electronic banking or Internet banking are gaining ground. Banks increasingly operate websites through which customers are able not only to inquire about account balances and interest and exchange rates but also to conduct a range of transactions. Unfortunately, data on Internet banking are scarce, and differences in definitions make cross-country comparisons difficult. Even so, one finds that Internet banking is particularly widespread in Austria, Korea, the Scandinavian countries, Singapore, Spain, and Switzerland, where more than 75 percent of all banks offer such services. The Scandinavian countries have the largest number of Internet users, with up to one-third of bank customers in Finland and Sweden taking advantage of e-banking.

In the United States, Internet banking is still concentrated in the largest banks. In mid-2001, as many as 44 percent of national banks maintained transactional websites, almost double the number in the third quarter of 1999. These banks account for over 90 percent of national banking system assets. The larger banks tend to offer a wider array of electronic banking services, including loan applications and brokerage services. While most U.S. consumers have accounts with banks that offer Internet services, only about 6 percent of them use these services.

- Concept of E-banking is more prevalent in the technologically developed parts of the world such as Europe and the US
- The number of online banks in Western Europe has mushroomed. As per Bluesky International Marketing, a US based research agency, the number is quoted at 1,845 in mid 1999.
- The scene is similar in the US where a recent Dataquest survey forecasts that the number of US households banking online will reach 24.2 million by 2004.
- 33 private banks and 43 foreign banks
- 27 public sector banks account for over 84 per cent of the total deposits and over 82 per cent of the total banking advances in India
- Rough estimates assuming teller at Rs. 1 per transaction put ATM transaction costs at 45p, phone banking at 35p, debit cards at 20p and Internet banking a measly 10p.

Most of the banks have combined the new electronic delivery channels with traditional brick and mortar branches ("brick and click" banks), but a small number have emerged that offer their products and services predominantly, or only, through electronic distribution channels. These "virtual" or Internet-only banks do not have a branch network but might have a physical presence, for example, an administrative office or non-branch facilities like kiosks or automatic teller machines. The United States has about 30 virtual banks; Asia has 2, launched in 2000 and 2001; and the European Union has several-either as separately licensed entities or as subsidiaries or branches of brick and mortar banks.

The digital divide between rich and poor and public and private banks and problems of security is widening. A multilayered security architecture comprising of firewalls, filtering routers, encryptions and digital certification is also playing an important role in e-banking.

Electronic banking also makes it easier for customers to compare banks' services and products, can increase competition among banks, and allows banks to penetrate new markets and thus expand their geographical reach. Some even see electronic banking as an opportunity for countries with underdeveloped financial systems to leapfrog developmental stages. Customers in such countries can access services more easily from banks abroad and through wireless communication systems, which are developing more rapidly than traditional "wired" communication networks.

THE RESERVE BANK OF INDIA

The Reserve Bank of India (RBI) has actively promoted the use of technology in the banking sector to achieve its goal of financial inclusion and bringing down transaction costs. This has resulted in increased spending by banks to upgrade information technology infrastructure.

The three major technology changes so far have been core banking solutions (CBS), automated teller machines (ATM) and electronic payment systems such as real-time gross settlement (RTGS) and national electronic funds transfer (NEFT).

While new private sector banks and foreign banks have the edge when it comes to computerisation, public sector banks have not lagged behind in making investments to computerise their operations. As of end-March 2010, 97.8 per cent of all the public sector bank branches have been fully computerised. Of them, 90 per cent provide CBS. This figure was 79.4 per cent at the end of the previous fiscal(Table 2 & Figure 2).

Table 2. Major return on investment by investing in online financial services *(% of banks in survey)*

Return on Investment in Online Financial Serivices	*Percentage*
1. Cost Savings	27%
2. Customer retention	22 %
3. Cross selling of services	19%
4. Customer acquisition and additional revenues (fees and interest)	15%

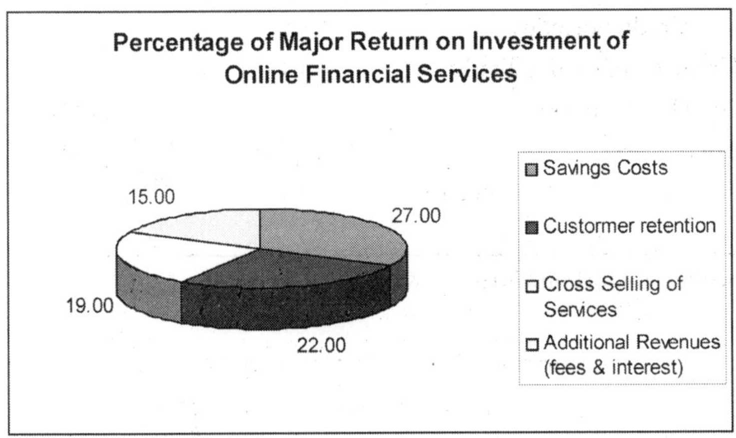

Fig. 2

Recently several policy initiatives have been taken by the Government/Reserve Bank to improve the credit flow to agriculture and the needy sectors. These measures had a significant positive impact on **financial inclusion** as revealed by the data for subsequent periodThe credit rate of SCBs has increased by 46.27 per cent during 2002 and 2007, which is followed by urban cooperative banks by 37.57 per cent, credit rate of RRBs has also increased by 12.33 per cent and the Self Help Groups has increased by 210.56 per cent. The increase of number of accounts has registered at 24.48 per cent (Table 3 and Figure 3).

Table 3. Number of Accounts with Institutions and Credit since 2002

Access to Credit Since 2002 Number of Accounts with Institutions in Millions			
	2002	*2007*	*% increase*
Scheduled Commercial Banks.	43.3	76.6	46.27
Regional Rural Banks	12.6	15	12.33
Sub Total	55.9	91.6	38.99
Others :Primary Agricultural Credit Societies	55.5	47.9	-9.35
Urban Cooperative Banks	4.4	7.1	37.57
Self Help Groups	7.4	40.5	210.56
Total	123.3	187.1	32.05
Number of Accounts per 100 Adults of all insti	18	25	24.48

Source: Report on Currency & Finance 2006-08

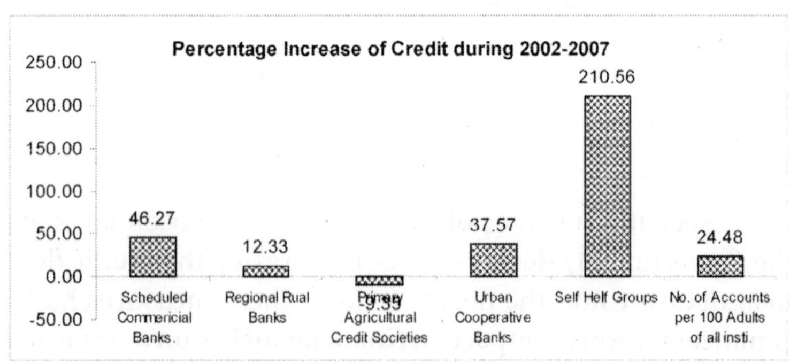

Fig. 3

Accessibility of the public to saving accounts of RRBs has increased by 27.28 per cent which is followed by SCBs with 19.23 per cent and Primary Agricultural Credit Societies with 14.93 per cent and Urban Cooperatives with 13.05 per cent. The lowest saving rate has registered from Post Offices by 0.66 per cent. Thus there is increasing of saving accounts at 9.06 per cent per annum (Table4 and Figure 4).

Table 4. Number of Accounts with Institutions and Savings since 2002

Access to Savings Accounts - Since 2002 Number of Accounts with institutions in Millions			
	2002	***2007***	***% increase***
Scheduled Commercial Banks	246.5	320.9	19.23
Regional Rural Banks	36.7	52.7	27.28
Sub Total	283.2	373.6	20.28
Others: Primary Agriculture Credit Societies	102.1	125.8	14.93
Urban Cooperative Banks	41.6	50	13.05
Post Offices	60.2	60.8	0.66
Total	487.1	610.2	16.21
No.of Accounts per 100 Adults of all institu.	72	82	9.06

Source: Report on Currency & Finance 2006-08

Another very important policy measure in January 2006 was to allow banks to adopt the agency model or what is known as the Business facilitator / Business Correspondent model for achieving greater outreach through intermediaries / agents. The results have been extremely impressive. In just two years the number of no frills accounts opened by banks has increased from around half a million accounts in March 2006 to 15 million in 2008. Going by the data from service providers offering smart card solutions , it may be assumed that smart card accounts probably account for 2 to 3 million of these no frills accounts. Evaluation by external agencies appointed by RBI has shown that while the first stage of opening no frills accounts has been quite impressive, due to

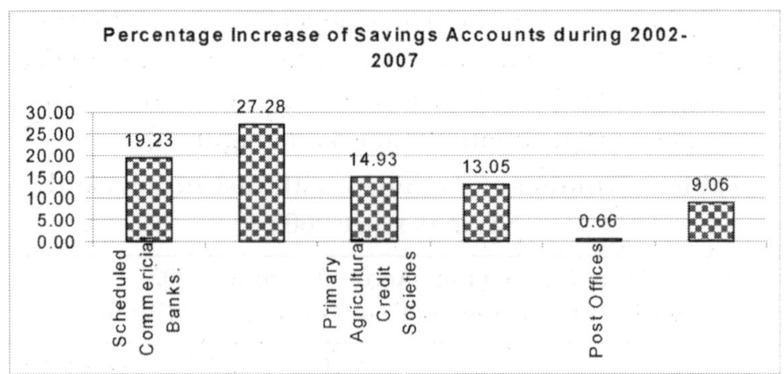

Fig. 4

inadequate of follow up, cost of transaction and access constraints, in many cases the accounts have not been operated upon at all after having been opened. In order to improve access and use of these accounts , banks will have to offer the services much closer to the customer either through mobile branches, satellite offices, extension counters or using intermediaries like SHGs/MFIs or through business correspondents using IT to increase scale , access and reduce cost.

In the past 10 years, public sector banks have spent close to Rs.22,000 crore on computerisation and IT upgrades. For the final half of the 2010 fiscal alone, spending on this account stood at Rs.1,370 crore (Table5).

STATE BANK OF INDIA

Thanks to core banking solutions Core Banking Solutions CBS technology, State Bank of India's capability to handle transactions went up more than three times. As of April 2010, SBI could handle 35 million transactions a day as against 10 million earlier.

Table 5. Number of Accounts opened by banks and No Frills Accounts

No Frills Accounts -Banks' Progress No. of Accounts opened by banks as on			
Category	*Mar 31 2006*	*Mar 31 2007*	*Mar 31 2008*
Public Sector Banks	332,878	5,865,419	13,925,674
% increase	-	1662.03	137.42
Private Sector Banks	156,388	856,495	1,879,073
% increase	-	447.67	119.39
Foreign Banks	231	2,753	33,115
% increase	-	1091.77	1102.87
Total	489,497	6,724,667	15,837,862
% increase	-	1273.79	135.52

Source: Report on Currency & Finance 2006-08

The bank started the move towards Core Banking Solutions CBS in early 2000, and the implementation was complete by 2008. The entire project was handled by Tata Consultancy Services (TCS), which was the systems integrator, while the other major technology partners in the project were Hewlett-Packard (HP), Data craft, Cisco and Microsoft.

Since 2003, SBI has witnessed a 60 per cent increase in customer account. Bank officials say this is primarily on account of quicker transactions.

All SBI branches are interconnected from a centralised IT department located at Belapur, Navi Mumbai. The bank has spent more than Rs.5,000 crore since September 1999 for the implementation of CBS and computerisation of its various branches. In the last half of the 2010 fiscal, it spent Rs.429 crore.

The advantages of the system are easier rectification of errors, minimisation of fraud and the elimination of human error. Bank of India has spent close to Rs.1,500 crore on technological upgradation and computerisation of its branches since September 1999.

AUTOMATED TELLER MACHINES (ATMS)

The Reserve Bank of India (RBI) has actively promoted the use of technology in the banking sector to achieve its goal of financial inclusion and bringing down transaction costs. This has resulted in increased spending by banks to upgrade information technology infrastructure. The growth of ATMs in the country has revolutionised cash advances made by banks. Off-site ATMs, in particular, have aided in the RBI's goal of financial inclusion.

"ATMs have been a big success. They have helped in banking services reaching different parts of the country," said Kalyan Sundar. Almost 75 per cent of Bank of India's cash advances are made through ATMs now.

Off-site ATMs of public sector banks witnessed a 70 per cent increase in the 2010 fiscal from the previous fiscal. The number grew from 9,898 in end-March 2009 to 16,883 by end-March 2010.

For private sector banks, the growth in the number of off-site ATMs in the 2010 fiscal has been around 19 per cent. The number stood at 9,844 in end-March 2010 as against 8,324 in the previous year.

The three major technology changes so far have been core banking solutions (CBS), automated teller machines (ATM) and electronic payment systems such as real-time gross settlement (RTGS) and national electronic funds transfer (NEFT).

While new private sector banks and foreign banks have the edge when it comes to computerisation, public sector banks have not lagged behind in making investments to computerise their operations. As of end-March 2010, 97.8 per cent of all the public sector bank branches have been fully computerised. Of them, 90 per cent provide CBS. This figure was 79.4 per cent at the end of the previous fiscal.

Thanks to core banking solutions Core Banking Solutions CBS technology, State Bank of India's capability to handle transactions went up more than three times. As of April 2010, SBI could handle 35 million transactions a day as against 10 million earlier.

The bank started the move towards core banking solutions CBS in early 2000, and the implementation was complete by 2008. The entire project was handled by Tata Consultancy Services (TCS), which was the systems integrator, while the other major technology partners in the project were Hewlett-Packard (HP), Datacraft, Cisco and Microsoft.

Since 2003, SBI has witnessed a 60 per cent increase in customer account. Bank officials say this is primarily on account of quicker transactions.

All SBI branches are interconnected from a centralised IT department located at Belapur, Navi Mumbai. The bank has spent more than Rs.5,000 crore since September 1999 for the implementation of core banking solutions CBS and computerisation of its various branches. In the last half of the 2010 fiscal, it spent Rs.429 crore.

The advantages of the system are easier rectification of errors, minimisation of fraud and the elimination of human error. Bank of India has spent close to Rs.1,500 crore on technological upgradation and computerisation of its branches since September 1999.

P.A. Kalyan Sundar, General Manager - IT, Bank of India, said, "Bank of India is now 100 per cent on CBS. This helps in quicker transactions in almost real time. Errors are minimised, and, overall, it is better for both the customer and the bank."

The number of on-site ATMs for public sector banks showed a growth of 36 per cent. The number grew to 23,797 as of end-March 2010 from 17,379 in the previous fiscal. In the past 10 years, public sector banks have spent close to Rs.22,000 crore on computerisation and IT upgrades. For the final half of the 2010 fiscal alone, spending on this account stood at Rs.1,370 crore.

NEW CHALLENGES FOR REGULATORS

The changing financial landscape brings with it new challenges for bank management and regulatory and supervisory authorities. The major ones stem from increased cross-border transactions resulting from drastically lower transaction costs and the greater ease of banking activities, and from the reliance on technology to provide banking services with the necessary security.

Regulatory risk : Because the Internet allows services to be provided from anywhere in the world, there is a danger that banks will try to avoid regulation and supervision. What can regulators do? They can require even banks that provide their services from a remote location through the Internet to be licensed. Licensing would be particularly appropriate where supervision is weak and cooperation between a virtual bank and the home supervisor is not adequate. Licensing is the norm, for example, in the United States and most of the countries of the European Union. A virtual bank licensed outside these jurisdictions that wishes to offer electronic banking services and take deposits in these countries must first establish a licensed branch.

Determining when a bank's electronic services trigger the need for a license can be difficult, but indicators showing where banking services originate and where they are provided can help. For example, a virtual bank licensed in country X is not seen as taking deposits in country Y if customers make their deposits by posting checks to an address in country X. If a customer makes a deposit at an automatic teller machine in country Y, however, that transaction would most likely be considered deposit taking in country. Regulators need to establish guidelines to clarify the gray areas between these two cases.

Legal risk : Electronic banking carries heightened legal risks for banks. Banks can potentially expand the geographical scope of their services faster through electronic banking than through traditional banks. In some cases, however, they might not be fully versed in a jurisdiction's local laws and regulations before they begin to offer services there, either with a license or without a license if one is not required. When a license is not required, a virtual bank—lacking contact with its host country supervisor—may find it even more difficult to stay abreast of regulatory changes. As a consequence, virtual banks could unknowingly violate customer protection laws, including on data collection and privacy, and regulations on soliciting. In doing so, they expose themselves to losses through lawsuits or crimes that are not prosecuted because of jurisdictional disputes.

Money laundering is an age-old criminal activity that has been greatly facilitated by electronic banking because of the anonymity it affords. Once a customer opens an account, it is impossible for banks to identify whether the nominal account holder is conducting a transaction or even where the transaction is taking place. To combat money laundering, many countries have issued specific guidelines on identifying customers. They typically comprise recommendations for verifying an individual's identity and address before a customer account is opened and for monitoring online transactions, which requires great vigilance.

In a report issued in 2000, the Organization for Economic Cooperation and Development's Financial Action Task Force raised another concern. With electronic banking crossing national boundaries, whose regulatory authorities will investigate and pursue money laundering violations? The answer, according to the task force, lies in coordinating legislation and regulation internationally to avoid the creation of safe havens for criminal activities.

Operational risk : The reliance on new technology to provide services makes security and system availability the central operational risk of electronic banking. Security threats can come from inside or outside the system, so banking regulators and supervisors must ensure that banks have appropriate practices in place to guarantee the confidentiality of data, as well as the integrity of the system and the data. Banks' security practices should be regularly tested and reviewed by outside experts to analyze network vulnerabilities and recovery preparedness. Capacity planning to address increasing transaction volumes and new technological developments should take account of the budgetary impact of new investments, the ability to attract staff with the necessary expertise, and potential dependence on external service providers

Reputational risk *:* Breaches of security and disruptions to the system's availability can damage a bank's reputation. The more a bank relies on electronic delivery channels, the greater the potential for reputational risks. If one electronic bank encounters problems that cause customers to lose confidence in electronic delivery channels as a whole or to view bank failures as systemwide supervisory deficiencies, these problems can potentially affect other providers of electronic banking services. In many countries where electronic banking is becoming the trend, bank supervisors have put in place internal guidance notes for examiners, and many have released risk-management guidelines for banks.

Reputational risks also stem from customer misuse of security precautions or ignorance about the need for such precautions. Security risks can be amplified and may result in a loss of confidence in electronic delivery channels. The solution is consumer education—a process in which regulators and supervisors can assist. For example, some bank supervisors provide links on their websites allowing customers to identify online banks with legitimate charters and deposit insurance. They also issue tips on Internet banking, offer consumer help lines, and issue warnings about specific entities that may be conducting unauthorized banking operations in the country.

REGULATORY TOOLS

There are four key tools that regulators need to focus on to address the new challenges posed by the arrival of e-banking.

Adaptation : In light of how rapidly technology is changing and what the changes mean for banking activities, keeping regulations up to date has been, and continues to be, a far-reaching, time-consuming, and complex task. In May 2001, the Bank for International Settlements issued its "Risk Management Principles for Electronic Banking," which discusses how to extend, adapt, and tailor the existing risk-management framework to the electronic banking setting. For example, it recommends that a bank's board of directors and senior management review and approve the key aspects of the security control process, which should include measures to authenticate the identity and authorization of customers, promote nonrepudiation of transactions, protect data integrity, and ensure segregation of duties within e-banking systems, databases, and applications. Regulators and supervisors must also ensure that their staffs have the relevant technological expertise to assess potential changes in risks, which may require significant investment in training and in hardware and software.

Legalization : New methods for conducting transactions, new instruments, and new service providers will require legal definition, recognition, and permission. For example, it will be essential to define an electronic signature and give it the same legal status as the handwritten signature. Existing legal definitions and permissions—such as the legal definition of a bank and the concept of a national border—will also need to be rethought.

Harmonization : International harmonization of electronic banking regulation must be a top priority. This means intensifying cross-border cooperation between supervisors and coordinating laws and regulatory practices internationally and domestically across different regulatory agencies. The problem of jurisdiction that arises from "borderless" transactions is, as of this writing, in limbo. For now, each country must decide who has jurisdiction over electronic banking involving its citizens. The task of international harmonization and cooperation can be viewed as the most daunting in addressing the challenges of electronic banking.

Integration : This is the process of including information technology issues and their accompanying operational risks in bank supervisors' safety and soundness evaluations. In addition to the issues of privacy and security, for example, bank examiners will want to know how well the bank's management has elaborated its business plan for electronic banking. A special challenge for regulators will be supervising the functions that are outsourced to third-party vendors.

THE MACROECONOMIC CHALLENGES

But the challenges are not limited to regulators. As the advent of e-banking quickly changes the financial landscape and increases the potential for quick cross-border capital movements, macroeconomic policymakers face several difficult questions.

1. If electronic banking does make national boundaries irrelevant by facilitating capital movements, what does this imply for macroeconomic management?
2. How is monetary policy affected when, for example, the use of electronic means makes it easier for banks to avoid reserve requirements, or when business can be conducted in foreign currencies as easily as in domestic currency?
3. When offshore banking and capital flight are potentially only a few mouse clicks away, does a government have any leeway for independent monetary or fiscal policy?
4. How will the choice of the exchange rate regime be affected, and how will e-banking influence the targeted level of international reserves of a central bank?
5. Can a government afford to make any mistakes? Will the spread of electronic banking impose harsh market discipline on governments as well as on businesses?

The answers to these questions fall into two emerging strands of thought. First, the technological revolution—particularly the expansion of electronic money but also, more broadly, electronic advances in banking practices—could result in a decoupling of households' and firms' decisions from the purely financial operations of the central bank. Thus, the ability of monetary policy to influence inflation and economic activity would be threatened.

Second, as electronic banking expands, financial transaction costs can decline significantly. The result would be tantamount to a reduction in the "sand in the wheels" of the financial sector machinery, making capital flows even easier to effect, with a potential erosion of the effectiveness of domestic monetary policy. In this regard, proponents of the Tobin tax—which would tax short-term capital flows to increase their cost and, thereby, the sand in the wheels—

would feel that electronic banking makes an even more compelling case for introducing such a tax.

ELECTRONIC BENEFIT PAYMENTS

Recognising the several advantages of using bank accounts for disbursal of government benefits, many State Governments have decided to disburse NREGA payments social security benefits electronically through no frills bank accounts and in some States with such accounts operated through smart cards with bio-metric identification. A Committee set up by RBI examined the various models through which such payments can be made and has recommended a bank led model with sharing of costs between Government and banks. Appropriate support from the RBI or the Financial Inclusion Technology Fund could also be thought of in the initial stages. Such accounts that have been opened to receive government benefits/payments can become the base for a host of other financial services and facilitate the objective of financial inclusion.

Difficulties

- The picture in India, however, is a bit grey. The RBI does not still allow inter-bank funds transfer through the Net since the cyber laws are still not in place. Once allowed, this could pave the way for smooth cash management.
- Security also continues to remain a major issue, especially in the case of corporates, as bulk transactions are done in a day.
- Bankers are aware of the fact reliable transaction technology as well as management of the security perceptions of customers are the keys to success.
- The infrastructural costs of providing such services are quite high.

- A bank not only has to automate its front-end systems which the customer interfaces with but also the back-end systems so that the bank is able to provide "robust functionality".

CONCLUSION

While electronic banking can provide a number of benefits for customers and new business opportunities for banks, it exacerbates traditional banking risks. Even though considerable work has been done in some countries in adapting banking and supervision regulations, continuous vigilance and revisions will be essential as the scope of e-banking increases. In particular, there is still a need to establish greater harmonization and coordination at the international level. Moreover, the ease with which capital can potentially be moved between banks and across borders in an electronic environment creates a greater sensitivity to economic policy management. To understand the impact of e-banking on the conduct of economic policy, policymakers need a solid analytical foundation. On the way forward the challenges are going to be banks using multiple channels for delivery of variety of financial services, developing synergies with MFIs and SHGs by introducing seamless ICT based models linked to such intermediaries, availability of skilled manpower to facilitate the adoption of IT on such large scale, use of IT for credit information and efficient credit delivery and risk management in a much bigger way, moving away from the use of cash and emergence of enough leaders in the banking system especially in the public sector banks/ RRBs and cooperative banks to recognize the opportunities and take advantage of their specific strengths including location.

REFERENCES

1. Abdul Hannan Mia , Mohammad Anisur Raham, Md,Main

Uddin, 2007, The Cost and Management, Vol.35, No.1 January-February, pp36-48.

2. *Bank for International Settlements, Basel Committee on Banking Supervision, 2000, "Electronic Banking Group Initiatives and White Papers," October (Basel); http://www.bis.org/publ/bcbs76.htm*

3. *Stijn Claessens, Thomas Glaessner, and Daniela Klingebiel, 2002a, "Electronic Finance: Reshaping the Financial Landscape Around the World,"* Journal of Financial Services Research, *Vol. 22, pp. 29-61.*

   – – –, 2002b, "Electronic Finance. A New Approach to Financial Sector Development?" World Bank Discussion Paper No. 431 (Washington).

4. *Benjamin M. Friedman, 2000, "Decoupling at the Margin: The Threat to Monetary Policy from the Electronic Revolution in Banking,"* International Finance, *Vol. 3, pp. 261-72.*

5. *Saleh M. Nsouli and Connel Fullenkamp, 2001, "The Regulatory Framework for E-Banking," keynote address at "e-Lebanon: Banking, Payments, and ICT" conference, Beirut, Lebanon, June 6-8.*

6. *Andrea Schaechter, 2002, "Issues in Electronic Banking: An Overview," IMF Policy Discussion Paper, No. 02/6 (Washington: International Monetary Fund).*

7. *Smt. Usha Thorat,2008," Financial Inclusion and Information Technology' by Deputy Governorat 'Vision 2020 - Indian Financial Services Sector' hosted by NDTV at The Ballroom, Taj Lands End, Mumbai .*

8. Reserve Bank of India 2008, Report on Currency & Finance 2006-08, Mumbai.

9. UNDP,2010, Real Wealth of Nations Pathway to Human Development HRD.

Section VI : Financial Inclusion and Priority Sector

32

Financial Inclusion in India: Emerging Trends and Challenges of Banking Services

K. P. Vipin Chandran
P. Sandhya

INTRODUCTION

The banking industry has shown tremendous growth in volume and complexity during the last few decades. Despite making significant improvements in all the areas relating to financial viability, profitability and competitiveness, there are concerns that banks have not been able to include vast segment of the population, especially the underprivileged sections of the society, into the fold of basic banking services. Internationally some efforts are being made to study the causes of financial exclusion and designing strategies to ensure financial inclusion of the poor and disadvantaged. The reasons may vary from country to country and hence the strategy could also vary but all out efforts are being made as financial inclusion can truly lift the financial condition and standards of life of the poor and the disadvantaged. The scope of financial inclusion can be expanded in two ways.

a) Through state driven intervention by way of statutory enactments.

b) Through voluntary effort by the banking community itself for evolving various strategies to bring within the ambit of the banking sector the large strata of society.

When bankers do not give the desired attention to certain areas, the regulators have to step in to remedy the situation. This is the reason why the Reserve bank of India is placing a lot of emphasis on financial inclusion. In India, the focus of the financial inclusion at present is confined to ensuring a bare minimum access to a savings bank account without frills, to all. Internationally, the financial exclusion has been viewed in a much wider perspective. Having a current account/savings account on its own, is not regarded as an accurate indicator of financial inclusion.

WHAT FINANCIAL IS INCLUSION?

"Financial inclusion may be defined as the process of ensuring access to financial services and timely and adequate credit where needed by vulnerable groups such as weaker sections and low income groups at an affordable cost". Holding a bank account itself confers a sense of identity, status and empowerment and provides access to the national payment system. Therefore, having a bank account becomes a very important aspect of financial inclusion. Further, financial inclusion, apart from opening and providing easy access to a No Frills account, should also provide access to credit, perhaps in the form of a General Credit Card (GCC) or limited OD against the no frills account. It should encompass access to affordable insurance and remittance facilities. It should also include credit counseling and financial education / literacy. While financial inclusion, in the narrow sense, may be achieved to some extent by offering any one of these services, the objective of "comprehensive financial inclusion" would be to provide a holistic set of services encompassing all of the above. The objective of financial inclusion is to extend the scope of activities of the organized financial system to include within its ambit people with low incomes. Through graduated credit, the attempt must be to lift the poor from one level to another so that they come out of poverty.

Financial inclusion is the delivery of banking services at an affordable cost to the vast sections of disadvantaged and low income groups. Unrestrained access to public goods and services is the prerequisite of an open and efficient society. As banking services are in the nature of public good, it is essential that availability of banking and payment services to the entire population without discrimination is the prime objective of the public policy. This simple definition encompasses the concept's two, primary dimensions (United Nations, 2006). Firstly, financial inclusion refers to a customer having access to a range of formal financial services, from simple credit and savings services to the more complex such as insurance and pensions. Secondly, financial inclusion implies that customers have access to more than one financial services provider, which ensures a variety of competitive options. Flowing from this definition, financial exclusion would mean the inability of the disadvantaged to access financial services. A range of obstacles could lead to financial exclusion; barriers include geography (limiting physical access), regulations (lack of formal identification proof or of appropriate products for poor households), psychology (fear of financial institution's staff, structures, complicated financial products, etc.), information (lack of knowledge regarding products and procedures), and low financial acumen (low income and poor financial discipline), among others (Figure 1).

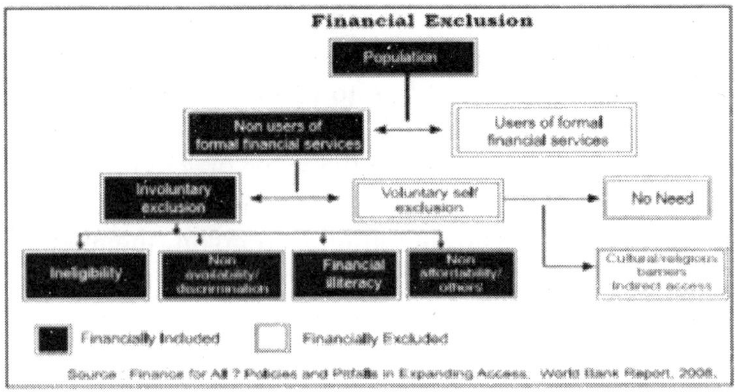

Fig. 1. Financial exclusion

The essence of financial inclusion is in trying to ensure that a range of appropriate financial services is available to every individual and enabling them to understand and access those services. Apart from the regular form of financial intermediation, it may include a basic no frills banking account for making and receiving payments, a savings product suited to the pattern of cash flows of a poor household, money transfer facilities, small loans and overdrafts for productive, personal and other purposes, insurance (life and non-life), etc. While financial inclusion, in the narrow sense, may be achieved to some extent by offering any one of these services, the objective of "Comprehensive Financial Inclusion" would be to provide a holistic set of services encompassing all of the above.

WHY FINANCIAL INCLUSION IMPORTANT?

One of the most important empirical relationships revealed in the last decade has been the establishment of the causal link between financial depth and growth (Honohan, 2004). Figure 2 shows a schematic representation of the theoretical basis for the link between financial depth and growth. Policy-makers would do well to recognize the relationships between well-developed financial systems and economic growth as well as economic growth and poverty reduction. Thus, the question becomes, does a well-developed financial system serve the poor?(Figure2)

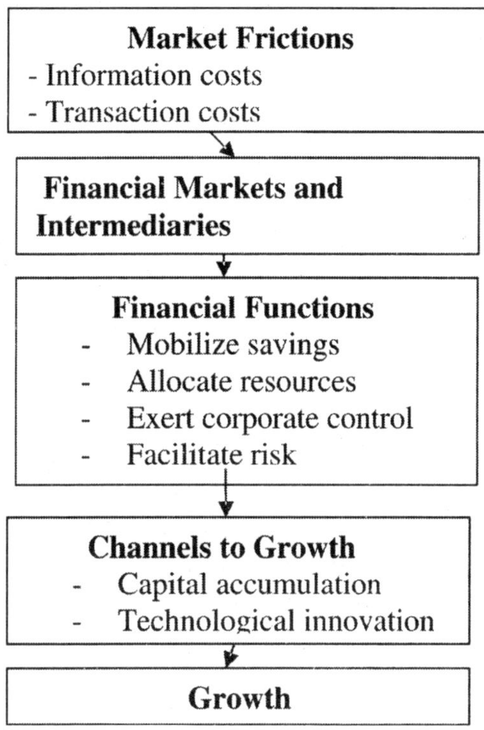

Fig. 2. Approaches to finance and growth

***Source*: Levine (2007)**

There are ample theoretical justifications and empirical evidence indicating that a well-developed financial system can be an effective poverty alleviation tool. For one, there are large costs to small and poor entrepreneurs for the market imperfections in a poorly developed financial system. These burdens include informational asymmetries, transaction costs, and contract enforcement costs, compounded by lack of collateral, credit histories, and contacts. For these entrepreneurs, broad access to financial services would smooth project financing, positively impacting growth and poverty alleviation (Galor and Zeira, 1993). Beck and de la Torre (2006) also refer to the Schumpeterian process of 'creative destruction' whereby a well-developed financial system is able to allocate resources to efficient newcomers. Empirical studies also show that small firms in countries with greater outreach and access face lower financing obstacles and grow at a higher rate (Beck et al, 2006). Access to finance is also an important incentive for new ideas and technologies (King and Levine, 1993). Additionally, a strong financial system encourages expansion in the market and competition for existing firms. It ensures that poor households and small entrepreneurs need not depend on middlemen. On the other hand, an underdeveloped financial system can be uncompetitive, conservative and inimical to poor or small entrepreneurs (Rajan and Zingales, 2003).

Although the causal link between financial depth (a well-functioning and well-developed financial system) and growth is well-established, the link between the breadth of financial services (outreach of financial services) and growth is less well-defined (Beck and de la Torre, 2006). The four central functions of finance are: mobilizing savings; allocating capital; monitoring the use of credit funds by entrepreneurs; and transforming risk by pooling and repackaging it. These functions need to be buttressed by legal, regulatory, and informational structures that enhance the quality of the financial system, which cannot be measured simply by looking at the scale or the breadth of the system (Honohan, 2004).

Economists like Joan Robinson (1952) opined that, "where enterprise leads, finance follows", thereby taking a position that economic development creates demand for particular types of financial arrangements and the financial system responds automatically to these demands. But economists such as Robert Lucas (1988) do not believe that the finance-growth relationship is important and assert that economists "badly overstress" the role of financial factors in economic growth. The literature has categorized the relationship between finance and growth into five links viz causal relation, demand following, supply leading, negative causal link from finance to growth and interdependence.

The primary function performed by financial systems can be classified into five basic functions: they are, facilitate trading, hedging, diversifying, and pooling of risks, allocate resources, monitor managers and exert corporate control, mobilize savings and facilitate exchange of goods and services. In the Indian context, both supply-side and demand side barriers have both been recognized as responsible for low level of access to financial services. Supply side constraints like poor banking infrastructure, low resource base of credit purveying institutions, security based lending procedures, lengthy and cumbersome formalities, low level of financial literacy, etc., are still dominant in the sector. Scores of demand side factors such as inadequate human capital, skewed distribution of land including lack of proper land reforms, presence of large section of landless labourers, poor state of physical infrastructure (road, bridges, irrigation structures, marketyards, cold storages), underdeveloped social capital (gram panchayath, local administration, commodity cooperatives, etc), low productivity leading to low level of profitability, poor linkages, poor risk mitigation mechanism, etc., in the country have adverse effects on the expansion of coverage of institutional credit. In short, access to financial services allows the poor to save money outside the house safely, prevents concentration of economic power with a few individuals and helps in mitigating the risks that the poor face as a result of economic shocks. Thus, providing access to financial services is increasingly becoming an area of concern for the policymakers for the obvious reason that it has far reaching economic and social implications.

MEASURING FINANCIAL INCLUSION

Closely related to financial inclusion is the idea of breadth of financial services. Breadth of financial services refers to the outreach of financial services in an economy. Although financial inclusion should signify access to a range of different financial services, the percentage of people in a given area with access to a bank account is the typical measuring stick for breadth of financial services, (Beck and De la Torre, 2006). This approach assumes that a bank account enables poor households to perform important financial functions such as saving money safely outside the house, accessing credit, making loan or premium payments, and transferring money (Mohan, 2006). Thus, in this framework, a bank account should determine access to and usage of many other financial services (Littlefield et al, 2006). Table 1

Table 1. Percentage of population with a bank account

Country/Location	*% with account*
U.K	87.7
U.S.A	91
Sweden	98
Denmark	99.1
Tanzania	6.4
India	59
Nagaland	21
Meghalaya	27
Bihar	33
Kerala	89

Source: Fedbank Hormis memorial foundation inaugural address by V.Leeladhar, Deputy Governor, Reserve Bank of India, December 2, 2005.

demonstrates the striking disparities in access to savings accounts between developed and developing countries. While in developed nations almost everyone has access to banking services, in less developed countries, access is often limited to small segments of the population.

METHODOLOGY

Financial inclusion index, which measures the degree of financial inclusion, has been developed by giving appropriate weights to the selected financial services. Financial Inclusion Index (FII) that can capture all dimensions of financial inclusion including "access" and "use" of financial services. Financial Inclusion Index (FII) compares the status and progress of financial inclusion across the states/ districts in India. The methodology for FII is similar to for constructing the Human Development Index (HDI). Firstly, a dimension index of the indicators used to capture financial inclusion is constructed and then the FII is computed as a weighted average of the dimensions. The form of the dimension index (Z) and the FII are given as under:

$$\text{Dimension index } (Z_i) = \frac{Ai - mi}{Mi - mi}$$

Where,

Z_i = Dimension Index

A_i = Actual value of ith dimension

m_i = minimum value of ith dimension

M_i = maximum value of ith dimension

Applying weights to the above Dimension Index, we have:

$$\text{Financial inclusion index (FII)} = \sum_{i=1}^{n} w_i Z_i$$

Where,

w_i = weight of the ith dimension

Z_i = dimension index

N = number of dimensions

The Financial Inclusion Index (FII) is the weighted average of the dimension indexes, where the weights assigned are equal.

$$\text{Financial inclusion index (FII)} = 1/n \sum_{i=1}^{n} Z_i$$

Where,

Z_i = dimension index

N = number of dimensions

The indicators selected for computing FII seek to cover various dimensions of financial inclusion are presented in Table 2.

Table 2. Dimensions of financial inclusion

Dimensions	*Indicators*
Number of rural offices	Coverage
Number of rural deposit accounts	Access and availability
Volume of rural deposits	Input of the banking system
Input of the banking system	Use/output of the banking system

The four dimensions have been converted (i.e. normalized) into ratios i.e. per office number of accounts, per office deposit amount, per account deposit amount, and per office credit amount. The ratios have been calculated for rural areas. The Banking Statistical Returns (BSR) Statement, published by RBI which provides population-based breakup in terms of rural, semi-urban, urban and metropolitan branch wise classification of various parameters was the basis for the analysis. The (lowest) unit level for which data is available is the district. The Index has been calculated at the district level. Aggregating the district level index gives us the state figure. The analysis was confined to scheduled commercial banks and does not include co-operatives.

The proposed Index theoretically takes values between zero (0) and one (1). The value 0 can be interpreted as indicating 'no financial inclusion' and the value 1 indicating 'complete financial inclusion'. For analytical purposes we have divided the range between the values 0 to 1 into four grades depicting different grades of financial inclusion (Table 3). The proposed FII can be used for ranking districts and

Table 3. Grades of Financial Inclusion

Financial inclusion index (value)

State	*Rank*		*FII Value*	
	2002	*2006*	*2002*	*2006*
Punjab	1	2	0.305	0.314
Kerala	2	1	0.295	0.318
Haryana	3	3	0.258	0.280
Jammu&Kashmir	4	5	0.252	0.252
Himachal Pradesh	5	4	0.251	0.262
Uttar Pradesh	6	8	0.217	0.216
Uttaranchal	7	6	0.216	0.226
Tamil Nadu	8	7	0.201	0.223
Andhra Pradesh	9	9	0.193	0.214
Gujarat	10	11	0.181	0.194
West Bengal	11	10	0.177	0.195
Jharkhand	12	12	0.168	0.183
Karnataka	13	13	0.154	0.173
Assam	14	14	0.151	0.162
Chattisgarh	15	16	0.137	0.151
Orissa	16	15	0.135	0.152
Bihar	17	18	0.127	0.140
Madhya Pradesh	18	19	0.122	0.138
Rajasthan	19	17	0.122	0.140
Maharashtra	20	20	0.116	0.134

adding the district wise FII values also provide the state FII values. The FII can be best interpreted if district ranks change over time.

The FII has been calculated for various districts in the country and based on FII values have been classified into various grades (of financial inclusion) for different periods of time (year 2002 and 2006) and the estimates are presented in Table 4. Note: For the year 2002 the FII calculated is for 524 districts and for 2006 it is for 510 districts. The estimated values of FII show that there has been a relative improvement in the status of financial inclusion between the period 2002 and 2006. In 2002, 378 districts (72 per cent) were in the lowest grade, however, in the year 2006, 330 districts figured in the lowest grade. Most of these districts have moved to the next grade where the FII ranges between 0.20 and 0.40.

Table 4. Financial inclusion values

FII Value (Grade)	*2002*		*2006*	
	No. of districts	*% to total*	*No. of totals*	*% to total*
0 to 0.20 (very low)	378	72	330	64.71
0.20 to 0.40 (low)	134	25.5	168	32.94
0.40 to 0.60 (medium)	09	1.7	09	1.76
0.60 to 1 (high)	03	0.8	03	0.59
Total	524	100	510	100

STATE WISE FINANCIAL INCLUSION INDEX

Ranking of state wise estimated FII for different periods of time revealed the growth and progress of financial inclusion in different states (Fig. 3). All states except Jammu & Kashmir and Uttar Pradesh for which the FII was constructed have improved in terms of the FII values between the periods 2002 to 2006. The doubling of agriculture credit programme may have also influenced this improvement. In terms of rank improvement Rajasthan has improved its rank by moving up by two ranks. Uttar Pradesh has moved down by two places although it has improved its FII values. At the top Punjab and Kerala have interchanged their positions.

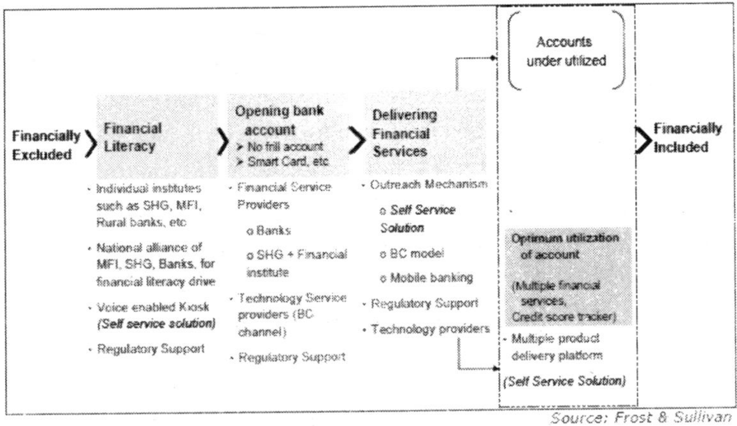

Fig. 3. Financial inclusion Lifecycle

FINANCIAL INCLUSION LIFECYCLE

The first step of financial inclusion is to educate customers and open an account. However, merely opening a bank account for a poor individual is not financial inclusion. This approach generally results in an inactive account or a repository for government benefits.

A three-step approach (figure 3) is required to bring financially underserved individuals into a financially inclusive society. After improving financial literacy and opening an account of some form, it is usage of that account, linkage with other financial services and access to all the financial instruments that are required to complete the financial inclusion lifecycle. Optimum utilization of an account should be another target for banking service providers.

Step 1: Financial Literacy

To begin the financial inclusion process, one needs to understand financial products, usage, operation and management of accounts. As defined by the Reserve Bank of India (RBI), financial education is 'the process by which financial consumers/investors improve their understanding of financial products, concepts and risks and, through information, instruction and/or objective advice, develop the skills and confidence to become more aware of financial risks and opportunities, to make informed choices, to know where to go for help, and to take other effective actions to improve their financial well-being'. Efforts for financial literacy can be driven through microfinance institutions (MFIs), self-help groups (SHGs), cooperative and rural banks. Collaboration between these parties would accelerate results.

Step 2: Opening a Bank Account

Opening a bank account is the second step towards financial inclusion. It provides access to financial facilities for the financially underserved through formal sources of banking. Financial services providers, technology service providers and regulators are the functioning participants in the system. As a major initiative to promote financial inclusion, the RBI has directed banks to introduce a basic 'no frills' banking account with either zero or very low minimum balances to better meet the needs of the poor. The RBI has also eased 'know your customer' (KYC) norms to minimize the procedural obstacles of opening a bank account.

Step 3: Delivering Financial services

The cost of delivery of service is considered to be the bottleneck in the value chain because, for the very consumer, anything but very low transaction costs are not feasible. Currently, the favoured delivery channel for microfinance and micro credit is via the business correspondent (BC) model, whereby an agent (who may or may not be a direct employee of the financial institution) personally travels within a wide geographical area to enroll customers, delivers loans, and collects repayments. The 'doorstep banking' model has obvious restrictions of scale as well as security. Agents may run away with their clients' funds or may themselves be the target of thieves.

CONVENTIONAL DELIVERY MODEL

Technology can improve conventional delivery channels such as the BC model by adding new levels of security, speeding up enrolment procedures or ensuring accuracy. Used in this way, technology offers conventional models the chance to increase scale, though to a limited degree. A conventional BC model will always be restricted by the amount of ground the agent can physically cover.

TECHNOLOGY-ENABLED DELIVERY MODEL

Alternatively, technology can actually become the direct delivery channel. Self-service technology, in particular, has already achieved this in the broader financial industry, through ATMs, the internet and user-driven mobile phone banking. With policy support, self-service technology can provide a feasible platform for the delivery of financial services to the financially underserved population. As well as technology providers, the other participants in this third step are the financial services providers.

FUTURE STRATEGIES

Important future strategies that will aid in furthering financial inclusion, especially credit inclusion.

DEMAND SIDE FACTORS

a. Grass root Level Organizations : Involvement of grass root level organizations like farmers' club and NGOs would lead to inclusion of the disadvantaged as they ensure local participation and help farmers in gaining access to credit and technology. The main advantage in involving such grass root organization is the large multiplier effects they generate along with the positive 'demonstration effects' among the target groups.

b. Rural Infrastructure : Infrastructure development is an essential prerequisite for attaining greater inclusive growth. Adequate rural infrastructure facilities and improvements in terms of availability of electricity, improved connectivity through provision of rural roads and telecommunications, construction of warehouses and market infrastructure are expected to lead to efficient supply chain management in agriculture and hence greater demand for banking activities in rural areas.

c. Financial Education : Lack of knowledge is an important reason for financial exclusion. Financial education is required to ensure that large sections of population in urban and rural areas that do not have access to formal banking and financial services are educated of the advantages of coming into the fold of such services.

d. Deceleration in Agricultural Growth : The yield of most of the agricultural commodities is low leading to less demand and supply of credit. For instance, the cultivation of commercial crops requires more funds due to increased cost of production. Similarly, irrigation also enhances the level of production. Hence, increase in area under commercial crops and increase in irrigated area to gross cropped area is expected to positively determine the supply of credit. Moreover, large investments in infrastructure are required for increased agricultural growth, which will also generate employment for semi-skilled workers.

SUPPLY SIDE FACTORS

a. Less Outreach : Due to insufficient branch networking in rural areas, banks are unable to reach the rural customers. This declining trend of the bank branches in rural areas has led to marginalization of the disadvantaged sections from accessing institutional credit, especially in the underdeveloped regions of the country. The relatively high transaction cost in dealing with a number of small accounts and small volumes of loans negatively impacts further expansion. Outreach can be increased through intermediaries like SHGs, MFIs, civil society organizations, etc., through the use of business facilitators and business correspondents. Mobile banks need to be promoted to resolve the problem of access to isolated and remote regions.

b. Mobile Banking : As elaborated in the section on role of technology, banks need to aggressively adopt mobile banking as a strategy for increasing their outreach in the rural areas.

c. Human Resource Constraints : There are human resource constraints also in rural bank branches.

d. Inefficient Financial Sector : Problems in credit access are routed in institutional weaknesses like absence of good credit appraisal, risk management tools in banks, etc. An efficient and organized financial sector contributes to growth by mobilizing savings for capital formation and investment and optimizes the capital allocation, which results in productive activities in the economy. Technology and computerization can reduce the operational cost in rural areas for public sector banks and customer friendly bank products can be developed with the help of technology. There are lots of challenges in reducing the adverse consequences of exclusion and including large sections of the society. A specific type of organizational ethos, culture and attitude (Rangarajan, 2005) is required. There is also a need for effective coordination among the various agencies (banks, NGOs, MFIs, Govt.) participating in inclusive growth.

CONCLUSION

There are a number of reasons why financial inclusion is not taking place in India. These include coverage, cost of small value transactions, infrastructure, suitable products, flexibility, weak delivery model for community enterprise and financial management support. Formal financial institutions such as, banks, insurance companies, mutual funds, pension companies will have to join hands with small NGO-MFIs, larger NBFC- MFIs, and technology providers to enable inclusion. The strengths of these institutions will have to be put together through sound collaborations for financial inclusion. Local and national presence organizations have to ensure that these partnerships look at both commercial and social aspects to help achieve scale, sustainability, and impact. It is becoming increasingly apparent that addressing financial exclusion will require a holistic approach on the part of the banks in creating awareness about financial products, education, and advice on money management, debt counseling, saving and affordable credit. The banks would have to evolve specific strategies to expand the outreach of their services in order to promote financial inclusion. This collaborative model will have to tackle exclusion in two main ways: By ensuring that there is a supply of appropriate and affordable services available to those that need them; and by stimulating demand for appropriate financial products, services and advice with appropriate delivery mechanism. The main findings of the study is that the banks need to redesign their business strategies to incorporate specific plans to promote financial inclusion of low income group treating it both a business opportunity as well as a corporate social responsibility. Financial Inclusion would help in bringing much needed access to the unbanked masses, which are the future growth engine of the economy.

REFERENCE

1. Beck, Thorsten and de la Torre, Augusto (2006): "The Basic Analytics of Access to Financial Services" Mimeo.
2. Committee on Financial Sector Reforms Draft Report (2008): Planning Commission, Government of India.
3. Das, V (2006): *Financial Inclusion Initiatives,* Inaugural Address for delivered at the
4. 'National Conference on Financial Inclusion and Beyond: Issues andOpportunities for India'. September 19-20, 2006, Cochin.
5. Dev, Mahendra S (2006): Financial Inclusion: Issues and Challenges, *Economic and Political Weekly,* pp. 4310 - 4313, October 14, 2006.
6. Honohan, Patrick (2004): *Financial Development, Growth and Poverty: How Close Are the Links?* In Charles Goodhart, ed. Financial Development and Economic Growth:Explaining the Links, Palgrave, London.
7. King, Robert G., and Ross Levine (1993): Finance and Growth: Schumpeter Might Be Right." *Quarterly Journal of Economics,* 108(3):717–37.
8. Mandira Sarma (2007): Index of Financial Inclusion, ICRIER, New Delhi.
9. Mohan, Rakesh (2006): *"Economic Growth, Financial Deepening and Financial Inclusion"* Address by Dr. Rakesh Mohan at the Annual Bankers' Conference 2006, at Hyderabad on November 3, 2006.
10. Nirupam Mehrota et.al (2009): *Financial inclusion, An overview,* Occasional paper No.48, Department of Economic analysis and Research, NABARD, Mumbai.
11. Priya Basu (2005): A Financial System for India's Poor, *Economic and Political Weekly,* No 37.
12. Rajan, R. and Zingales, L. (2003): Savings Capitalism from the Capitalists, *Crown Business,*New York.
13. Rana Mitra (2007: Financial Inclusion: Meeting the Challenge, *People's Democracy,* Vol. XXXI - II, No. 17,April 29, 2007.

14. Ross Levine (1997): Financial Development and Economic Growth: Views and Agenda, *Journal of Economic Literature,* Vol. XXXV.

15. Subba Rao K. G. K (2007): Financial Inclusion: An Introspection, *Economic and Political Weekly,* Vol. 42, No. 05, February 03- February 09.

16. Thorat, Usha (2007): *Financial Inclusion – The Indian Experience,* Text of speech by Deputy Governor, Reserve Bank of India at the HMT-DFID Financial Inclusion Conference 2007, Whitehall Place, London, UK, June 19.

17. United Nations (2006): Building Inclusive Financial Sectors for Development, New York.

33

An Analysis of Agriculture Credit and Capital Formation in Indian Agriculture: Pre Reform and Post Reform Comparison

M. Michael Raj

INTRODUCTION

Agriculture plays a crucial role in the development of the Indian Economy. The prosperity of people in India is very much inter-related with progress in her agriculture in view of predominantly agrarian character of the economy.(Mani 2007).It accounts for about 18 per cent of GDP and still about two third of the working population depends upon this sector for their livelihood. Any change in agriculture production and productivity creates spill over effects on other sectors and all over growth rate of the economy. The higher overall growth witnessed during the eighties and nineties was inter-alia, on account of higher agricultural growth. (Asha P Kannan, 2005) Agriculture development depends upon a number of factors-favourable monsoons, availability of irrigation, high yielding seeds; credit etc, however the adequate and timely availability of credit is the crucial factor which augmenting agriculture production and productivity. In the colonial period the lack of institutional credit facilities persuaded the peasant to depend the money lenders both for consumption and investment credit. The money lenders provided credit on the basis of the security of land provided by the borrowing peasants. In most cases the money lenders giving loans less than the actual value of mortgage land. Thus the land mortgage increase during the colonial period leads the forced commercialisation of Indian agriculture by the way of forcing the farmers to sell more portion of the farmers produce in the market or to the money lenders to get the interest and principle loan amount.(Raj,Mridula Mukherjee,1985).Thus after independence the government of India take concrete steps in the financial sector with the help of RBI to provide a broad based institutional frame work to ensure adequate and timely availability of credit to agriculture. The RBI perhaps the first bank in the world to have taken interest in the matters related to agriculture and agriculture credit and it continues to do so (Reddy, 2001).However the financial sector reforms as a part of new economic policy produce serious impacts in rural agrarian economy in terms of giving more autonomous power to financial institutions their lending activities and steps taken for strengthen agriculture credit. Thus the present study tries to analyse (a) Changing structure of institutional credit in India in the pre and post reform period.(b).Growth of production Credit and Investment Credit in pre reform and post reform periods.(c)to study the relationship between long term credit and private capital accumulation in Indian agriculture.

DATA AND METHODOLOGY

The study is based on secondary data collected from various issues of RBI publications, Agriculture statistics at a Glance, Economic Survey. The time period of study is 1970 to 2010, but changes with the time series availability of data with the same base year. Average growth rate, Correlation, Regression methods are used for data analysis. To find out the determinants of private capital formation multiple regression analysis has been worked out taking private capital formation as depended variable and public capital formation, long term credit, terms of trade as independent variables.

TREND OF INSTITUTIONAL AND NON INSTITUTIONAL CREDIT IN INDIA

Agriculture policies in India have been reviewed from time to time to maintain the pace with the changing requirements of the agriculture sector, which forms an important segment of the priority sector lending of scheduled commercial banks and target 18 percent of the net bank credit. The practice of extending institutional credit to agriculture could be traced back to 1870s, when farmers were provided such credit during the drought years by the Government. The genesis of institutional credit in agriculture could be traced back to the enactment of the co-operative societies act 1904.The evolution of institutional credit to agriculture could be broadly classified into four distinct phases-1904-1969, predominance of co-operatives and setting up of RBI, 1969-1975 nationalisation of commercial banks and setting up of Regional Rural Banks (RRBs), 1975-1990 setting up NABARD and from1991 onwards financial sector reforms. Over the sixty three years after independence with the concrete steps of government and RBI helps to increase agriculture credit in quantitative terms although the qualitative aspect still a debated issue. The growth of institutional credit from 1951 to 2002 is clearly understand from table 1.

Table 1. Relative Share of Borrowing of Cultivator Households from Different Sources

Sources Credit	*1951*	*1961*	*1971*	*1981*	*1991*	*2002*
1	2	3	4	5	6	7
Non-Institutional	**92.7**	**81.3**	**68.3**	**36.8**	**33.9**	**38.9**
Of which						
Money Lenders	69.7	49.2	36.1	16.1	17.5	26.8
Institutional						
Of which	**7.3**	**18.7**	**31.7**	**63.2**	**66.1**	**61.1**
Cooperatives Societies/banks	**3.3**	**2.6**	**22**	**29.8**	**23.6**	**30.2**
Commercial Banks	0.9	0.6	2.4	28.8	35.2	26.3
Unspecified						
Total	**100**	**100**	**100**	**100**	**100**	**100**

Source: All India Debt and Investment Survey and NSSO

One of the major achievements in the post independence India has been widening the spread of institutional machinery for credit and decline in the role of non institutional sources, however some reversal trend occurred i.e. increasing trend of no institutional sources particularly in the 1990s.The share of institutional credit, which was only little over 7 percent in 1951 increased many fold to 66 percent in 1991, reflecting concomitantly a remarkable decline in the share the non-institutional credit decreased from 93 percent to 31 per cent during the same period. However after 1991 the trend reversed, the institutional credit declined from 66.3 percent in 1991 to 61 in 2002 and non institutional credit increased from 30.6 in

1991 to38.9 percent during the same period. Thus the analysis of agency wise institutional credit to agriculture helps to understand the pattern of change in agriculture credit after 1990s.

GROWTH AND CHANGES IN AGENCY WISE FLOW OF AGRICULTURE CREDIT IN PRE AND POST REFORM PERIOD

The all India Rural Credit Survey Committee (1954) stated the first time in its report the needs for strengthening the credit delivery system to ensure timely availability of agriculture credit. Accordingly, a three -pronged strategy of developing rural financial or agricultural services have been followed comprising of (i) broad basing the institutional frame work; (ii)directed lending policies, and (iii)concessional or subsidised credit(Rengarajan,1996).To achieve the above mentioned three pronged strategy, India has adopted a multi agency approach consisting Co-operative banks, Regional Rural Banks and Commercial banks to augment the adequate and timely availability of agriculture credit. The multi agency approach helps to increase the total institutional credit from 24.23 crore from 1951 to 248510 crore in 2010. But the agency wise allocation shows shifting the role of co-operative banks in agriculture credit to Commercial and RRBs. This was strengthened after the nationalisation of 14 Commercial Banks in 1960s , followed by 6 banks in 1980 and the financial sector reforms implemented in 1990s.The agency wise change in the flow of institutional credit can be understand from table 2.

The analysis shows that the total institutional credit to agriculture increased from 885.15 crore in 1970-71 to 248510 crore in 2009-10 with an average percentage growth of 33 percent per decade, the largest percentage growth occurred between the period 1991 to 2010.Of this the share of Co-operative banks in total credit to agriculture shows a

Table 2. Agencies wise flow of institutional credit in pre and post reform period.

(Rs. crore)

Agency	*Pre reform period*			*Post reform period*		
	1970-71	*1980-81*	*1990-91*	*1991-92*	*2000-01*	*2009-10*
Co-operative Banks	678.79 (77)	2126.31 (63)	3973 (44)	5800 (52)	20718 (39)	38578 (15)
Regional Rural Banks				596 (5)	4219 (8)	23932 (10)
Commercial Banks	206.37 (37)	1262.8 (37)	5010* (56)	4806 (43)	27807 (53)	186000 (75)
Total	885.16 (100)	3389.11 (100)	8983 (100)	11202 (100)	52744 (100)	248510 (100)

*Include medium term and long term loans

Source: Statistics at a Glance various issues, Ministry of Agriculture and Economic Survey 20.

declining trend, declined from 77 percent in 1970-71 to 15 per cent in 2009-2010.At the same time the Commercial banks share increased from 37 to 75 percent. In the case of former the largest decline occurred after 1990's, 37percent and in the case of latter the largest change occurred in the post reform period, 32 percent. The RRBs contribution also increases from 5 to 10 per cent in the post reform period. Thus the financial sector reforms as a part of new economic policy redefined the role of commercial banks and Co-operative banks, RRBs in the total credit allocation to agriculture sector. Although the government take special programmes to strengthen the Co-operative credit system in India through the financial sector reforms giving more autonomous power to their credit operations but the maintaining of over dues and non performing assets and high transaction cost adversely affected the credit operations of Co-operative banks. The Co-operative banks role in the total agriculture credit decreased and Commercial Banks and RRBs role has increased. This produces serious implication in agrarian rural economy because small and marginal farmers mostly depend the Co-operative banks for their credit requirements. The redefining role helps to increase the total credit generation capacity of commercial banks in the post reform period but its lending to the agriculture has showing a declining trend in the post reform period. This is clearly understood from table 3.

From the table it is clear that the growth rate of total credit (agriculture and other sectors) during the reform period was higher than that during the pre reform period. However in the case of agriculture credit, the growth rate during the reform period was lower (10.9 per cent) than that during the post reform period (15.2 per cent).A comparison of growth rates of credit to agriculture between pre and post reform periods reveals that most of the states registered higher growth rates of credit to agriculture during the pre and post reform period as compared to the later period except Punjab and Maharashtra. This clearly shows that the commercial banks share in the total credit increased after 1990's but the rate at which credit was disbursed to agriculture slowed down during the reform period.

SHORT TERM AND LONG TERM CREDIT TO INDIAN AGRICULTURE IN PRE AND POST REFORM PERIOD

Short term credit and long term credit has due importance in accelerating agriculture production and productivity. Short term credits are production credit on the other hand long term credit is mainly used for investment purposes. The long term growth rate of agriculture is highly correlated with investment in agriculture which in terms depends upon public and private investment in agriculture. However recent studies questioned the complementary

Table 3. State wise annual average growth rates of outstanding credit by SCBs (per Cent)

States	*1981-1991*		*1992-2000*		*1981-2000*	
	Agri-culture	*Total*	*Agri-culture*	*Total*	*Agri-culture*	*Total*
High Income						
Gujarat	14.7	16.5	7.5	16	12.4	15.4
Haryana	14.3	14.9	9.3	14.7	9.9	13
Maharashtra	13.8	13.5	13.9	18.9	12.2	16.2
Punjab	10.6	12.8	10.7	14.8	9.2	13.1
Group Total	13	14	10.9	17.8	11	15.5
Middle Income						
Andhra Pradesh	13.5	17.9	12.2	15.3	11.4	15.9
Karnataka	17	16.6	13.8	17.7	13	15.3
Kerala	15.2	14.8	12.6	16.1	12.1	14.1
Tamil Nadu	17.3	17.6	10.3	17.2	13.2	16.7
West Bengal	17.5	14.5	3.5	11.5	10.1	13.3
Group Total	15.9	16.4	11.4	15.6	12.2	15.3
Low Income						
Bihar	16.2	15.9	4.3	10.6	12.2	13.8
Madhya Pradesh	19.2	20.8	12.5	15.3	14.1	16.3
Orissa	15.9	20.7	9.9	11.5	10.1	13.9
Rajasthan	16.1	15.8	12.2	15.6	12.7	14.9
Utter Pradesh	15	16.8	9.8	11.8	12.8	14.3
Group Total	16.3	17.6	10	13	12.7	14.7
All major states	15.2	15.7	10.9	16	12	15.3

Source: Ganan Bihari Sahu (2007), Indian journal of agriculture Economics.

between private and public investment in agriculture. After the 1990 the growth of investment in Indian agriculture deviated from the complementary nature at the same time the growth rates of private investment is not enough to compensate the decline of public investment. Thus the analysis of growth rate of short term and long term credit is very important because the former determines the present productivity and the later determined the private investment and long term productivity of Indian agriculture. Thus the table 4 gives a clear idea about the decadal growth of short and long term credit in Indian agriculture.

Table 4. Decadal Average Growth rate of Direct Institutional Credit to Agriculture and Alaid Activities

(Per cent)

Period	*C-operatives*		*RRBs*		*Commercial Banks*		*Total*	
	Short term	*Long term*	*Short term*	*Long term*	*Short term*	*Long term*	*Short term*	*Long term*
1970s	10.6	13.9	334.8	426.8	28.2	29.9	14.5	20.2
1980s	12.5	11.0	19.8	18.5	16.3	18.6	13.9	14.8
1990s	11.9	13.1	32.7	10.6	17.8	12.1	14.6	11.9
2000s*	11.6	5.0	23.6	15.7	20.2	18.1	17.1	13.4

* Up to 2007-08

Source: Handbook of Statistics on Indian Economy 2008-09

The decadal growth rate of short term and long term credit to agriculture and allied activities shows that while short term (production) credit to agriculture has remained around 14.5 percent up to the seventies and nineties, and then shows a slight improvement(from 14.6 to 17.1) percent. On the other hand there was deceleration in the expansion of medium and long term credit (investment credit) to agriculture from 20.2 per cent to 13.4 percent during the above period. The agency wise flow of short term and long term credit shows in the case of short term credit the largest decline occurred in the case of RRBs (334.8 in 1970s to23.6 in 2000s) followed by commercial banks from28.2 in 1970s to20.2 percent in 2000s.But in the case of Co operative banks the decadal growth rate of short term credit shows a slight improvement from 10.6 per cent in 1970s to11.6 percent in 2000s.In the case of long term credit the decade growth rate of co-operative banks 'share continuously declining, RRBs and Commercial banks' 'share declined up to 1990s and then shows an increasing trend. Although the RRBs' and Commercial Banks' contribution in the long term credit increased in the recent period, the decadal growth rate of total long term credit is continuously falling in 1990s and makes a slight improvement in recent years. This has serious implication in agriculture production and rural progress of Indian economy because the long term private investment partly depends upon long term credit flow to the agriculture.

LONG TERM CREDIT AND PRIVATE CAPITAL ACCUMULATION IN INDIAN AGRICULTURE

The problem of investment in Indian agriculture and the substitutability and complimentarily nature of public and private investment is still a debated issue in Indian agriculture. Although the gross investment in agriculture increased from 1668 crore in 1960-61 to 54539 crore in 2005-06, the percent share of public investment in gross capital formation in agriculture declined from35.5 per cent in 1960-61 to 24.2 in 2005-06.At the same time the growth of private investment in agriculture does not fully enough to compensate to the declining public investment in gross capital formation. Public investment, terms of trade for agriculture and the flow of long term institutional credit to agriculture are found to be strong determinants of private investment in agriculture. The relationship between these independent variables and private capital formation of Indian agriculture understand from the following table.5 it was hypothesized that private investment in agriculture is affected by (i) public investments; (ii) institutional credit provided for medium and long term purposes i.e. loans for creation of asset and (iii) terms of trade (TOT) for agriculture.

Table 5. Correlations between private Capital formation in agriculture and other related variables (1980-81 to 1999-00)

	Private Capital Formation	*Public Capital Formation*	*Long term credit*	*Terms of Trade*
Private capital Formation Pearson Correlation	1	-.522*	.921**	.717**
Public Capital Formation	-.522*	1	-.321	-.591**
Long Term Credit	.921**	-.321	1	.684**
Terms of trade	.717**	-.591**	.684**	1

* Correlation is significant at0.05level (2-tailed)

** Correlation is significant at the 0.01 level (2 tailed)

Among these three variables, terms of trade for agriculture is measured in several ways. There are mainly three kinds of sectoral terms of trade between agriculture and non agriculture sectors available in literature. These are: one, ratio of implicit price deflator for agriculture to non agriculture sector; two, ratio of price index of agricultural products to price index of manufactured products, as published in Economic Survey (Government of India); and three, ratio of prices received to prices paid by agriculture sector i.e. barter terms of trade. Out of the three measures the ratio of price index of agriculture products to price index of manufactured products is used to study the impact of TOT on the private capital formation. From the table 5 it is clear that the Private capital formation in agriculture long term credit and terms of trade are positively correlated and private capital formation is negatively correlated to public capital formation in Indian agriculture. The correlation between long term credit and private capital formation is high (0.921 with 0.01 level of significance as compared to terms of trade (0.684

with 0.01 level of significance). Thus it is very significant to analyses the strength of long term credit in augmenting private capital formation in agriculture in pre reform and post reform period.For this purpose multiple regression analysis worked out taking private capital formation as depended variable, public capital formation, long term credit and terms of trade as independent variables. Separate analysis is done to understand the effect of long term credit in private capital formation in agriculture in the total time period under study, the pre reform and post reform periods.

A. Regression equation of the period under study. (1980-2000)

PVTCFA = 3004.885 - 1.212 PBCFA + 0.257LTCA
(1.036) (-3.190) (6.412)
+ 16.365 TOT ... (1)
(0.536)

R^2 = 0.908 Adjusted R^2=0.891 N=20

2579.469+0.262LTCA ... (1.1)
(14.841) (10.063)

R^2 = 0.849, Adjusted R^2=0.841

B. Regression equation pre reform period. (1980-1990)

PVTCFA = 1292.652 – 0.664PBCFA + 0.080LTCA
(0.520) (-0.711) (0.421)
+ 28.635.TOT ... (2)
(1.691)

R^2 = 0.673 Adjusted R^2=0.509 N=10

2545.638 + 0.184LTCA ... (2.1)
(14.230) (2.820) **

R^2 = 0.499 Adjusted R^2=0.436

C. Regression equation post reform period. (1991-2000)

PVTCFA = – 2822.894 – 1.396PBCFA + 0.303LTCA

(-0.706) (-0.909) (3.678)**

- 84.913TOT ... (3)

(1.200)

R^2 = 0.855 Adjusted R^2 = 0.782 N=10

3552.956 + 0.322 ... (3.1)

(12.323) (5.398) **

R^2 = 0.758, Adjusted R^2=0.758

Where

PVTCFA – Private Capital formation in agriculture.

PBCFA – Public Capital formation in agriculture

LTCA – Long term Credit to agriculture.

TOT – Terms of Trade

(Figures in parentheses aren't' values ** are significant at .01 level)

The above analysis shows that during whole the period under study (1980 – 2000) the three independent variables taken for analysis is capable for explaining 84(R^2 value) percent changes in dependent variable and private capital formation in agriculture predicted to increases 0.257 when long term credit goes up by one per cent. Although this amount is negligible, shows a positive influence on private capital formation in agriculture. As compared to the pre reform period in post reform period the power of long term credit in determining the value of private capital formation increased from 0.080 to 0.303.The adjusted R^2 value is also higher in post reform period as compared to pre reform period. To find out the effect of changing long term credit and its impact on private capital accumulation single regression equations are worked out (equations 1.1, 2.1, 3.1) shows the prediction capacity long term credit and corresponding R^2 values has increased in the post reform period as compared to pre reform periods. Thus although the growth rate of long term credit decreases in the 1990s, it is not possible to say that the total long term credit to agriculture decreases over the period. This is clearly understood from table 6 also.

Table 6. Private Capital Formation and Pattern of Long term Credit

(Rs. in Crore)

Year	*Private Sector Capital formation*	*Investment Credit*	*Proportion*
1980-81	2843	1335	47
1990-91	8402	4208	50
2000-01	12979	6624	51
2002-03	38861	24529	173

Source: Central Statistical Organisation national Income Accounts.

It is clear from the table 6 that the long term credit as a share of private investment has also been raising in the1990s. Thus it is possibly fair to say that even though the decadal growth rate of decrease, the long term agriculture effort has not really been slacking in the 1990s.

CONCLUSION

Agriculture credit is the crucial input which helps to increase agriculture production and productivity. The multi agency approach consisting Co-operative Banks, Commercial Banks and RRBs followed by the government helps to increase the adequate and timely availability of credit to agriculture in quantitative terms over the 60 years after independence, but its qualitative aspect is still a debated issue. The adequate and timely availability of credit to agriculture reduces the role of money lenders in agriculture credit markets this in turn helps to increase their production without force from the lending institution. The agriculture credit policy changes from time to time to cope with the changing needs of the sector. Thus the bank nationalisation in 1969, followed by 1980 and financial sector reforms as a part of new economic policy redefines the role of Co-operative banks in agriculture credit lending at the same time the share Commercial Banks and RRBs in the total credit has increased. But although the share Commercial Banks in total agriculture credit increases over the years, in most of the states the growth agriculture credit disbursed by Commercial banks shows decreasing trend in the post reform period. Reduction of Co operative Credit and slow growth of Commercial banks credit to agriculture in the post reform period leads to the re- emergence of money lenders in rural agriculture credit marketing system in recent years. This increases the debt problem among the marginal farmers, and increases farmer suicides in many parts of the country. Thus a further policy initiative is needed to strengthen the co-operative credit system along with reducing the disparities of commercial banks in agriculture credit allocation across the states.

REFERENCES

1. Braveman,A and J L Guasch (1986),"Rural Credit Markets and Institutions in Developing Countries: Lessons for Policy analysis from practice and modern theory, Word Development, Vol. 14, No.10, pp 1253-1267.
2. Bell Clive (1990),"Interactions between Institutional and Informal Credit to Agriculture", Indian Journal of Agriculture Economics
3. Dadibhavi R V (1998) "Dimensions of Regional Disparities in Institutional Credit to Agriculture". Indian Journal of Agriculture Economics, Vol.43, No.3, July September, pp 374-380
4. Gadgil M.V(1994)"Formal Agriculture Credit System In India: Shape of things to Come", Indian Journal of Agriculture Economics,Vol.4,9,No.3,July September,pp476-490.
5. Government of India, Economic Survey various Issues.

6. Handbook of Statistics on the Indian Economy, Various issues.

7. Kannan P Asha (2005) Agriculture Finance in India: Experience and Lessons, Artha Vijnana, Vol.XLV11, No.1-2, March June, PP 105-116.

8. Mani K.P (2007), Institutional Credit For Agriculture Reflections Since Reforms, Financing Agriculture, Vol.39, Issue No.5, pp 33-37.

9. Mohan Prakash (2004) "Agriculture Credit in India: Status, Issues and Future Agenda "RBI Bulletin, November.

10. Mridula Mukherjee (1985), Commercialisation and Agrarian Change in Pre Independence Punjab, edited by K.N Raj in Essays on the Commercialisation of Indian Agriculture published Oxford University Press, New Delhi.

11. NABARD (2001), Report of the Expert Committee on Rural credit.

12. Raj K N (1985) Essays on the Commercialisation of Indian Agriculture, Oxford University Press, Delhi.

13. Rangarajan.C (1996) Rural India: The role of Credit, The first Ravi Matthai Memorial Lecture organised by Academy of Human Resources Development in Indian Institute of Management,Ahmedabad on March 8,1996,Publised in the RBI Monthly Bulletin, May.

14. Reddy.Y V (2001),"Indian Agriculture and Reforms: Concern Issues and Agenda" RBI Bulletin, March.

15. Report on Currency and Finance Various Issues,Mumbai.

16. Report on Trend and Progress of Banking in India, Various issues, Mumbai.

17. Reserve Bank of India Annual Report, Various Issues, Mumbai.

34

Financial De-regulation and Financial Exclusion with Special Reference to Priority Sector Lending

N. Madhava Menon

The present paper examines the financial exclusion in the era of liberalization in India. The first section deals with the meaning, causes and consequences of financial exclusion. Second section deals with the extent of financial exclusion in the priority sectors, especially farm sector and small scale industries.

FINANCIAL DE-REGULATION IN INDIA

Indian financial system functioned in a relatively regulated and controlled environment over the first few decades of the country's independence in 1947. As with the rest of the economy, the financial sector operated in a state supervised environment, imposing an administered interest rate structure, restrictions on credit flows, high reserve requirements and with the pre-emption of a significant proportion of lendable resources towards 'priority' and government sectors. There were several restrictions on flows of overseas capital. As for the exchange rate of the rupee, it was linked to movements in major currencies while subject to close monitoring by the RBI.

Financial sector in India had been subject to gradual de-regulations over the subsequent decades and has been finally subjected to extensive transformation since the launch of sweeping economic reforms in 1991, which introduced three major changes such as liberalization of the capital market (which included the introduction of current account convertibility, easier access of foreign capital and managed float of the rupee with interventions in the foreign exchange market by the RBI), changed norms of operation for banks in terms of the Basel norms which now has led to a near dissolution of priority credit by making it possible to borrow for housing and other purposes under the head of priority credit and marketized borrowing by the fiscal authorities and an end to official borrowings from the RBI in terms of Fiscal Responsibility and Budget Management since 2003.

FINANCIAL EXCLUSION

According to K.C.Chakrabarty "Financial Exclusion is the lack of access by certain consumers to appropriate, low cost, fair and safe financial products and services from main stream providers."Financial exclusion thus means the people those living on low incomes cannot access mainstream financial product such as bank accounts, low cost credit, remittance and payment services, financial advisory services, insurance facilities etc.... Financial exclusion therefore means: No Savings, No Insurance, No access to money advice, No affordable credit, No Bank account and No assets.

There are three types of exclusions: (a) people who do not have any access to a regulated financial system; (b) people who have limited access to banks and other financial services; and (3) individuals who have inappropriate products. The financially excluded sections largely comprise marginal farmers, landless labourers, self employed and unorganized sector enterprises, ethnic minorities, socially excluded groups, senior citizens and women. Mostly low income, unemployed and illiterate people, women and disabled are excluded from the formal financial services.

Lack of Banking habits, high transaction cost, lack of banking knowledge and insufficiency of knowledge on banking products prevents the unbanked people from knocking the door steps of banks. There are people who desire the use of financial services, but are denied access to the same. In countries with a large rural population like India, Financial Exclusion has a geographic dimension as well. Inaccessibility, distance and lack of proper infrastructure hinder financial inclusion. Going by the available data on the number of savings bank accounts and even assuming that one person has only one account, on an all India basis less than 60 per cent of adult population in the country has bank accounts. To compound matters, there are regional disparities among different regions of the country in this respect. In the rural parts of the country, where the farming community is living, the farm households having bank accounts is showing a miserable picture (51.4 per cent of farm households have no access to formal or informal sources of credit, while 73 per cent have no access to formal sources of credit).The unbanked population is higher in the North Eastern and Eastern Regions as compared to other regions. Further the extent of credit inclusion is even lower at 14 per cent of adult population. While there are pockets of large excluded population in all parts of the country, the North-East, Eastern and Central region contain most of the financially excluded population. (chart 1).In short, according to NABARD top official, around 60 per cent of India's population was deprived of access to financial institutions. In developed countries, this financial exclusion was less than 15 per cent.

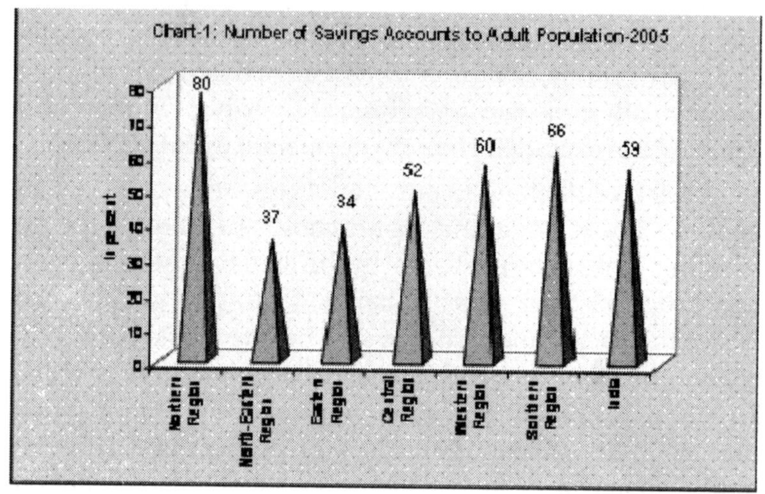

Chart 1

CAUSES OF FINANCIAL EXCLUSION

In general financial exclusion arises from

a) Problems with the **supply of** appropriate financial service products and

b) Problems with **demand for** financial services among potential customers

SUPPLY PROBLEMS

The main supply problems are

1. The financial institutions not supplying products to appropriate consumer needs
2. The financial institutions not supplying products with adequate consideration of consumers interests

3. The financial institutions not making appropriate products easily accessible.

A lack of appropriate products is a common supply problem. For example, low income customer often requires credit which provides small sums over a short period. Because of the high set-up cost of mainstream credit agreements, it may not be profitable for Banks and other commercial lenders to provide such loans. Similarly, most mainstream insurance products such as home contents or car cover are designed for payment or premiums directly from a bank account automatically excluding unbanked consumers. And some people choose not to engage in financial services for religious or cultural reasons. For example, Islamic Shari'a law prohibits payments or receipts of interest, meaning that most saving or credit products are not appropriate for those who follow Shari'a law. Products may be provided with inadequate consideration of consumers interests. Non-mainstream credit products providing basic features required by financially excluded customers are available. Accessibility problems can arise in a number of ways. For example, basic bank accounts were created to increase access to appropriate banking products in the UK. But these accounts were inaccessible for many financially excluded customers. Apart from these, distance from branch ,branch timing, cumbersome documentation and procedures, language, staff attitude etc. are some other supply problem responsible for financial exclusion.

DEMAND PROBLEMS

From the demand side, lack of awareness, low income or assets, social exclusion, illiteracy etc... act as barriers. Even when financial products do meet the needs of excluded customers, they may be unaware that these products exist or of the benefits they can bring and therefore be unwilling to invest the time and effort needed to take them up. Often, lack of demand results from people believing that they will not be served by financial services providers. This belief can be based on prior experience of having been turned down, or on hearsay or prejudice. In many cases it is reinforced by social or cultural preferences or alternatives, such as Christmas hamper saving schemes in US. Lack of demand for financial products may rise because people do not have the financial capability to make well informed decisions. In these circumstances, many opt out altogether, and operate primarily in cash

FINANCIAL EXCLUSION AND PRIORITY SECTOR LENDING

The new norms of bank lending have adversely affected the volumes as well as the terms of credit for those who are only marginally bankable like the poor and the SMEs. Thus credit is being denied to a large segments of small and medium sized enterprises and especially for those whose credit rating do not qualify the eligibility criterion in terms of Basel capital adequacy norms. The percentage share of the SMEs in aggregate bank advances has dropped from 36% to 23% between 2000 and 2004. Advances to priority sector as a whole have also been de-regulated, both in terms of interest rates and also in terms of additional types of priority credit as have been made eligible. Moreover no target as such is set for lending to the small sector industry on a priority basis. With advances to agriculture and to weaker sections set respectively at 18% and 10% of net bank credit, it effectively leaves 12% as a residual of the 40% priority credit for SSIs. With the new dispositions relating to credit, the share of bank credit from public sector banks to the small sector and the SMEs has fallen from 17% (1999-2000) to 7% (2002-03) and to even lower proportions during the following years.

INSTITUTIONAL CREDIT TO PRIORITY SECTORS

Directed credit programmes involving loans on relatively preferential terms and conditions to priority sectors have been major tools of development in our country. Prior to the nationalization of banks in 1969, banks lending was confined primarily to big business and trading, with operations predominantly confined to the metropolitan and urban centers. After nationalization, the government of India undertook corrective measures for such lop sided lending by the banks. Indian banks were expected to contribute towards economic development of the country by extending credit for the activities undertaken in the areas, which were considered to be "priority sectors". Under the prescriptions for priority sector lending in India a target of 40% of net bank credit has been stipulated for lending by domestic commercial banks. Within this, sub- targets of 18 per cent and 10 per cent of net bank credit, respectively, have been stipulated for lending to agriculture and weaker sections. Of the total net bank credit of foreign banks operating in India, aggregate credit to small scale industries sector should not be less than10 per cent of net bank credit and that to the export sector should not be less than 12 per cent of net bank credit.

LENDING TO AGRICULTURE AND FARM SECTOR

Lending to priority sector, although recorded a significant progress in the 1970s and 1980s, started falling short thereafter. There was rapid expansion in institutional credit in the post-bank nationalization period from Rs.1,675 crore in 1975-76 to Rs. 1,80,486 crore in 2005-06. During 1975-76 to 2005-06, the share of co-operatives in total credit to agriculture declined from 69.5% to 21.8%, whereas the share of scheduled commercial banks increased from 24.2% to 69.5%. But there was a distinct slowdown in the flow of agriculture credit during the 1990s; it declined to an average annual growth rate of about 10 % from 20% in the 1980s. Although there was an improvement in growth of agriculture credit in the decade beginning in the year 2000 to about 26%, its relative share came down to about 12% of total bank credit(Table-1).

Table 1. Annual average growth rate of credit (percent per Annum)

Period	*Priority Sector*	*Agriculture*	*SSI*	*Industry*
1980-81to 1990-91	20	20	19	17
1990-91 to 2001-02	13	10	13	15
2000-01 to 2006-07	26	27	13	22

Source: Handbook of statistics on Indian Economy 2006-07, RBI

Credit to farmer households is one of the important elements of financial inclusion. In order to know the extent of financial inclusion, we use farmer's indebtedness as a proxy. According to NSSO data, at all India level around 49 percent of the farmer households were indebted. As per the report of the Committee on Financial Inclusion, 51 per cent of the farmer households are financially excluded from both formal and informal sources as of 2007 and nearly 73 per cent of farmer households have no access to formal sources of credit. These exclusion varies from state to state. For example, Andhra Pradesh has the highest percentage of financial inclusion (82 per cent of farmer households in AP are indebted).On the other hand, Meghalaya has the lowest percentage of financial inclusion (only 4 per cent of farmer households are indebted). See the table 2.

Another issue is the inclusion of credit for small (land holding up to 1 ha) and marginal (land holding 1-2 ha) farmers. Table 3 shows that the share of formal loan sources increases with the size of land. At the all India level, the share of loans from formal sources varies from 22.6 per cent to 58 per cent for small and marginal farmers, while it varies from 65 to 68 per cent for medium to large farmers. Dependence of small and marginal farmers on informal sources is higher formal source.

Table 2. Percentage of Indebted Farming Households by All Sources of Loans and by Source of Loan (2003)

State	*Percentage of Indebtedness Farming Households in Total Rural Households (All sources)*	*Percentage of Indebted Farmers Household by Source of Loan*	
		Formal	*Informal*
Andhra Pradesh	82	54	77
Arunachal Pradesh	6	14	103
Assam	18	15	88
Bihar	33	23	84
Chhattisgarh	40	66	56
Gujarat	52	63	49
Haryana	53	76	50
Himachal Pradesh	33	57	65
Jammu& Kashmir	32	9	94
Jharkhand	21	44	60
Karnataka	62	57	55
Kerala	64	96	40
Madhya Pradesh	51	64	66
Maharashtra	55	92	30
Manipur	25	6	99
Meghalaya	4	2	97
Mizoram	24	33	67
Nagaland	37	20	79
Orissa	48	68	46
Punjab	65	58	70
Rajasthan	52	38	81

Sikkim	39	18	89
Tamil Nadu	75	59	67
Tripura	49	46	55
Uttar Pradesh	40	47	70
Uttarachanchal	7	65	44
West Bengal	50	51	73
Group of UTs	51	42	71
All India	49	56	64

Source : Calculated from NSSO (2005)

LENDING TO SMALL SCALE INDUSTRIES

Apart from agriculture, lending to other priority sectors such as SSI and Village industries has also registered a significant slowdown in the 1990s both in terms of loan account as well as credit supply. Even in 2000s the deterioration continued in the form of relative as well as absolute numbers. On the other hand, a definitional change in the priority sector has allowed a number of activities, which otherwise were not included and may not actually represent the small and weaker sections of the society. Consequently, about 45 to 48 per cent of priority sector advances belonging to the miscellaneous categories in2006 as against about 20 per cent during 1990s (table 4). Thus, a large part of increase in priority sector lending could be attributed to 'others' but not agriculture and rural small-scale sector.

Thus, despite renewed focus in the recent years, the credit needs of a large number of rural households have not been met and they are excluded from the benefit of institutional financing.

It is further noted that even as the priority sector lending includes small enterprises as a vital recipient, the reluctance to serve them is apparent from the date for the period 1990-2007. As given in the table 5. The proportion of

Table 3. Percentage Distribution of Outstanding Loans by Formal and Informal Source across Size Classes of Land in 2003.

	Size Class of Land Owned							
	0.01	*0.01-0.40*	*0.40-1.00*	*1.01-2.00*	*2.01-4.00*	*4.01-10.00*	*10.00+*	*All Size*
Formal Sources All India	22.6	43.3	52.8	57.6	65.1	68.8	67.6	57.7
Informal Sources All India	77.4	56.7	47.2	42.2	34.0	31.2	32.8	42.3
Percentage of total Indebted Households	1.3	30.0	29.8	18.8	12.5	6.4	1.2	100
Incidence of Indebtedness (Percentage)	45.03	44.4	45.6	51.0	58.2	65.1	66.4	48.6

Source: Calculated from NSSO (2005)

Table 4. Bank credit for SSI and Village Industries

Period	*No. of Loan Account (in Lakh)*	*Amount Outstanding (Rs. Crore)*
June 1981	11.35 (5.5)	3158 (12.7)
March1991	46.79 (7.6)	16446 (13.2)
March 2001	30.88 (5.9)	38977 (7.2)
March 2006	21.84 (2.6)	62454 (4.1)

Source: Shetty, 2008. (Figures in the bracket are percentages to total bank credit).

Table 5. Bank credit to SSI and Tiny Sector, 1990-2007 (Rs. millions)

Year (as on end March)	*Net Bank Credit*	*Credit to SSI*	*Credit to Tiny Sector*
1990 - 91	1,56,320	167,830(15.9)	
1991 - 92	1,121,600	173,980(15.5)	
1992 -93	1,327,820.	193,880(14.6)	
1993 -94	1,409,140	215,610(15.3)	
1994 - 95	1,690,380	258,430(15.3)	77,340(4.6)
1995 – 96	1,843,810	294,850(16)	81,830(4.4)
1996 – 97	1,896,840	315,420(16.6)	95,150(5.0)
1997 -98	2,182,190	381,090(17.5)	102,730(4.7)
1998 -99	2,462,030	426,740 (17.3)	88,370(3.6)
1999 – 2000	2,929,430	457,880(15.6)	227,420(7.8)
2000 – 01	3,408,880	484,450(14.2)	260,190(7.6)
2001 – 02	3,969,540	497,430(12.5)	270,300(6.8)
2002 – 03	4,778,990	529,880(11.1)	269,370(5.6)
2003 – 04	5,588,490	582,780(10.4)	308,260(5.5)
2004 – 05	7,187,220	676,340(9.4)	280,630(3.9)
2005 – 06	10,177,037	824,340(8.1)	361,870(3.6)
2006 – 07	13,087,875	1,047,030(8.0)	443,110(3.4)

Source : Alternative Economic Survey, India 2007 - 2008

credit to SSI (as percentage of net bank credit) has been on the decline since 1997-98 and has touched a low of a mere 8 percent in 2006-07. Such figures for the tiny sector (for the period 1994-95 to 2006-07) have been hovering around a low level of 4 to 5 percent till 2004-05, with the exception of a jump from 3.6 percent to 7.8 percent from 1998-99 to the subsequent year. The fall has continued and touched 3.4 percent in 2006-07, the lowest so far. This shows that the priority sector lending has failed to cater to the most crucial needs of loan finance to small and tiny enterprises.

The growth in the total bank credit to SSI also reveals the fact that there is a decline trend in the total bank credit disbursed to SSIs. The average annual growth in credit to SSI sector was 11.4 per cent during 1991-92 to 2003-04. The credit to SSI witnessed a slow growth rate during these periods. It is also observed that the annual growth rate in credit to SSI sector fluctuated widely between -3.6 per cent and 21.7 per cent. The share of SSI declined continuously from 13.9 per cent in 1992 to 8.1 per cent in 2004 (Table 6).

Table 6. Growth in Total Bank Credit to SSI Sector

Year (end March)	*Growth Rate in Bank Credit to SSI sector*	*Per Cent Share in Total Bank Credit to SSI Sector*
1992	5.6	13.9
1993	10.8	12.9
1994	14.3	13.6
1995	21.7	13.8
1996	17.4	13.5
1997	11.5	13.4
1998	19.8	13.8
1999	12.9	13.5
2000	10.4	12.4
2001	5.5	11.2

2002	11.6	10.2
2003	-3.6	8.6
2004	10.7	8.1

Source: Basic Statistics Return of Scheduled Commercial Banks(Various Issues) and Handbook of Statistics, 2003-04, RBI

Apparently, the focus on priority sector has got diluted in the post-financial sector reform period. The reduction was seen not only in the credit growth but also in terms of the number of bank branches. In the first two decades (1970-1991), 53,537 branches were added, that is 2,550 branches per year. But, thereafter, in about 16 year period only 8,987 branches have been added, that is, 562 branches per year or about one-fifth of what was achieved until the 1990s.

Economic Survey 2009-10 reveals the fact that though public, private-sector and foreign banks achieved the overall priority-sector lending targets as on March 2009, there were shortfalls in all the categories included in the priority sectors.

CONCLUSION

The coverage of priority sector lending has increasingly been diluted, crowding out small borrowers and opening gates for big borrowers. The decline in the share of priority sector lending clearly shows that the people working (or owning a small assets) in the agricultural and tiny sectors are really excluded from the organized financial system.

REFERENCES

1. Throat Usha (2007): ***Financial exclusion – The Indian Experience,*** RBI Bulletin, Vol L XI, No.7
2. Alternative Survey Group (2008): ***Alternative Economic Survey, India 2007 – 2008***
3. Roy Mohua (2006): ***A Review of Bank Lending to Priority and Retail Sectors,*** Economic and Political Weekly, Vol XLI, March 18-24.

4. Rao Ramachandra KS, Das Abhiman and Kumar Singh Aravind(2006) : ***Commercial Bank Lending to Small - Scale Industry,*** Economic and Political Weekly, Vol XLI, March 18-24.

5. Dev Mahendra S (2006): ***Financial Inclusion: Issues and Challenges,*** Economic and Political Weekly, Vol XLI, October 14-24.

6. NSSO (2005**):** ***Indebtedness of* Farmer *Households2003,*** NSS Report 498, CSO, Government of India.

7. Shetty, S L (2003**):** ***Credit Flow to Rural Poor,*** mimeo, EPW Research Foundation, Mumbai